RAISE HELL AND SELL
NEWSPAPERS

RAISE HELL AND SELL NEWSPAPERS

Alden J. Blethen & The Seattle Times

SHARON A. BOSWELL
AND LORRAINE McCONAGHY

Washington State University Press
Pullman, WA 99164-5910
(800) 354-7360

Washington State University Press, Pullman, Washington 99164-5910
©1996 by the Board of Regents of Washington State University
All rights reserved
First printing 1996

Front cover illustrations courtesy Museum of History and Industry (Seattle) and The Rainier Club (Blethen). Back cover illustrations courtesy Gilbert Duffy (Blethen) and *The Seattle Times*.

Library of Congress Cataloging-in-Publication Data

Boswell, Sharon A.
     Raise hell and sell newspapers : Alden J. Blethen and the Seattle Times / Sharon A. Boswell, Lorraine McConaghy.
          p.   c.m.
      Includes index.
      ISBN 0-87422-126-9. — ISBN 0-87422-127-7 (pbk.)
      1. Blethen, Alden Joseph, 1845-1915. 2. Newspaper editors—United
States—Biography.   3. Seattle Times.   I. McConaghy, Lorraine.
II. Title.
PN4874.B555B67   1996
070.4'1'092—dc20
[B]   96-3480
                                                                             CIP

Washington State University Press
Pullman, Washington 99164-5910
Phone: 800-354-7360
Fax: 509-335-8568

CONTENTS

PREFACE

In 1916, *The Seattle Times* moved into a home of its own, a modern skyscraper on the northern outskirts of the city's business district. Alden Joseph Blethen had been dead for little more than a year, and his family conceived the Times Square Building as a monument to his memory. The building offered mute testimony to Blethen's faith in Seattle's future, his indomitable spirit, and his magnificent ambitions for his newspaper. Packing for the move from the old plant, C.B. Blethen—Alden Blethen's younger son and then editor of *The Times*—had run across a birthday telegram from his father. Rereading the message, C.B. smiled at Alden Blethen's brash and infectious optimism. In 1913, the old man had written:

> Congratulations on your part in the upbuilding of this great newspaper. Hope you echo my desire that one hundred years hence *The Times* may be a more powerful newspaper than today and be published among five million people, and in the control of your great great grandsons.[1]

From the vantage point of 1996, one hundred years after Alden Blethen bought *The Seattle Times*, his visionary wishes may yet be fulfilled. Today, daily circulation stands at nearly a quarter-million copies, and Sunday circulation at more than half a million. *The Times* is the Seattle metropolitan area's dominant newspaper, one of a handful of surviving afternoon papers that serve a large United States city. Seattle has not reached a population of five million, but with more than five hundred thousand people living within its boundaries and an additional two million in the surrounding area, the city has become a major urban center. However, *The Times* has reached out beyond the hard-copy newspaper to a new and growing readership, developing an electronic information subsidiary, including telephone audiotext services and on-line computer access to *The Seattle Times*.[2]

The use of these innovative technologies at *The Times* is coupled with a deep affection and respect for the heritage of the newspaper and the Blethen family. The Seattle Times Company has resisted industry trends toward consolidation into national newspaper chains, and remains family controlled and independent, a Pacific Northwest institution with vital traditions. Looking to its history with pride and care, the newspaper undertook in 1993 the task of gathering and arranging an archive of corporate and family material. As the research and organization proceeded, the photo albums, oral histories, and dusty files yielded dozens of stories, each more intriguing than the last, about the Blethens and their newspaper, where corporate, family, and community history have grown inseparable.

The current *Seattle Times* publisher, Frank Blethen, is Alden Blethen's great grandson and has led this effort to reclaim the newspaper's past. At the family's yearly meetings, he and his cousins, Bob, Will, Alden, and John Blethen, share their perspectives on the newspaper with their children. Gathered at *The Times'* historic headquarters in downtown Seattle or its state-of-the-art publishing facility in the suburbs, young men and women of the fifth generation learn about their family's long newspaper heritage, its current management philosophy, and the challenges the company will face heading into a new century. At this intersection of past, present, and future lie the core values that the Blethen family has adopted for *The Seattle Times:* to remain family controlled, private, and independent, to serve the community through quality journalism, to maximize the workplace satisfaction of all employees, and to be the country's best regional newspaper.

The centennial of Blethen family ownership of *The Seattle Times* is a particularly fitting time to look back to the beginnings of this notable Northwest business enterprise so strongly marked, even today, with the complex character of Alden Joseph Blethen. The values of his descendants do not always reflect those of Alden Blethen, whose stormy career as publisher and editor-in-chief of *The Times* lasted from 1896 through 1915. But the family's interest in his remarkable story demonstrates their conviction that this heritage is worth preserving, understanding, and sharing.

Alden Blethen was a failed man of fifty when he arrived in Seattle. As a boy, he had clawed his way out of a hungry, lonely childhood to pursue his life with a ferocious and relentless energy. As a young man, he twice walked away from easy success, bored and restless, eager for risk. In his middle age, he moved impatiently from venture to venture, from newspapers to politics to banking, until he arrived in the Northwest, disgraced and broke. In Seattle, he was living on the charity of his wife's family, literally penniless, at the end of his rags-to-riches-to-rags trail when he bought into *The Times* with

$3,000 in borrowed capital. In 1896, *The Seattle Times* was a drab little eight-page paper, losing money. At his death, twenty years later, Blethen left a thriving newspaper business to his sons and daughters—a tribute to his own vitality and determination.

During the two decades that he ran the paper, Alden Blethen infused *The Seattle Times* with his unmistakable personality—belligerent, decisive, and obstinate. He was a man of deep and enduring contradictions. He combined rank opportunism with deeply held principles: no one was more patriotic or more generous. Likewise, the most hardheaded of men, he lavished sentimental affection on the boys who sold *The Times*, often homeless or abused. His judgment often seemed capricious but once he made up his mind, his allegiance never wavered. He was critical to a fault but formed unquestioning loyalties to casual and unworthy acquaintances. He seldom sheathed his own weapons, though he was easily wounded. Possessed of a long memory for favors and for insults, he could forgive with childlike eagerness or punish with vindictive energy.

And he projected himself through his newspapers. *The Seattle Times* was a fierce competitor, ruthless and boastful, focusing its owner's own aggressive ambitions. *The Times'* principled crusades were largely his own, as were its whims and misjudgments. Its exaggerated language of outrage or praise was his, as were its "speckled editorials," whose bold and hectic typesetting embodied his vehemence. Driven by conviction or eccentricity to hold unpopular opinions, Blethen courted public outrage and turned his notoriety to advantage to build *The Times'* circulation.

But this book is not just the story of how Alden Blethen made a success of *The Seattle Times*. It is his biography, the narrative of his life, the distinctly American tale of a self-made man whose path lay westward from Maine to the Midwest, and then on to Seattle. It is the story of his family and boyhood, the people he knew, and the experiences that shaped his character; it is an honest exploration of some of the mysteries and ambiguities in his past. Though research in Maine, Minneapolis, and Kansas City has solved some of the puzzles, Alden Blethen, a relatively obscure figure for much of his life, left little evidence for his biographers. Few of his contemporaries remembered him in their own published reminiscences; fewer still of his distinguished correspondents kept his letters among their papers. His voluminous files of correspondence burned in a series of disastrous fires, in Minneapolis and in Seattle. Although Blethen was interested in family history and edited a genealogy, he wrote little of an autobiographical nature, and his own son doubted the truthfulness of his after-dinner-speech reminiscences, reported in his newspapers and obituaries.

Yet there is a great story in his life, from farm to city, from ploughboy to publisher, across the country and across the centuries. In an era of accelerating change, Blethen's world was linked by correspondence, telegraph, and then telephone; illuminated by candles, oil, and then electricity; powered by animals and water, steam, and then gasoline engines. He came to maturity during the Civil War, and the issues of his lifetime ranged from the abolition of slavery to socialism, women's suffrage, and prohibition. From the gold rush to World War One, from boomtown to metropolis—in Seattle's liveliest decades—Blethen's life became entwined with the city he claimed as his last home.

In Seattle, Alden Blethen raised hell and sold newspapers, achieving a remarkable success that both fulfilled and redeemed his tumultuous life.

The earliest known photograph of Alden Joseph Blethen is a studio portrait taken during his last year at Abbott Family School or soon after he moved to Portland, Maine. He was about twenty-seven years old.

(Courtesy of Gilbert Duffy)

1 A YOUNG MAN OF GREAT PROMISE

Alden Joseph Blethen was born and spent his boyhood in the broken uplands of Maine's Waldo County, a great sweep of land that rose above the seacoast towns, westward to the distant mountains. Harbor and hill, ridge and valley, the land was buffeted by the wind in every season, scoured by the bitter gales and blizzards of winter, raked by wind-blown rain in spring and fall. In springtime, streams raced downhill to the sea, threading swift silver among the hills, powering gristmills and sawmills as they flowed. Once a dark forest of elm, maple, and oak, with stands of pine and spruce, in Blethen's day only the ridge crests flamed red and amber in the autumn, aglow above the green hillsides dotted with sheep, the thin soil planted to orchards or potatoes. Long runs of stone wall edged farm fields, setting maple sugar bush apart from sheep fold, one neighbor's land from the next.

All his life, this harsh and beautiful country was never far from his thoughts; it had demanded so much of him and yielded so little. When he was an old man, Alden Blethen remembered boyhood visits to his grandfather Joseph Blethen at the family homestead near Thorndike, Maine. In the snug house, the boy listened as the old man told the family's history late into the night, tales of Welsh princes, Ethan Allen's Green Mountain boys, and the Blethen Quaker heritage. He remembered the stories all his life and retold them to his own sons and daughters.

Alden Blethen's grandfather had built the homestead with his brother Isaiah and their father Job in the 1810s, when the three men moved from Durham, Maine, to the northern frontier. They joined Job's sister and her husband who had settled thirty years earlier in the new town of Unity, but the three Blethen men purchased property a few miles east of town—out in "the wild lands," as townsfolk termed them. They built a crude log house the first year, then, over time, constructed a solid farmhouse and a large barn of hand-hewn timbers, connecting the structures with a sheltered passageway, a concession to the severe winter weather. Job, Isaiah, and Joseph Blethen felled and burned the trees, opening land for orchards and hayfields and grazing range for their sheep and cattle. When Thorndike township incorporated, father and sons registered their herds' earmarks with the town clerk, for despite the stone walls the animals strayed far and wide.[1]

By 1820 the men's wives had joined them, and the three Blethen families were gathered together, established in this beautiful yet unforgiving place. With time, they chose the knoll up behind the house as the family burial ground, marking the graves with simple fieldstones. After Job Blethen's death, Alden Blethen's grandfather Joseph stayed on in the original homestead and his great uncle Isaiah built his own place nearby.

Confident and opinionated, Joseph Blethen became established as a powerful

This headstone marks Joseph Blethen's grave in the small Blethen family cemetery. The marker, not in the Quaker tradition, was likely placed later in the century.
(Boswell/McConaghy)

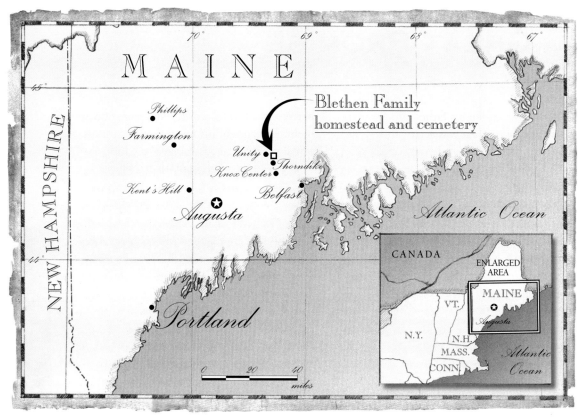

The rural setting of Waldo County, Maine, remains in the 1990s much as it was when Alden Blethen was a boy.
(Boswell/McConaghy)

figure in the little farming community of Thorndike. Chosen to moderate town meetings as early as 1814, in middle age he acted as assessor, school agent, overseer of the town poor, and selectman. But as he grew older, he became obsessed with the lost family fortune, an inheritance of many millions of dollars unclaimed at the death of his grandfather's grandfather. Joseph Blethen's own letters provide a vivid self-portrait of him, scheming by candlelight in the lonely Maine farmhouse, avid to claim his birthright. In 1850, when Alden Blethen was five years old, his grandfather hired an agent to plead the family's case before the English royal court. The unsuccessful effort seemed an extravagant folly to those around him. Chastened, Joseph Blethen became an earnest Quaker

convert in his old age, adopting biblical speech and plain dress, and forsaking his dreams of riches. An old man, lame and nearsighted, he nevertheless cut quite a figure, tall and slim in a long gray coat and broadbrimmed hat, lecturing town meetings with "thee's" and "thou's."[2]

He and his wife reared nine children: a stepson, six daughters, and two sons, Philip and Alden. Philip, the elder, knew that he would eventually inherit the old place. Alden, with fewer prospects, married Abigail Lamson, a woman from a distinguished country family in nearby Knox. Their wedding took place in the spring of 1837; six months later, Abigail's brother James married Alden's sister Jane, and the two families became closely entwined. James D. Lamson worked his farm in the summer, taught school in the winter, and successively represented his district in both houses of the Maine legislature. One of the most prominent men in Waldo County, he distinguished himself by learning, property, and modest political power. Like his father and brother-in-law, Alden Blethen was active and respected in the community and held the office of justice of the peace. He and his father-in-law invested in a town shop together, but Blethen was a carpenter and dairy farmer as well.[3]

Living in the Knox backcountry, Alden and Abigail Blethen had six children within ten years—four sons and two daughters. Alden Joseph Blethen, named for his father, was born on a bitterly cold day, December 27, 1845, the fourth son in the family. Then, three years later, disaster struck when the elder Alden Blethen died in the prime of life. He incurred medical bills of $93 in his "last sickness," as the estate's probate described it—a huge sum for the day and more than 10 percent of his total worth. No records document the cause of his mysterious death; his son always remained strangely silent on the subject. It is clear, though, that his death shattered the family.[4]

Alden Blethen died in November 1848. His wife, Abigail Lamson Blethen, struggled through that winter with the help of her oldest children, only eleven and nine years old, to keep the house warm, food on the table, and the youngest—Alden, Jr. not yet three and two-year-old Arabel—out from

Here in ruins, the foundations and cellar hole of the Blethen homestead were built about 1820 by Job Blethen and his sons, Isaiah and Joseph.

(Boswell/McConaghy)

One of the old country schoolhouses, typical of those in which Alden Blethen taught. This building served in the 1990s as the town hall, in Knox, Waldo County, Maine.
(Boswell/McConaghy)

underfoot. In nineteenth-century fiction, noble widows rose above impossible odds; in real life, Abigail Blethen did not. She may have tried to run the farm with hired help—if so, Maine's 1849 drought was the final straw. That hot dry summer destroyed the potato crop, and the local wheat harvest fell by two-thirds. Farmers slaughtered their heifers and lambs because there would be no winter fodder for them. By the time the Blethen estate was inventoried, in the fall of 1849, the house was nearly bare. Abigail Blethen's rocker, spinning wheels, and loom remained, as did a few other necessities: the milk pans and churns, the featherbeds and worn coverlets. The mantel clock was the only luxury left in the house—the rugs, books, and pictures were all gone. There was no stock left on the farm except an old milk cow and a single heifer. A sleigh and wagon remained in the barn, but there were no horses left to pull them.[5]

Everything else had been sold to pay debts and provide immediate support for the six children. In fall 1849, she sold the farm itself. At her husband's death, the widow had received an allowance of about $300 to care for her family; at settlement, in 1850, she received the balance of $200. Then she disappeared, leaving even five-year-old Alden and three-year-old Arabel behind. The town records were filled with references to such "sworn off" or orphaned children as "town paupers to be Supported by the lowest bidder at Auction." Successful bidders agreed to feed, clothe, and train these pauper children on pittances paid by the town, and were encouraged to sweeten their bargain through the use or sale of the children's labor. Abigail Blethen's six children found places with neighbors and family members. In Alden's case, that good fortune did not ensure a loving home.[6]

In 1850, he was five years old, living on a farm with his aunt and uncle, separated from his mother, far from his brothers and sisters. When the boy was ten, his aunt—his father's sister—died. After her death, Alden Blethen's uncle bid the boy's labor out to neighboring farmers. Blethen often recounted the tale of ploughing a furrow and milking a cow, demonstrating his skills before a speculative group of farmers who were his prospective masters. Then, as Blethen later put it, "I was put up at auction, to be knocked down to the highest bidder." He went to a farmer who promised him room and board, two suits of clothes and three months schooling each year, with $1 spending money each Fourth of July. Neither his grandfather nor his mother's family intervened, and the boy grew up in loveless homes, a pauper on the town dole and a stranger within the household, valued only for his muscle. As an old man he told his younger son his story of these years. It was a

bitter tale of abandonment and drudgery.[7]

Year in, year out, the farms in Thorndike and Knox moved with the rhythms of the seasons, of August heat and January freeze, of lambing and shearing, of calving and milking, of plowing and threshing. In 1859, Waldo County temperatures ranged down to 38° below zero in January; more than twelve feet of snow fell during that winter. As a teen-aged farm laborer, Alden Blethen mixed corn with molasses for winter feed and shoveled mountains of manure out of the barn onto the snow. In the spring, summer, and fall, he split firewood, spread manure in the fields, hoed corn, drove stock to market, milked cows, and helped with the harvest. Most county farmers practiced "low farming" and

grubbed out a subsistence living. Farming was simply a way of life and not a science or a business; ill-conceived efforts to grow surplus crops of oats, potatoes, and hay brought quick cash, but exhausted the soil. Folks got along, but they never got ahead.[8]

The roads away from Thorndike began to draw Alden Blethen's attention, pulling his dreams of distant possibilities. When the boy straightened, easing his back from work in the fields, he could spot passersby on horseback, outward bound along the country lanes. Stagecoaches rattled past, carrying the mails or bringing the springtime wool-buyers from Massachusetts mill towns, eager to pick over the upcountry fleece. The boy saw ox teams pulling sleds of lumber from the

Harvesting potatoes in the 1880s, near Thorndike, in Waldo County, Maine. As a boy, Alden Blethen was "farmed out" by his guardian to work as a field hand on such harvests.

(Unity Historical Society)

sawmills in Unity, headed for Belfast and the open sea, or returning with loads of flour, molasses, and bolts of cloth for the northern country stores.[9]

When he was thirteen or fourteen, life and work out on the farm became unbearable and Alden Blethen ran away along one of the country roads. Remembering his experience as a pauper farm laborer, Blethen always maintained that he had nothing but cast-off rags to wear and that the snow drifted onto his blankets through cracks in the attic walls. His master did not abide by even his miser's bargain and kept the boy from the little schooling he was entitled to by law. Alden Blethen talked back, and his master beat him. In later years, he told his sons little about his run; he always said that he couldn't remember the details. He recalled that he had worked in logging camps for a while, as saw-

yer and cook, and that he had worked in a small town hat factory, as foreman on the line. He didn't go very far, and he soon came back—homesick, hungry, and out of luck.[10]

His mother had returned, too, and was living on a farm south of Unity. She had remarried a younger man, Reuben Gould, and they had a new baby; she wanted to gather the family back together. At fifteen, sulky and resentful, Alden Blethen was living with his mother and stepfather, his older brother Charles, and his younger sister Arabel, as well as his half-brother Samuel, the baby. It was a home of sorts but Alden Blethen never fit in, never wanted to fit in. His brother Charles soon left for military service in the Civil War, and Alden grew restless and unhappy, estranged from his mother. Avid to learn and make up for lost time, he attended the little one-room school

The school building and dormitory of Maine Wesleyan Seminary, or Kent's Hill, in about 1865. Alden Blethen graduated from Kent's Hill in 1868, intent on a career in law and eager for a life in the city.
(Kent's Hill School Archives)

Early Blethen Family Genealogy

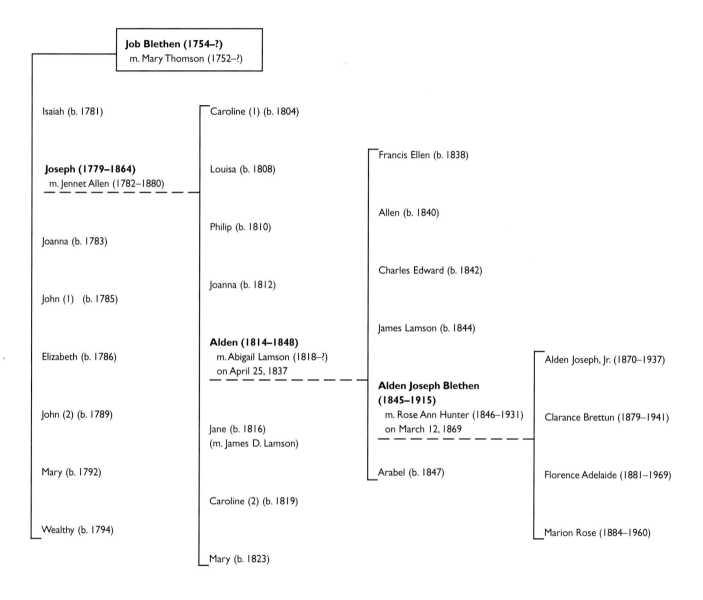

Job Blethen (1754–?)
m. Mary Thomson (1752–?)

Isaiah (b. 1781)

Joseph (1779–1864)
m. Jennet Allen (1782–1880)

Joanna (b. 1783)

John (1) (b. 1785)

Elizabeth (b. 1786)

John (2) (b. 1789)

Mary (b. 1792)

Wealthy (b. 1794)

Caroline (1) (b. 1804)

Louisa (b. 1808)

Philip (b. 1810)

Joanna (b. 1812)

Alden (1814–1848)
m. Abigail Lamson (1818–?)
on April 25, 1837

Jane (b. 1816)
(m. James D. Lamson)

Caroline (2) (b. 1819)

Mary (b. 1823)

Francis Ellen (b. 1838)

Allen (b. 1840)

Charles Edward (b. 1842)

James Lamson (b. 1844)

**Alden Joseph Blethen
(1845–1915)**
m. Rose Ann Hunter (1846–1931)
on March 12, 1869

Arabel (b. 1847)

Alden Joseph, Jr. (1870–1937)

Clarance Brettun (1879–1941)

Florence Adelaide (1881–1969)

Marion Rose (1884–1960)

near the farm, reading voraciously. At sixteen he began teaching in the rough schoolhouses scattered throughout the north county. The independent work was not new—he had been earning his way all his life. But school teaching was his first step to a wider range of possibilities, far from the mindless tedium of the farm or the heavy labor of the woods camps. Much later, Alden Blethen told his son that he had decided to prepare for the study of law while teaching as a teenager in these schools.[11]

Backcountry Maine schools were only in session during winter and summer terms, releasing students to work when they were most needed on their family farms. Fewer than half the eligible students ever attended school at all. Rural schoolteachers were often poorly trained, and rural schoolhouses were often little more than shacks. A Maine school superintendent's report wryly said of one such school that "with proper repairs it might make a respectable pigpen," and suggested that arson was the only responsible solution. From township revenues, local school agents hired teachers like Blethen, bought supplies, and delivered the firewood. Pupils aged six to twenty-one crowded onto benches to copy lessons onto their slates, read aloud from the Bible, and learn arithmetic and geography from a ragtag assortment of books. It was a hard way to learn or to teach.[12]

Blethen taught in these country schools for three years and then in 1864, at the age of nineteen, enrolled in the Maine Wesleyan Seminary and Female College in Kent's Hill, a few miles west of Augusta. The nation had been at war since 1861 and Blethen's three older brothers had all enlisted in the Union Army, but Alden went to school instead of joining his brothers at the front. Throughout his life, he hastened to justify his lack of service in the Civil War, the greatest conflict of

his generation, saying that his mother had forbidden his enlistment because she needed his financial support. Perhaps so. Whatever his reasons, many years later, he would claim the honorary title of "colonel" with great eagerness, seldom pointing out that it had not been earned on the battlefield.[13]

Kent's Hill, as the academy was best known, followed a forty-year tradition of liberal education in a Methodist context. Nearly two hundred young men and women attended the school, as both day students and boarders. In these years before public high schools in rural Maine, such private academies provided graded secondary instruction as well as advanced preparation for the professions and for admission to Bowdoin, Colby, and Harvard Colleges. They also prepared teachers who then scattered into the ungraded country schools. A personal contact with one of these Kent's Hill graduates almost certainly introduced Alden Blethen to the academy.[14]

Under vigorous administration, Kent's Hill bustled during Blethen's time there. Like all students, he was required to present letters of recommendation for acceptance, as well as "a certificate of good moral character," usually supplied by the family minister. At this time, Kent's Hill expected students to testify to a vibrant spiritual life and to attend mandatory religious meetings every day of the week except Friday. Indeed, a visitor noted, "the atmosphere of the whole place breathes with religious influences." The school could expel students for the use of alcohol or tobacco, profanity, "indecorous deportment," or for their general "pernicious influence." Each year's catalog listed the ne'er-do-wells who had been sent home in disgrace. But, as far as is known, Alden Blethen was not particularly devout and was not a Methodist in his later life. His choice of the academy at Kent's

Hill—and its choice of him—remains mysterious.[15]

When he arrived, two campus buildings had been recently constructed: the brick Seminary Building and "the college," or Sampson Hall. The Hall housed parlors, lecture and recitation halls, and a chapel; indeed, it also included a dormitory and "bathing rooms." In the 1860s, the big drafty rooms were still heated by cast-iron barrel stoves, and had wood boxes, ash pails, and water buckets. Students each brought a half-gallon can of whale oil to keep the study lamps ablaze by night and also prepared their own pens from goose quills. Blethen, like other students, paid quarterly fees for his room and board.[16]

Kent's Hill, simple and frugal, had no boarding school frills and kept its education practical. Generally, the school trained Methodist farm girls to play the piano and teach school; it trained Methodist farm boys in mathematics and rhetoric. Kent's Hill students cheerfully referred to themselves as "diamonds in the rough," and many did not graduate. Alden Blethen was among the few who successfully earned a degree in the seminary course. For him and others like him, Kent's Hill provided an open door to opportunities and possibilities, to the world far from the fields of Waldo County. But it was hard work. He attended only spring and fall terms at Kent's Hill, apparently teaching at country schoolhouses during the other seasons to earn his way through school.[17]

Blethen considered education after Kent's Hill a luxury beyond his grasp and pursued a "terminal" degree that did not prepare him for college entrance. At Kent's Hill he studied arithmetic, algebra, and geometry, Latin, French, and English composition, natural and moral philosophy, and rhetoric. The first half of the course was at the secondary level

and the second half, collegiate. Eventually, as important as his studies were the friends and connections he made. At the Hill he roomed with William Pattee, who would one day head the law school at the University of Minnesota. He met Stilson Hutchins, who would later own *The Washington Post*, and Edwin Haskell, editor of *The Boston Herald*. He long cited Henry Torsey, the dynamic president of Kent's Hill, as a personal reference. With the assistance of one of his teachers, Blethen came to the attention of George Davis and Josiah Drummond, prestigious Maine attorneys, in whose Portland offices he would fulfill his long-held goal of studying the law.[18]

At Kent's Hill, Alden Blethen became prominent as a star debater in the Calliopean Society, the oldest of the academy's literary fraternities and sororities. The Society operated the Kent's Hill library and reading room and published *The Calliopean,* a journal of essays, poetry, and short stories. In joint public meetings each month with the women of the Adelphian Society, the Calliopean men contested the issues of the day in formal debate. Invited to join in the spring term of 1865, Blethen became secretary and publications editor and was elected president within six months. His Byronic good looks, barrel chest, booming voice, and sarcastic wit were all perfect instruments of classical rhetoric, and he often engaged in the "forensic debates" of the mock courts or the competitions in declamation.[19]

Set against the solemn celebrations of victory at the war's end, President Abraham Lincoln's assassination in 1865 catalyzed the political consciousness of this student generation. Kent's Hill plunged into mourning, prayer, and eulogy. The Calliopean Society, which had debated every nuance of abolition and slavery, of war and compromise, passed on to the issues of political terrorism and

Dr. Henry P. Torsey served as president of Kent's Hill for many years. Alden Blethen was one of Torsey's many protégés among the "diamonds in the rough" at the little local academy. Blethen later repaid his debt of gratitude by acting as Kent's Hill trustee for nearly thirty years, and endowing Blethen Hall on campus.

(Kent's Hill School Archives)

reconstruction. The Civil War and its aftermath shadowed the lives of these young people at Kent's Hill; the toll was tremendous. Blethen's brother Charles died in 1865 at the Battle of Cedar Creek, while James was severely wounded at Gettysburg. But Alden Blethen chose to take his stand on the divisive issues of his day in debate rather than in battle and he gained a reputation in the Calliopean Society as a premier debater, emerging a leader of the student body.

Blethen's prominence at Kent's Hill is clear from his public role in a tragic affair. He was one of six students chosen by his classmates in May 1867 to investigate events surrounding the suicide of a young woman student, Louise Greene, and her father's subsequent accusations against Kent's Hill president, Henry Torsey. During the previous spring, Miss Greene had been accused of stealing several items of clothing. School authorities then searched her room and found a substantial sum of money and a master skeleton key. Confronted, the girl tearfully confessed stealing the money and other items and, following interviews with Preceptress Frances Case and President Torsey, left Kent's Hill. After Louise Greene had been missing for five months, her body was finally discovered in a lonely stretch of woods, an apparent suicide by poison. Heartsick, her father accused Torsey of sectarian fanaticism, cruelty, and neglect in expelling his distraught daughter, driving her to flee the Hill on foot. In turn, Torsey claimed that Louise Greene had herself decided to leave Kent's Hill, and that she was afraid to face her angry father. Torsey claimed that he had not barred her from graduating with her class, but had done his best to comfort her, give her good advice, and send her home to her family.[20]

After the discovery of the body, the students asked their teachers to withdraw from chapel one evening and chose Alden Blethen and five others to investigate Jonas Greene's charges. The committee soon reported back its findings: Louise Greene was guilty of the thefts and Dr. Torsey had behaved with kindness and restraint. Infuriated, Greene wrote a letter to each of the six students and asked a series of questions, probing their "wicked and uncalled-for attack on our dead child" and their exoneration of "the old angler," Henry Torsey. Alden Blethen returned Greene's letter unanswered with this derisive phrase penciled across the top, "Should advise a careful perusal of English grammar...." Greene found the judgment of these "sprigs of learning" deeply flawed by "fear or favoritism," and pointed out that these six students received one-third of all the prizes awarded to their entire class at graduation, in 1868.[21]

Against tremendous odds, Alden Joseph Blethen graduated from Maine Wesleyan Seminary at Kent's Hill. Blethen came to Kent's Hill a rough ploughboy, ambitious and angry; he left a young man of great promise, possessed of a network of influential mentors and a group of friends, young men like himself, eager to make their way in the world. His path lay clear before him, to rise from rural drudgery and poverty to the wealth and influence of an urban career. The Portland law firm of Davis and Drummond had already accepted him as a legal apprentice, and he began to read law there, working in the library.

For an ambitious young man, admission to the bar was a license to succeed; as Blethen later reminisced, "in the good old state of Maine, the lawyer was the man who did things." Reading law as an apprentice was a less expensive and more practical training for the profession than legal study at college, and it was a common route to the bar for disadvantaged young men. Like all law clerks,

Blethen chafed at monotonous office duties, studied the state statutes, and assisted his mentor in preparing arguments and researching case law and precedent. Though George Davis fell ill and soon died, his partner Josiah Drummond argued frequently before the Maine Supreme Judicial Court, and Blethen saw practice at its best.[22]

Whether young men trained in law at a college or as apprentices in a law office, their admission to the profession depended on passing the bar examinations. It was customary to read law and observe practice for three years before attempting the exam, and clerks received very modest stipends. Alden Blethen either did not have the family money to support him or did not wish to ask for it, and he continued to earn his own way. He taught in the village school at Phillips, Maine, either in the summer term of 1868 or during the following winter. As an old man, he recalled that when he took the stagecoach to this new teaching job, he was struck by the dark-eyed good looks of one of the passengers, a young woman with sharp features and a lively glance. He awkwardly "attempted a flirtation" with her, the prettiest girl he had ever seen, Rose Ann Hunter. They rode through to the same destination, and Blethen was both embarrassed and delighted when they met each other the following day, teachers in the same school. They fell in love, courted, and then married at her father's home in Strong on March 12, 1869.[23]

At twenty-four, Alden Blethen was no longer a solitary law clerk but a married man. He and Rose were soon expecting their first child. Throughout his life, Blethen sheltered his family with a fierce protective love, and their physical security was of great importance to him. He never forgot or forgave his own boyhood. Under no circumstances would he allow that cycle of hardship and

NOTICE.
THE ABBOTT FAMILY SCHOOL,
At Little Blue,
FARMINGTON, · · · ME.

WILL re-open on the 8th of October, under the most favorable auspices. Mr. Abbott, who has been entirely disconnected with the school for the past four years, will henceforth be intimately connected with all its vital interests; and the new Principal will be guided by Mr. Abbott's judgement, gained by seventeen years experience as Principal and Proprietor of this school. Send for a circular, or address the Principal, A. J. BLETHEN.
Farmington, Sept. 20th, 1869.   6w39

This advertisement in The Farmington Chronicle *for the Abbott Family School announced the reorganization of the school with Alden Blethen as principal and proprietor.*
(The Farmington Chronicle, October 21, 1889)

neglect to recur in his own family circle, and he provided for his wife's financial well-being, taking a life insurance policy when their first son, Joseph, was an infant. Alden Blethen rejected his own close relatives as hard, stingy, and selfish, but he found a warmth and generosity of spirit among Rose's kin. Her roots were deep in Franklin County, and the prolific Hunter clan included substantial farmers in the countryside and prosperous merchants in town. Blethen went trout fishing with his brothers-in-law, talked politics with Rose's father, and basked in the homely pleasures of a real family.[24]

But he could not afford a home for Rose on a law clerk's wage, and he had to leave her behind with her parents in Strong while he returned to the city, eighty miles away. Blethen's legal mentor, Josiah Drummond, had helped the young man find work, suggesting that the Portland school committee hire him to complete the unexpired term of the principal at North School in the spring of 1869. After working in unpainted one-room schoolhouses, managing this large urban school proved a challenging experience for

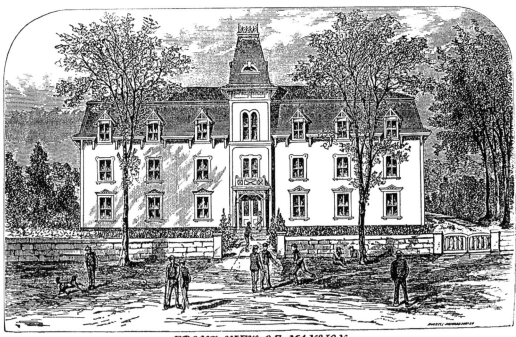

FRONT VIEW OF MANSION.

Blethen. North School was brand new, built after the great Portland fire of 1866, designed to accommodate its frankly experimental system of education. Rather than the mass ungraded instruction provided in other Portland schools, North School offered a strictly graded curriculum. Each of North's twenty-six teachers taught classes limited to fifty, and students moved from grade to grade based on their age and performance. For the time and place, it was a novel system of education, and Blethen found it fascinating.[25]

But the position was temporary, and after three months the Portland school committee turned to a more experienced man to replace Blethen as principal. It seems likely that Drummond could have helped him find a teaching position in Portland, but schoolteachers' salaries were very low—too low to support a wife and family. Blethen later maintained that Henry Torsey, president of Kent's

Hill, had encouraged him to continue teaching. Perhaps Torsey suggested a practical solution to his financial difficulty as well, and helped him find his next position, building on his North School experience.[26]

Alden Blethen reluctantly set aside his law studies and left Portland in the summer of 1869, moving with Rose to Farmington, Maine, to work as teacher and principal at the Abbott Family School, better known as Little Blue. Farmington, a bustling Yankee market town on the Androscoggin Railroad seventy miles north of Portland, boasted a productive farm district, a cheese factory, manufacturers of plows and wagons, a tannery, a spool and shoe-peg factory, nearby mica mines, and slate quarries. As Franklin County seat, Farmington had attracted a substantial community of professional men as well as a thriving retail center, weekly newspaper, and many fraternal organizations, churches, and schools.[27]

Founded in 1844, the Abbott Family School boarded boys from families of some means. Pupils came from Cuba, Uruguay, and Spain, as well as throughout New England for a secondary education in a disciplined family atmosphere. The school was built on the grounds of the estate of Jacob Abbott, an eminent historian and writer of the popular "Rollo" books for children. The school's distinguishing feature—"Little Blue"—was a small sandy knob that resembled nearby Mount Blue. The grounds were carefully landscaped, and *The Farmington Chronicle* often remarked that townspeople enjoyed strolling along the paths and over the bridges, past picturesque Rollo Pond. At the first "old boys" reunion at Little Blue, organized by Alden Blethen in 1870, the alumni bought stereopticon views of the school buildings and grounds, and walked out in the countryside as if they were students again. Like Kent's Hill, Abbott Family School offered a strong sense of place and custom, and many of its graduates long remembered it with sentimental nostalgia.[28]

Arriving in August 1869, Alden and Rose Ann Blethen became part of the tradition of Little Blue, managing the school as principal and matron. The young couple made their first home in the headmaster's quarters. He taught modern languages and natural sciences one year, Latin and the sciences the next. Beginning a lifelong pattern of bringing family into his ventures, Alden Blethen hired two of Rose's cousins to teach piano and oil painting while three of her brothers and sisters worked at the school as waiters and gardener. During Blethen's tenure at Little Blue, he also brought friends and family into the student body: his own half-brother Samuel Gould, his wife's brother David Hunter, and the grandson of his wife's wealthy uncle, Soranus Brettun.[29]

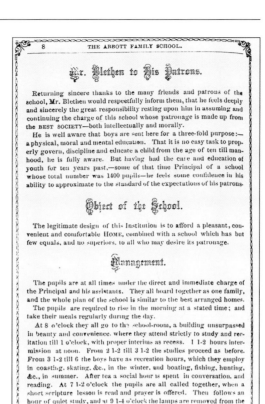

Alden Blethen wrote this page in the Abbott Family School catalog, 1870, describing the "physical, moral, and mental education" offered at Little Blue for boys of the "BEST SOCIETY." It is Blethen's earliest known prose.

(*Special Collections, Bowdoin College Library*)

The following year, in 1870, Alden Blethen borrowed money from Rose Ann's father and leased Little Blue from A.H. Abbott. Determined to achieve prosperity, he assumed responsibility—at age twenty-five—for the success or failure of the entire enterprise. In the school's catalog, he reprinted Abbott's testimonial:

Mr. and Mrs. Blethen have now been long enough in charge of the school at Little Blue to enable me to judge of their qualifications for the position.... It gives me, therefore, very great satisfaction to state, that my expectations of their success have been more than realized. Always at the post of duty, untiring in their efforts to promote the

An advertisement for the Abbott Family School appeared in The Farmington Chronicle *in 1873, signed by Alden Blethen after he had received his honorary Master of Arts degree from Bowdoin.*

(The Farmington Chronicle, September 11, 1873)

physical, intellectual and moral improvement of their pupils, they are entitled to the
fullest confidence by those who have sons to
educate away from home.[30]

In Blethen's day, the boys at Abbott Family
School ranged from eleven to seventeen, but
nearly all were thirteen, fourteen, or fifteen.
Many of them passed the Christmas recess at
school and spent the summer camping out in
the mountains with their teachers and classmates. Some of them never went home and
grew up at Little Blue. These boys were
sometimes angry and bullying, sometimes
homesick and lonely. All his life, Alden
Blethen would claim a bond with unhappy
boys, whether his pupils at this boarding
school or newsboys lost on the streets of Minneapolis or Seattle. Blethen acknowledged in
the school catalog that it was "no easy task to
properly discipline and educate a boy from
childhood to manhood." Acting as surrogate
parents, Alden and Rose Ann Blethen spent
five years at Little Blue.[31]

Abbott Family School prepared many boys
for distinguished careers but it was also a
place for troubled boys. Nat Goodwin—who
would become one of America's premier
comic actors—was one of Blethen's most
difficult pupils, one who would reenter his
life far later, in distant Seattle. In 1872, the
school catalog noted that Goodwin had been
expelled "for gross misconduct" and Blethen
later remembered that the boy had three
times tried to burn the school down.

Goodwin's escapades offer a rare glimpse of
Rose Ann Blethen. She was a busy woman
during the years at Abbott Family School,
caring for little Joe, managing the kitchen
and laundry, and acting as mother to a hundred rambunctious boys. She certainly had
her hands full with Goodwin, in the rough-
and-tumble family life at this boys' boarding
school. As her son later wrote:

The one pupil [my mother] loved best to
describe was Nat Goodwin. She had to do
various things to him besides attempting to
educate him.... She had to bang him about
no little, and in later years Nat himself used
to howl with joy when Mother told of
breaking Goodwin's big toe. Rose snatched
at Nat to prevent his harming another pupil; Nat resisted, [and] his toe caught in a
crack in the floor.[32]

In brochures, Blethen promised parents
their sons would live together in "a convenient and comfortable HOME," as well as
study together "as one family" at a superior
school. Family discipline assured parents that
the Blethens would employ "every humane
method" to maintain good order, and to
"develop a moral sense of duty." Pupils like
Goodwin, who broke the family rules, were
sent home to their parents. In fact, expulsions
became common enough from Abbott Family School that *The Farmington Chronicle*, the
town's long-established newspaper, twice
reassured its readers that such tactics would
not endanger the school's success.[33]

At Abbott Family School Blethen applied
many of his successful strategies from Kent's
Hill to foster "physical, moral, and mental
education." Though Little Blue was non-
sectarian, it, too, offered daily Bible reading
and prayers. Like Kent's Hill, Little Blue
presented its headmaster as a hero, a larger-
than-life man after whom boys might model
themselves. Both schools offered many opportunities for gymnastics, games, and team
sports, including the new game of baseball.
And Little Blue students especially distinguished themselves, in the eyes of *The
Farmington Chronicle*, in their oratory and
"declamations." At Kent's Hill, Blethen had
discovered a lifelong love of rhetoric—language and persuasion, pose and bombast—
and he taught it to the boys at Little Blue.[34]

ABBOTT FAMILY SCHOOL.

The 1872 Little Blue catalog provides a panoramic view of the Abbott Family School and grounds.

(Special Collections, Bowdoin College Library)

However, Little Blue differed from Kent's Hill in its superb laboratory and apparatus for physics, physiology, chemistry, and astronomy—areas of study that interested the owner, A.H. Abbott. The school offered a thorough preparation in the natural sciences and housed a far more extensive library than Kent's Hill. *The Little Blue Times*, written and edited on campus and published in the school's printshop, chronicled Abbott Family School life. In 1871, the Blethens completely renovated the student rooms, hanging new wallpaper and laying new carpets, and refurnished them with black walnut bedroom suites. The student residences were centrally heated with steam radiators in each room, and Little Blue boasted an enclosed gymnasium for wintertime team sports. Compared to Kent's Hill, Abbott Family School's personal accommodations were luxurious.[35]

Under Alden Blethen's administration,

more students boarded at Little Blue than at any time in its history. In Farmington he had become a big man—a popular and substantial citizen and a well-respected educator. In 1870, Blethen had been asked to be guest editor of Maine's *Journal of Education* and two years later was elected to the board of trustees of Kent's Hill, at age twenty-seven surely one of the youngest graduates to have that honor. In that same year, he received an honorary master of arts degree from Bowdoin College, an achievement of which he was most proud throughout his life. Blethen was very young to join the gray-haired fraternity of distinguished educators, clergymen, and jurists who had received such an honor from Bowdoin. Doubtless, his network of Kent's Hill mentors helped him, and A.H. Abbott, current owner of Little Blue, was a graduate of Bowdoin College. But by 1872, Blethen had impressed many influential men in

Maine as student, educator, and businessman; his award may well have reflected a consensus about this young man of great promise.[36]

Blethen was active and energetic in Farmington's community affairs. According to the local newspaper, he was one of the "few wide awake members" who revived the local chapter of the Oddfellows fraternal order in 1873. Also in that year, Blethen joined with two other local boosters to organize a town subscription for instruments and uniforms to outfit the Farmington Cornet Band, so it could provide "open air concerts during the Summer Season." Finally, at an 1873 caucus of the Farmington Republicans, friends proposed Blethen as a write-in candidate for the Maine state legislature, although in the end the caucus did not choose him as its nominee.[37]

Engaging, competitive, and self-assured, Blethen took readily to local politics. He and Rose Ann hosted a number of parties and open houses, described in *The Chronicle* as polished and delightful social experiences. Blethen mastered the Abbott Family School and Farmington, as he had mastered Kent's Hill. The success that Alden and Rose Ann Blethen crafted at Little Blue contributed solidly to community well-being, and the local newspaper was proud of it:

> We are pleased to note the unprecedented growth and prosperity of this popular family school for boys, under the able management of Mr. Blethen.... Fifty boys are now in attendance and more are on their way, so that Mr. Blethen was obliged Wednesday morning to make arrangements for furnishing three additional rooms for their accommodation. The present income of the school is $2500 per annum larger than at any period since its foundation.[38]

However, Blethen was not satisfied with his success in Farmington. By 1873, he had begun to study law again, late at night, preparing to sit for the Maine state bar exams and to resume his legal career. Still, at Little Blue's commencement, there was no sign of a change in the air. Alden Blethen's own students—in physiology, advanced mathematics, and rhetoric—acquitted themselves well in their public oral examinations. The graduating seniors presented a varied program of poetry, dramatic readings, and declamations.

HOME NEWS

Mr. and Mrs. Blethen's "At Home" on Friday evening last, at "Little Blue," was one of those occasions which, the more frequently they occur, tend to render life more enjoyable. Indeed, they are an occasional necessity, and when not carried to excess, as we are happy to say was the case in this instance, the party breaking up at the very seasonable hour of quarter past ten, they serve as educators of the social qualities in young and old as indispensable to those who would please and benefit all with whom they come in contact. Mr. Blethen made the party especially for his pupils, to whom he gave the privilege of extending invitations to their young lady friends and acquaintances in the village, Mr. and Mrs. B. inviting a large number of older persons of both sexes.

As might have been expected, a large and social company of old and young was gathered in the spacious drawing room at "Little Blue" at an early hour. The usual "chit-chats," friendly gossipings and pleasantries were indulged in by the older ones, while the young folks delighted all present with their songs, and games. Some of the young lady guests had kindly prepared printed programmes for the musical entertainment, which were a novelty we never before saw produced on such an occasion, but they proved great helps by way of reminders of the rich treat just a little in advance. The young ladies executed the parts assigned them very finely.

The dining-room doors were thrown open about half past nine, through which the party passed to refresh the "inner man." The provision which Mr. B. had made in this quarter was sufficiently abundant for a company twice as large. The long table was just loaded with everything that mortal appetite could crave—cold tongue, chipped beef, chicken, pressed meat, sandwiches, cake, in endless variety—all nice and well set-on, with tea, coffee, and pure, sparkling cold water to wash it down with.

After becoming fully satisfied with their treatment in the dining-room, the party returned to the parlors, where the final exchange of compliments took place, and the "good-nights" and "good-byes" were repeated, when the company dispersed to their several homes, to remember with pleasure in the coming future Mr. and Mrs. Blethen's "At Home" Friday evening, February 10, 1871.

The Farmington Chronicle, February 16, 1871

The church hall was lush with flags and flowers, the music lovely, the food wonderful. Everything seemed as usual. And, throughout the summer and fall, Blethen continued to run the usual advertisements for the Abbott Family School in Farmington and Portland papers, listing his name as headmaster.[39]

But back in the city, *The Portland Press* soon published an article headed "A Loss to Education," which reported that Alden Blethen had passed the bar, would soon begin his practice in Portland, and intended to leave his position at the Abbott Family School. In December, *The Farmington Chronicle*'s editor wrote a lengthy hail-and-farewell article, frankly noting that Blethen's efforts had nearly tripled attendance at Little Blue in five years. It quoted from his parting letter to friends and patrons that he was "retiring from the profession of teaching altogether." His decision was a considerable gamble, as the family left behind the solid certainties of the Abbott Family School in Farmington for the untried possibilities of a new life in the city. Driven by restlessness and ambition, Alden Blethen abandoned his successes in a small pond for opportunities in a larger one.[40]

Just at this time, Blethen wrote a revealing letter to Joshua Chamberlain, president of Bowdoin College, recommending two Little Blue graduates. Though neither his position nor his honorary degree merited it, he wrote as a colleague to Chamberlain. The prose was headlong and precipitate, arranged in incomplete sentences, marked by dashes, underlinings, and exclamation marks. Blethen confided his career plans to Chamberlain; indeed, he essentially solicited his legal business. Most unfortunately, Blethen clearly misspelled "Bodoin." Passionate, careless, and over-confident, the letter pairs well with Blethen's piercing eyes and eager face, his tumble of curly dark hair, his petulant mouth, his quick gestures and rapid walk.[41]

In December 1873, the Blethen family—Alden, Rose, and little Joe—said their farewells in Farmington and Strong, shipped their things to Portland, and moved into their new home on Bramhall Street, just off the Western Promenade. Bramhall Hill was the most fashionable neighborhood in the city and, although the first Blethen home was quite modest, there were elegant mansions within a block or two. An evening stroll under the elms, past formal gardens, took the Blethens out to the Promenade that curved along the crest of Bramhall's Bluff.[42]

Of an evening, seated on the grassy ridge with a picnic supper, Alden and Rose Blethen finally had a private life, away from Little Blue's hundred noisy, quarrelsome, needy boys. Far below them, the Back Cove of the sea met the Fore River as the tides moved in and out. Beyond toward the sunset stretched field and woodland, with church spire and curling smoke, to the hills of southwestern Maine and the White Mountains of New Hampshire. Leaning back on his elbows, watching Joe play, Alden Blethen forgot the past and conjured the future, weaving prudent strategies with wishful thinking.

Blethen's first "business card" advertisement appeared in *The Portland Press* two days before Christmas, in 1873. Through this ad—in Portland's premier Republican daily newspaper—he not only hung out his professional shingle, but also announced his entrance into other spheres of this new world. As an ambitious young attorney-at-law in Portland, active in fraternal organizations and interested in Republican politics, he had the opportunity to rub shoulders with a most remarkable group of Maine men of similar interests,

Alden and Rose Ann Blethen began their own family while they managed the Abbott Family School. Alden Joseph Blethen, Jr., always known within the family as Joe, was born in 1870, and is here pictured in a portrait at three or four years of age.
(The Seattle Times)

Office of—
Alden J. Blethen,
Attorney and Counselor at Law,
49 1-2 Exchange St.

Alden Blethen used this letterhead in 1873.
(Special Collections, Bowdoin College Library)

Centennial Block, Exchange Street.

This engraving of the Centennial Block on Exchange Street is from Edward Elwell's history of Portland, published during Blethen's stay in the city. Alden Blethen established his law offices here in the 1870s.

Alden Blethen's earliest advertisement for his law practice appeared in December 1873 in The Portland Press.

(The Portland Press, December 23, 1873)

including prominent politicians James G. Blaine and Thomas Brackett Reed. At a time when "As Maine went, so went the Nation," Portland Republican politics was a high-stakes game of influence, friendship, and professional connection.[43]

Alden Blethen was already acquainted with James Blaine because of their shared interest in the Kent's Hill academy, Blethen as trustee, Blaine as benefactor. Blaine had been a newspaperman in Portland and Augusta and had also long been chairman of Maine's Republican State Committee. When Blethen arrived in Portland, Blaine was Speaker of the U.S. House of Representatives and soon would represent Maine in the U.S. Senate. Portland native Thomas Brackett Reed, a Bowdoin graduate, was at the time Blethen

knew him a brilliant and acerbic attorney and former state attorney general, then acting as Portland's city solicitor and running hard for the 1876 Republican nomination to the U.S. House of Representatives. Blethen would long retain his connection with these two men, entertaining Reed at his home in Minneapolis during the 1892 national Republican convention, and—all his life—calling himself a "Blaine Republican."[44]

In 1874, Portland was a city of considerable commercial vitality, with a population of thirty-five thousand. Sixty-five daily trains carried passengers and freight to and from Boston, New York, and Montreal through this transportation hub for the Northeast. From the docks, passenger steamers departed daily for Boston and weekly for Europe, and in the 1870s, cargo worth nearly $50 million passed each year through Portland's commercial wharves and warehouses. Young men made reputations in law and politics but they made fortunes as entrepreneurs, bankers, and manufacturers. The countryside had formed Blethen's character; Kent's Hill encouraged his dreams; Farmington offered him the opportunity to demonstrate his abilities; but Portland opened dozens of possibilities.[45]

The very air pulsed with enterprise. Portland's 1866 fire had burned fifteen hundred buildings in the commercial and professional heart of the city: the docks, the warehouses, the shops and eating houses, the banks, schools, and offices. Downtown Portland was entirely rebuilt by 1874 and new "handsome business blocks" of brick, stone, and marble replaced the old colonial buildings. Blethen's law offices were on Exchange Street, as were the headquarters of the Board of Trade, the United States Superior Court, the Merchants' Bank, and the Printers' Exchange where the daily *Argus, Advertiser,* and *Portland Press* were published. All along

Exchange and Middle streets, the four dozen attorneys who practiced law in Portland maintained their offices, saw their clients, prepared cases, and huddled over deals. It was the city's vital center.[46]

The practice of law in Portland was extremely competitive and many lawyers stitched their livings together by dabbling in commerce, real estate, and other ventures. Blethen's first newspaper advertisements had indicated that he maintained a general legal practice, but would gladly handle local collections and the prompt execution of legal documents. He had, by some means, also secured the office of justice of the peace. By March 1874, he entered into partnership with William H. Motley, as MOTLEY & BLETHEN, Attorneys At Law, and the two young lawyers moved into new offices together on Exchange Street. They pled a case together in superior court in November 1875, but soon had a falling out and Blethen then worked alone.[47]

He was, in the slang of the day, a "warm man," aggressive and enterprising. He had repaid his loan to Rose Ann's father and arrived in Portland, according to his older son, with nearly $5,000 in cash. Rose Ann Blethen owned their home on Bramhall Street; in fact, she owned the family's three increasingly luxurious homes, all within two blocks of one another. Although the significance is not clear, it was highly unusual for a married woman to own property in her own name at this time. Alden Blethen also speculated in real estate in Portland, buying city houses as rentals. His son, Joseph, ten years old in 1880, remembered vaguely that his father was involved in any number of business ventures. Joe's brother, Clarance Brettun Blethen, born in Portland in 1879, was named in gratitude to rich uncle Soranus Brettun, who had made substantial loans to Alden and Rose Ann Blethen. It took money

to make money in Portland deals, and it took influence to gain influence. Alden Blethen wove his friendships, his wife's family connections, his profession, his politics, and his fraternal memberships into business relationships.[48]

Though Josiah Drummond, Blethen's patron, was a very active Mason in Portland, there is no clear indication that the young man joined any Masonic lodge in the city. He continued to attend the Oddfellows meetings

The busy heart of downtown Portland, looking down Exchange Street, taken from a contemporary engraving in Elwell's 1876 Portland and Vicinity.

BUSINESS CARDS.

MOTLEY & BLETHEN,

ATTORNIES AT LAW,

49 1-2 EXCHANGE STREET,

(Over Dresser & McLellan's Book Store.)

WM. H. MOTLEY.   ALDEN J. BLETHEN.
mar5-3m

ALDEN J. BLETHEN,

Attorney at Law,

PORTLAND,   -   -   MAINE.

Prompt attention given to all business sent from Franklin County. Practice in all the courts of the State, and special attention given to practice in the United States Courts.

Above left: This Portland Press *advertisement documents the short-lived legal partnership between Alden Blethen and William Motley.*

(The Portland Press, March 4, 1874)

Above right: In early 1879, Alden Blethen broadened his legal business to include nationwide collections, as here explained in The Portland Advertiser.

(The Portland Advertiser, January 3, 1879)

Lower left: Alden Blethen sought legal business from residents of rural Maine in brother-in-law Otis Moore's weekly newspaper, The Phillips Phonograph.

(The Phillips Phonograph, December 21, 1878)

Legal Claims.

THE undersigned takes pleasure in calling the attention of business men to his new plan for FOREIGN collections.

I have reliable correspondents in any county in nearly all the States of the Union, New Brunswick, Nova Scotia, the Provinces of Quebec and Ontario.

Parties residing in Portland holding demands against persons in Chicago, St. Louis, San Francisco, &c., can send claim through my office and enforce collection just as well as if the debtor resided here.

ALL LEGAL business promptly executed at fair compensation.

We attend promptly to all business, whether foreign or local, charge fair prices for services rendered, satisfy all, and pay over all funds to creditors immediately on collection.

ALDEN J. BLETHEN,
Attorney at Law,
Centennial Block, Portland, Me.

---

and participated in their many outings and excursions. He was also active in the Portland Provident Association, organized to provide charitable assistance to "needy and deserving persons" in the city.[49]

In addition to his fraternal and benevolent involvement, Alden Blethen continued his political activities. He submitted articles occasionally to the Portland Republican press, fiercely partisan pieces to suit the taste of the day, and once casually remarked to a friend that the newspaper business intrigued him. Blethen was also "in demand as a political orator," whipping up excitement among the Republican faithful. During the 1876 elections, the Republicans of Portland pulled out all the stops, mounting a nighttime parade of thousands who walked in companies past brightly illuminated homes, hung with placards picturing James Blaine and Thomas Reed. The marchers rallied in the park for hours of patriotic music and tableaux, punctuated with Republican oratory. Blethen's "political speeches" were extraordinary performances, heavy with historical allusions and rhetorical flourishes, alternately flaying his opponents with razor-sharp sarcasm and calling down thundering denunciations on

their heads. A man of only moderate height, Alden Blethen nonetheless possessed the platform and filled its space. He grasped the lectern and gathered the audience with his eyes, lowering his voice to a stage whisper; or strode back and forth, slashing the air with his arms, trumpeting his outrage.[50]

Professionally, Blethen was most successful working from this rhetorical strength and pleading his case before a jury. In later years, he told his sons that he became a successful trial lawyer in Portland, and his obituaries and biographies have echoed that claim. Blethen's younger son Clarance was satisfied that his father had been "well launched on a sound legal career" in Portland, and that he had gone toe-to-toe in court against the distinguished Thomas Brackett Reed on many occasions. The Blethen genealogy, edited by Alden Blethen himself, claimed that he pursued a legal career "winning distinction both in criminal and bankruptcy proceedings."[51]

An anecdote later recounted in an obituary captures Blethen's reputation for courtroom tenacity. One day the young lawyer was walking his dog in a Portland park when the dog chased after a cat. A passerby intervened on behalf of the cat, but Blethen's dog knocked the man down and tore his clothes. Enraged, the fellow ran up to Blethen, not recognizing him, and heatedly demanded to be reimbursed for the damage. As a final argument, he threatened to "go straight to Blethen's office," hire the attorney to represent his interests, and "let him sock it to you" in court if payment for the trousers was not instantly forthcoming. Smiling, Blethen was said to have settled the matter at once.[52]

He was at his best in a courtroom, as a trial lawyer—dramatic, sarcastic, and wheedling at turns, and the sensational Witham murder case seemed to offer the voluble and flamboyant attorney the chance of his lifetime.

In May 1879, Portland newspaper readers were shocked and titillated by the arraignment of a prominent local physician, Charles H. Witham, on charges of fornication and murder. A domestic, Annie Small, accused him of murdering their baby after the infant was born in a botched abortion attempt. She said tearfully that early in their affair he had written her letters and claimed that he loved her; he had made plans to elope; he promised to always take care of her. Instead, she charged, he repeatedly administered ergot to induce an abortion, then, when the infant was born alive, murdered the baby and hid its body. After trusting him, she found herself a bereaved and ruined woman. She didn't know whether she had given birth to a son or a daughter.[53]

Dr. Witham claimed to be the innocent victim of a blackmail scheme, and retained Blethen as his attorney. Blethen and Sewall Strout, vice president of the Cumberland County Bar, undertook Dr. Witham's defense amidst considerable uproar and publicity. Maine newspapers from Phillips to Farmington noted Witham's arrest and his selection of Blethen as his attorney; the Portland newspapers looked forward to a long and well-fought case, and provided prominent daily coverage of THE MURDER CASE, as it was called.[54]

First, Witham was tried on the murder charge. Under Maine law at the time, an abortion was a felony; however, if Witham were convicted of murder, he would almost certainly be hung. The issue turned, then, on whether the baby had been born living and when life should be said to begin, at conception or with respiration. "The turning point of this case," as Alden Blethen argued in court, "is, was this child born alive?" As the case unfolded, the tiny body was recovered from the privy vault into which Dr. Witham

had thrown it, and placed in a glass jar filled with alcohol. An autopsy concluded that there were no severe injuries to the body, but it proved impossible to determine whether respiration had taken place—and whether life existed—because of the effect of alcohol on the lungs. That method of preserving the body was "by direction of Mr. Blethen," and the prosecution attempted to prove that he had known that alcohol-storage would likely save his client's life. Despite testimony closely followed by the medical and legal fraternities, this issue was never resolved in court.[55]

The Portland Advertiser reporter described the orphaned Annie Small as "a small girl with a pleasant face" and "somewhat weak-minded," while characterizing Charles Witham as "a good-looking man with brown hair and red side whiskers and mustache... carefully dressed and calm." On the stand, the servant girl appeared timid and awkward; the physician confident and well-spoken. Annie Small claimed that she heard her baby's cry; Charles Witham insisted that the fetus was born dead. On trial for his life, Witham's attorneys advised him to save himself by "shielding a greater crime with the lesser," as the prosecution put it, and essentially admit to inducing an abortion with ergot rather than murdering the infant. The prosecution could not prove that the baby had been born living; therefore, it became very difficult to convince the jury that a murder had actually taken place, and impossible to prove Witham's guilt for that crime.[56]

After days of testimony and argument, the jury retired and found Witham not guilty of murder. Blethen had conducted much of the examination and cross-examination of witnesses, and *The Advertiser*'s reporter found his two hours of closing argument "very able." The verdict was a professional triumph for him. However, Witham's conviction in his

During their stay in Portland, Alden and Rose Ann Blethen frequently bought and sold real estate to supplement the family's income. Blethen placed this ad for building lots in The Portland Advertiser.

(The Portland Advertiser, November 24, 1878)

second trial, for fornication or "criminal intimacy," was a foregone conclusion. Despite the defense's efforts to portray Annie Small as promiscuous, a parade of witnesses enthralled the court with sensational testimony about Witham's own promiscuity. Annie Small had produced a sheaf of his passionate letters. During his wife's absences, he had invited not only Annie Small but her friend to his bed—on the same night. Witham was a libertine by the standards of 1879 Portland; his way of life "revolting to any human being." Blethen, then, had successfully defended a man against a murder charge whose personal conduct outraged the standards of community morality. In high irony, his stunning professional success may have led to professional failure. Blethen became notorious rather than famous.[57]

During this same summer of 1879, Blethen's sudden celebrity was matched by a new political prominence as he emerged from Republican ranks to a conspicuous position within the Maine Greenback Party. American farmers experienced hard times throughout the 1870s as their debts increased and prices for farm products declined. A grass roots movement arose to boost prices by putting more money into circulation, including the $450 million in emergency paper money—"greenbacks"—that had been issued throughout the Civil War years. During Reconstruction, conservatives wished to "retire" this currency, unsupported by the gold standard, as inflationary and unstable. Members of the Greenback Party disagreed and argued that the supply of paper currency should instead be increased. The Greenbackers swept Maine in a frenzy, drawing enthusiastic converts from both established parties. A backcountry zealot explained the party's economic proposals to a political rally in Portland:

I am a farmer and raise three hogs every year for market. Time was when I got 11 cents a pound, then 9, then 7, then in 1878, 4 1/2 cents a pound for what cost me 5 cents to produce. By raising 1000 pounds of pork I was $10 poorer.... We don't farm for fun. When we get no growth, we can hire no labor.... Scale down the gold dollar.... Make paper and silver the peers of gold. We want all the money we can get. We want more money and higher prices.[58]

In the spring of 1879, the Greenbackers' arguments and their startling success convinced Blethen to support them. People responded enthusiastically to their simple solutions to enduring and complex economic problems. The previous fall, the Greenbackers had swept into the Maine statehouse with a majority in both houses and elected their own governor, Alonzo Garcelon, promising reform and a transfer of political power from the moneyed elite. Hopping on the bandwagon, longtime Republican James D. Lamson, Blethen's uncle, ran for the state senate from rural Waldo County as a Greenback candidate. He was not alone. Blethen stumped Franklin County making speeches for a number of old Farmington friends who had abandoned the Republican Party to run for office on the Greenback ticket. By summer, Alden Blethen's name appeared in the Portland newspapers every day, arguing the Witham murder and fornication cases, and identified as a well-known local attorney who had joined the Greenback ranks.[59]

The Greenbackers were forerunners of the Populists, opponents of a nation grown increasingly urban and industrial. In Maine, their greatest strength was in the rural counties, and the city press made fun of Greenback spokesmen as "Farmer This" or "Brother That," mocking their pronunciation and grammar. Alden Blethen's distinction as a

Greenback convert lay, in part, in his city professionalism; very few Portland attorneys were identified with the Greenback Party. But Blethen had spent a tough boyhood in the farm country; he understood the hard work, long hours, and poverty, and could express the simmering agrarian discontent. Indeed, Portland itself was not immune to the consequences of the agricultural depression, and Blethen's old partner William Motley was one of a number of people in the city to face bankruptcy. However, Blethen perceived himself as a reformer rather than a revolutionary, and his political roots were firmly in the Republican Party. He mistrusted the alliance—or "fusion"—between Greenbackers and Democrats that some political realists saw as the only way to beat the Republicans, once and for all.[60]

Blethen concluded his Franklin County political barnstorming by joining Rose Ann and the boys, Joe and Clarance, for a vacation trip to Strong. His brother-in-law Otis Moore, editor of *The Phonograph* published in nearby Phillips, teased Blethen in print, rejoicing that he had made "no political speeches" while fishing and relaxing with the family. It was the calm before the storm.

Maine's Counting Out crisis received national attention. This engraving of the dramatic scene in the Maine state senate is taken from Leslie's Illustrated Newspaper *of January 1880.*

(Maine Historical Society)

On his return to Portland, election day eve, Blethen was enraged to find that Democrats had infiltrated and seized control of the city Greenback Party. Overnight, he and purist Greenbackers created a write-in slate to run alongside the Republican and Fusion tickets in his ward. This "straight Greenback ticket" listed Alden Blethen as candidate for Cumberland County attorney. But the quixotic Greenback crusade garnered few votes in suburban Portland, and Blethen and his friends met easy defeat at Republican hands. Statewide, too, the Republicans ran very well. When the legislature convened, the Greenbackers would surely lose their majority in the statehouse and the opportunity to select the governor; instead, all hell broke loose in the respectable state of Maine.[61]

Seeking to retain political power, lameduck Greenback Governor Alonzo Garcelon and his council refused to seat duly-elected Republican candidates from more than fifty towns and cities in Maine. They argued that there were procedural irregularities in many races and that more than twenty Republican senators and representatives should not be seated and should be "counted out." The great Counting Out scandal of 1879-80 placed Augusta under virtual martial law and brought Maine to the verge of civil war, as two antagonistic state governments stood parallel to one another. Companies of armed civilians ringed Augusta and prepared to attack the regular militia and capture the statehouse. Politicians received dozens of death threats; someone ran a fuse into James G. Blaine's hayloft on his farm near Augusta. The Greenbackers had proven far more radical than Blethen anticipated, and he found himself identified with a lawless party of violence and anarchy.[62]

On the night of December 23, 1879, Portland held a great non-partisan meeting of indignation in response to the Counting Out. The city's own Republican representatives had not been seated in Augusta, and infuriated citizens overflowed the city hall to listen to hours of speeches decrying "this dangerous and wicked scheme." Once a reform Republican, recently a purist Greenbacker, now an outraged voter, Alden Blethen was the final speaker of that long and angry night. Standing on the platform with Thomas Brackett Reed and other prominent Portland Republicans, Blethen told the crowd that he had been invited to participate because he no longer represented any political party. He said he had been persuaded in the spring that the Greenbackers "had principles of reform and independence of action at heart," but confessed that he had "made a woeful blunder." He deplored the Counting Out as irresponsible, fraudulent, and insurrectionary, and concluded his remarks with the plea that there be no bloodshed, that the supreme judicial court be allowed to decide the matter. He ate crow well, but he doubtless did not eat it happily.[63]

Blethen's humiliation and anger must have been compounded when the Greenbackers nominated his uncle, James D. Lamson, perennial Waldo County legislator, as President of *their* Senate. Lamson became Maine's acting governor on January 10, 1880. The explosive situation in Augusta continued throughout January, as five hundred Greenback irregulars camped near the capitol. Governor Lamson remained resolute, unfazed by the anarchy. He officially declared the Republican legislators to be a "mob," and directed the commander of the state militia to eject them from the statehouse. As the supreme judicial court considered the varying suits and counter-suits, Blethen left Portland for a business trip to Kansas City, Missouri. While he was gone, the court declared the

Greenbackers' efforts to "count out" their successful opponents unconstitutional. Slowly, the situation grew calm, and the armed citizens returned to their farms.[64]

In February 1880, Blethen announced he would leave Maine for reasons of health and establish a legal partnership with William Carlile, a prominent attorney of Kansas City, Missouri. He promptly placed his home on the market, characteristically describing it as "the most desirable house and lot in the city." *The Portland Advertiser* noted his decision to leave with a paragraph of biography, and concluded with regret, mentioning Blethen's "attack of hemorrhage of the lungs" the preceding fall. Likewise, brother-in-law Otis Moore specifically noted Blethen's "present poor health" in his own article in *The Phillips Phonograph*.[65]

Throughout his life, Alden Blethen maintained that he had left Portland in 1880 because of illness. His older son Joe—who was then ten years old—remembered that his father returned from a successful trial proceeding and "collapsed with a hemorrhage of the lungs." In their reminiscences, both of Alden Blethen's sons related their Portland doctor's recommendation that the family move to a dry climate to relieve his "severe bronchial trouble." Yet Missouri seems a peculiar destination for a Yankee invalid. Its muggy summers and stormy winters would not have offered a substantial improvement over Maine's own climate. Missouri and Maine also differed radically in character and heritage. Missouri was the slave state that had balanced Maine's admission as a free state in the Compromise of 1820; it was contested ground during the Civil War. When Farmington and Portland newspapers mentioned Missouri, they described a lawless place, packed with wild, unreconstructed Democrats, good whiskey, and bad men and women. In contrast, Maine had been dry since 1851; it was a Methodist and Republican stronghold and—usually—upright and respectable. But perhaps Blethen had truly fallen ill; certainly he had undergone tremendous stress. Perhaps he had grown bored and footloose. At thirty-five, he may simply have wanted to try his luck in the West, impatient with his life in Maine.[66]

Blethen had earned a modest legal reputation, at best. In early 1879, in a strategy to bring in business, his newspaper ad introduced a "new plan for foreign collections," naming "reliable correspondents" throughout the U.S. and Canada who could assist clients in collecting delinquent debts. This new enterprise suggests either an entrepreneurial mind or too little legal business; after his death, an anonymous colleague coolly judged that he had practiced law in Portland "without a marked degree of success." He had an unimpressive record before the Maine Supreme Judicial Court. Blethen argued his first case in 1874 with then-partner William Motley and won the decision. Likewise, Blethen's arguments persuaded the court in a bankruptcy proceeding in 1877. However, thereafter, he argued three appeals from superior court or the court of insolvency decisions, all dealing with bankruptcy issues, and lost all three. Reading the justices' opinions, Blethen was faulted on his preparation and interpretation of existing case law. He was not a lawyer's lawyer, not a legal intellectual.[67]

In six years, Blethen had argued perhaps four dozen cases before the superior court; occasionally his name was mentioned as counsel in municipal court. Though his obituary claimed that many of his cases were settled out of court because opposing counsel feared his skills, the infrequency of his court appearances is striking. His reported cases were humble, bread-and-butter matters, and the judgments were small. They were argued on behalf of ordinary people who had kept an open shop on Sunday or were short-changed on the purchase of a suit of clothes. Arguing to juries, relying on his rhetorical skill, flashing his temper and wit, he won more of these cases than he lost, and earned a reputation as a dogged litigator though not as the "great pleader" he claimed in retrospect. Perhaps he would find more opportunity in the West.[68]

Everywhere Alden Blethen had lived and worked—Unity, Kent's Hill, Farmington, even Portland—the newspapers were full of letters home from successful Maine men who had ventured west to the gold fields of California or to the cities of the Midwest, and later to the sheep ranges of the Western plains. In 1873, a historian of Waldo County noted that the rural population had steadily fallen for three decades and regretted the "restless roving spirit of the Yankee" that sent men off to the sea, to the city, and to the West. The historian counseled "adherence to our native place," but the land was played out; it was losing its sons and daughters. And, in the wake of the Witham case and the Greenback scandal, Blethen may have been especially glad to leave Maine behind.[69]

In six months, Blethen's political and professional plans had gone awry. He had always been one of four dozen bright young attorneys in Portland, but now he was no longer so young and he had flouted community sentiment. His Greenback politics had alienated powerful Republicans like Thomas Reed and James Blaine. It was time to leave. In the spring, Alden Blethen argued his last losing case before the Maine Supreme Judicial Court, sold or leased the Portland houses, closed his practice, and packed up his law books.[70]

In the late afternoon of May 26, 1880, Blethen leaned forward on the window sill,

staring down at the throng on the crowded sidewalks. He knew nearly all of them—the lawyers walking side by side in earnest conference, the knot of newspapermen arguing about a *Press* editorial, the portly bankers heading to their club. This was Exchange Street, the heart of Portland, Maine, where law, influence, and money came together in one grand and powerful embrace. Blethen had arrived here as a young man of twenty-nine, newly admitted to the bar, fierce with ambition; he was leaving at thirty-five, an

uncertain success, plagued by ill health.

Behind him, his office was stripped and a row of bulky packing crates stood along the wall. The desk drawers were empty; the shelves cleared. Soon, he would lock his office door for the last time. The next day, Alden Blethen would take the train and head west. For two hundred years the Blethens had made their homes in New England, but familiar scenes, familiar gains and losses, familiar friends and enemies would soon all slip away.

In the morning, the Blethens left Maine behind. Alden Blethen stopped in Chicago to attend the Republican National Convention, while the rest of the family traveled through to Missouri. When the census was taken later that summer, Rose Ann Blethen, ten-year-old Joseph, and baby Clarance were listed with the new arrivals in Kansas City, wide-eyed newcomers in that astonishing Western boomtown. Soon, Alden Blethen joined them, and the family started all over again.[71]

The Western Promenade of Bramhall Hill, a block away from the Blethen home in Portland, offered a spectacular view of the sunset to the West. This engraving is from Edward Elwell's 1876 Portland and Vicinity.

In 1880, Alden and Rose Ann Blethen
and their two sons left Maine to travel by
train to a new life in Kansas City,
Missouri. Union Station was brand new,
the pride of this wild little cattle town
with aspirations to be a big city.

(University of Missouri at Kansas City)

When the Blethen family arrived in
1880, Kansas City was riding an
extended wave of dramatic growth. Only
ten years earlier, the town's pretentious
opera hall and the Coates House hotel
had presided over a cow pasture.

(The Kansas City Star)

2 GOING WEST

In the summer of 1880, Alden and Rose Blethen, and their sons Joe and Clarance, were living in rented rooms at the Coates House, the only good hotel in Kansas City, Missouri. The Yankee tenderfeet from Maine were astonished by the Western town's sights and sounds, its boisterous vulgarity, crude boomtown buildings, cowboys and Indians, and the "Battle Row" of saloons, brothels, and gambling dens. By comparison, Portland seemed clean, quiet, and refined.

Once a river town, Kansas City had become a railroad city, the point of interchange for thirteen railroads, as well as a bewildering array of short-lines. Thriving on Eastern investment, Kansas City was dominated by huffing steam locomotives, huge grain elevators, and twenty-six acres of feedlots and stock pens. Each year, more than one million cattle and hogs passed through town, either sold to local packers or shipped by rail to distant buyers. Kansas Citians listened all night long to the grinding squeals of the rail cars and inhaled the fierce odors of the stockyards—the sounds and smells of Western prosperity.[1]

The city's population had doubled in ten years to nearly sixty thousand, and would continue this rapid increase during Blethen's years there. Kansas City had been a wild little cattle town; it became a Western center for rail and river shipping; it aspired to be the legal, financial, and manufacturing capital of the West, a city of good schools and elegant suburbs. But, in 1880, Kansas City was raw and ugly, torn between identities, boasting a garish opera house and one decent hotel. Townsfolk sweltered in the summer's muggy heat and shivered in the winter snow storms. When the earth wasn't frozen, it liquefied to a distinctive clinging mud or dried to a gritty red dust. The city was all bluffs and gulches in an endless upheaval of grading and filling, regrading and refilling.[2]

In the entire city, there were a few dozen newly planted trees, two board sidewalks, and only one paved street. But 1880 bank clearings—the total amount of money flowing through the city's financial institutions—exceeded $100,000,000. The largest city between St. Louis and San Francisco, Kansas City ran full-throttle seven days a week, a wide-open boomtown. Proprietors of the "Sodom at the mouth of the Kansas" operated brothels openly and paid hefty licensing fees for dozens of saloons, burlesque houses, and gambling halls. Kansas City's sinners—its soiled doves, card sharps, train robbers, and tired cowpokes—were good business. But not, it seemed, for an attorney from Maine.[3]

Alden Blethen always maintained that he had moved to Kansas City to recover his health and to build a successful law practice. Certainly, William Carlile, his intended partner, was well-educated and well-connected; the scrabbling Westerners were gratifyingly litigious. But Blethen practiced very briefly with Carlile and their partnership was

This studio portrait of Joseph Blethen and his little brother, Clarance (C.B.), was taken soon after the family's arrival in Kansas City.

(The Seattle Times)

Kansas City was built in terraces along the river's steep western bluff. During the years that the Blethens lived here, the city underwent constant regrading, as hills were leveled and gullies filled in.
(The Kansas City Star)

Opposite: Farm and ranch families rode many miles into town on public market days. Here, in Kansas City's market square, folks "parked" their wagons while they shopped and visited.
(University of Missouri at Kansas City)

stormy, ending in hard feelings. As the arrangement dissolved, Carlile angrily accused Blethen of a lack of sincerity and integrity. But Blethen had always viewed the law as an avenue to other opportunities, and his allegiance to the legal profession had grown uncertain.[4]

Much later, in Seattle, Blethen wrote that he was shocked to find a legal code in force in Missouri "so vicious in its character that it did not require any legal acquirements nor study to practice." Maine's common law tradition depended on centuries of legal precedent, but Missouri attorneys practiced according to a civil code that substituted honest argument and plain English for obscure Latin antiquities. Blethen had decided to leave Kansas City when he "received a tempting offer," as his son later explained it. He changed his mind and remained in Missouri, but abandoned his law career for the rest of his life.[5]

One evening in the Coates House bar, Blethen was relaxing away from the crowded upstairs room that he and Rose shared with the boys. He overheard a conversation between two men who were seeking a third investor to buy an interest in *The Kansas City Journal.* He listened, then introduced himself and joined their table. After some discussion, Blethen offered to raise $40,000 for the venture, intending to borrow most of the money from his wife's wealthy uncle Soranus Brettun. According to Blethen's son, the two men—publisher Robert T. Van Horn and editor John Lawrence—agreed to his father's proposal and waited while Blethen journeyed up to Illinois by train to persuade Uncle Soranus. Certainly, the newspaper was a sound investment opportunity. *The Journal* was a Kansas City institution, the oldest newspaper in town, published continuously since 1854.[6]

Blethen had become interested in newspapers back in Maine in the 1870s, when the daily paper was the focus of popular intellectual life and editors had as great an effect as ministers on public opinion and behavior. He was drawn to newspapers as he had been drawn to teaching, to the law, to real estate speculation—as another avenue toward success and influence. And he knew a little about the business, too. His brother-in-law, Otis Moore, published the weekly *Phillips Phonograph,* and Blethen had been close friends with the owner of *The Farmington Chronicle* during his years at Little Blue. In Portland, Blethen wrote occasionally for the newspapers, and the city press provided increasing coverage of his professional and political activities. He was acquainted with many of the city's publishers, editors, and reporters. Like all men of affairs, Alden Blethen read the newspapers every day and paid a great deal of attention to them.

Newspapers were the primary mass communication medium of the nineteenth

century—people's daily source for information, gossip, and opinion. In 1870s Portland, readers eagerly devoured column after column of stale news recast in drab prose, in hand-set papers of two sheets, or eight pages. There were no headlines, no columnists, no comics; editors made little effort to please or amuse the reader. The Portland newspapers remained openly partisan, their reporting of events highly colored by their political points of view. Bogus, even dangerous, claims filled the advertisements, and engravings in these ads often served as the only illustrations in the paper. Yet publishers of the daily press wielded enormous power—contested only by one another—to promote political candidates, civic crusades, or their own ventures. In 1880, newspaper publishing was an exciting and profitable business enterprise, on the verge of dramatic change.[7]

Alden Blethen negotiated for a one-fifth share of *The Kansas City Journal* during the fall of 1880, and came to work as business manager. One week after his arrival, *The Journal* began to publish a redesigned newspaper on a brand-new press, and rivals noted that "it has changed not only its management but also its dress." Proudly, *The Journal* introduced its two new partial owners, Alden Blethen and John Lawrence:

> The gentlemen who assume their new duties...are young, active men, of trained business habits, and come with the very best endorsements of the very best men in their former homes, and we bespeak for them the good offices of our patrons and people, until all become better acquainted. *The Journal*, like Kansas City, receives fresh and vigorous blood from the new conditions and populations that have made her the first among the rising cities of the West, and it is by this method that it renews its youth as it renews its years.[8]

Blethen had made a shrewd and lucky investment. *The Kansas City Journal* was a sound business proposition, printing a nickel daily for city readers as well as weekly editions for subscribers scattered across the booming New West from Arizona to Montana. Newsboys rushed out the city edition before breakfast, and mailers hurried the country edition onto the early trains. *The Journal* boasted a daily circulation of ten thousand and a Sunday circulation of fourteen thousand, double that of any other Kansas City paper. Through its contract with the Kansas and Missouri Associated Press (KMAP), *The Journal* purchased telegraph news from across the nation and around the world. The physical plant was housed in a downtown building less than two years old and boasted a brand new Scott-Webb press.[9]

The Journal hoped to maintain a competitive edge among the dailies in Kansas City and the weeklies throughout the rural West by making a substantial investment in the "new journalism" of the 1880s, a potent mixture of new technology, brighter content and style, and more sophisticated business methods. Successful newspapers appealed to a mass readership thrilled by the immediacy of telegraph and telephone news. Readers also preferred lively design—more illustrations and decked headlines, entertaining features, and broad news coverage, with attention to accuracy, timeliness, and vivid expression. And they wanted newspapers easy to read, cleanly laid out, with sharp, clear print.[10]

Since 1865, *The Journal* had purchased three new presses, one after the other, rushing to keep pace with changing technology. In only fifteen years, *The Kansas City Journal* increased production from four hundred single sheets an hour to fifteen thousand eight-page newspapers an hour. In 1865, cut paper had been fed sheet-by-sheet into a

Robert T. Van Horn was the long-time publisher and editor of The Kansas City Journal *and majority owner during Blethen's years on the paper. A power in Missouri Republican politics, and in the economic and civic development of Kansas City, he used his newspaper to further his personal agenda.*

hand-operated press, directly imprinted by movable type locked into a flat form. Then, each sheet was peeled off by hand and placed on a stack. In 1880, paper flowed off a roll in a continuous "web," as it was called, and was printed front and back from curved stereotype plates, cast for each edition from the impression of the composed page into a *papier maché* mat. This versatile machine—called the "perfecting press"—cut the web into sheets, sorted the sheets into sets, and then folded the finished newspapers.[11] Its "complications of tapes and pulleys, flying cams, vibrating creasers and switches, and an endless train of fine gearing" required the constant vigilance of an oiler and mechanic, but *The Journal* boasted that the press produced newspapers almost automatically:

> Everybody has read of the machine, that by throwing brush and tree tops in at one end, delivered rakes, ax handles and agricultural implements at the other. Our new press is a first cousin to that machine. It don't quite take a bundle of rags and make newspapers of them, but it does take hold of an endless web of white paper at one end, and delivers perfect *Journals* at the other, folded, cut and pasted, and the rate of fifteen thousand per hour.... We are simply *fixed*, and that is all of it![12]

During Alden Blethen's tenure as business manager, the wonderful new press was pushed to its limit to meet *The Journal*'s soaring circulation. Blethen introduced a number of novel promotional stunts, like offering a pocket watch as a subscription premium. The most expensive innovation added an eight-page supplement to the weekly *Journal*, featuring illustrated fiction, lists of produce and stock prices, and lavish retail and mail order ads. Much of this material was produced by national syndicates in the distant cities of New York and Chicago, then shipped to

KANSAS CITY JOURNAL BUILDING.

In 1881, a year after Alden Blethen's arrival, W.H. Miller's History of Kansas City *printed this engraving of* The Kansas City Journal *building on the busy corner of Sixth and Delaware.*

The brief legal partnership of Carlile and Blethen is noted in Kansas City's 1880 city directory.

A Magnificent Premium ! The JOURNAL.

The Celebrated "WATERBURY" Watch, made by the Waterbury Watch Co., Waterbury, Conn.,

NOW OFFERED AS A PREMIUM FOR THE SUNDAY OR WEEKLY KANSAS CITY JOURNAL.

Here is an opportunity for every school boy, mechanic and laborer to procure a first-class "time keeper" at ridiculously low prices. Read carefully what the makers say about this watch; and then read the offer below:

We will send the WEEKLY JOURNAL one year to any address for $1.00, and a Watch, in an elegant satin-lined case, for $3.00, registry fees prepaid by us; WATCH and PAPER for $4.00.

TWO Copies of the WEEKLY and one WATCH as above for - -	$4.90.
THREE Copies of the WEEKLY and one WATCH as above for - -	5.75.
FIVE Copies of the WEEKLY and one WATCH as above for - -	7.50.
EIGHT Copies of the WEEKLY and one WATCH as above for - -	10.00.
TEN Copies of the WEEKLY and one WATCH as above for - -	11.50.
FIFTEEN Copies of the WEEKLY and one WATCH as above for - -	15.00.
TWENTY Copies of the WEEKLY and one WATCH as above for - -	18.50.

All remittances must be made at SAME TIME. For example: Suppose you desire to send three subscriptions and get a Watch. Go to your nearest postoffice and purchase a money order for $5.75 and remit with full directions as to the postoffice address of the persons who are to receive the papers, and your own address. Give names in full, with Town, County and State. Address all communications to the "JOURNAL CO., Kansas City, Mo." You would also remit for any other number, from one to twenty copies, in a like manner.

To those persons who would prefer the SUNDAY JOURNAL, we make the following offer:

ONE Copy of SUNDAY JOURNAL one year and one WATCH,	$5.00.
TWO Copies of SUNDAY JOURNAL one year and one WATCH,	6.80.
THREE Copies of SUNDAY JOURNAL one year and one WATCH,	8.50.
FIVE Copies of SUNDAY JOURNAL one year and one WATCH,	12.00.

EXACT SIZE OF WATCH.

With Solid Plate and Full Dial.

All watches, previous to this date, made by us, have had open dial and skeleton plates, showing all the moving parts of the watch through the dial. The demand for a full dial, enabling the position of the hands to be more readily seen, has of late been so great, we have concluded to make all watches in future (unless specially ordered otherwise) with *full dial* and *solid* (not skeleton) plates. We are fully satisfied, from tests made, that the solid plates now used will result in making the *Waterbury* a much more reliable time-keeper, being less liable to damage, both in transportation and in the hands of the wearer.

In this new, *solid plate* movement the position of the regulator has been changed; it will be found projecting beyond the plate, immediately under the bezel holding the glass (see cut). The danger of injuring the hair-spring in regulating is hereby obviated, which is a most desirable feature in this full dial watch.

All watches are cased in cases made of an entirely new metal called Nickel-Silver. For the purpose, this metal is the nearest to silver yet attained, will wear white, and, although more expensive than the one abandoned, we shall make no change in the price of the watch.

Each watch will be put up in our handsome new improved spring-box, satin-lined, which will carry the watch safely through the mails.

WE GUARANTEE

As business manager of The Journal *during a period of circulation growth, Alden Blethen was responsible for a number of successful advertising campaigns. This one, which ran in 1883, was designed to promote the Sunday or weekly edition of the newspaper by offering a pocket watch as a premium to subscribers.*

(The Kansas City Journal, April 5, 1883)

The Journal as readyprints and stereotypes. Blethen pushed the weekly as "The Cheapest Paper in the West!", an affordable necessity for every reading family. A weekly news magazine, *The Journal* made the Great New West a smaller and more comfortable place as far-flung subscribers shared a common reading experience with each mail.[13]

One of the sensational stories Western readers shared in the early '80s concerned the daring train and bank robberies of Frank and Jesse James. These violent young men, guerrilla sons of Missouri's Civil War, intrigued the popular mind, and many found romance in the lives of the "boy rogues." *The Journal* never pandered to this fascination, but agitated continually for the James brothers' arrest and trial. Indeed, according to Blethen's youngest son, Jesse James took personal exception to *The Journal's* vendetta, and the bandit confronted the business manager one afternoon on a lonely street in Kansas City:

Alden had the cane that was characteristic of his outdoor attire throughout his life but no other weapon. Excepting for Jesse James there was not another human being in sight. Alden explained his ensuing movements solely on the ground that there wasn't anything else to do. If he stood still he was sure to be murdered in his tracks. If he attempted to run he was almost as sure to be shot down. Apparently without the slightest hesitation, Alden stormed straight across the street toward the bandit whose right hand rested on the butt of his gun. I have seen him in later years start after someone who had outraged him and I know what a fury he must have looked.... Simultaneous with his first movement in James' direction he commenced to shout orders to the bandit to get out of town and stay![14]

James did get out of Kansas City, and within a few months one of his gang members shot him in the back while he hung a picture in his modest frame house in St. Joseph, Missouri. *The Journal* declared, "Jesse James died like a dog, as he deserved to die, at the hands of a boy whom he had doubtless led into crime." Speaking for the rule of law and order in a metropolitan West, *The Journal* was bucking widespread public sentiment.[15]

The Kansas City Journal wasn't the only newspaper in town. In the 1880's, *The Journal* competed against another morning nickel paper, *The Kansas City Times*. The Democratic *Times* and the Republican *Journal* fought an endless war with countless volleys of hot words, and boosted one another's circulation. A third newspaper started in 1880, *The Kansas City Star,* a four-page evening paper. *The Star*, independent politically and beholden to no one, merrily exposed Kansas City's sweetheart contracts and corrupt candidates "utterly unfit for the positions to which they aspire." *The Star* practiced the new economics of mass circulation, selling newspapers cheap and advertising high. The keen competition made Kansas City a good school in the newspaper business for Alden Blethen.[16]

As business manager of *The Journal,* Blethen directed the newspaper's revenue side, working closely with publisher Van Horn, and an associate editor, commercial editor, telegraph editor, and city editor, as well as five local reporters. Blethen supervised the work of the company secretary and the chief bookkeeper, and planned the advertising and promotional campaigns that boosted circulation and kept ad rates high. Under his management, *The Journal* assigned an advertising clerk to the newspaper's telephone and sent six men knocking on doors to solicit ads.

Blethen had plenty of business headaches. *The Times* and the brand-new *Star* threatened circulation and ad accounts. Each week, payroll and expenses amounted to $2,000, and there was the new building and press to work off, too. *The Journal* stabled sixteen horses for the use of its road men and reporters, the "intelligent, active and tireless news gatherers." Blethen was concerned with securing newsprint, type metal, and ink, winning local and national advertising, negotiating labor contracts, and making arrangements with wire services for news and with national agencies for fiction, puzzles, and other features. Alden Blethen was at the center of conflict with Kansas City's labor unions and at the center of power within the new regional wire services.[17]

In the United States, the first news dispatches were sent out over a leased telegraph wire in 1850; twenty-five years later, the New York Associated Press in combination with the Western Union Telegraph Company supplied European cable news and national telegraph news to its affiliates, like the Western Associated Press (WAP). In turn the WAP then sold the wire service to regional auxiliaries, like the Kansas and Missouri Associated Press, which then sold the news to its own members, like *The Kansas City Journal.* The KMAP restricted the distribution of wire service franchises within the region to one morning and one evening newspaper in each city. No newspaper could be admitted to the

This portrait shows Jesse James at about thirty years of age, just a few months before he was murdered. James looked much like this when he confronted Alden Blethen on a lonely Kansas City street.

(Kansas City Public Library)

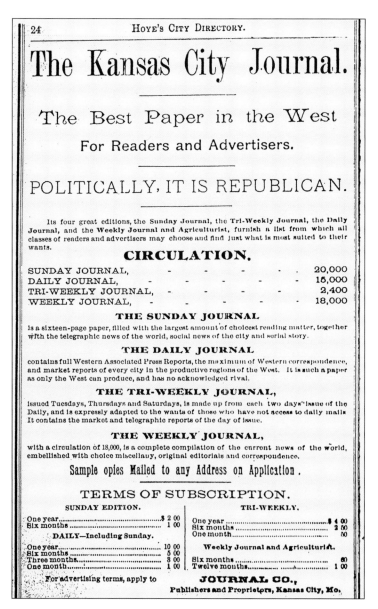

The Kansas City Journal *placed a full-page advertisement in the 1884 city directory, reassuring readers of its political orthodoxy and boasting of its circulation. Alden Blethen would soon come to a parting of the ways with his fellow owners of* The Journal.

(Kansas City Public Library)

regional organization without the unanimous agreement of the current members. Their lock on hot news virtually assured a newspaper's success in the new journalism wars.[18]

When readers grabbed their paper in the morning, they wanted to learn what had happened overnight around the world. In 1884, *The Kansas City Journal* telegraph editor and his assistant received fifteen thousand coded words each day over the wire, and laboriously transcribed the dispatches onto the newly invented typewriter—"the mill," as press telegraphers termed it. The morning *Journal,* off the presses at 6:00 a.m., took the last telegraph reports at 4:00 a.m. Hastily rewritten, the latest international and national wire service news was the last type set and locked into the front page every day by the typographers.[19]

Wire service newsbrokers shaped the information revolution of the new journalism. Attracted by the merger of influence, money, and technology, Blethen helped revise the bylaws of the Kansas and Missouri Associated Press, and then became that organization's director and president. His regional wire service activities placed him at the vital center of the newspaper business in the 1880s, and brought him to the attention of powerful allies. Alden Blethen acted as liaison between the KMAP and the Western Associated Press, negotiating directly with the WAP's general manager—and Blethen's future business partner—William Henry Smith.[20]

The Journal recognized and rewarded Blethen's accomplishments and he was promoted to vice president. In 1883, he completed the delicate business negotiations with Smith that led to his newspaper's full membership in the Western Associated Press. Building his widespread network of friends and contacts, Blethen made annual visits to Chicago, Minneapolis, and New York; he didn't miss an Associated Press annual meeting for more than thirty years. Moving from the small stage of the Kansas and Missouri Associated Press to the regional and national organizations, Alden Blethen positioned both *The Journal* and himself for wider success in the new journalism.[21]

In Missouri, the regional associated press also acted as a trade association for newspaper owners and managers. Throughout the industry, the rise of labor unions paralleled the rise of such business organizations, attempting to balance the concentration of power. The International Typographical Union (ITU) had organized in 1852, and later joined the growing American Federation of Labor.[22]

The Journal had developed a troubled relationship with Local 80 of the ITU during the business management of Alden Blethen's predecessor. In 1877, he had peremptorily cut wages by 20 percent, and gave Local 80 one hour to decide whether to accept or be locked out. The local capitulated and disbanded itself, and many of its members joined the radical Knights of Labor. Just before Blethen's arrival in Kansas City, the printers reaffiliated with their national craft union, regained the charter, and presented wage demands. In retaliation, *The Journal* locked out the union printers and Blethen permitted ITU members to work at the newspaper only if they deposited their union cards with him. If there were no problems, he promised to return the cards in six months. According to Local 80 meeting minutes, he did not do so. A standing disagreement between *The Journal* printers and the pressroom foreman erupted into angry shouts. Blethen blamed the ITU men.[23]

From then on, Blethen refused to permit any members of Local 80 to work at *The Journal,* and the union responded by declaring the newspaper—and eventually *The Kansas City Times* and *The Kansas City Star,* too—an unfair employer. For years, Local 80 fined or expelled printers who "ratted," or worked in *The Journal*'s composing room and pressroom without a special permit. Blethen refused to meet with their representatives, let alone negotiate with them, and *The Journal* was long printed by non-ITU men.[24]

At this time, the Printers' Protective Fraternity organized in Missouri as a "company

Looking along Main Street in downtown Kansas City in about 1883. This view shows the city as Alden Blethen knew it.
(Kansas City Public Library)

The Blethen family home on Pennsylvania Avenue, one of the principal residential streets of "Quality Hill," overlooking Kansas City. When the Blethens lived in this house, their oldest son Joe was a young teenager, attending commercial college downtown. C.B. Blethen's earliest memories were of this house, and the Blethen girls Florence and Marion were born here.

(The Seattle Times)

Alden Blethen had become a trustee of Kent's Hill in 1872 when he was still teaching at the Abbott Family School. Ten years later, as the successful business manager of The Kansas City Journal, he donated the funds to erect Blethen Hall on campus, as a home for the school's headmaster. This photograph was taken shortly after the house was completed in 1883.

(Kent's Hill School Archives)

union" rival to the ITU, which considered the Fraternity a "rat" union. The Fraternity's constitution endorsed negotiation and labor peace; it expressly prohibited strikes and walkouts. Although many typographers considered the Fraternity "a standing menace to free labor," the organization provided many of the same social and financial benefits available to Local 80 members. Spreading throughout the West from its Kansas City core, the Fraternity was encouraged by newspaper management and became a serious rival to the ITU.

International Typographical Union men refused to work in the same shop with the Fraternity men; and there was considerable violence. It was hard to know who to trust. In the shop, union printers identified themselves by standing next to a type tray and casually sifting lower case "i's" through their fingers; a "square man"—an ITU member—would respond by sifting "k's." As tensions ran high, Local 80 charged that *The Journal*, when Alden Blethen was business manager, had provided $500 to found the Printers' Protective Fraternity, and that the newspaper's management had "cradled" this organization of "long-tailed schemers."[25]

In Maine, Missouri, Minnesota, and Seattle, Alden Blethen considered himself an advocate of the laboring man, but he drew a sharp line between organized labor and radical labor. He perceived the members of ITU Local 80 as stubborn hotheads, possibly criminals; he perceived the Printers' Protective Fraternity as reasonable and respectable, good family men. The Kansas and Missouri Associated Press members, under Alden Blethen's presidency, struck back against the ITU printers in management resolutions distributed in their *Proceedings*, placing any strikers on a permanent black list with "drunken tramps" and other disreputable workmen.[26]

Blethen and his business partners in *The Kansas City Journal* disagreed over his handling of the ongoing labor problems with the printers. Although the details are uncertain, an exasperated Blethen eventually proposed a "give or take, fish or cut bait" offer to his partners that they either buy out his interest at $350 per share or he would buy theirs at $400. Blethen parted company from *The Journal* with $100,000, a small fortune in 1884.[27]

Though *The Journal*'s farewell editorial spoke of Blethen's pleasant association and valuable contributions, it is clear that there were conflicts among the owners. The rival *Kansas City Times* claimed Blethen had wielded virtually complete control of *The Journal* for the previous three years, and that he had single-handedly "taken *The Journal* out of the narrow rut of personal journalism in which it had floundered for years." Widening the rift with *The Journal*, Blethen gave an expansive interview to *The Times*, taking personal credit for replacing *The Journal*'s "old style" and for the increased circulation of both the daily and weekly editions. When asked his plans, Blethen genially indicated that he was considering a "very flattering proposal from New York soliciting [him] to take the editorial and business management of a well-established daily newspaper." Also, he said that he was in negotiations to become a partner in a "leading northwestern newspaper," in Minnesota or Wisconsin. He had not yet made up his mind, he said, but first he intended to take some time off. He could afford to.[28]

By the spring of 1884, Alden Blethen was a wealthy man and proud of it. Besides his newspaper earnings, he had "profited largely in real estate speculation" in Kansas City, riding the boom as town lots and suburban tracts increased their value one hundred fold in five years. Blethen was mindful that he had made his fortune as a capitalist, not a journalist, attorney, or educator. He interrupted his son Joseph's elite schooling with a practical stint at a local commercial college to study bookkeeping, business law, and general office practice.[29]

Prosperous and influential, Blethen had become prominent in Kansas City political, benevolent, and fraternal organizations. The family lived in "a private, handsome residence" on Quality Hill, the most exclusive neighborhood in the city. Blethen repaid his debt to Rose Blethen's uncle, Soranus Brettun, and made charitable gifts of his own. He continued his relationship with Kent's Hill as trustee, donating about $3,000 toward the construction of a home for the headmaster, to be named Blethen Hall. It delighted him to return to Kent's Hill as a philanthropist.[30]

The Blethen family had visited Maine during the summer of 1883, spending time at the school as well as with friends and relatives. Two family reminiscences suggest that Alden Blethen remained estranged from his mother and avoided a visit to Waldo County because there was "too great a risk in view of the danger in encountering Mrs. Gould." However, *The Phillips Phonograph* clearly noted that the Blethens had visited his mother and stepfather before traveling to Strong for the usual happy round of hiking, fishing, and picnicking in the mountains. It seems likely that family accounts omitted this visit because it was the occasion of a violent quarrel about the Kent's Hill philanthropy.[31]

Joseph Blethen alluded to this argument in his own brief reminiscences, writing that someone in the family had protested the extravagance of Blethen Hall, saying "if Alden had any money to give away he better give it in the family so long as any member

remained poor." Alden Blethen could scarcely believe his ears. He retorted that "he was the only one in the crowd to break out of the grind of farm work," and that they would do better to encourage their young people to follow in his footsteps than to "scold him for what he had done." If this argument took place between Alden Blethen and his mother or stepfather, it was the last straw. His visits to Maine grew less frequent, and he did not resume contact with Abigail Gould until her husband's death.[32]

During the family's visit to Maine, four-year-old Clarance fell ill with malaria. Blethen always maintained that he decided to move his family to a colder climate from Kansas City on a doctor's advice, after his son's illness. However, one must wonder whether Missouri's malarial environment would have been as great a concern if he had been able to buy out his *Journal* co-owners in the "give or take" offer. The Blethen family seemed settled in Kansas City; Maine visitors remarked that the boys spoke with a Western twang. Fourteen-year-old Joseph was in school, and Clarance was about to begin first grade. The Blethen girls were both born there—Florence was a toddler and Marion a tiny baby in 1884. There were good reasons to stay, but more persuasive reasons to go. Joseph believed that his father wanted "to command a daily paper in a large city" as editor and publisher, not just as business manager. Alden Blethen was convinced that such a man "became a power in the community." Then thirty-nine, he wanted more than wealth—he wanted influence.[33]

Clarance Blethen claimed that his father virtually threw a dart at the map to settle on Minneapolis as the family's next destination. His story is certainly not true. At this time of his life, Alden Blethen had been in the newspaper business long enough to develop

An artist's rendering of the elegant red brick Tribune Building. Completed in 1885, it housed all of the newspaper's facilities as well as other offices and retail businesses.

(Minneapolis Public Library)

strategic business connections around the country. He may well have had a close newspaper contact in the city, perhaps someone he had met through his activities with the Western Associated Press. A friend may also have convinced him to make the move, as the Minneapolis area had a strong contingent of Maine men, including Blethen's Kent's Hill roommate, William Pattee, an attorney and state legislator. Minneapolis, in fact, was virtually an outpost of Maine, and events sponsored by the Sons of Maine or Bowdoin College alumni drew the city's best-connected residents.[34]

Alden Blethen was a guest at the annual Sons of Maine dinner his first week in Minneapolis, and he gave the appreciative audience a speech "full of journalistic bite" on the important contributions of Maine newspapermen. The occasion was also a personal celebration, for on the previous day he had made a decisive career move. As his son later reminisced, "with more ready money at hand than had been in his wildest dreams when he left Maine, ...he chose to re-enter the newspaper game." On December 1, 1884, just six months after he left *The Kansas City Journal*, he purchased a half-interest in *The Minneapolis Tribune*, another morning paper. Not quite a year later, he also became an owner of the afternoon *Minneapolis Journal*.[35]

Blethen invested in both *The Tribune* and *The Journal* with another Kent's Hill alumnus Edwin Haskell, editor and part owner of *The Boston Herald*, whose son Will would become *The Tribune*'s editor. It was a rapid career advancement for young Haskell, whose only previous experience was running the Harvard University student newspaper. But Blethen agreed to the bargain, so *The Tribune*'s new masthead identified him as general manager and Will Haskell as managing editor. Rounding out the organization were "Blethen's cowboys," a rowdy, hard-drinking group of eleven writers and reporters from *The Kansas City Journal* and other Kansas City papers who had followed Alden Blethen to Minneapolis.[36]

In Kansas City, Blethen had been *The Journal*'s business manager, but he cultivated the friendship of local editors and writers. The kind of allegiance he inspired went beyond the camaraderie fostered by sharing too many rounds of drinks in the dingy bars frequented by the press crowd. His drive overshadowed the brash excesses of his personality and earned him respect and affection among the newsmen. As one of his loyalists later wrote, "Blethen had the punch and after all, punch is what captures a young man's imagination."[37]

The *Minneapolis Tribune* certainly needed some "punch." For many years, the paper's ownership had been characterized by turnover and careless management. The most recent editor had changed its course, purchasing a morning Associated Press franchise and providing strong editorial direction. Yet he had earned the nickname "Deacon" along Newspaper Row in Minneapolis because he ran *The Tribune* with the firm hand of a Christian moralist, avoiding any hint of scandal, frivolity, or humor. In fact, a police reporter from a competing paper once claimed that he never worried about being scooped by *The Tribune* because it was "about as sensational as a Sunday school leaflet." The paper was also dull to look at—seven columns of small type, with advertising frequently occupying more than half of the front page.[38]

When Blethen and Haskell arrived, they promised that *The Tribune* would have a completely different appearance and tone. Their "model daily paper, progressive and fearless" would be staunchly Republican, but offer "editorial enunciations and criticisms [that will] be liberal, broad-gauge, and

The new Tribune Building was erected on the outskirts of the main downtown business district in anticipation of rapid growth brought by development of the city's street railway lines.

(Minneapolis Public Library)

A rough-and-tumble crew of very young newsboys handled street sales of The Minneapolis Journal, *an afternoon paper purchased by Alden Blethen and his partners in 1885.*

to-the-point, and no effort will be made to curry favor with any clique or combination." The new owners also vowed to practice the new journalism, offering readers "the fullest and most accurate news, the brightest and most brilliant correspondence and the choicest and most interesting original literary productions." Slowly, ads began to disappear from the front page, replaced by wire service news from around the world. The Sunday editions soon contained sports coverage, humor, and even syndicated short stories. Headlines became larger and more daring.[39]

A new aggressiveness swept through the paper from the newsroom to the business office and Blethen, as general manager, was primarily responsible. He discharged tradition-bound employees, and had no trouble attracting younger staffers, like his bright, eager, and hungry Kansas City transplants. He also brought some of Kansas City's successful promotional schemes to Minneapolis, pushing *The Tribune's* rural weekly, *The Farmers' Tribune,* for example, with premiums of Saskatchewan Fife Wheat or packets of garden seeds. He even began to feature the newspaper's circulation figures prominently on the editorial page, challenging his competitors to a real race.[40]

To add to the excitement, the newspaper almost immediately moved from the old City Hall into new headquarters—the prestigious *Tribune* Building. The eight-story red-brick structure itself became a marketing tool, as *The Tribune* hailed it as "the most complete and best arranged building for newspaper purposes west of Philadelphia." The building's basement housed *The Tribune's* state-of-the-art press and mailing facilities; the business offices opened onto an elegant arcade at street level. The news and editorial departments, as well as the composing and stereotyping rooms and a job printshop occupied several upper floors. Other newspapers and commercial tenants, including Western Union and a number of attorneys and engineers, leased additional space. Much was written not only about the building's design, but also its safety, as it was said to be the first entirely fireproof commercial structure in Minnesota. This claim would later echo with terrible irony.[41]

In the spring of 1885, *The Minneapolis Journal* moved into one of the leased spaces at *The Tribune* Building, and because of their different publishing schedules, the two newspapers profitably shared printing facilities and the composing room. However, when Blethen and Haskell along with several partners negotiated to purchase *The Journal* in November of 1885, it was considered a hostile takeover. Despite their shared facilities, the owners of *The Journal* had been openly disdainful of the new *Tribune* management, publicly expressing their regret that "*The Tribune* had fallen into the hands of men who seem to possess neither dignity or brains and who are rapidly degrading that once respectable paper." Now these same *Tribune* investors, perceiving the potential value of an evening newspaper in the expanding metropolitan market of Minneapolis, made a "no holds barred" bid for *The Journal*. Blethen threatened to drive *The Journal* out of business with another evening paper if its owners did not sell out. With "regret," they sold.[42]

Blethen, in addition to his duties at *The Tribune*, was named the general manager of *The Journal,* while Will Haskell had the title of corporate president; yet neither appeared to be deeply involved in their new paper. Blethen appointed experienced newspapermen who made almost all of the day-to-day decisions. *The Journal* was initially the smaller of the two Haskell-Blethen properties in

Minneapolis, with a circulation of about eleven thousand at the time of the purchase.[43]

Yet the potential of *The Journal* was clear. As an afternoon paper it could take better advantage of the speedier technology of the "new journalism," providing news on the day it happened to people who only had time to read the paper on a streetcar commute or during leisure hours after dinner. Between 1870 and 1890, total daily circulation of newspapers in the United States tripled, and nearly 90 percent of that increase was in evening editions. During the same time period, the country's urban population more than doubled and the metropolitan press eagerly responded to the needs of this diverse, increasingly sophisticated, constituency. Newspaper technology met social change to create an eagerness for "today's news today," as *The Journal* proclaimed on its pages. Besides, *The Journal* owned the evening franchise of the AP wire; *The Tribune* owned the morning, and neither offered significant competition to the other. Between the two, they conveniently covered the market, and that market was booming beyond everyone's expectations.[44]

Alden Blethen, always the self-made man looking for opportunity, had found it in another of the young, rising cities of the West. Like Kansas City, Minneapolis was a river town, situated at the great falls below the confluence of the Minnesota and Mississippi rivers. Lumber and flour mills lined the banks, and used the river's water power to drive their saws and grindstones. Industry had given Minneapolis its start, but the city was poised to grow, with grandiose visions of the commercial hub it could become. Where Kansas City had been distinctly Southern, Minneapolis was "a New England town on the upper Mississippi," though with a growing population of Irish and Scandinavian

Alden Blethen launched his newspaper career in Minneapolis at the beginning of a period of tremendous urban expansion and rivalry with neighboring St. Paul. This view taken about 1885 from Third Street down busy Hennepin Avenue illustrates why Minneapolis gained a reputation for its "hustle."

(Minnesota Historical Society)

immigrants. In 1880, the Flour City had been smaller than Kansas City, but a tremendous boom began in 1885 that would increase its population in ten years by 250 percent. The excitement was electric.[45]

Every conversation centered on land investment and getting rich. The newspapers were indispensable guides to the boom, boosting it, tracking it, and helping speculators anticipate it. Each year, the Minneapolis papers published an annual edition celebrating the industrial and financial achievements of the previous year. Bank clearings rose from $20,000,000 in 1881 to more than $304,000,000 in 1890.[46] The city was moving:

> Everything from the cradle to the grave, from cable car to hearse, goes at top speed. Nothing living can dawdle in the constant whir of those rushing mills.... They say you

never see a dog stop to scratch himself in Minneapolis. Its newspapers, prompt to make a point in favor of the town will tell you it is because there are no fleas on a Minneapolis dog. The truth is, he has not time.[47]

Minneapolis looked like "an overgrown village" in the 1880s, sprouting brick and stone office buildings on its crazy-quilt site, a prairie suffering an urban convulsion. Residents and visitors found the city haphazard and inconvenient, with few public services, no downtown core, nor even a coherent city plan.[48]

Across the river, St. Paul, the state capital, perceived itself a city of grace, dignity, and heritage, scorning the ambitions of brash upstart Minneapolis. The two cities were side-by-side in geography, but a world apart in character. St. Paul, on the river's bluffs, was peopled by "staid burghers," lawyers, and wholesale merchants while Minneapolis, down on the prairie, was filled with railroad and lumber workers, millers, and artisans. Soon, however, as Minneapolis began to grow beyond its working-class roots, St. Paul's patricians could no longer merely dismiss the efforts of the Minneapolis hustlers. A fierce civic rivalry ensued, promoted by the press and fueled by unrestrained boosterism.[49]

The rivalry between the two cities was mirrored in the intense competition between their daily newspapers—particularly Blethen's *Minneapolis Tribune* and St. Paul's morning paper, *The Pioneer Press*. As the champions of their respective communities, the newspapers used civic pride to increase their own circulation. They praised hometown attributes with exaggerated prose, constantly compared growth, and lobbed insults indiscriminately as they attempted to undercut the other city's achievements. The newspapers also engaged in direct attacks on each other, battling over readership and advertising rates as ferociously as Minneapolis and St. Paul battled over population figures. Alden Blethen continued to bait his rivals by trumpeting daily and weekly circulation figures beneath *The Tribune*'s masthead.[50]

The Pioneer Press claimed a daily Minneapolis circulation of about four thousand. *The Tribune* claimed eleven thousand, and *The Pioneer Press* attacked these figures as inflated by nearly one-quarter. If the figures were correct, *The Tribune* had made astounding progress, doubling circulation in three months. To prove his honesty, Blethen opened *The Tribune*'s pressroom to visitors and offered $1,000 to anyone who could discover a discrepancy between the press register and the published figures. Additionally, *The Tribune* claimed that its advertising "lineage"—or line count—had surpassed *The Pioneer Press,* and pointed out that while all of *The Tribune*'s ads came from Minneapolis businesses, only a quarter of *The Press* ads came from Minneapolis.[51]

Later, Alden Blethen would return to many of these circulation stunts in both Minneapolis and Seattle—they were standard newspaper war tactics. But when *The Pioneer Press* claimed to be "published simultaneously in St. Paul and Minneapolis," the competition took on a new dimension. Alden Blethen, as an active member of the Western Associated Press, knew *The Tribune*'s rights: if *The Pioneer Press* claims were true, the paper had violated the expensive territorial exclusivity conferred by the AP franchise. Blethen reprinted on the editorial page a letter from William Henry Smith, the Western Associated Press' general manager, who confirmed that no morning newspaper could use the wire service's reports in Minneapolis without *The Tribune*'s consent. Blethen also lodged a formal protest against *The Pioneer Press* at the

1885 annual meeting of the WAP's board of directors, and the group agreed to launch an investigation.[52]

The pages of each paper bristled with antagonism as *The Tribune* lashed out at the "habitual duplicity and hypocrisy" of *The Pioneer Press,* which in turn lambasted the "hallucinations" and "flagrant fraud" of the paper it chose to satirize as *The Kansas City-Minneapolis Tribune.* With what *The Tribune* characterized as "elephantine playfulness," *The Pioneer Press* commented on the inability of the Wild West newcomers to report city news. *The Press* specifically extended this critique to "the cowboy manager of *The Tribune,*" Alden Blethen.[53]

Baited by *The Tribune*, *The Pioneer Press* personalized the newspaper conflict and mounted a direct attack on Blethen, calling him a "colossal liar," among other epithets. Alden Blethen came to personify *The Tribune,* emerging from a modest role in the business office to eclipse Will Haskell and the other able editors on the newspaper. His belligerent personality dominated the paper, attracting attention and acting as a lightning rod for controversy.

An incident in July 1885 illustrated Blethen's complete identification with *The Tribune,* and—if *The Pioneer Press* is to be believed—his aggressive efforts to promote his newspaper and himself. That summer a party of Minneapolis residents, including the former mayor, his wife, and three children, drowned in a boating accident on Lake Minnetonka, a nearby resort. At first news of the tragedy, Blethen and a host of other prominent Minneapolitans rushed to board a train to the lake, hoping to assist the bereaved families. Later, *The Pioneer Press* denounced Blethen for his ghoulish behavior at the scene and for violating "all rules of decency under the cloak of reportorial necessity." *The Press*

THE CENSUS RIVALRY BETWEEN ST. PAUL AND MINNEAPOLIS

A prodigious popular place is Pad City. It is peopled with plotters and padders, their prompters, promoters, protectors, and procurers; with pursepround plunderers of pine lands, with pestilent pothouse political prigs, with their packers of precinct primaries, and their pap-fed and place-hunting parasites; with pimps and panders and prostitutes; with the pals of pickpockets and pluckers of pigeons; with picayune peddlers of peanuts and popcorn; with petty plebeians and puffed up pirates patrician; with prodigal paupers and penurious plutocrats; with pig-headed patriots, the poll-parrot puppet of the pushers and puffers of Padville. These are the princes of Padville, so preponderant in plural proportion, so potential with public opinion, that its pure and its pious, its patterns of prudence and probity, its politic parsons and puritanic professors, its pluperfect pinks of propriety, its prim, impeccable prudes and prosicians in preaching and practice, its prayerful pewholders and pre-emptors of the prizes predestinate of paradise, are powerless to protest against palpable padding, and lie prostrate and prone—not in propitiatory penitence proclaiming for Padville "peccavi"— but in passive and palsied pusillanimity putting forth paltry piteous pleas palliative for the pushers and puffers and padders— the predominant powers of Padville.

The St. Paul Pioneer Press,
August 15, 1890

charged that Blethen had accosted the two surviving sons of the victims at their lakefront home and then insisted on making the train ride back with them to Minneapolis, badgering them with questions until they fled, grief-stricken, to a private car. *The Pioneer Press'* editor was shocked and appalled, or pretended to be.

Blethen retorted with outraged indignation and published an array of signed letters that attested to his friendship with the family and his exemplary journalistic behavior. *The Pioneer Press* issued a grudging apology, but would not back off from its judgment of Blethen's character:

> Nobody at all acquainted with Mr. Blethen could suppose that [publication of his behavior] would wound his feelings. That he should object to appearing in the columns of *The Pioneer Press* in a light in which he has studiously striven to place himself in business and social circles in Minneapolis could not have occurred to the most vigilant and scrupulous editor. It is difficult to understand his attitude even now, unless some over officious acquaintance has whispered to him that the figure he cut at the Rand cottage was not exactly one of which considerate gentlemen are apt to be proud. [54]

Blethen did not have the finesse or polish of a true gentleman, but he had moved onto center stage as the head of *The Tribune*. He frequently made his own news, and *The Tribune* publicized his emerging persona, delightedly responding to *Pioneer Press* insults on its editorial page. Time and again, *The Tribune* mustered a righteous indignation, insisting that *The Press'* editor should be horsewhipped, or insinuating that he had been drunk when composing his editorials. The editor of *The Pioneer Press* retaliated by citing *The Tribune* manager's "ineffable stupidity." *The Press* even charged Blethen with

using obscene language on the telephone to female operators, dubbing him "Bully O'Blethen." It was outrageous, and it sold newspapers. [55]

And it wasn't just *The Pioneer Press*. *The Minneapolis Times* and *The St. Paul Globe* also joined the fray, for Alden Blethen was soon regarded as a renegade throughout Twin Cities newspaper circles. Even private citizens got in on the insults. The plaintiff in one of many libel suits brought against Blethen and *The Tribune* wrote in *The Minneapolis Newsletter,* "Mr. Blethen was such a fearful and reckless mud-slinger and stench-slinger that [his victims] would rather do almost anything or refuse to do it than to have him open his skunk batteries on them." In response, Blethen expressed indignant contempt on the editorial pages of *The Tribune,* and simply went back to work. [56]

He continued to throw himself into Minneapolis boosterism, self-promotion, and politics. The Minneapolis Industrial Exposition became one of Blethen's pet projects, and he maintained a "just pride" that *The Tribune* had originated the Exposition idea in an 1885 editorial. Rival St. Paul had staged a coup by acquiring the site for the state fair. Within a week Minneapolis boosters decided to stage their own extravaganza. Alden Blethen was an active member of the Exposition's board of directors, a driving force within this group of prominent local businessmen. In March 1886, Blethen encouraged his fellow directors, who were developing cold feet at the cost of constructing the Exposition Hall, to move forward, urging "that there must now be some hard and rapid work and no time wasted." His pleas yielded results, and the first Exposition was held in the fall, attended by more than 300,000 visitors. For six years thereafter, the products of Minneapolis art, industry, and enterprise

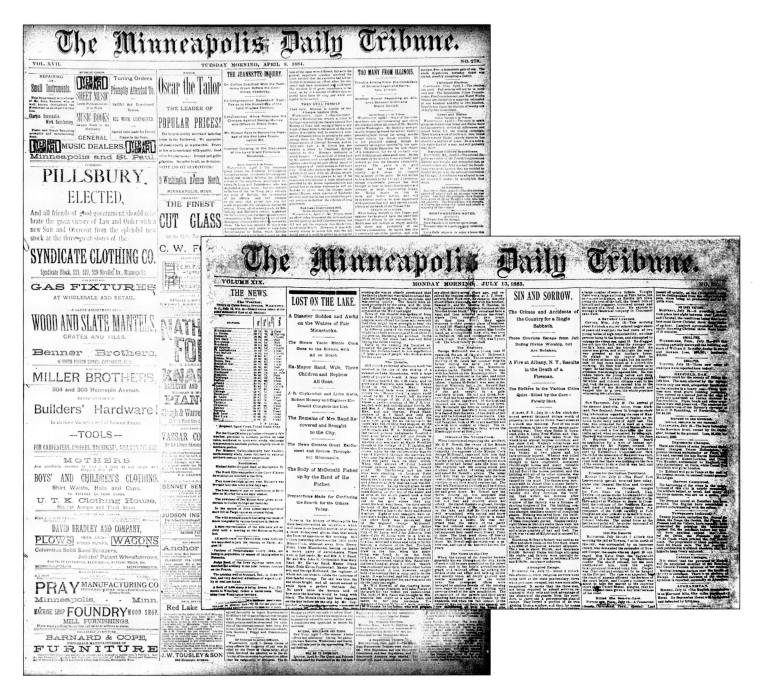

The Minneapolis Tribune *was "as sensational as a Sunday school leaflet" when Blethen and Edwin Haskell took over the paper from its former editor, Colonel A. B. Nettleton in 1884. Advertisements claimed half of the front page before the new owners made changes. As the Tribune's general manager, Alden Blethen put his own very personal stamp on the newspaper, adding many features of the "new journalism" and making it more lively, sometimes even sensational, reading. Rival papers frequently attacked Blethen for his handling of news events.*

(Minneapolis Daily Tribune, April 8, 1884; July 13, 1885)

Alden Blethen was a founder and director of the Minneapolis Exposition, an annual display of the industrial and trade products of the city. The Tribune helped launch a subscription drive to pay for a lavish building to house the exposition, seen here from a vantage point across the Mississippi River near St. Anthony Falls.

(Minneapolis Public Library)

went on annual display in this lavish hall overlooking the river.[57]

The Minneapolis Exposition was a solid contribution to the city's well-being, one of which Blethen and *The Tribune* could be proud. However, on the closing day of 1887's Exposition, President Grover Cleveland visited Minneapolis, precipitating a disgraceful incident that aroused public outrage against Alden Blethen and *The Minneapolis Tribune.* During Cleveland's race for the presidency, Republican newspapers had bashed the Democratic candidate's private life. Press critics railed against the invasive—sometimes inventive—reporting of a partisan press that slandered Cleveland as a drunken reprobate. When he married his ward, a young woman thirty years his junior, his enemies delighted

in portraying him as an aging rake who had seduced an innocent. Aggressive reporters even trailed the pair to their honeymoon cottage in the Virginia woods. America reveled in this journalistic sensation, as the press exploited the private life of a public figure with suggestive innuendo.[58]

Minneapolis press reaction to the Cleveland 1887 visit was very partisan. The president, his wife, and a large entourage arrived by train and toured the city, concluding with Cleveland's oration at the Exposition Hall. Republican newspapers reported that the president had received a cold and undemonstrative reception; Democratic papers delighted in Cleveland's warm and enthusiastic welcome. The Republican *Pioneer Press* contrasted the president's "middle-aged and dull obesity" with his wife's "youthful grace and sprightliness and beauty." The Republican *Tribune* reported that observers in the crowd exclaimed, "That's Mrs. Cleveland, she's beautiful!" and "That's Grover. My, isn't he fat, though!"[59]

Alden Blethen, seated with other city notables on the platform at Exposition Hall, joined the presidential party at a lavish reception after Cleveland's speech. The following morning, an editorial entitled "Mr. and Mrs. Cleveland as Mere People" appeared in *The Tribune*. The anonymous writer justified his personal remarks about the president and his wife—ordinarily insulting to the highest office in the land—because the couple were simply tourists on a pleasure trip. Musing that Mrs. Cleveland was "several years older than she is said to be," the editorialist continued:

> At least she was old enough to have exercised her own free choice in marrying Grover Cleveland. It is inconceivable that she should have married him except to obtain the position of mistress of the White House.... It is hard to have respect for a woman who would sell herself to such a gross and repulsive man as Grover Cleveland, and one with a private record so malodorous, for the bauble of a brief social ascendancy.... If she can secure reelection for Grover, she will have four years more of the gratification which the highest social prominence gives, and the delight of unflagging newspaper notoriety. After that she will simply have to put up with being the wife of as insignificant a man as an ex-president could possibly be.[60]

No Minneapolis Republican newspaper had provided favorable coverage to the Cleveland visit, but by attacking the president's wife, *The Tribune* editorial went too far. *The St. Paul Globe* denounced *The Tribune*'s stan- dards of taste, calling the editorial "an abuse of journalistic decency," and *The Pioneer Press* agreed. *The Press* was shocked at the vulgar insults directed at the first lady, "whose graciousness and womanliness have been...most pleasing...and for whom the people entertain feelings of chivalrous regard." Referring to commonly held standards of press ethics, *The Press* called the editorial "a disgrace to journalism." *The Tribune*'s censure by the Minneapolis press was matched by public outrage.[61]

Outcry over the scandalous *Tribune* editorial was directed at Alden Blethen personally. Throughout the day of October 14, 1887, the rumor spread through Minneapolis that Blethen was to be burned in effigy that night. Led by one of Blethen's local political enemies, Democratic Mayor A.A. "Doc" Ames, a crowd of several hundred gathered downtown. A bewhiskered dummy of straw bearing the placard, "A.J. Blethen, the Dog," was set afire. When half consumed, protesters kicked the straw man around the street. With Ames at its head, the mob then marched on *The Tribune* Building and parodied various ditties, including "Let's hang old Blethen from a sour apple tree." They concluded the evening with three rousing groans in honor of the first lady's defamer.[62]

The next day, *The Tribune* went on the offensive, deriding the "notorious Doc Ames" and his hooligans, depicting them in front page cartoons as drunken street toughs. On the editorial page, a letter from "A Disgusted Citizen" defended Blethen, claiming that the newspaper's manager "neither inspired, consented to, or knew of that article until he read it, greatly to his personal regret, in his paper on the day of its appearance." Behind the scenes at the newspaper, trouble brewed between Alden Blethen and his partner, young Will Haskell, "whose father pays *The Tribune*'s bills." As the personality of

The Tribune, Alden Blethen was blamed for the unsigned editorial. But who had really written it? Blethen, Haskell, or Albert Shaw, the paper's customary editorial writer?[63]

The Pioneer Press speculated on the authorship of the editorial, noting on the one hand its raw "Kansas City flavor," and on the other its clear technical superiority to much of Blethen's prose. *The Press* reprinted negative comment from newspapers throughout the region that judged Blethen a tasteless fool and "a cowardly editor" who would not own up to a mistake. The critical press reaction generally seconded *The Pioneer Press'* conclusion that "everybody who has ever conversed with Mr. Blethen knows that he is the responsible and authoritative editor of *The Tribune.*" After the Minneapolis city council passed a resolution condemning *The Tribune* "in the publication of its libelous and insulting editorial," Blethen hired a personal bodyguard. Fairly or not, he personified the newspaper and had to shoulder the blame.[64]

On October 20, *The Minneapolis Tribune* printed an article, signed by Will Haskell, in which he acknowledged responsibility for reading and accepting the editorial for publication. On the same page, unusually subdued, Blethen expressed regret over the incident but denied involvement. He described his role at the newspaper as general manager and treasurer, an infrequent contributor to the editorial page who had no actual authority over its content. Edwin Haskell, Will's father, was said to be en route from Boston.[65]

The Pioneer Press, delighted by the public evidence of disunity at *The Tribune,* printed a long interview with Blethen, the "Kansas City hero," which allowed him to set out his side of the story:

> That editorial on Mr. Cleveland and his wife was published without my knowledge or consent, and after the wrong was done I urged an immediate and complete apology, but Will Haskell opposed such a course as cowardly.... Mr. Shaw stopped in [my office] and informed me that he intended to write an editorial on President Cleveland as a man, but I advised him to postpone it until Sunday, as the president was the guest of the city.... I thought the editorial would drop then and there, and was utterly surprised the next morning to see the attack not only on the president but on his wife. I never yet insulted a woman, and you can imagine my feelings when I read the article.... Dr. Shaw wrote the article under W.E. Haskell's instructions.... I am tired of being wrongfully blamed in this matter, and am ready either to step out, sell my interest in the *Tribune* or buy Mr. Haskell's.[66]

Alden Blethen steadfastly maintained that he neither wrote nor approved the scandalous Cleveland editorial of October 11, 1887, but recriminations from the piece followed him for the rest of his life. The Blethen family portrayed Will Haskell as a wild and dissipated boy, sent west by his father to train in the newspaper business under Blethen's watchful eye. Alden Blethen's younger son later characterized the editorial as a juvenile prank, a trick played by a ne'er-do-well on a patient older mentor. Albert Shaw, who later confirmed that Haskell had asked him to write the editorial, claimed that he had shown the incendiary piece to Alden Blethen, who made light of it. Blethen's enemies, of course, always maintained that he wrote the editorial himself, and was a notorious scoundrel. Whatever Alden Blethen's role, the incident effectively ended the partnership with the Haskells. Will Haskell would soon become his bitter enemy.[67]

In May 1888, Blethen sold his share in *The Tribune* but vowed that he would not leave Minneapolis. "My newspaper interests are too

large," he wrote in his farewell editorial, "and this city presents too many journalistic opportunities to warrant a different course." He initially planned to devote himself to his other local newspaper property, *The Journal*, but it, too, was owned in partnership with the Haskells. As he had done at other critical junctures in his life, Blethen took his family on a long trip to Maine—going back home always seemed to clarify his thinking. When he returned to Minneapolis, he had changed his mind and soon announced an agreement allowing Edwin Haskell to purchase his share

in *The Journal*. It was "purely a business transaction," he maintained. "I have parted from this property simply because a capitalist offered me more spot-cash than was ever before paid for any western newspaper property." And the sale *was* lucrative. Altogether his shares from both newspapers netted him more than a quarter of a million dollars. He had nearly tripled the nest egg he had brought from Kansas City.[68]

Rumors continued to circulate that Blethen would invest his wealth in an Eastern newspaper, but he consistently denied he had

Will Haskell, the son of Alden Blethen's business partner Edwin Haskell, had little newspaper experience before he became the editor of The Minneapolis Tribune. *He and Blethen became bitter enemies over the handling of a notorious editorial about President Grover Cleveland and his wife. Haskell, in the dark coat and hat, is pictured in the front seat of this early electric car, joined by other Minneapolis dignitaries including S. E. Olson, a department store owner in the top hat, and* Minneapolis Journal *manager Lucian Swift to the right of Olson in the second seat.*

(Minneapolis Public Library)

Alden and Rose Ann Blethen pose for a family portrait in about 1888 with their eldest child Joe standing in the rear, younger son, C.B., and their two daughters, Florence, on the left, and Marion on her father's knee.

(Courtesy of Gilbert Duffy)

ture. He had gained wealth; now he turned his attention to securing political influence.[69]

Running for office seemed a natural step for the outspoken publisher who had waged so many political battles through the pages of his newspaper. In his years at *The Tribune* the paper consistently used the editorial page and even its news columns to tout favored candidates and causes. Alden Blethen had accepted most other tenets of the "new journalism," but maintained his strong political partisanship born of an earlier era of personal journalism. He had sought elective office in Maine, but now, unlike his Greenback Party days, his views were much more within the mainstream. He was a staunch Republican at a time when Minnesota was a stronghold of the Grand Old Party. Every governor of the state had been Republican since 1860, and the city of Minneapolis, despite its working-class populace, usually voted heavily Republican in its municipal elections.[70]

With the bravado of a more experienced politician, Blethen expressed ambition for national office: "I may run for Congress if the Republican party manifests a disposition to secure the services of a good man and a finished statesman for that high position," he confidently told an interviewer. His friends encouraged him to consider a municipal position first, and Alden Blethen finally settled on the race for the Republican mayoral nomination. The Republican city convention was slated for early October 1888, and during the preceding months the candidate was highly visible around Minneapolis.[71]

Nothing in his life capitalized on his hunger for self-display and his talent for self-promotion like politics. Blethen loved it, and he was good at it. He gave a major address at the opening of the Minneapolis Exposition, sat on the platform at a huge rally attended by the Republican faithful, danced with the

any plans to leave the area. As he told one reporter: "I propose to stay here where four years of hard labor for the newspapers with which I have been identified have made some impression on the public and the city which has done so much for me. Here I have made a good fortune and here I propose to spend it." Blethen, however, was in no hurry to spend his money on another newspaper ven-

city's social elite at a charity ball, and toasted Henry Villard, the railroad magnate, while standing alongside the city's most influential business leaders. He also threw a large banquet for two hundred former employees at *The Tribune* and *Journal*, primarily the typographers and compositors. He genuinely appreciated their services, but they also represented the core of an important labor constituency.[72]

Alden Blethen's brand of Republicanism was based on a belief in—as he put it—"protection to American labor and the fundamental principles of the old Republican party." However, the 1888 campaign dealt less with these grand issues than with restoring honesty to city affairs. Republican municipal candidates promised to reform the graft-ridden administration of "Doc" Ames, the highly popular Democratic mayor, a friend of the poor but also of the city's gamblers and saloon keepers.[73] As one partisan Republican paper summed up the contest:

> A host of loyal citizens think it is about time Minneapolis had a mayor for whom they are not obliged to blush 365 days a year and 366 on leap year. They naturally look to the Republican Party to deliver them from the present thralldom...to put at the head of its ticket a man who shall be as complete a contrast as possible to the present incumbent...a mayor who is level-headed, well-balanced, well-behaved, conservative but broad-gauge, conscientious and clean business man.[74]

Alden Blethen thought he could fill the bill, and he drew his strongest backers from the Minneapolis elite who had no sympathy with the city boss methods of "Doc" Ames. To win, however, Blethen needed a broader base, and his campaign strategy involved building a coalition of varied interest groups. Blethen counted on the votes of the typo-

graphical union members, while one of his closest advisors, influential Minneapolis merchant S.E. Olson, confidently maintained that he could also obtain the backing of the Scandinavian community. As they drew towards the nominating convention, Blethen moved from merely being a candidate to being the man to beat.[75]

When the Republican city convention opened, the Blethen forces predicted victory with "characteristic modesty," as *The Pioneer Press* jabbed. But when the nominations began, there was a surprising surge of enthusiasm for Captain E.C. Babb, a Civil War officer and respected Minneapolis businessman who had been active in veteran's affairs. The convention elected Babb on the second ballot, even though Blethen had thrown his sixty votes to another candidate. Alden Blethen, gracious in defeat, spoke to the crowd and pledged his support for the Republican ticket:

> Somebody [said] today that Blethen would be a sorehead. I want to say that, although men may cast stones on me, as they have done in this campaign already, that no power on earth, not even an effigy burning, could make me go back on the Republican party.... I have a little time and a little money, and no man shall outdo me in helping Capt. Babb to be mayor of Minneapolis.[76]

An observer in the convention remarked that if Blethen had made the well-received speech at the beginning of the proceedings, he might have secured the nomination for himself.[77]

Alden Blethen kept his promise, enthusiastically speaking on Babb's behalf at Republican rallies throughout the city. No longer a candidate, Blethen still seemed to relish the political husting which put him into the thick of party activity. After the local elections, Blethen moved on to national politics, stumping throughout Minnesota on behalf of Republican Benjamin Harrison, who was running for the presidency against Grover Cleveland in 1888.[78]

Despite Blethen's apparent enthusiasm for campaigning, rumors started almost immediately after his loss in the mayoral race that he was back in the market for a newspaper. As *The Pioneer Press* suggested:

> Brother Blethen is evidently getting homesick. He sighs for the joys and glories and manifold emoluments of the proprietorship of a newspaper. He would mold public opinion some more. He finds that Mr. Blethen, the private citizen, is not nearly so great a gun as Mr. Blethen, the manager of *The Tribune*. He proposed to buy up *The St. Paul Dispatch*, but he didn't bid high enough.[79]

Blethen's acquaintances in the journalism business knew of his "betwixt and between" status, and William Henry Smith of the Western Associated Press tried to interest him in another newspaper venture. Smith's son had been slow to choose a career and his father hoped to buy a newspaper that would provide him with an appropriate livelihood. The elder Smith wanted to control whatever paper he purchased for his son, but was looking for a "first class managing editor" with money to invest as a minority partner. As early as August 1888, when Blethen was testing the waters for his mayoral run, Smith had been in contact with him about several East Coast newspaper properties. Alden Blethen expressed definite interest.[80]

To Blethen, Smith had important attributes as a potential business partner. He was experienced, respected, and very well connected in the newspaper industry; a member, along with several top-flight publishers, of the inner circle that controlled the lucrative business arrangements of the Western Associated Press. Smith also had extraordinary political connections. Earlier in his life he had parlayed his prominence as the editor of *The Cincinnati Gazette* into his own political career, winning election twice as Ohio's secretary of state. Smith also became a close advisor of Ohio governor Rutherford B. Hayes, and continued as a trusted counselor when Hayes became President. Since 1869 he had maintained his position as the WAP general manager.[81]

William Henry Smith was a man of influence—wealthy, polished, and socially prominent—everything the ambitious Maine farm boy had hoped to become. Alden Blethen had known Smith since he had first negotiated *The Kansas City Journal*'s entrance into the Western Associated Press in 1883, and he could not help but be flattered that this powerful man would initiate an alliance with him. The arrangement would put Blethen back in a position as guide and mentor to the young, relatively inexperienced son of a business partner. Such a relationship had proven disastrous with the Haskells, but Blethen simply dismissed his misgivings.

Despite repeated declarations that he would never leave Minneapolis, Blethen expressed his eagerness to join the Smiths at two papers they were considering—one in Providence, Rhode Island, and the other in Washington, D.C. The latter was *The Washington Post* whose owner, Stilson Hutchins, wanted desperately to sell out and devote himself to his interests in a linotype company. *The Post* was a potentially valuable property in the nation's capital, but it had not yet distinguished itself. Smith had the idea of combining *The Post* with two other smaller Washington papers to form one strong and influential operation. Smith negotiated with Hutchins to secure a six-month option on

The Post, proposing to run the paper during that period in order to assess its financial health and competitive position.[82]

Alden Blethen made a visit to Washington to review the situation in mid-November, but many details remained to be settled. Despite ongoing negotiations over *The Post*, the Smiths and Blethen continued to explore the purchase of newspapers in cities as far-flung as Toledo, Omaha, Providence, Milwaukee, and even St. Paul. After the first of the year, *The Post* deal seemed to be on track, as Minneapolis papers reported that Blethen's former city editor had left *The Tribune* to join the Washington, D.C., enterprise. Yet on January 6, 1889, *The Washington Post* reported the sale of the paper—but not to the Smith group.[83]

On the evening before *The Post's* surprise announcement, Alden Blethen returned to Minneapolis, refusing to give the local press any indication of the status of his newspaper ventures. For a few weeks he resumed his normal habits, attending several meetings of the Minneapolis Board of Trade and allowing his name to be placed in nomination as one of the organization's directors. In February 1889, however, Blethen took Rose Ann, Clarance, and the girls to Washington, D.C., for a few months, leaving Joseph to continue his studies at the University of Minnesota.[84]

A move to Washington, no matter how temporary, put Blethen at the heart of the political world he loved. He told friends in Minneapolis that the trip was just for the winter, to rest and to attend the inauguration of his candidate, Benjamin Harrison, who had won the November election. Perhaps he thought he could salvage *The Washington Post* prospect or seek other newspaper opportunities more effectively with his family by his side. He may even have dreamed of a political appointment from President Harrison, just reward for his campaign efforts.

The winter of 1889 passed. No patronage positions were offered him, and he could make no firm decision about the future because William Henry Smith had taken an extended trip to Europe. Alden Blethen grew bored and restless. Rumors floated back to the Minneapolis papers that Blethen's Washington negotiations had ended, and that he was shopping around for another paper.[85]

Initially, Blethen's interest was *The St. Paul Globe*. He had evidently been alerted to the opportunity by the respected Minneapolis financier and streetcar magnate, Thomas Lowry, who owned stock in *The Globe* building. Lowry sought someone to purchase and run the paper while he took majority interest in the real estate. Blethen encouraged the Smiths to participate, and the WAP general manager met with Lowry in New York late in April 1889. As William Henry Smith subsequently remembered their conversation, Lowry also had other motives for encouraging the purchase:

> Mr. Lowry said that he and Mr. Blethen had been talking over the matter of the purchase of *The St. Paul Globe*.... He was anxious that it should be in the hands of parties who would be friendly to him, and went on to detail his own situation there at the 'Twin Cities'...; that he had street railway interests in both of them; that he had just gotten through with a strike and was mortified to find that the press was disposed to be in opposition to him. He said that he was trying to give the two cities the very best service that was possible, and that he felt that the press ought to give him cordial support in the general interest of the community...he was anxious that I should go into this, if, upon examination, I considered it a good thing to do. He said if I would do so, that he would stand at the back of it, and he thought it would be a good investment.[86]

Blethen's behind-the-scenes backer in his re-purchase of The Tribune *in 1889 was Thomas Lowry, a well-known financier who also owned the Minneapolis Street Railway Company.*

(Minneapolis Public Library)

As sole editor and publisher of The Minneapolis Tribune, *Alden Blethen was finally able to make the paper his own. He also purchased* The Minneapolis Evening Star *in 1889, adding afternoon coverage so that he could boast in this advertisement, placed in the city directory of 1890, that* The Tribune *was the only "all day newspaper" in Minneapolis.*

Lowry thus promised his financial backing in return for "cordial support," or favorable coverage of his enterprises. Neither Blethen nor Smith seemed to find the proposed arrangement improper or unusual, and they proceeded to negotiate for *The Globe*. Despite Lowry's pressure for a resolution, the deal stalled. Purely by accident, however, another opportunity arose that promised Blethen even greater satisfaction than any other potential acquisition—an opportunity to take back *The Minneapolis Tribune* from his nemesis, Will Haskell.

William Henry Smith later recounted the story of the chance encounter that led to *The Tribune* purchase. He and Blethen were on the train heading to St. Paul for a last-ditch effort to salvage *The Globe* deal when they met C. M. Palmer, one of the minority partners of *The Minneapolis Tribune.* "[D]o you want to buy a paper in a dead city and of a different political character from your own politics?" Palmer had asked when told about the pending *St. Paul Globe* purchase. Why not come to Minneapolis and buy *The Tribune* instead, he encouraged them, indicating that Will Haskell had grown tired of the business and wanted to sell.[87]

Excited, Smith and Blethen hastened to tell Lowry of *The Tribune*'s availability. Tom Lowry, enthusiastic about the purchase, suggested that the two men secure *The Globe* as well and cover both the Minneapolis and St. Paul markets. *The Globe* buyout never materialized, but *The Tribune* negotiations did rapidly proceed, with Blethen and Smith as primary investors. A contract was drawn up in late May of 1889, but at the last moment Smith fell ill and could not sign the final agreement by its expiration date. Blethen feared that *The Tribune*'s major stockholder, Edwin Haskell, would back out entirely because he had already expressed concern that the property was undervalued. Unwilling to see this opportunity slip away, Blethen offered to make the full $100,000 cash payment personally, with the balance in notes.

Possibly intending to offend, Haskell insisted that Blethen's notes be backed by someone reputable, or he would not agree to the sale. Thomas Lowry, still desiring friendly press for his streetcar enterprises, stepped in and offered his endorsement, thus allowing the purchase to proceed. Lowry was a silent

and secret partner, and announcements of the sale listed Alden J. Blethen as *The Tribune*'s sole proprietor.[88]

For the first time in his life, Blethen had complete editorial and business control of a newspaper. The masthead of the new *Tribune* proudly stated, "***The Tribune*** by Alden J. Blethen." Blethen immediately set out to make the paper truly his own. He brought in trusted staffers, revived his aggressive circulation contests, and put his own contentious but colorful stamp on the editorial page. He even announced that the following summer the paper would move out of *The Tribune* building and into a brand new home on Newspaper Row.[89]

Alden Blethen had worked hard and paid his dues. As a boy in Maine he had clawed his way from a pauper's childhood into respectability; as a man his pride and ambition had matured and hardened. His opportunism had been schooled by harsh necessity, and it was refined in the volatile newspaper business of the great Midwest. He had constantly pushed for new authority, to be more than a manager of money and men. Yet always tied to partnerships, he had never fully realized his ambitions. Now was the time. As editor-in-chief and publisher of *The Minneapolis Tribune*, he believed he could now, at last, control his own destiny. Instead, he would enter the crucible and be tried.

After losing The Tribune *to Lowry, Alden Blethen considered other opportunities, but chose to remain in Minneapolis, where he was at the center of a thriving business community. The downtown had continued to grow, as seen in this 1890 photograph of Fourth Street at Nicollet Avenue.*

(Minneapolis Public Library)

The Minneapolis Tribune *Building was touted as fireproof, but a devastating blaze in November 1889 destroyed the structure and claimed the lives of seven, all of them newspapermen.*

(Wheller and Haas, Landscape Photographers, Minnesota Historical Society)

3 THE CRUCIBLE

On a bitterly cold November night in 1889, five months after Blethen's second purchase of *The Minneapolis Tribune*, lights blazed in urban splendor from the upper floors of *The Tribune* Building. It was a skyscraper of the 1880s—eight stories tall, built of red brick and supported by an internal structure of iron girders and I-beams. Only four years old, the building had been publicly touted as "the first fire-proof commercial structure...in Minnesota." Up on the seventh floor, *Tribune* staffers worked in the editorial and composing rooms, feverishly preparing the twenty-four pages of the Sunday morning paper before deadline.[1]

On the darkened third floor, the offices were closed for the day. Until recently, the Republican League campaign headquarters for the 1889 elections had occupied a suite of rooms at the end of the hallway. Many cans of paint for political signs lay among the piles of banners and old campaign literature. It was here that the fire started.

At about 10 o'clock, a *Tribune* reporter rushed into the office of managing editor Charles Alfred Williams and told him there was a fire four floors beneath them. Williams was one of the Kansas City cowboys, and had begun his career on *The Kansas City Journal* as a reporter, following Blethen from Missouri to Minnesota. Williams told the reporter to keep an eye on the fire and let him know if there was any danger. The editor turned back to the work on his desk and the reporter went downstairs. Neither man showed much concern because the building was known to be fireproof.

By the time the reporter reached the third floor, the fire raged completely out of control. Intense heat drove him back up the stairs. The campaign rooms were completely ablaze. Flames spread down the hall, feeding on the varnished wood trim on the plastered walls, reaching toward the wooden staircase. The fire caught the gas used to light the building, and a series of small explosions followed.

Even then, many just kept working. Some hastened down the stairs, but fire soon blocked that path of escape. The elevator made a few runs up and down through the inferno, and then it quit operating. Outside, the volunteer fire department had arrived and a crowd gathered in the snow.

In the adjoining composing room and newsrooms, the air began to heat up and fill with smoke as the fire chimneyed up the elevator shaft and the open stairwell. With every normal escape route blocked, terrified men headed for windows on the sixth and seventh floors. On the east side, fire department volunteers erected their ladders, which only reached the sixth floor. In the frozen darkness, newsmen inched their way along the building's narrow and slippery cornice, trying to reach the safety of the ladders. The building's single fire escape—a series of narrow metal stairs—zig-zagged down the west side.

after them in the draft toward the open window. Desperate, Williams slammed the door, and its glass window shattered to the floor. The fire swirled through the room and ignited the newspapers, proofs, and galleys that littered the office.

In frantic haste, the men in Williams' office scrambled out onto the fire escape and down the ladder. One of the last to leave slipped or lost his balance just outside the window. Falling, he struck a telegrapher, who in turn lost his grip. The two men hit two others farther down the building, and all four plummeted to their deaths on the snow-covered sidewalk. Heartsick, Williams watched helplessly from his window while an Associated Press telegrapher tried to pull himself hand over hand along the telephone wire to another building. As the thin copper sliced into his palms, he struggled to pull his legs up over the wire to relieve the agony in his hands. With a despairing cry, he let go and fell between the buildings, into the alleyway far below.

Williams fainted on his own window sill, his head and arms hanging outside. The fire rushed in behind him and climbed his back, burning off his clothing and hair. He gasped in pain and the frigid air knifed him into consciousness. He crawled out onto the fire escape and made his way down the ladder. The injuries from his burns and the damage to his lungs from the smoke and searing heat confined him to bed for eight months. Yet he was lucky; he survived.

Alden Blethen was working in the building that night, in his office on the sixth floor. He heard someone yell, "Fire!," and rushed out, alerting Albert Shaw on his way to the stairwell. He meant to hunt for a fire extinguisher, but fire drove him from the building.

It had all happened so fast. Seven men died in an inferno that completely demolished

After the fire, Alden Blethen quickly built this expensive new facility for The Tribune, *but the cost of construction as well as other debts and poor business decisions severely strained his financial resources.*

(Minneapolis Public Library)

Fourteen men from the news and composing rooms crowded into the sixth floor office of Charles Williams, hoping to reach the safety of the fire escape outside his window. He closed his door and tied the transom shut; the flames flickered on the other side of the door's glass window. Panicky, men climbed one by one over the window sill, out onto the icy metal rungs. Williams urged them on; he said he would be the last to leave. Then came a knock at the door, and two more men staggered blindly into the office, pulling flames

The Tribune Building. Insurance covered only a third of the total $300,000 loss. The following day, *The St. Paul Globe* offered the use of its presses to publish *The Tribune*.[2]

An investigation followed, with many recriminations, as *The Minneapolis Times* demanded, "Who Is To Blame?" The building was *not* fireproof; in fact, it was declared "a firetrap"—its open stairwell and unenclosed elevator shaft had acted as highly efficient flues. After the tragedy, *The Tribune* and other newspapers reported that labor unions, the chief of the Minneapolis fire department, and tenants in the building had repeatedly requested additional fire escapes. The volunteer fire department had not been prompt and its equipment proved inadequate to fight the fire. *The Tribune* itself carried an insurance policy of only $25,000, and the newspaper presses in the basement as well as all composing, newsroom, and editorial room fixtures were completely destroyed. It was a catastrophe.[3]

Alden Blethen, devastated by the ruinous

The Tribune *was in competition with several other Minneapolis dailies, most of which had offices along 4th Street, often called "Newspaper Row." Crowds gathered there for the latest information on news and sporting events—in this photograph they are waiting for updated football scores.*
(Minneapolis Public Library)

fire, fought back with characteristic tenacity. Always at his best in a crisis, he was everywhere at once in the days following the disaster—arranging with other newspapers to share printing facilities, ordering new presses and other machinery, and organizing relief funds to benefit the families of those men killed in the blaze. In later years he would remember with pride that *Tribune* subscribers never missed a single issue of the paper, even on the morning after the fire. But he would also bitterly describe the deep financial distress that the disaster brought him. It was the beginning of his Minneapolis nightmare.[4]

Blethen, financially extended even before the losses of the fire, had made matters much worse by a series of business ventures that seem increasingly speculative, even reckless. The purchase price of *The Tribune* was $250,000, and Blethen had personally contributed $100,000 of this sum, signing promissory notes endorsed by local financier Thomas Lowry for the balance. These notes were payable in one year, although Blethen later maintained that Lowry promised to extend payment for as long as necessary. In September 1889, only three months after this initial transaction, Blethen also bought *The Minneapolis Evening Star*, which merged with *The Tribune* to become its evening edition. *The Star* was purchased with *Tribune* stock, increasing the company's debt load to nearly $137,000.[5]

Now, on top of this heavy financial burden, the fire-ravaged *Tribune* needed new quarters as soon as possible. Blethen set out to build what he termed "a proper plant," equipped with the very latest in machinery, as was always his practice. *The Tribune* construction project took nine months. When completed, Blethen could boast that the new facilities "in point of convenience and complete adaptability to the newspaper business

have very few equals and probably no superior in the country." The five-story structure was devoted exclusively to newspaper publishing, an advantage in Blethen's mind, but one that meant there would be no rental revenues from other tenants. The fixtures, labor, and materials for the building were also quite expensive, perhaps extravagant: Blethen later claimed that the final costs exceeded $130,000.[6]

Mindful of his huge debt load, Alden Blethen wasted no time in reviving the journalistic bombast that in the past had helped him sell newspapers and advertising. Within two weeks of the fire, he began to tout his newspaper's upcoming annual review edition and disparage his competitors' versions as clearly inferior "advertising fakes." He was also not above capitalizing on the sympathies of his readers, printing and then reprinting the gruesome details of the fire as well as lengthy tributes to the victims and their families.[7]

In the first few weeks after *The Tribune* fire, there was an outpouring of public sympathy for Blethen in recognition of the severity of his losses. One of Blethen's most scathing critics, who had filed dozens of libel suits against the editor, expressed deep regret and dropped all charges against him. Even Blethen's fiercest competitors joined in congratulations when *The Tribune* began printing again from temporary quarters, with the usually venomous *Times* complimenting *The Tribune* for the "unprecedented" speed of its recovery. But Blethen's ill-fortune scarcely blunted his rivals' dislike of him, and he continued to provoke them at every opportunity. Within three months of the tragedy, the personal insults resumed their former intensity, with *The Minneapolis Times* referring to Blethen as the "diseased mind now dominating the unfortunate *Tribune*," and quoting

Despite their financial difficulties, Alden Blethen and his family continued to live in their large home on South 10th Street in one of Minneapolis' more elegant residential neighborhoods.

(Courtesy of Gilbert Duffy)

The Pioneer Press' contention that he was "the greatest blatherskite who ever struck the northwest."[8]

Blethen's critics in the press increasingly ridiculed him for episodes of public drunkenness during this period. Maine had been a dry state where most educated men advocated strict temperance, so Alden Blethen had little temptation to drink as a young man. After the move to Kansas City, however, Clarance Blethen recalled that his father began "to spasmodically turn to alcohol during fits of loneliness or depression." On an insurance application form, Alden Blethen later indicated that he had started drinking on doctor's orders: his Kansas City physician had prescribed a teaspoon of whiskey in water before meals and beer for his nerves. Blethen, who had left Portland weighing 134 pounds and suffering from tension and digestive problems, claimed that following this medical advice, he had gained 50 pounds and seen his health fully restored. "At no time, either day or night...did I ever drink to intoxication," he claimed. "I sometimes drank sufficiently to show it, both in my face and language; but no man ever saw me off my feet in the world."[9]

Despite his fervid denials, other newspapers, and particularly Edwin Haskell's paper, *The Minneapolis Times*, frequently portrayed him as intemperate, even describing a drunken brawl in *The Tribune* offices:

BLETHEN AS A SCRAPPER

The Editor of an Obscure Morning Sheet Gets Into a Fight

The proprietor of the *Tribune* was on the rampage yesterday. During the afternoon, he had been engaged in discussing the medicinal and bibulous qualities of Holland gin...and as is usually the case in those arguments, he got the worst of it. When he arrived at the *Tribune* business office, he found a burly collector for the Edison Electric Light Company waiting for him with a bill. When Mr. Blethen had read over the bill he was mad....

"You —— —— —— —— ——! You and your company are the biggest robbers on earth. You are trying to blackmail me!" shouted the newspaper magnate, prancing about the composing room.... "You —— —— ——! You ——! I can lick you!" shouted the *Tribune* man, frothing at the mouth.

But the big collector would not take a bluff and began to strip for a fight, and so did Blethen. The two pranced around in a highly undignified and pugilistic fashion for the space of five minutes.... It is understood the Alden Jay finally settled the account, after which he went in and made another reduction in the salaries of all the employees in the business office.[10]

Whether or not his drinking habits impaired his judgment, as his detractors implied, Blethen seemed plagued by one setback after another. The Minneapolis land boom, which had profited him so handsomely in the past, began to slow, and the Blethen family lost a great deal of money in their "widely scattered speculations in real estate." In the spring, a rumor spread around Minneapolis that *The Tribune* could not meet its heavy financial commitments. Blethen still claimed steadily increasing circulation, but the actual figures, once so prominently displayed to provoke his competitors, no longer appeared below the masthead. Blethen lost his bragging rights, as *The Tribune*'s gains slowed substantially. *The Times*, which facetiously began calling the struggling editor "the one man power," also reprinted reports of a pending sale, advising Blethen that he had better lower the price because no one would pay top dollar for "a paper that is on its last legs."[11]

The rumors quieted at the end of May 1890 when the news became public that Blethen had negotiated a new loan from the Minneapolis Trust Company to tide *The Tribune* over until better days. The bank loan staved off immediate disaster, but it merely postponed the inevitable. Blethen scrambled for the money to meet his commitments. And, his personal disappointments continued. Still eager for public office, he campaigned vigorously throughout the fall of 1890, speaking at numerous Republican functions to boost his candidacy for the state legislature. His efforts proved unsuccessful; the Democrats captured all the seats in his district. Among the Republican candidates, Alden Blethen ran dead last.[12]

In addition to politics, Blethen's duties with the Western Associated Press also distracted him. He had been active in the WAP since his days at *The Kansas City Journal*, serving on numerous committees before his election to the organization's board of directors in August 1890. He took his place on the board at a very contentious time, and was immediately asked to serve on a fact-finding board investigating possible WAP collusion with the upstart wire service, the United Press. Rumors circulated that the two rivals had made a "gentlemen's agreement" to limit ruinous competition and that several WAP directors—including general manager William Henry Smith—had secretly purchased UP stock. Blethen joined Smith and one of the general manager's most vocal enemies, *Chicago Daily News* publisher Victor Lawson, on the three-man investigating committee. Blethen represented the swing vote and when the group presented its findings to the full membership, it was clear that he had sided with Smith, his former business partner. The report did not condemn the directors' actions but merely called for another

committee to explore "a plan of reorganization of present relations."[13]

All the time Blethen spent on WAP matters and his political campaign took a heavy toll on his precarious newspaper empire. After a difficult struggle to keep the newspaper alive, Blethen found himself faced in February 1891, with a $60,000 note due to the Minnesota Trust Company. He could not pay it and the bank refused to give him any more time. He went in desperation to silent partner Thomas Lowry, seeking a new infu-

sion of capital, but this time Lowry balked. He would only pay off the note if the beleaguered editor turned over all his shares of the paper for Lowry to sell and agreed to step down as editor and publisher of *The Tribune.* Blethen, understandably bitter, had little choice but to agree. Only a year and a half after the fire, he faced another devastating loss, this one most damaging to his pride. Blethen was out of *The Tribune,* so financially and emotionally drained by the experience that for two years he abandoned newspaper

The Blethen children played with the sons and daughters of the Minneapolis elite, including the Pillsbury and Eustis families. Here Marion and Florence, who are in the dark dresses and hats at the center of the photograph, and C.B., second from left, pose on bicycles with some of the neighborhood children at the South 10th Street house.

(The Seattle Times)

work entirely. At loose ends, he turned instead to banking and local politics.[14]

In 1891 Minneapolis was still riding high. The city had expanded and diversified. Lumber and flour mills, which had dominated the Minneapolis cityscape and her economy in the booming 1880s, were pushed to the periphery where lower land prices allowed more room for expansion. In their place at the city's center rose new office buildings and a retail district catering to the new wealth of the growing middle classes. Railroads had made Minneapolis a transportation hub of the old Northwest, and the rich resources of the surrounding region—iron, grain, and timber—poured into its mills and warehouses. Local entrepreneurs expanded the industrial base into production of machine tools, steam engines, and farm equipment.[15]

To meet the needs of business and satisfy the constantly growing demand for investment capital, the number of banking houses in the city multiplied with dizzying speed. By 1892, with a population approaching 200,000, Minneapolis had several dozen banks and nearly as many savings and loan associations. Bank clearings, always a popular gauge of economic growth, had soared 2,000 percent in the city during the previous ten years.[16]

Banking lay at the heart of the city's industrial and commercial expansion, a fact that appealed to Alden Blethen's avid boosterism. Many of his political friends were involved in finance, and they encouraged Blethen to try his hand. In the spring of 1892, when Minneapolis' prospects seemed particularly bright, Blethen became a founder and the first president of the Bank of New England and its companion institution, the New England Dime Savings Bank. The names sounded conservative and reliable, reminiscent of home and heritage for Blethen as well as for thousands of others transplanted from the Northeast to Minnesota. The headquarters for the two banks occupied part of the ground floor in the most prestigious office space in Minneapolis, the twelve-story Guaranty Loan Building. The bank directors included many of the city's most prominent businessmen, lawyers, and civil servants.[17]

Banking seemed a radical change in professions for Alden Blethen. He had no direct experience in the field, although as business manager at *The Minneapolis Tribune* and *The Kansas City Journal* he had taken primary responsibility for all financial decisions. He may have regarded his legal training and

Minneapolis had grown and diversified by 1892. New stores and offices dominated the downtown core, pushing industry to the periphery. This view shows Nicollet Avenue from Fourth Street.

(Minnesota Historical Society)

Even as Alden Blethen changed careers, satiric cartoons of him continued to appear in rival Minneapolis newspapers.

(The Minneapolis Times, January 24, 1892)

Alden Blethen entered the banking business in 1892, after giving up his interest in The Minneapolis Tribune. *Blethen became president of the Bank of New England and its companion institution, the New England Dime Savings Bank. Other investors, as this advertisement from the Minneapolis city directory suggests, were important members of the business community.*

successful real estate speculation as good preparation for a banking career, but above all he just seemed ready to try something new. The horrible *Tribune* fire still haunted him, and he had become disillusioned by the daily grind of the newspaper business and the bitter negotiations that ended his partnership with Thomas Lowry. As son Clarance remembered, he wanted to leave journalism and find a new profession with predictable hours and "nights without worry."[18]

Blethen became convinced that banking offered him the means to recoup his personal fortune, so much diminished after losses at *The Tribune*. Joe Blethen remembered that his father converted "a few odds and ends of the wreck into cash" to provide his share of the banks' capitalization costs; later accounts suggest the family's initial investment was $20,000. Alden Blethen claimed his stake eventually climbed to well over $100,000. Whatever his own financial role, he convinced several wealthy Minneapolis businessmen to join him as principal shareholders. He then launched into banking with great optimism.[19]

The Bank of New England had its offices on the ground floor of the tallest and one of the most elegant new buildings in downtown Minneapolis, the Guaranty Loan Building. Blethen also ran his political campaigns from headquarters here.

(Minneapolis Public Library)

The state-chartered Bank of New England did well enough in its first year of operation, but despite its upscale quarters, the bank remained a modest operation by local standards. Advertising his institution as "young, energetic and liberal," Blethen applied to this banking enterprise some of the talent for promotion that had served him so effectively in the newspaper business. Convinced that Minneapolis had room for a bank catering to the needs of individuals and small businesses, he worked hard to attract this kind of depositor. The savings and loan arm of the bank appealed for deposits from 10 cents to $5,000, claiming to value the accounts of its smallest depositors as much as the largest. The Bank of New England advertised itself as the understanding financial advisor for ordinary working people in the city and even their children:

> The object of this institution should be understood by every person desirous of saving his small earnings, by every child anxious to lay aside the pennies he may take or have given to him, and the wage earner who wishes to make a practice of laying a small portion of his weekly or monthly payments aside and place them where they will bear the highest rate of interest possible with absolute safety.

Blethen's detractors remained unpersuaded and later sarcastically accused him of courting unsuspecting "widows, clerks and mechanics."[20]

The Bank of New England also served as the staging ground for Blethen's varied political activities. In 1892 Minneapolis basked in worldwide attention as the site of the Republican national convention. The rather brash notion that this young boomtown could host such a prestigious event had originated at the planning meetings for the Minneapolis Exposition back in 1886, when Alden Blethen and other civic boosters argued that the huge exposition building they were proposing would also be a perfect venue for the Republican convention. Representatives of the city made an unsuccessful bid for the 1888 convention, and in November 1891, a group of prominent Minneapolitans, including Alden Blethen, headed to Washington, D.C., to plead the city's case again before the Republican National Committee.[21]

During that visit, the Minneapolis delegation tried to gain the support of leading presidential candidates, including James G. Blaine, one of Blethen's old Maine acquaintances. Blaine was especially cordial, joking and chatting with them, noting that the city should be "thawed out" by the June convention date. The Minneapolis papers later reported that one delegate had replied enthusiastically, "We have always been warm toward you," and that Alden Blethen had chimed in, "And when the convention is held you will find a greater warmth towards you than ever."[22]

The bid this time proved successful, and, as promised, Alden Blethen and other Minneapolis men were "warm" to Blaine. They sported red lapel ribbons stating "BLAINE: The People's Choice," and strong-armed other delegates to join his contingent. Blethen had also been involved in convention planning, serving on the executive committee and on the press committee, which made arrangements for the hundreds of journalists converging on the city to cover the event. The Maine delegation had headquarters near Blethen's bank in the Guaranty Loan Building, and he joined fellow Maineites in enthusiastic support of "their" candidate. The convention proved to be a great success for the city, but not for Blaine and his backers, as Benjamin Harrison received the nomination on the first ballot.[23]

Blethen continued to have his own personal political ambitions in Minneapolis, and soon after the convention he announced that he would join the 1892 mayoral race. Campaign headquarters were located in the Bank of New England offices, and some of the institution's directors were also his principal political supporters. Visitors frequently commented on the "semi-political" atmosphere that surrounded the bank, unusual even for those times of limited regulation. Yet in the highly charged climate of this national election year, the strong network of associations Blethen had built through his work for the Republican Party must certainly have increased his customer base and the prominence of his institution.[24]

Blethen threw himself wholeheartedly into the 1892 campaign, perhaps regarding it as his best chance to redeem past failures. He had announced his candidacy for mayor in late July, focusing his oratory on the need to curb the city's wide-open policies on saloon licenses. Blethen favored what were known as high licenses—expensive fees charged yearly to saloon keepers that would, in theory, stop the proliferation of low-class establishments. Blethen's stance attracted the backing of a distinguished group of Republican businessmen, equally reluctant to shut down the city's highly profitable liquor trade or to permit Minneapolis to become a wide-open town.

Two other well-known party loyalists, A.J. Boardman and C.P. Lovell, quickly joined the race against Blethen for the Republican nomination. The press described Lovell, a city councilman with four years of experience, as politically conservative and rock solid, while Boardman was well known as a successful businessman and shrewd ward

Politicians from throughout the country converged on Minneapolis for the Republican convention in 1892. Colorful campaign ribbons boosted everything from local products to presidential candidates.
(Minneapolis Public Library)

In 1892 Minneapolis was caught up in the political fever as it hosted the Republican National Convention. Alden Blethen was part of the delegation of civic leaders who lobbied for the convention to come to Minneapolis.
(Minneapolis Public Library)

THE MAYORALTY RACE.

Boardman Leads by a Nose.

Alden Blethen had failed in two previous attempts at public office, but was a leading candidate for the Republican nomination for mayor in 1892. In this cartoon Blethen in the striped jersey is seen neck and neck with political rival A.J. Boardman. An unidentified dark-horse candidate looms behind them.

(Minneapolis Times, September 8, 1892)

politician. Many observers considered this mayoral contest as one of the most spirited in recent memory, as the candidates lambasted the Democrats and no less enthusiastically sniped at each other. Blethen, still as outspoken and controversial as he had been on the editorial pages of *The Tribune*, was certainly the most colorful candidate, although his opponents mocked his "brass band" hustling as more wind than substance.[25]

The long weeks of intensive campaigning, speech-making, and behind-the-scenes maneuvering built toward the Republican city convention, which would select candidates for city office. On September 7, 1892, the convention came to order at Normanna Hall, the standard meeting place for the city's large Scandinavian community. An anxious crowd of three hundred official delegates, as well as numerous reporters, Republican leaders, and other political types filled the hall.

As the hours passed, excitement built toward the mayoral contest, the convention's climax. At nearly six o'clock in the evening the hall was just as crowded as it had been in the morning when the session was first called to order, with the delegates now standing knee-deep in trampled ballots, bunting, and campaign broadsides. No one noticed the heat or the litter as they jostled for space and stood on their chairs, focused on the dramatic battle unfolding on the stage before them.[26]

At the foot of the lectern, Blethen conferred with his supporters, whispering and smiling to one, patting the shoulder of another, leaning over to wink knowingly at a third. Squinting into the cigar smoke, he waved and smiled to a friend out working the floor and quickly surveyed the churning room. Alden Blethen, no longer a young man, was still vigorous and powerful. His curly hair and distinctive side-whiskers had grayed slightly, but they still bristled around his face, embodying the energy of the man. Many observers described his head as leonine, and noted the power of his chest and shoulders. At forty-six, he had relinquished none of the physical presence that had commanded attention all his life—he stood ready to accept his party's nomination, to possess the stage, and deliver an acceptance speech that no one would ever forget.

Blethen's delegates, intensely loyal, remained committed through four ballots. Lovell's men deserted him after the third, but instead of crossing over to Boardman or Blethen, they chose to support the so-called "dark horse" candidate, William Henry Eustis. Eustis, a successful real estate developer and civic booster in Minneapolis, had earned wide respect for his integrity and level-headedness. He had not sought this nomination, but it was common knowledge he would accept it if offered. Surprisingly, at the end of the fourth ballot he was the leading candidate, just twenty votes short of victory.[27]

Backroom negotiations were frantic. Boardman, realizing that he had no hope of winning, agreed to withdraw in favor of Blethen. The Blethen forces then began to canvass the hall, trying to keep Boardman delegates in line. But Eustis had the momentum, and the pleas of Blethen supporters could not dissuade a majority of the Boardman delegates from joining the Eustis camp. When the fifth ballot votes were tallied, the chairman of the convention stepped up to the podium, called repeatedly for quiet from the excited crowd, and then announced the victor. William Henry Eustis had triumphed. All the other candidates came to the stage in a show of Republican unity, but when the call rang out for Alden Blethen, he did not respond. The former editor and his backers had stormed from the convention immediately after hearing the results.[28]

Alden Blethen had much at stake in this campaign, and it is not surprising that he responded to defeat without the grace and good-will that had marked his two previous runs. His fascination with politics had grown and intensified since his early support of political causes in Maine. In Minneapolis he had used the pages of his newspapers to wage fierce political battles, taking strongly partisan positions on many local issues and loyally supporting the Republican Party's nominees. He had tirelessly devoted his own time to the city's Republican organization and used his widely recognized speech-making abilities to stump for favored candidates. But a supporting role never satisfied him; he wanted the power to make decisions and shape policy, to be recognized for his singular contributions. Alden Blethen had lost his

platform as the influential editor of *The Tribune*, but as the mayor of Minneapolis he could have satisfied his personal political ambitions, as well as his sincere desire to be a potent force for the growth and development of the city. Now, instead, he would be branded a three-time loser.

Blethen reacted bitterly, first charging Eustis with deceit and fraud, and then retreating into uncharacteristic silence. He never talked about his failed campaigns or ran for political office again. The following winter he did receive one valued political reward—the title of Colonel and a place on Minnesota governor Knute Nelson's honorary military staff. The honor recognized his services to the party and to the newspaper profession, and Alden Blethen would be known as "the Colonel" for the rest of his days. But the title served only as a poor substitute for the real political influence that he sought, and, with regret, he turned his attention back to banking. In studied understatement one of the local newspapers said it best: "Mr. Blethen was a very much disappointed man."[29]

But Blethen soon faced even greater disappointments in his banking career. If the maxim "timing is everything" has any validity, he could not have picked a worse period to learn the banking business. Early in 1893, soon after Blethen had wound up his mayoral campaign, the first bellwether of a slowing national economy appeared. A small railroad in Pennsylvania went bankrupt, the victim of overexpansion, heavy debt, and dwindling profits. The same kinds of problems plagued the country's other railroads as well as many of its leading manufacturers. Unemployment grew as more businesses failed or cut back. Consumer spending declined and people fell back on their savings. The financial dominoes began to topple.

Despite a spirited contest, Blethen lost the mayoral nomination to William Henry Eustis, the dark-horse candidate who went on to win the November election. Blethen, extremely bitter about this loss, never ran for public office again.
(Minneapolis Public Library)

In this precarious economic climate, banks quickly felt the pinch as debtors began to default on loans and depositors lined up to withdraw their money. In the first six months of 1893, more than one hundred banks across the nation collapsed. The Panic of 1893 hit Minneapolis hard. As Horace Hudson, a historian and former *Tribune* reporter, wrote, "It had seemed that prosperity was a thing which belonged to Minneapolis as a right; in many people's minds, continued growth and constant advance in values of property and volume of business were assured." Hudson could well have been describing Alden Blethen's attitude. Although humbled by his own political misfortunes, Blethen had always possessed unflagging self-confidence and optimism. He, too, believed that the Minneapolis boom would continue, and the Bank of New England would provide capital to fuel that growth. He had gambled heavily on that boom, but he had bet wrong.[30]

The forces of economic collapse proved too powerful, and Blethen's own financial house of cards too unstable. The huge industrial and technological surge that had led America to remarkable prosperity during the 1870s and 1880s ground to an agonizing halt. The large cities of the East and Midwest felt the shock first, and then Minneapolis, with its important railroad connections and heavy concentration of industry, was hard hit. The Bank of New England had secured its capital stock with notes held by two Chicago banks that failed early in the crash; the Minneapolis bank lost access to cash and essential lines of credit.[31]

Rumors circulated that the Bank of New England also had numerous unsecured loans, as many as half of them to development companies the Blethen family controlled. Alden Blethen, ever the confident speculator, had continued his real estate ventures in Minneapolis. The bank had provided capital for at least two companies—the New England Investment and Realty Company and the West Minneapolis Land Company—in which he was an officer or principal shareholder. Their loans were collateralized with property that Blethen had purchased around the city, sometimes at inflated, boom-time prices. He had backed other personal or family loans with bonds from the Briar Bluff Mining and Stock Company. The Briar Bluff Company controlled 1,200 acres of Illinois farmland, once owned by Rose Ann Hunter's uncle Soranus Brettun, and the mining company hoped to exploit the reputedly rich deposits of coal lying beneath the surface. Whether this corporation was just another grandiose sham or a legitimate venture mattered little; the value of its bonds collapsed as real estate prices tumbled down with the economy.[32]

In late June 1893, with heavy liabilities and no place else to borrow, the Bank of New England suspended operations. The courts named judge John Rea, an old Blethen friend and a bank shareholder, as receiver. The Bank of New England became the seventh financial institution in Minneapolis to fail that summer. By the time the economy finally rebounded in 1897, that number had risen to thirteen. In fact, of all the banks that opened during the Minneapolis boom years, only one survived. Later legislative investigations determined that a few of these banks had never been solvent, and others had been raided by greedy corporate officers before the end came. The committee did not name the Bank of New England as one of these "rotten" institutions, but the stigma of his bank's failure plagued Alden Blethen for the rest of his life.[33]

Blethen's enemies in the Minneapolis press periodically dredged up the details of the

bank's insolvency and the fate of depositors who were bilked out of "every red cent." The papers made much of the fact that Alden, Rose Ann, and Joseph Blethen had all received loans from the bank, with *The Minneapolis Journal* snidely commenting that "the only member of the family that didn't get in on the divy was the pony." In response, Blethen fiercely defended himself, arguing that the collateral he had lost, including the Briar Bluff bonds, far exceeded the amount of these loans. He claimed that he had made a heroic effort to protect small investors, and vowed that his Bank of New England would eventually liquidate all of its debts. Years later he made good on this promise. Joseph Blethen attributed his father's banking misadventures to his character: he was "just too good-natured to be a banker." But others, perhaps more dispassionate, blamed his inexperience and questionable financial judgment.[34]

The bank's collapse fundamentally challenged Alden Blethen's views on the economic and the social order of the United States. The financial disaster of 1893, as startling and severe an economic downturn as the country had ever experienced, pushed many patriotic Americans into a critical re-evaluation of their most basic beliefs and goals. The crisis forced staunch Republican Alden Blethen to reconsider old doubts about his party's elitist hard money stand; it forced ex-banker Blethen to take on the new role of debtor and champion of the masses. But Alden Blethen, the family man, was simply out of work.

In Minneapolis, Blethen had spent a great deal of money to live in the right neighborhood, to send his children to the right schools, and to belong to the right clubs. He dressed well and dined well; he cultivated his taste for fine art and good books. His

The Blethen family followed the Minneapolis elite to the suburbs, building this large mansion on Pleasant Avenue in 1893.

(Courtesy of Gilbert Duffy)

Alden Blethen made sure that his children had every advantage while growing up in Minneapolis. The boys, including C.B. on the left in this photograph, were expected to be tough, however, while the girls, Marion, in the center, and Florence, standing to her right, were pampered and protected.

(Courtesy of Gilbert Duffy)

fraternal, political, and booster activities brought him into the highest circles of Twin Cities society, even though his bitter feuds and journalistic bad taste kept him from fitting in comfortably. In their first home, on fashionable South Tenth Street in the city, the Blethen family lived side-by-side with the industrialist Charles Pillsbury and his family; their children grew up riding bicycles together. In later years, they followed the elite to an exclusive suburban neighborhood, where they built a large and gracious home of stone and Minnesota red brick.[35]

Rose Ann Blethen loved spending time with her young daughters in the family's home and garden. Shy and uncomfortable in company all her life, she attended charity

balls and society functions at her husband's side with considerable reluctance. Otherwise, she retreated behind his bluster into her own private life, avoiding luncheons, musicales, and charity functions with other matrons, preferring the company of her children, her sisters, and a very few close friends.[36]

In Alden Blethen's family, the men and boys stood out—they lived public lives and shielded the women. To his sons he was a demanding father who could withhold approval and affection, controlling them to toughen them for life. The girls, Florence and Marion, were petted and admired, dressed in fine silk frocks and fur-lined winter coats. Blethen never pampered or indulged the boys, but prepared them for the battle to grasp and keep their share of life's rewards. C.B. Blethen—Clarance—was thirteen when the Bank of New England crashed and his world came to an end; his father told him to keep his chin up. In Kansas City, Blethen had sent his son Joe to business school so he would know how to do something useful; in Minnesota, Blethen decided that Joe would attend the University of Minnesota in Minneapolis, not some effete Eastern school. By 1893, Joe was a talented writer of light comic verse and escapist plays set in exotic locales; he had been class poet and historian. He soon began to publish his work, but after he graduated, he joined his father and went to work as a teller at the Bank of New England. Yet Joe and C.B. loved Alden Blethen, and spoke of him through the rest of their lives with fierce pride, defending him against every critic, long after his death.[37]

Blethen depended on the security of his family's trust and affection; he had lost his public influence, his good name, and his fortune by the summer of 1893. The legal maneuverings over the liquidation of Bank of New England debts tied up his remaining

assets. The new suburban mansion, a monument to better days, now seemed one more burden to bear, binding him to high mortgage payments. He had to find new job opportunities. At the age of forty-six, what he knew best was the newspaper business. But Blethen's caustic editorial exchanges with other Twin Cities journalists effectively barred him from working for any of the city's established papers. He had limited alternatives: move and begin anew or stay in Minneapolis and start another newspaper of his own.[38]

Although the fall of 1893 might seem like the worst of times to begin a new publishing venture, Alden Blethen did it anyway. He saw the risks, but he was too experienced in the newspaper business (and probably still

too chastened by his recent financial losses) to plunge ahead without some reasonable chance of success. Shrewdly assessing the Minneapolis news market, Blethen had a strong intuition that shifting popular attitudes caused by economic hard times would prompt increasing challenges to the status quo. He had changed his own mind; perhaps he could change the minds of others. New voices struggled to be heard and there might be room for another newspaper to represent their views. The idea of *The Penny Press* was born.

The concept of an inexpensive paper catering to the masses was certainly not new. The first penny press began in the 1830s during the democratic upheavals of the Jacksonian era, pioneered and popularized by big-city

Joseph Blethen showed a literary flair and was named class poet and historian at the University of Minnesota. He was also the author of several plays, including The War of the Roses, *which was produced in 1894. Joe is seen here, third from the left, playing the role of a doctor in the production.*

(Minnesota Historical Society)

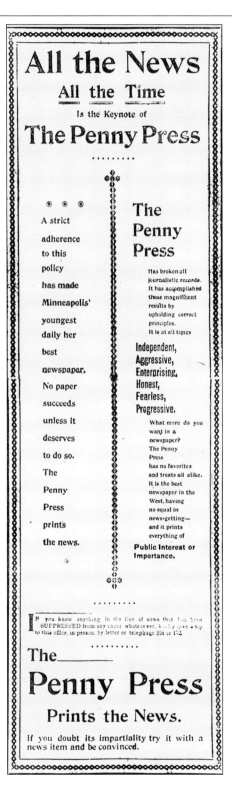

editors like Benjamin Day and Horace Greeley. At that time of turmoil in American history, a new urban middle class arose, demanding an end to monopoly by special interests as well as an expanded role for the common man in the political and economic direction of the country. Blethen undoubtedly saw striking parallels in his own era, and used some of the rhetoric of the earlier penny press to carve a new niche for himself in the Minneapolis of the depressed 1890s.

The original penny press publishers often had strong working class origins and sympathies, but the radicalism of their columns had quickly disappeared, replaced by practical or human interest stories with broader middle class appeal. In contrast to the sober city dailies, which relied on the patronage of particular parties or interest groups, the new mass-market papers trumpeted their fearlessness and independence from partisanship, while expanding their coverage beyond financial and political news to crime, entertainment, romantic fiction, and scandal. The penny papers became increasingly audacious, developing a bold new style marked by sensational headlines and flowery prose. Reaching back beyond the drab newspapers of the 1870s, Alden Blethen revived and restyled the penny press to a new purpose, responsive to the technological opportunities of the new journalism.[39]

Blethen's *Penny Press* echoed these early penny sheets. In his first issue, October 21, 1893, the new editor laid out some of the goals of this upstart enterprise and the new urban audience of workingmen and immigrants it hoped to attract. Minneapolis was a manufacturing town, Blethen argued, and its largely working-class population regarded morning newspapers as a luxury they could not afford. *The Penny Press*, by publishing an evening paper that was bright, brief, and above all, cheap, would "transform luxury into necessity." It would entertain and it would educate. It would train good citizens. It would take on the issues of the growing city—public transportation, municipal parks, free libraries, safe drinking water. *The Penny Press*, strongly independent in its politics, avoided the heavy partisanship of its competitors and freely criticized or promoted any cause it chose. Its only loyalty, according to its editor, was "to the best interests of the great metropolis." No one had ever tried a penny paper in Minneapolis, making it both an innovation and a gamble.[40]

The Penny Press was no Jacksonian antique, but the journalistic child of the nineties. It was the extraordinary expression of its editor's desperate situation, his bruised ambitions, and his changing political ideas, blended with the old egalitarian city newspaper, the brand new urban readership, and cutting-edge newspaper technology. Alden Blethen hedged his bets by making sure that this inexpensive daily would still be able to provide "red hot" news coverage from around the country. The sudden availability of a United Press membership offered him a compelling and possibly decisive reason for proceeding with *The Penny Press*. In September 1893, a newly restructured Associated Press peremptorily ordered its clients with UP service to discontinue it or face sanctions. Most complied, and suddenly several UP memberships became available in Minneapolis.[41]

In the days of the early penny press, timely reporting of world news had not been possible, but in the 1890s, a wire service franchise became a prerequisite for a "real" newspaper. Newsbrokering associations like UP or AP carefully guarded their membership and usually admitted only one morning and one evening paper in each metropolitan area. Based on his experiences at *The Kansas City Journal* and *The Minneapolis Tribune*, Alden Blethen knew the value of exclusive access to telegraphic news services and acted quickly to purchase the daytime UP rights in his own name. Awed by his own luck, he wrote, "a few months ago neither service could have been obtained at any price by a new organization. Such is war."[42]

It still remained to establish the business apparatus and install production facilities for this new enterprise, so Blethen organized *The Penny Press* Company. Machinery, payroll, and other start-up expenses cost approximately $25,000, which he evidently solicited in small sums from friends, relatives, banks—wherever he could beg or borrow the money. In all ways, the early *Penny Press* was a shoestring operation. With low salaries, many employees took part of their pay in stock. Some of the Kansas City cowboys left other newspapers to join Blethen on *The Penny Press*, sympathetic to their old boss and glad to write for him again. Joe Blethen went to work on the newspaper, doing rewrite, reviewing plays, roughing out features—whatever needed to be done. C.B. helped in the mailroom after school every day, bundling papers for the newsboys to sell. Production facilities were jammed into several first floor rooms of a small commercial building, formerly a carpenter's shop. The carriers who supplied subscription holders operated out of the building's basement, while the city newsboys picked up their consignment of papers from an unheated shed in the back. Blethen had bought some new production equipment, including the presses, but it was the dead minimum needed to publish a "respectable sheet."[43]

The first issues of *The Penny Press* ran four pages. The front page featured local and national news, although it usually included a few display ads touting clothing sales or special purchases on such popular items as "Professor Winsor's electric insoles." Promising readers "All of the news of the day in condensed form," *The Penny Press* instructed its reporters to provide the basic facts, enlivened with short, pithy commentary and plenty of quotes. Bold one word headlines—**Blood!! Lost??** or **Storm!**—emphasized the drama of the news, followed by as many as four or five stacked sub-heads summarizing story content. For its debut edition, *The Penny Press* was fortunate to have a breaking local news story —the mysterious suicide of a Bank of Minneapolis cashier and the disappearance of one of the bank's tellers with $100,000 in embezzled funds. The fugitive was eventually apprehended in South America, but the details of his extradition and trial provided fodder for months of columns.[44]

On the editorial page, Alden Blethen usually kept his commentary brief with dozens of pithy one- and two-line observations and a few lengthier pieces on national and international issues. Obsessed with economic news, he wrote daily updates and weekly reports on the state of the economy—analyzing bank clearances, employment figures, and the state of gold reserves. Initially, his tone was subdued, decidedly pessimistic about any rapid financial improvement. When the Minneapolis street car operators threatened a strike, Blethen discouraged such rash measures and counseled patience and caution among his working class readers: "Steady wages that will keep the wolf from the door during the next six months will be vastly better than no employment." Speaking for himself as well as for *The Penny Press'* readers, Blethen's 1894 New Year's editorial wished that "the winter of discontent now lowering over us [would] soon give way to a glorious summer of prosperity and sunshine!"[45]

THE

VOL 1. NO. 117.

DEATH.

Horrible Accident at a Coal Mine in Pennsylvania.

Four Men Out of a Crew of Nine Meet Almost Instant Death.

Three of them Are Crushed to Death and One of Them Burned.

Due Warning Had Been Given But It Was in Some Way Neglected.

Scranton, Pa., March 6.—Four men out of a gang of nine were killed in the Richmond shaft, in the northern part of the city, this morning at 5 o'clock. The accident was caused by the fall of a shelf of rock from the side of the shaft near the bottom and a consequent explosion of a blower of gas. The victims are: Thomas Holwill, charge man, married, wife and child, burned to death; Richard Hughes, single, 27 years; James Northen, single, 20 years; Albert Richards, single, 24 years.

Hughes, Northen and Richards were crushed to death by the rock. The two latter had but recently come here from the copper mines of Michigan and were

WHAT THEY WA

Board of Trade Men and Views on Municipal Government.

Some Excellent Suggestio Made for Running the C Properly.

There was a good audience at ceum last evening at the mass in the interest of municipal refo der the auspices of the Board of F. N. Stacy presided.

President Crocker made a re the Philadelphia municipal refo vention. S. M. Owen urged th sity for a citizens' organizati the municipalities were well g then the state and the nation w well governed."

N. F. Hawley enlarged upon t men charter law, and Prof. W. well discussed: "What a Charte Give Us." He said he thought trying to conduct business here mediaeval constitution. He w vise a number of experiments, not holding the municipal elec the same day with the state and n making the big cities one and he would like to experiment tried of only prope ers exercising authority, becau had property and were not goir He would have the number of a limited to 13, and matters so a that by a proper combination th ing men could get their represe in the city council. Important tions should be submitted to th for a popular vote.

Rev. M. D. Shutter said there together too much party politic up in public affairs which placed he official elected by one particul between hell and the iron work

Rev. F. L. Hayes did not be commissions for city employ thought salaries should be so a

The Penny Press *also relied on bold headlines and sensational stories to create excitement and attract readers, a technique that soon came to be known as "yellow journalism."*
(The Penny Press, March 6, 1894)

PENNY PRESS

EAPOLIS, MINN., TUESDAY, MARCH 6, 1894—5 O'CLOCK EDITION.　　　　PRICE ONE CENT.

BLOOD.

lows at the Troy Mayoralty Election Today.

cratic Gangs Are in Charge of the Polls.

itate a Riot, and a Leading Republican Is Sent Into Eternity.

s Are Badly Wounded in the Terrible Conflict Which Ensues.

. N, Y,, March 6.—There is un-nted excitement concerning the test is between Senator Murphy's Moloy, and Mayor Whelan, who dependent-Democrat indorsed by cans.

s, alleged to be in the employ of uy faction began their work upon ning of the polls in the Thirteenth In some cases the name of a nan was voted on by repeaters six times.

Republican inspectors vigorously d, but being in the minority in trict they were overruled and the nt ballots were shoved into the

FIENDS.

West Virginia Miners Are Evidently a Blood-thirsty Lot.

They Are Hunting for a Man Who Disclosed a Plot.

It Is Said the Jail at Fayette-ville Will Be Set on Fire.

Two Gatling Guns Are Sent There to Protect Property.

Charleston, W. Va., March 6.—An ex-citing 24 hours has passed in the mining region. The disclosure of a plot to blow up the troops with dynamite had an electrical effect on the strikers and they are bloodthirsty and determined to find the man who "peached."

A mob thronged Handley; spies were in every house and the man's life was in the utmost danger and how he escaped detection is a miracle. This morning he was taken secretly from Handley to Eagle on a locomotive and there placed under the protection of the military. The strikers do not yet know where he is. Alarming reports come Fayetteville that the jail, if not already

BOOZE.

Frank Floyd Says He Loved the Demi-john.

Sorry for a Letter Which He Sent His Mother.

No One Could Find Anything Dis-honest in His Past Life.

He Admits That at Times He Con-sidered Phil Scheig Somewhat Eccentric.

Mrs. Eleanor Floyd, surrounded by comforting lady friends, was the center of all feminine eyes at the trial of her sons today.

Frank Floyd again took the stand.
"How did you put in the time at St. Louis between April and September?" asked Mr. Nye.
"I was breaking the horses, training them to go double or single or with saddle."
"What else did you do?"
"I passed away the time the best way I could."
"Did you spend the time in sporting houses?"
"Some of it."

PISTOL.

Manager Clark Has an Exciting Experience This Afternoon.

He Was Seated at His Desk When Attorney Clay Called.

The Lawyer Puts a Revolver in His Face and Demands $100.

Clark Proposes to Get a Check Book and Locks Himself in His Vault.

Manager Clark, of the Minneapolis Grain Commission Company, had a dra-matic time of it this afternoon.

The offices of the company are at 312 Guaranty Loan building.

Mr. Clark was at his desk at 1 o'clock, when looking up he found a 38 calibre eevolver pointed toward his face.

The gun was cocked and leveled with-in an inch of his forehead by B. B. Clay, a well known attorney of this city.

"Give me $100, d——n you," shouted Clay, or I'll blow your brains out.'

Mr. Clark looked his assailant in the eye and believing he meant business

PLOT.

Catholics of Costa Rica Charged With Planning a Revolution.

The Authorities Said to Be in Hourly Expectation of Attack.

Bishop Thiel Is the Head and Friend of the Proposed Uprising.

He Has Been Arrested and With Others Will Be Ex-pelled.

New York, March 6.—A special from San Jose, Costa Rica, dated Feb. 23, says:

Bernardo A. Thiel, bishop of Costa Rica, and several other prominent Cath-olics, clerical and lay, have been arrested here, charged with plotting revolution.

At this writing the authorities are in hourly expectation of an attack. The police have been armed with rifles and militia are under arms, prepared to turn out at a moment's notice. Bishop Thiel's purpose is said to be the establishment of a government of the Catholics under his direction. For a similar attempt in 1885 he was expelled by President Fernandez. It is expected that the bishop and his associates will be

The Penny Press *waged bitter circulation battles against other Minneapolis dailies, but advertising revenue kept a penny paper in business.*

(The Penny Press, June 19, 1895)

Opposite: Even The Penny Press' *classified section was lively with plenty of illustrations.*

(The Penny Press, August 17, 1895)

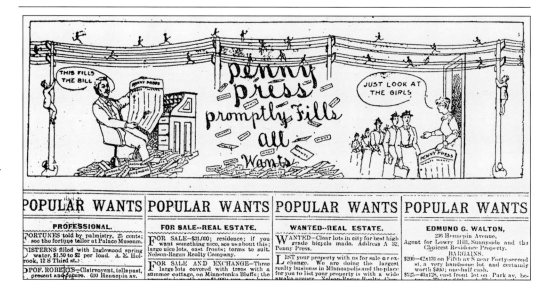

The paper, like its earlier penny press counterparts, did not offer a partisan political voice. Blethen had not only failed three times as a Republican candidate, he had also become disillusioned by the Grand Old Party's ineffectual response to the catastrophic financial circumstances of the 1893 Panic. Yet the Democrats did not quickly embrace him; he had been too outspoken a critic in years past. In *The Penny Press,* editor Blethen chose to speak as an independent, "not bound by corporate chains or held tight in the grip of monopoly." In his national political commentary, Blethen criticized the Cleveland administration's monetary policy; locally, he could not resist frequent jibes at Republican political nemesis, Mayor William Henry Eustis, for his views on vice and police corruption. But, far more than in the past, his commentary dealt with the pressing issues of the city and the character of candidates and office holders, rather than with party loyalties or petty jealousies. In Minneapolis, his was the voice of the new urban populist, the progressive. Alden Blethen loved to claim "Pro bono publico"—for the good of the public— as the motto of *The Penny Press.*[46]

What did he really think? Did the public editor and the private man hold different views? Alden Blethen's heart and mind are hidden from us, as they were hidden from his contemporaries. Certainly, his transition from Republican standard-bearer to champion of the masses made good business sense, as two of the city's established dailies were already Republican papers. A few cynics openly doubted the sincerity of Blethen's new-found populism. The city's notorious Democratic political boss, Doc Ames, whom Blethen had harshly criticized as a demagogue during his *Tribune* days, publicly questioned his new conviction. In a letter to Blethen reprinted on *The Penny Press'* editorial page, he wrote: "It is a difficult job, is it not, friend Alden, to hide your long Republican ears under the lion skin you put on when you re-entered the newspaper field?" But Blethen, somewhat uncharacteristically, did not rise to the bait, and, in fact, adopted a new, more conciliatory attitude toward the highly popular Ames:

My dear doctor... You have proved yourself too much of a man in a great many ways to be reminded of any mistakes you may have made while mayor; and I know I have made too many mistakes to have any desire to remind you of your errors...we are not here for the purpose of stirring up animosities, by alluding to unsavory things of the past, but are here for the purpose of gaining new friends by our future work, and holding all those we have had in the past.[47]

If *The Penny Press* was to become the voice of the people, Blethen did have to make new friends.

The Penny Press initially remained aloof from dogged editorial criticism of rival papers and refused to imitate their circulation stunts and promotions. Yet while Blethen sarcastically poked fun at the "premium schemes" of *The Journal* and *The Tribune*—schemes he himself had once embraced—he made aggressive and innovative efforts to build *Penny Press* readership. Alden Blethen had a decade of experience running the business side of newspapers and he knew that at a penny a copy, his only chance of success against the established dailies was to boost circulation figures quickly in order to attract steady commercial advertisers. He gave away thousands of papers during the first few weeks of publication and allowed patrons to insert classified advertisements free of charge. Blethen confided to friends that the venture would succeed only if it reached a circulation of ten thousand within six months. By the paper's third week Blethen bragged that *The Penny Press* had an average daily readership of over eleven thousand people.[48]

Soon, circulation figures began to appear daily at the head of the editorial columns. Those figures grew steadily, reaching fourteen thousand by the end of February, but advertising, the lifeblood of the paper's financial health, declined during the slow winter months of 1894. Blethen needed controversy or high drama to create new interest. Conflict between laboring men and local industrialists

afforded Blethen his best opportunity to hook the new reading audience his penny paper needed for survival.

The Penny Press considered itself a friend of labor. Blethen, usually an eager purchaser of the most up-to-date equipment, remained the only newspaper owner in town who did not install typesetting machines, claiming that they would result in too many layoffs and cause hardship for his employees. The paper displayed the emblem of the International Typographers Union on its editorial page and proudly reprinted commendations from local unions and ethnic societies. During his days in Kansas City, Blethen had battled with the ITU, blacklisting its members and supporting a "company union," the Printers' Protective Fraternity. Then, he had considered ITU members wild-eyed radicals; now, they were family men just trying to keep their jobs.

Great Northern Railroad workers went out on strike in April and May, and the intense public interest in this battle between labor and management gave the paper a needed boost. During the strike, the paper claimed a high middle ground, always sympathizing with the plight of the workers whose salaries were cut, but urging reasonable and respectful dialogue with management. While most of the city's other papers uncritically supported the railroad, *The Penny Press* persistently encouraged negotiation and compromise. When the strike was settled through arbitration, the paper modestly claimed some credit for serving its constituency so well. "90% of the railroad men... believed that *The Penny Press* was their friend during the late unpleasantness," an editorial commented. And there were other more tangible rewards—during the height of the strike, workers in one Northern Pacific shop sent in almost two hundred new subscrip-tions, helping circulation to peak at twenty-five thousand.[49]

As *The Penny Press* fought to establish itself in the competitive Minneapolis market, its distinctive personality emerged. The paper tried to build a new city readership with intensive coverage of local immigrant news, from Norwegian dances to Irish prize-fights. *The Penny Press* recognized that Minneapolis, no longer just an outpost for displaced New Englanders, had grown increasingly diverse. The city should be clean, safe, and convenient, the paper argued; good municipal governance was just good management, and political party had become irrelevant. The paper took strong but non-partisan stands on controversial urban issues, exposing the "dangerous and monopolistic practices" of Tom Lowry's street railway company or the "self-serving calumnies" of the Minneapolis police chief. A full-page exposé on vice in the city—**Places of Sin**—prompted a grand jury investigation. *The Penny Press* effectively explored the problems of a rapidly growing city and brought them to the community's attention.[50]

As Alden Blethen drew conclusions based on his own experience, the political and economic analyses of *The Penny Press* also became more confident. On the editorial page, Blethen increasingly explored populist economic arguments and became a strong advocate of the free coinage of silver as the best solution for the country's continuing financial woes. When it came time to make endorsements for the November election, *The Penny Press'* slate included a mixture of Republicans, Democrats, and Populists "because it is the right of an 'independent paper' to select the best men from all parties." Despite Blethen's formerly close ties to Republican governor Knute Nelson, *The Penny Press* in 1894 endorsed his populist opponent.[51]

In the eyes of the established dailies, *The Penny Press* was an insignificant upstart and its editor a journalistic renegade. The Minneapolis papers initially ignored *The Penny Press*, refusing to mention it by name in their columns. When a leading merchant included brief excerpts from a *Penny Press* review in his advertisement for a popular book, no other Minneapolis papers would run the ad. *The Tribune* always referred to it as the "Puny Press," but as its circulation figures and editorial voice grew stronger, all the dailies were goaded into action in the battle for readership. They started new circulation promotions, offering the latest popular literature, Bibles, histories, works of art—even dress patterns—to gain new subscribers. *The Penny Press* eventually forced *The Minneapolis Times*, followed by *The Tribune* and *The St. Paul Globe* to lower their single copy prices to one cent.[52]

Penny Press competitors and Alden Blethen's enemies directed personal attacks against the outlaw editor. Blethen's most

Alden Blethen tried a variety of promotional schemes to build readership. Crowds like this one gathered on Newspaper Row to see election returns as they were posted in the windows of Minneapolis dailies. Blethen went one better by projecting them on the side of a building the evening of the election.

(Minneapolis Public Library)

PERSONAL JOURNALISM IN MINNEAPOLIS.

"Compliment's' of Col. Haskell to Col. Blethen.—From the Times of Oct, 16.

Blethen had personal feuds with many in Minneapolis, but possibly the most bitter was with his former Tribune *partner Will Haskell, who had become the editor of* The Minneapolis Times. *In this editorial cartoon published on the front page of* The Times, *Haskell lampooned Blethen for all of his failed business ventures.*

(*The Minneapolis Times, October 16, 1894 as reprinted in The Penny Press, October 20, 1894*)

vicious opponent was his former *Minneapolis Tribune* partner, Will Haskell, now editor of *The Minneapolis Times.* The two had been on bad terms since the infamous Grover Cleveland editorial. Nearly ten years later, Blethen had Haskell's paper on the run. Haskell published almost daily attacks lampooning Blethen in *The Times'* editorial columns. One edition included a particularly insulting cartoon of Blethen, with trademark sidewhiskers

and waistcoat, flying tattered kites labeled as *The Tribune*, the bank, and the mayoralty bid. Responding to the insult, Blethen reprinted *The Times'* cartoon on the front page of *The Penny Press* along with a companion one showing Haskell with his own array of kites, representing heavy debts, intemperate drinking, and irresponsible editorializing. In an editorial Blethen excused this lapse into "personal journalism:" "When one journalist makes a personal attack through the columns of his paper against another, the public [will] justify the reply, even though it may be along the same lines of the attack."[53]

With the other papers newly alert and on the offensive, *The Penny Press* tried new strategies. During the 1894 elections, Blethen stretched a huge piece of canvas across a nearby bank building and hired a projectionist to screen election results as they came in over the telegraph. Later in the month he announced that *The Penny Press* would introduce a Sunday edition, *The Sunday Review*, at no extra charge to subscribers. He explained that the new publication was a "matter of self protection" to preserve his circulation and advertising gains, but he would not call it *The Sunday Penny Press* until "opportunity and facility would permit the enlargement of *The Penny Press* to such a standard as would satisfy its patrons."[54]

Alden Blethen had always taken pride in the appearance of his newspapers, and the rag-tag facilities of *The Penny Press* bothered him. Since his earliest newspaper days in Kansas City, he had believed that a good newspaper required state-of-the-art equipment. *The Penny Press* was a modest success, but Blethen—hungry for a thunderous one—had grown impatient with the newspaper's makeshift facilities. Despite the precarious financial position of *The Penny Press* and his previous pro-labor stance, he finally ordered the latest linotype machines and a "Three Deck Walter Scott Perfecting Press," capable of producing twenty-four page papers at an extremely rapid rate. The new equipment was in place for the eighteen-month anniversary of *The Penny Press*, which marked the occasion with a special edition that included a full-page description of the new machine and a history of the paper, illustrated with drawings of the plant and the paper's top brass.[55]

Reading about *The Penny Press* in mid-1895, one would have thought that Alden Blethen was on top of the world, back on the road to wealth and influence. The reality was more sobering. The extravagant improvements had cost Blethen over $30,000—money he didn't have. Less than a month after the changes, Blethen announced the formation of a new corporation, *The Penny Press* Publishing Company. Several "gentlemen of wealth" had agreed to invest $50,000 in new working capital, he wrote, which would place *The Penny Press* on sound financial footing. In another piece of good news for the paper, the city awarded its publishing contract to *The Penny Press*, and the paper "crowed" on its editorial page that its bid had saved city taxpayers at least $7,000 over the previous year.[56]

For a time, *The Penny Press* could continue to boast that "everything seems to be coming our way." Figures released by a Boston advertising firm confirmed that the paper's circulation had surpassed the city's leading evening publication, *The Minneapolis Journal*. More than 41,000 readers bought *The Penny Press* daily, while *The Journal's* sales lagged behind at 38,000. Blethen was beside himself; this was his kind of success, and he gleefully rubbed it in: "Now please put that in your pipe and smoke it, Mr. Editor of *The Journal*."[57]

Compliments of Col. Blethen to Col. Haskell.

The Journal and the other Minneapolis papers began to take *The Penny Press'* threat much more seriously. The major dailies had hoped that reducing their street price to a penny would quickly drive Blethen out of business. Instead, many of their readers switched to *The Penny Press*. Another circulation war erupted. Blethen complained bitterly about the cutthroat tactics of his competitors, calling them "circulation liars" and "fakirs." He became incensed when they sent salesmen around the city claiming *The Penny Press* was too risky a venture to trust with advertising. His rivals also argued that Blethen's readers were working class men—millworkers and railroad laborers—who had little money to spend in city shops. Angry, he offered to wager the price of a month's

Blethen responded in kind to Haskell's public attacks, publishing The Times *cartoon as well as one of his own which satirized all of Haskell's faults. He apologized to readers for this brief foray into personal journalism, but both men continued to lambaste each other in print.*

(The Penny Press, October 20, 1894)

The Penny Press *offered extensive coverage of local theater news, including a comedy playing at the Bijou called "A Gay Old Boy."*

(The Penny Press, February 8, 1896)

display ad to any advertisers who did not get as large a return from *The Penny Press* as they did from any other Minneapolis paper. The controversy got so hot that all of the city's newspapers finally agreed to contribute $250 apiece and hire an outside auditor to examine circulation claims.[58]

The Penny Press had first suggested the idea of a circulation examiner, but when the deadline came for presenting deposits, Colonel Alden Blethen did not appear. He did not have the money. In December of 1895, just over two years after its founding, *The Penny Press* went into receivership—the "gentlemen of wealth" had failed to come through, Blethen said. The paper claimed $25,000 in liabilities, but *The Minneapolis Times* and other rivals speculated that the sum was much higher. *The Penny Press* "scooped" its competitors by putting news of its own default on the front page, and in an editorial

blamed the paper's financial straits on the country's continuing depression. More likely, *The Penny Press* had fallen victim to Alden Blethen's impatience, rash judgment, and wishful thinking.[59]

Shortly before *The Penny Press* went into bankruptcy, Blethen had initiated a bitter lawsuit against his secret backer in the repurchase of *The Tribune*, Thomas Lowry. Blethen claimed that when he turned over his interest in *The Tribune* to Lowry in 1891, the streetcar magnate had verbally promised to guarantee him the return of his original investment when the newspaper was sold. Lowry had then reneged on his promise. Blethen had waited four years, but now in the spring of 1895 he filed suit to recoup $100,000 of his losses at *The Tribune*. On the verge of bankruptcy, the beleaguered editor grasped for any straw he could find.[60]

The case went to trial in February 1896 and became the single biggest news story in the city for several weeks. Virtually all the daily papers reprinted verbatim accounts of trial testimony, adding their own strongly partisan commentary and occasional cartoons of the principal players in the drama. Day by day the newspapers conducted the Minneapolis reading public through the intricacies of the Blethen and Lowry financial dealings. Blethen proved disarmingly frank in his descriptions of their verbal arrangement: Lowry had agreed to become a silent partner in the 1889 repurchase of *The Tribune;* in return, Blethen had provided friendly coverage of Lowry's many business enterprises. These revelations kept the town buzzing.[61]

The outcome of the lengthy trial added to Blethen's string of disappointments. After only two hours of deliberation, the jury found in favor of Thomas Lowry, relieving him of any legal responsibility to repay Blethen for losses at *The Tribune*. Recouping this money was Blethen's last best hope of extricating himself from the financial sinkhole that had been swallowing him since 1893. In his editorial comment on the jury's decision, he lashed out at the lack of justice with his own remarkable logic: "Never before in the annals of civil jurisprudence... has a plaintiff with an apparently 'just, equitable and moral cause,' if not an exactly legal one, been subjected to such personal abuse."[62]

Alden Blethen's career in Minneapolis ended with the verdict in the Thomas Lowry lawsuit. He struggled to maintain *The Penny Press* for a few more months, buying the rights to the paper when they were auctioned in the bankruptcy proceedings. His rivals at the other Minneapolis papers loudly questioned the ethics of his purchase of the bankrupt *Penny Press*, instigated a grand jury hearing on his role in the Bank of New England debacle, and filed a legal challenge to the award of the 1896 city printing contract to *The Penny Press*. Blethen, in turn, damned the editors of *The Times, Journal,* and *Tribune* for their "diabolical scheme to destroy the property of *The Penny Press* and the character of its Editor and founder in the community."[63]

Alden Blethen officially retired from *The Penny Press* on April 11, 1896, turning over his assets to a new entity, *The Penny Press* Cooperative Printing Company. The bold and independent little paper survived as an employee cooperative through the election of 1896, then quietly closed its doors, without any of the ballyhoo that Colonel Blethen had created for its debut. *The Penny Press* was a creditable experiment in creating a newspaper for an urban mass market. Blethen brought to his small Midwestern daily a spicy and innovative style that strongly suggested the controversial journalism practiced by his contemporaries, William Randolph Hearst

As The Penny Press *struggled and Blethen's suit against Thomas Lowry went to trial, rival editors stepped up their personal attacks. Blethen was frequently accused of drunkenness, as in this parody of the advertisement for "A Gay Old Boy."*
(Minneapolis Times, February, 1896)

and Joseph Pulitzer. Like many other small businessmen, he tried to expand too fast, becoming the victim of debt and legal entanglements in the wake of the economic downturn of 1893. Blethen's silence reflected his assessment of *The Penny Press* experience—he never mentioned the paper in public again.[64]

In the spring of 1896, Alden Blethen was truly broke. As soon as the school term ended, Blethen borrowed the money to send his wife Rose, son Clarance and daughters Florence and Marion to Seattle where they moved in with relatives. Alden Blethen and his son Joe stayed behind to clear up the wreckage and salvage whatever they could. Most of the family possessions—the fine furniture, the jewelry and furs, the elegant carriage—were put up for auction. While Joseph remained in Minneapolis, Alden Blethen left to search for new opportunities.[65]

One can only guess at his state of mind. He squandered so many chances in Minneapolis; he had so many good ideas and he worked so hard. He held success time and again, only to see it slip from his grasp. His enemies numbered some of the most well-respected and powerful men in Minneapolis—Will Haskell, Tom Lowry, William Henry Eustis—and he relied on his friends once too often. They didn't return his phone calls; he couldn't get appointments. But he refused to give up, nor was he content to live an ordinary life. In 1896, with no money, no prospects, and a history of failures, he puffed great schemes, trying to ensnare old associates to invest in him once again. He cast about the country for one more great opportunity.

Why did Blethen choose Denver as his next destination? It could have been anywhere. He probably searched for a place that resembled Kansas City or Minneapolis in their boomtown years—a small city ripe with potential, possessing good transportation facilities, rich resources, and an energetic frontier spirit. Denver was such a town, and Blethen managed to talk his way into a purchase contract with the majority owner of *The Denver Times*. He would buy a minority interest and take over the duties of editor and general manager of the paper, with an option to purchase more capital stock within a year. The contract set June 8, 1896, as the date for first payment to be made.[66]

But this time, Alden Blethen's financing agility failed him. He couldn't raise the needed $5,000 in time. Complicated land swaps, mortgages, notes—nothing worked. The June 8 deadline passed and was extended; negotiations verged on completion numerous times, only to fail. Weeks went by in this pattern until June 25 when Blethen, cooling his heels in Denver, received word that the owner of *The Denver Times* had accepted another offer.[67]

Alden Blethen may have had one more chance to acquire a newspaper in Denver. Two colorful and rather shady characters, Frederick Bonfils and Harry Tammen, owned *The Denver Post*, a rival paper to *The Times*. According to a story later told by Clarance Blethen, they welcomed his father to Denver with open arms, trying to entice him into a poker game, with *The Denver Post* and his remaining cash reserves as the stakes. "Fortunately for Alden," claimed Clarance, "he had never touched a card in his life." He refused to take this one last gamble and headed out of Denver on a train to join his family in Seattle.[68]

During the previous twelve years Alden Blethen had gained and lost public trust, private regard, and a brilliant newspaper career. He had willingly, perhaps eagerly, become a magnet for professional jealousy and popular controversy in Minneapolis.

Alden Blethen was nearing fifty and nearly broke when he left Minneapolis in 1896 looking for new opportunities, first in Denver and then Seattle.

(Courtesy of Gilbert Duffy)

A bulldog of a man, he possessed driving energy and worked harder and longer than any of his employees. Blethen learned the newspaper business in an age of increasing press professionalism and sophistication, but he did not make his mark as a prudent manager or brilliant journalist. Rather, his erratic and controversial newspaper career in Minneapolis reveals an ambitious man of modest talents whose character led him to resemble the great editors of late nineteenth century popular journalism—Hearst and Pulitzer.

As a former reporter who knew him in Minneapolis—one of many who "hated him fondly"—reflected years later:

> [Blethen] couldn't write, he couldn't spell, he was more ignorant of grammar than Macauley's celebrated sixth-form boy, he never had any original ideas, he was coarse and intemperate and harsh and hasty and unreliable—but he was [a] great [newspaperman.][69]

In Seattle he would have one more chance to prove it.

Facing north from Beacon Hill, Seattle looked this way when Alden Blethen arrived in 1896. The tide flats gave way to a mixed neighborhood of homes and factories, and the metropolitan corridor moved north toward the new affluence of Queen Anne Hill.

(The Seattle Times)

4 THE BATTLE OF LIFE

*I*n the summer of 1896, Rose Ann Blethen and the three younger children were staying with her brother-in-law, Otis Moore, at his Seattle home. They had nowhere else to go. To get by, the Blethen family spent their last $3,000, netted from loans and the auction sale of their furniture in Minneapolis. As C.B. Blethen bitterly remembered, living on family charity was a "precarious existence": they owned the clothes on their backs and had no prospects. In early July, Rose received word that a warehouse fire destroyed their few stored household goods and books. It must have seemed the final, crushing disappointment in their rags-to-riches-to-rags story.[1]

When the Blethen family came to stay with relatives, Seattle was rough, raw, and busted, a frontier seaport on the long downside of a boom-and-bust economy, shipping timber products, coal, grain, and fish. With little local capital, the city was the plaything of distant investors. During the nationwide panic of 1893, Seattle banks foreclosed on mortgages and investors withdrew their funds from proposed industrial schemes, real estate development, and retail and commercial ventures. Businesses let workers go and cut wages as much as 30 percent. The city of Seattle couldn't meet its own payrolls. Those who could leave, did, and the city lost half its population.[2]

Even so, optimistic boosters of the mid-1890s touted Seattle's meager industrial base,

pointing to soap and candy factories, breweries, and a furrier. The great fire of 1889 had been fortunate, they argued, clearing the way to replace the hodgepodge disorder of the old city, releasing the triumphant "Seattle Spirit." And new buildings of brick and stone did rise downtown, served by street railways and cable cars. Then, too, in 1893, Seattle gained its first direct transcontinental connection—Jim Hill's Great Northern Railway—and could finally compete head-to-head with rival Tacoma. However, Seattle's boomlet of immigration and construction soon slowed, and a lingering recession took its place.[3]

Seattle hoped to become the commercial hub for a great hinterland, from the

Here, saltwater canoes are drawn up on Seattle's waterfront. In the 1890s, Indian people often visited the city, traveling from their homes up Puget Sound, in the islands, and on the peninsula.

(Special Collections, University of Washington Libraries, LaRoche Collection, No. 43)

grainfields and rangeland of eastern Washington through the woods, mines, and fishing grounds of the west. Viewed from a Beacon Hill pasture, the 1896 city sprawled along the shore of Elliott Bay, bounded by the tide flats on the southwest and by precipitous hills to the north and east. Metropolitan Seattle was no more than a few blocks of dense urban construction between First and Third Avenues, on either side of Yesler Way, also known locally as the Deadline. Although suburban corridors ran out along the streetcar lines, "downtown Seattle" was still a walking city in which factories, offices, shops, and residences of every class were within an easy stroll of one another. As new Seattle grew steadily northward up the hilly avenues, old Seattle—the heart of the pioneer city—lay below Yesler, the city's moral boundary.[4]

South of the Deadline clustered the cheap boardinghouses, saloons, gambling dens, and brothels of the city. Seattle was known as the Northwest's Barbary Coast, and vice—gambling, sex, and booze—provided the city's most reliable source of income. The Tenderloin, as this area of the city was known, offered a seasonal home, companionship, and recreation to the men who worked throughout the Northwest orchards and farms, in the clay pits and mines, in the woods, in the mills, on the fishing boats, and on the docks. In 1896, Seattle's red light district was the most distinctive section of the city and its most profitable, just as it had been in Kansas City.[5]

In 1896, the city where the Blethen family found safe haven was as young, crude, and ambitious as Kansas City had been in 1880 or Minneapolis in 1884. Puget Sound echoed with reminders of Missouri and Minnesota: boom and bust, vulgarity and respectability, twin city rivalry, Western risks and Western opportunities. The previous summer,

Blethen's sons, Joseph and C.B., had attended the meetings of Washington's press association in Seattle. Visiting their uncle, Otis Moore, who had long ago edited Maine's *Phillips Phonograph* and now served as the association's secretary, the Blethen boys—then twenty-four and sixteen—were listed in the conference bulletin as representatives of *The Penny Press.* Joe Blethen later spoke of the romantic attraction that the Great Northern's distant Puget Sound terminus had for his group of college friends in Minneapolis. Writing back to *The Penny Press,* he had enthusiastically praised Washington's lakes and forests, the mountains and the coast. It seemed to him "a paradise"; it became the setting for his father's greatest battles.[6]

In July 1896, Alden Blethen frantically juggled the Denver deals, firing off telegrams and letters to wary friends, promising them the investment opportunity of a lifetime, pressing them to get in on the ground floor of a sure thing. Sick at heart, Joe Blethen tidied the shambles in Minneapolis. Restless and worried, C.B. Blethen sat idly in his uncle's Seattle home and thumbed through *The Seattle Daily Times,* counting up inches of advertising, critically eyeing the layout and typography. The current publisher and editor, C.A. Davies and T.A. Hughes, had only owned the paper for fifteen months. They bought it for a song from a feckless investor who combined the old *Press*—with its valuable option on an Associated Press franchise—with the old *Times.* Indeed, the lineage of *The Seattle Times* could be traced back to the 1881 *Chronicle* through a complex "game of battledore and shuttlecock" among failed newspaper entrepreneurs.[7]

In 1896, Davies and Hughes published a modest four-page evening newspaper, quietly Republican. They considerably inflated their weekday circulation to six thousand;

four thousand was more like it. Encumbered by a mortgage against the circulation lists, machinery, goodwill, and the wire franchise, the owners stayed solvent only by operating a printing shop in conjunction with their newspaper. *The Times* was a pale evening imitation of the big morning Republican daily, *The Seattle Post-Intelligencer*, whose circulation nearly equaled all the other state papers combined. C.B. considered *The Times* a dreadful newspaper and he wrote to Denver and told his father so; he didn't know that *The Times'* owners were fed up and ready to sell.[8]

In his biography of Alden Blethen, C.B. recounted a story his father once told to a gathering of *Seattle Times* employees. Alone in his Denver hotel room, Alden Blethen had considered suicide. He hadn't raised the money to buy into any Denver paper, and the game was up. His life insurance policies would benefit his family more than he could. Worth more dead than alive, Blethen went for a walk through the streets of Denver, mulling this decision, and returned to the hotel determined to take his own life. As he claimed his key, the desk clerk handed him a letter from his younger son deriding the "flabby morning *Post-Intelligencer* and the decrepit little ...(Seattle) Times." He said he hopped the next train to San Francisco, jumped on a steamer to Seattle, and the rest was history.[9]

Reminiscence sometimes provides unreliable evidence; little of Blethen's correspondence has survived from this period and none of it reveals his state of mind. We cannot know whether he intended to commit suicide. However, he did suddenly leave Denver for San Francisco, and headed straight north for Seattle to glad-hand the local editors and offer confident interviews to reporters. Both *The P-I* and *The Times* reported the arrival of this "well-known newspaper proprietor" from Minneapolis. Blethen disguised his desperate financial situation and spent his dwindling resources on cigars, lunches, and drinks for new-found friends. "A solid Free Silverite," he expansively discussed his political views, predicting an exciting presidential contest between Populist William Jennings Bryan and

The front page of The Seattle Times *on Monday, August 10, 1896, the evening that Alden Blethen first edited the newspaper.*

(The Seattle Times)

When Alden Blethen first purchased a share in The Times, *the newspaper's offices were on Yesler Way. In this illustration, the building is marked as the home of* The Evening Times, *a title that Blethen's predecessors had changed to* The Seattle Daily Times.

(The Seattle Times)

Republican William McKinley. Blethen declared that goldbug McKinley would face a fierce uphill battle in Colorado, casually mentioning to reporters that he "was negotiating for the purchase of the *Denver Times.*" He successfully flimflammed everyone, setting out the "Denver deal" as a ploy in his scheme to join with local capitalist and aspiring kingmaker Charles Fishback to acquire *The Seattle Daily Times* from its present owners.[10]

Blethen was all bluff; the Denver deals were dead. Seattle offered the last chance at wealth, influence, and respectability for this failed man of fifty.

Seattle provided a wide open field for an evening daily, especially for a lively and inexpensive paper—like *The Penny Press*—that gave working men and women the opportunity to read the news of the world on the day it happened, at home after work. Alden Blethen's daughter Florence remembered her father's excitement about the possibilities of the Associated Press franchise, which he believed Davies and Hughes underestimated. Certainly *The Times* was available at a bargain basement price—reportedly only $30,000—and much of the contract luckily hinged on promises rather than cash money. The discussions advanced rapidly and Blethen fired off a telegram to his son Joe in Minneapolis stating, "Purchased *Times*/start by Friday/get money Dave/will remit." Living in one brother-in-law's Seattle home, Blethen asked another brother-in-law, David Hunter, to mortgage his Minnesota home and wire the money to Seattle.[11]

It isn't clear how Charles Fishback—attorney, mining entrepreneur, self-styled "colonel"—met Alden Blethen. Their paths may have crossed in Colorado, where Fishback had mining interests, or in Free Silver circles, or they may have encountered one another

for the first time in Seattle. Together they took over *The Seattle Times* on August 10, 1896, when Fishback announced in the editorial columns that *The Times* would change its political course and advocate "bimetallism and the immediate return of the government to the free coinage of silver." Colonel Fishback's political convictions were less than disinterested, as he used his newspaper both to announce his silver mining discoveries and to push the political program that would make the ore far more valuable. Of the two men, Fishback owned the lion's share of *The Times*, but he was no newspaperman and left Alden Blethen in complete charge of editorial policies, business decisions, and news coverage. The "two colonels" took over *The Times* in the restless political year of 1896, when the Fusion Party of Populists, Democrats, and Silver Republicans ran a full slate in Washington. Nationally, William Jennings Bryan mounted his quixotic presidential campaign to end the economy's torture on "this cross of gold," to soften the gold standard's hard money by expanding silver coinage.[12]

Since his Greenback days in Maine, Alden Blethen had flirted with one eccentric monetary scheme after another, each designed to increase the money supply with soft paper or silver currency. At times an eager machine politician, at others a zealous progressive reformer, Blethen was a political chameleon who identified himself at different times in his life with both the Democratic and Republican parties, with Greenbackers, with rural Populists and urban Progressives, and with various Fusion alliances. In Seattle, in 1896, out of conviction or necessity, newcomer Alden Blethen became one of the most outspoken advocates for the free coinage of silver, both in *The Times* and on the speaker's platform. Then and later, Blethen went through extraordinary contortions to claim political consistency, seeking to reconcile his loyalties to Republicans James Blaine and Thomas Reed with his role as Fusion champion of soft money for the common people. The Republican Party, he wrote, had strayed from its principles. In the heat of the 1896 campaign, *The Times'* rhetoric grew quite radical, and fanned class-driven mistrust between poor and rich, workingmen and capitalists, Free Silverites and Goldbugs.[13]

Overnight, *The Times* became Seattle's populist voice, brandishing the platform and ticket of the People's Party on its masthead, speaking out on behalf of laboring men against "the silk-stockinged gentlemen" glutted with wealth. Blethen's *Times* eagerly took on the role of David against *The P-I's* Goliath, of ragged upstart against the well-heeled "organ" of the state's entrenched Republican ring. The "Ring," bloated and unscrupulous, would stop at nothing, *The Times* maintained. Claiming unspecified threats by unnamed enemies, Blethen valiantly declared that *The Times* would not be cowed.[14]

The Times—newly named *The Seattle Evening Times*—moved in the fall of 1896 from a "hole in the wall" on Yesler Way into space in the Boston Block on Second Avenue between Cherry and Columbia. Announcing "new and commodious quarters," *The Times* installed the press below street level, and crowded business, composing, news, and editorial offices on the ground floor and onto a hanging balcony halfway up one wall. Promising a "fully-equipped metropolitan newspaper," *The Seattle Evening Times* ordered two new linotype machines from New York, and lowered the street price to three cents "to place the newspaper more largely in the hands of the common people."[15]

Blethen was determined "to make *The Times* the most popular publication in the

state of Washington" by producing a bigger, better, and cheaper paper that would attract more readers and in turn more advertisers. *The Times* announced its lower price in an editorial that described the magnificent success of three-cent and penny papers in the 1890s, including Joseph Pulitzer's *New York World*, Victor Lawson's *Chicago News*, and Blethen's own *Penny Press* as examples. However, William Randolph Hearst really claimed Alden Blethen's admiration. Between 1895

Alden Blethen had known and admired James J. Hill in Minneapolis. Hill's Great Northern Railway crossed the continent to the docks of Seattle, forwarding freight for the ports of Asia. The Times provided support for Hill's many ventures, including the Nippon Yusen Kaisha (Japanese Steamship Line) in which the railroad magnate had invested. A Times furniture ad hails the August 1896 arrival of the Miike Maru, the first steamship to maintain a regular schedule between Japan and Seattle.

(The Seattle Times, August 31, 1896)

Shortly after Alden Blethen joined The Times, *the newspaper moved from its Yesler Way office to this storefront in the Boston Block, at Second Avenue and Columbia. Passersby are reading news bulletins posted in the windows. Other dispatches are visible above. As the paper prospered, it doubled and then tripled its rented space in this building.*

(The Seattle Times)

and 1896, Hearst, in a war with Pulitzer, built the circulation of *The New York Journal* from 77,000 to 417,000 readers and cut its price. The new mass market newspapers claimed to speak for the people; they were brightly written and beautifully produced on the most up-to-date equipment. But in clumsy or grasping hands, the new journalism easily became yellow journalism, fraudulent and sensationalistic, selling violence, sex, and scandal, and preoccupied with nothing but circulation.[16]

As in Minneapolis, Blethen began to print the newspaper's daily circulation over a "sworn statement," unconvincingly signed by

The Times' mailroom manager—an effort to enlist the public's interest in the steadily climbing numbers. With the promotional motto, "Circulation is Swelling Daily— Watch It Grow!" Blethen mounted a mechanical counter on the folder of *The Times*' press. He invited passersby to inspect the counter—visible through a window of the Boston Block business office—and loudly promised a cash reward to anyone who could discover any fraud. Blethen's editorials— which combined social and political commentary with the newspaper battle he was waging single-handedly—ridiculed *The Post-Intelligencer*'s circulation claims and encouraged advertisers to switch over to *The Times*.[17]

Suddenly, *The Times* no longer seemed a dull, perfunctory echo of the morning paper. Blethen, not content to quietly share the Seattle market and earn a modest living, wanted to win big. He wanted to goad *The P-I* into a fight; he did not want a competitor—he needed an enemy. *The Times* became militant and insulting. The 1896 political campaign provided the substance and drama for this newspaper battle, and political rhetoric became its language. Both Fishback—the "silver-tongued orator of King County"—and Blethen stumped for the Fusion slate at rallies throughout Washington. The political contest offered a metaphor for the newspaper conflict: the plucky *Times* underdog taking on the strapping *P-I* bully.[18]

Blethen was the "speaker of the evening" for a full house at Seattle's Masonic Hall in early October. He argued that "a struggle was on between organized greed, corporate monopoly and the people," and that Fusion would protect the people's interests. Blethen had cultivated his physical likeness to William Jennings Bryan, shaving his muttonchop whiskers and growing out a mane of unruly hair; *The Times* dutifully noted that his "remarkable resemblance to Bryan was much commented on." Later in the month, Blethen shared a Seattle podium with gubernatorial candidate John R. Rogers. As *The Times* reported the event, when Blethen began to speak, "an ovation such as a public speaker seldom receives" washed over him. The audience, the article continued, received his remarks with great enthusiasm, and he often had to pause and allow fresh outbursts of applause to die down. "In a masterful manner," he denounced the goldbug press'— meaning *The P-I's*—tactics of "intimidation, coercion, fraud, and suppression" against the free silver cause.[19]

During the election campaign, both papers practiced shamelessly partisan news reporting. *The Times* consigned coverage of Seattle's huge Republican demonstration to the back page, and reported that **THE GOLDBUG PARADE** was a farcical disaster of unenthusiastic men "hired to march." As Blethen's *Times* reported:

> At the head of [last night's] great "demonstration" were...the corporations public and private, more especially the railroads, which employ men and think they own them body and soul.... The coldness of last night shows that the self-respecting masses of the people are in favor of law, order and decency and will vote for Rogers, the "friend of the workingman."
>
> The plain people were there, in the halls, on the streets, everywhere, ready and willing to hear honest argument and fair discussion of the burning issue, the money question.
>
> They heard everything else. They heard that they were patriots, that they were the bone and sinew of this nation, that they were old soldiers who had saved the Union.... Not a word of living interest to the great toiling masses, not a breath of freedom from the shackles of trust and corporations. All palaver, all evasion, all—talk.[20]

Four days later, *The Times* proclaimed a Populist rally the **GRANDEST DEMONSTRATION OF THE YEAR!** with a ten-deck headline on page one.[21] *The Times'* reporter counted more than six thousand "hard-handed, heavy-hearted" workingmen in a "spontaneous" demonstration for Fusion candidates Bryan and Rogers, and continued:

> This parade...sprang from the hearts of the people. No one man—no set of men— could have organized it. Those who were in it looked at each other in amazement. Where did so many people come from? Nobody could tell. They seemed to have sprung from the earth.

In 1896, when Alden Blethen purchased a share in The Seattle Times, *he was in desperate financial circumstances. This page from the stock ledger of* The Times *shows the initial investments of Charles Fishback, Alden Blethen, and his friend Frank Hunter.*

(The Seattle Times)

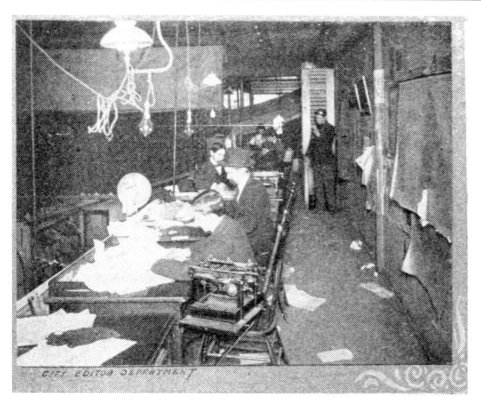

The city editor and reporters worked in the "newsroom" of The Times' *Boston Block office, situated on a balcony suspended halfway between floors. This photograph has been reproduced from a screened image in* Seattle and the Orient, *published in 1900, and is the earliest known photograph of the workplace at a Blethen newspaper.*

(The Seattle Times)

And the goldbugs should have heard them cheer!...They knew that solid phalanx, stretching over thirty-two solid blocks, meant the downfall of corporation and ring influence in King County....

And these crowds meant something. They knew how they were going to vote and they said so. They cheered and yelled for the whole ticket from top to bottom. *The Evening Times* takes off its hat to the citizens who joined in the ovation whenever its name was mentioned in so complimentary a manner.[22]

Despite its own dubious journalism, *The Times* regularly dubbed *The P-I* the "captive organ" of the Republican ring, spreading exaggerations and falsehoods as news. *The Times* claimed that the morning paper filled its accounts of local political rallies with "gross misstatements of enthusiasm, number

of people in attendance, etc.," and took *The P-I* to task for low journalistic standards, for not being a real *newspaper*. In an editorial, Alden Blethen argued that a good newspaperman had a responsibility to print "all the news and not be partial with reference to treatment of actual news." He admitted that, in a political campaign, this policy might "be disagreeable to [the publisher's] tastes," but loftily insisted that "it is never right to suppress the news." Incited by *The Times*, a mob of Populists gathered outside *P-I* editor James Hoge's office one evening, yelling that they wanted to hang him from "a sour apple tree"—and not in effigy, either. In the heat of the campaign, *The P-I* responded with "The Truthful *Times*," its own outraged recital of exaggerations and falsehoods. But that was virtually the only direct reply to Blethen's repeated sallies. While *The P-I* often sneered at the "Populist evening paper," it seldom dignified *The Times* by naming it.[23]

The P-I ignored *The Times* gadfly, its carpet-bagging editor, and its ragtag readership. The big morning paper continued to patronize Bryan, Rogers, and the other "Popocrat" candidates as uneducated bumpkins. But, in the heat of the 1896 campaign, *The Times'* circulation soared and Alden Blethen trumpeted his rising numbers day by day on the editorial page. If the figures are reliable, *The Times* nearly doubled its sales in three months. Blethen threw himself at this opportunity. He was everywhere in and around *The Times*—making Fusion speeches, writing editorials, covering political events, thinking up stunts and contests, soliciting advertising, organizing parades, making news, and becoming the personality of *The Times*. During the dramatic political campaign his frenzied efforts paid off.[24]

In November 1896, John Rogers won the governorship and William Jennings Bryan lost the presidency. After the election, *The Times'* readership fell sharply. Seattle remained what it had been, an opportunistic frontier town waiting for the opportunities to arrive. Alden Blethen and his wife and children were crowded into a rented house with old friend Wilson Hammons, his wife and their two children, as well as Otis Moore and his own family. C.B. Blethen always remembered this "Christmas of grim necessity," and his boyish disappointment at finding boots and mittens instead of toys under the tree, and hard candy in his stocking. His only real treat that year was a second-hand sled.[25]

In his New Year's editorial, Blethen referred gloomily to 1896 as "a miserable failure" for United States business in general, continuing the hard times that began in 1893. During the quiet winter months of 1897, *Times* circulation and advertising declined; Blethen later admitted that *The Times* lost more than $500 each month. The newspaper couldn't meet its payrolls, and family members and friends worked for free. Fishback's promissory notes to Hughes and Davies fell due and he was unable to pay, nor could Blethen afford to buy out his partner and their creditors. The cycle of indebtedness threatened to pull down this version of *The Times* as it had pulled down its predecessors—too many newspapers, too few readers, not enough money.[26]

Nevertheless, in December 1896, Alden Blethen secretly bought up all available shares of *The Times* from Davies and Fishback.[27]

The P-I had maintained a dignified silence against *The Times'* gibes because its editors expected the evening paper's imminent collapse and Alden Blethen's hasty departure. It had happened before—Blethen's *Times*, a contemporary wrote, was just the most recent product of the "wrecks...along the journalistic highway" in Seattle. But the city's Republican weekly, *The Argus*, eagerly took on the new *Times* and noisily investigated its financial mysteries. Harry Chadwick, editor of *The Argus*, had a reputation for his "blistering satire" and his prose "that had the sharp reality of a skinning knife." Chadwick attacked *The Times*, and that meant attacking the man who so readily personified the newspaper.[28]

Rumors flew around Seattle about Blethen's stake in *The Times*. Everybody knew that Fishback was broke, his "big mining deals" just hot air. Had the Minneapolis adventurer gained control of the paper? How? *The Argus* thought it had the answers. In 1896, years before direct election of senators to the United States Congress, the majority party caucus simply presented its candidates to the state legislature for approval. That senatorial nod was the ultimate slap-on-the-back of clubby, good-old-boys politics conducted behind closed doors in smoke-filled rooms. *The Argus* charged that U.S. Senator Watson Squire, who had bolted the Republican Party for Fusion in 1896, bought *The Seattle Times* outright in January 1897 and owned editor Blethen "body, soul, and breeches." Squire wanted to influence the selection of the second Washington senator and to advance his own political career by controlling a newspaper.[29]

The Argus also charged that James J. Hill, president of the Great Northern Railway, had provided money to keep Blethen in control of *The Times*, and that the two were so tight that when Hill sneezed in Minneapolis, Blethen wiped his nose in Seattle. *The Argus* gleefully reported, then, that Squire and Hill had secured the support of *The Seattle Times* by giving its editor enough money to pay his debts, buy out Fishback, and gain sole ownership of the newspaper. They owned *The Times*, *The Argus* claimed, and it became their mouthpiece.[30]

Two Men "A Head of The Times."

In February 1897, Alden Blethen bought out his partners in The Seattle Times *and became the newspaper's publisher and editor-in-chief. Here, a triumphant engraving on the editorial page of February 20, 1897, shows Alden Blethen and his son Joe as the two men "A Head of The Times."*

(The Seattle Times)

Alden Blethen did have a long-standing friendship with James Hill, dating from their Minneapolis days. As C.B. Blethen later wrote, Hill credited Blethen with helping to "break up a Minneapolis real estate syndicate which had endeavored to hold Jim Hill up when he found it necessary to establish a real railroad terminal...." Hill told Blethen that he had saved him nearly a million dollars and "that if ever in this life he needed help, to let him know."[31]

From the day Blethen began to edit *The Seattle Times*, the paper pushed Hill as "the greatest railroad man of the age," knocking his Northern Pacific competitor, promoting his steamship venture, backing his plans for a Seattle depot and docks, and encouraging preferential treatment from the city. Blethen even tied Hill into the early down-to-earth Populism of the paper and portrayed the multimillionaire as a regular guy, writing that

he "is a good talker and there is much meat in all that he says." In interviews, Hill told Blethen he believed the newly opened Japanese markets would take "all the wheat Washington can raise" and that Washington timber, sold in Asian markets, would offer more wealth than any gold strike. Blethen made it sound like plain common sense to support Hill's business plans. However, in 1897, *The Argus* publicly charged that "the Great Northern owns...*The Seattle Times.*" In 1919, with the benefit of hindsight, Upton Sinclair's *The Brass Check* also judged the turn-of-the-century *Seattle Times* a paid railroad mouthpiece.[32]

In the 1890s, the standards of responsible journalism were more widely acknowledged than practiced. During the 1896 campaign, Alden Blethen articulated clearly the responsibility to publish *all* the news, without bias; he justly skewered *The P-I*'s slanted reporting and attacked the morning paper as a tame organ of moneyed interests. However, few American newspapers of the 1890s had the financial security to practice editorial independence and impartial news reporting. Instead, many newspapers provided favorable coverage in return for cash payments or less tangible benefits. In Minneapolis, Blethen had provided support to friends and patrons, based on both conviction and obligation. This commonplace practice of nineteenth-century journalism was a disreputable necessity, and Blethen sold his newspaper's influence in Seattle as he had done in Minneapolis. In the spring of 1897, Watson Squire and James Hill became heroes in *The Seattle Evening Times*, daily quoted, celebrated, and lionized. As Blethen would later describe the situation in a letter to Squire, he agreed "to provide [you] the entire support of the paper editorially, publish all the special service from Olympia which you desired, and to promote your candidacy locally without charge." As Blethen continued:

> The contract under which I borrowed three thousand dollars of you in the winter of 1897 was a mutual contract and there were therefore mutual obligations. You wanted the support of *The Times* both locally, editorially, and specially from Olympia where the contest for United States Senator was going on.... Moreover to have accepted a right-out cash proposition of even the amount of money which I received from you and have the same liquidated by the kindly work I did for you would have been a direct sale of the editorial influence of the paper, whatever it was—and I have never made such a trade in my life.[33]

In his own mind, Alden Blethen drew a delicate distinction between the outright sale of editorial influence and the contract for "kindly work" he had made with Squire. Blethen, also aware of the developing standards of his profession, was never proud of the arrangements with his patrons. In print, he vehemently denied *The Argus* charges of taking money from either Squire or Hill in that grim winter. He loudly declared that he was indignant and insulted; he called Chadwick a whelp, a blackmailer, a cur. Nevertheless, Blethen clearly sold the influence of *The Times* to Squire for a consideration of $5,000, of which the senatorial candidate actually paid $3,000. He himself acknowledged in a 1911 editorial that he had requested and accepted $23,000 from Hill—and later paid it all back. With this money, Times Company stock passed entirely into the hands of Alden Joseph Blethen, his son Joseph Blethen, and Otis Moore. In return for selling approving publicity to wealthy benefactors, the family owned the newspaper.[34]

In 1897, Alden Blethen's name appeared as editor-in-chief on *The Times*' masthead, and

THE FIRST CONSCRIPT ON "QUALITY HILL."

Let every twenty blocks in the residence portion of the town organize, conscripting one man from each block to serve one night in a week and as many more for the next night and so on—and let them be armed to the teeth, with proper signals, and patrol their blocks with the distinct understanding that the first highwayman that is caught shall be hung to the nearest telephone pole the moment that it shall be determined that he is a highwayman, and pursuing his unlawful profession.—Alden J. Blethen's Seattle Times, March 19, 1898.

In the list of personal notes in the very defunct New England Bank occur the following: A. J. Blethen, $7,999.09; Rose Blethen, $6,542.07; A. J. Blethen, Jr., $1,717.44, and J. L. Blethen, $551.97; a grand total of about $17,000.

The only member of the family that didn't get in on the divy seems to have been the pony.—Minneapolis Journal, April 26, 1897.

A notorious bank robber has been killed in New Mexico. The most dangerous bank robber, however, is the scamp on the inside.—Tacoma Ledger.

engravings of Alden and Joe Blethen appeared side by side on the editorial page, captioned "Two Men A Head of the *Times*." At twenty-seven, the younger man owned 25 percent of the newspaper's capital stock. Joe Blethen had left his literary career behind in Minneapolis and followed his father to Seattle in August 1896 "to take up newspaper work." Alden Blethen wanted and needed his eldest son by his side. *The Times* introduced him as "one of the cleverest young writers in the twin cities," who had worked since 1893 as a drama critic for a Minneapolis

Harry Chadwick of the weekly Argus *was, for a time, a bitter enemy of Alden Blethen. As one in a series of such caricatures, this March 26, 1898,* Argus *cartoon poked fun at a* Times *scheme for vigilante crime fighting and kept alive the old accusations of fraud and mismanagement in the collapse of Blethen's Bank of New England in Minneapolis.*

(University of Washington Libraries)

newspaper—*The Penny Press*—and written dozens of poems and short stories. His greatest success, however, came as a lyricist and playwright, and his fifth play, "The Chinook," was considered especially "bright and witty," and toured on the theatrical circuit. Joseph Blethen had performed on stage in the twin cities as an actor and comedian. In the 1890s, he continued to write, publishing a light opera, two plays, and a series of short stories—sentimental, charming, exotic—and also worked on *The Seattle Times.* Slender, fair, and tall, well-spoken and amusing, he didn't share his father's hot temper and rough edges. Pressed into service as *The Times'* drama critic, reporters remembered him as a "good fellow" who liked to have a drink after work and talk shop.[35]

In May 1897, Alden and Joseph Blethen formed the Times Printing Company and signed a long-term contract for the new Associated Press "day report," a news service designed for the booming evening newspapers of the West Coast. Working from loans and a line of credit, *The Times* suddenly had money to spend and boasted of its new typesetting machines and "model composing room." To meet *The Times'* challenge, *The P-I* lowered its price. But *The Times* declared that the day of the morning paper had passed, never to return. Seattle's three-hour time difference with the East Coast meant that "all the news of the world would be published and laid at [the] door, down to within an hour of delivery." Alden Blethen continued to market *The Times* to wage-working people who only had time for reading at day's end. He wrote, "The morning paper of the future will be the paper of the aristocrat while the evening paper will be the paper of the masses...the one will be limited to the few while the other will be limited only by that multitude who win their daily bread in the sweat of their brow." Nev-

ertheless, in spring 1897, *The Times* continued to lose money each month.[36]

The Argus never forgot that "Jim Hill owns *The Times*," and wouldn't let Alden Blethen leave the Minneapolis crucible behind. Chadwick wrote that the time had passed when "a person could come to Seattle, set up as a saint, and there would be very little inquiry" about his past. *The Argus* reprinted articles from the Minneapolis papers concerning the collapse of the Bank of New England and the messy Thomas Lowry scandal. In *The Argus*, Seattle readers learned about Blethen's "promiscuous and dazzling career" in Minneapolis as publisher, capitalist, politician, and banker. Chadwick taunted Blethen, begging him to make amends for his past and "live down the reputation he brought with him."[37]

The Post-Intelligencer chimed in. When Blethen wrote an editorial critical of Garret Hobart, McKinley's vice president, *The P-I* revived the scandalous Cleveland editorial from *The Tribune.* Blethen believed that Will Haskell was in cahoots with *The P-I's* editor—that "contemptible whelp wholly unfit to occupy any public position"—and with Chadwick—"one of the most contemptible curs in the state of Washington." In fact, *The P-I* contacted Albert Shaw, *The Tribune's* old editorial writer, to gather hot quotes for the Blethen roast while Blethen bewildered his Seattle readers with front-page exposés of Will Haskell's failings, and vicious editorial diatribes against his former partner. Blethen eventually ran AN APOLOGY to *Times* readers for the Haskell vendetta.[38]

But Alden Blethen didn't want to leave Minneapolis behind; he wanted to refight it and master it. In Seattle, he constantly reminded his readers that he had been a newspaper publisher in Minneapolis. He often compared Seattle's urban concerns with parks, public transit, and vice to those of the Twin Cities, even dubbing the common scheme of limiting saloons through expensive licensing fees the "Minneapolis Plan." When *The Argus* provoked Blethen with his past, he eagerly retaliated. Refighting his Minneapolis demons in Seattle, he called *The Argus* a "blackmailing sheet," "filled to the brim with filth and falsehood"; Chadwick was a blackmailer and a liar, henchman for the "exboodlers and criminals of King County," Republicans driven from the public trough by the 1896 Fusion victories. Blethen published a front-page array of testimonials, signed by prominent Minneapolis residents. He blustered and demanded apologies; he pronounced himself outraged; he vowed lawsuits; he threatened violence.[39]

The feud escalated between the two men. Chadwick frequently attacked Blethen's foul language, vicious temper, and heavy drinking, describing "a tough-looking guy" "with dissipation written on every feature," whose presence shamed his "accommodating church" in Seattle. Chadwick twice joked in print that Blethen's memory had been muddled ever since he took the Keeley cure, a popular turn-of-the-century treatment for alcoholism. *The Argus* continually claimed that Alden Blethen had no principles. When he won appointment to the state university's board of regents, his Republican opponents called him a "red-hot carpetbagger" who earned his place by boosting Governor Rogers and his Populist cronies into office. *The Argus* reprinted a snide Minneapolis commentary—written by Will Haskell—which declared that "Alden J. Educator's" academic credentials were negligible and his appointment disgraced the university. *The Argus* repeatedly claimed that the Abbott Family School had been a reformatory and Alden Blethen its head jailer. His "students" were delinquents sent off by their families for rehabilitation; they grew up to be rogues or criminals.[40]

Certainly, former student Nat Goodwin turned out to be something of a rogue. When Goodwin came to Seattle, he always stayed with the Blethen family, no matter how crowded or impoverished they were. He had been Alden and Rose Ann Blethen's student at Little Blue a quarter century before; a wild and difficult boy, Rose had broken his toe

---

ALDEN BLETHEN'S DREAM OF A FOURTH OF JULY CELEBRATION, ACCORDING TO *The Argus*

The Times has expressed itself on several occasions as dissatisfied with the officers selected to run the Fourth of July celebration, and not without cause. I cannot see how the committee could have been so dense. When there are plenty of good men who have as *The Times* put it, had "experience," laying around loose, waiting for lightning to strike them, it seems almost preposterous to think that such selections should have been made.... It was impudence in the first place for them to even assume to accept the offices.

Of course, it is not more than right that I should suggest another ticket.... Now, for instance, how would this suit?

President—A.J. Blethen

Vice President—Hon. A.J. Blethen

Marshall—Col. A.J. Blethen

Treasurer—Mr. A.J. Blethen

Secretary—A.J. Blethen, Esq.

Finance Committee—Col. Blethen, chairman, Alden J. Blethen, A.J. Blethen, Honorable Mr. Blethen and Blethen

President A.J. Blethen to appoint all committees

There might be objection to this ticket in some locations but I think it would be perfectly satisfactory to *The Times*.... It might then be in order for the finance committee to instruct the president and secretary, after the celebration was over, to "loan" any funds that might remain on hand, on "good security."

The Argus, June 12, 1897

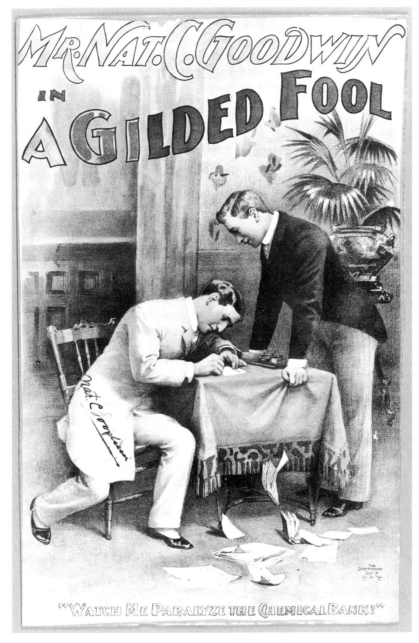

Nat Goodwin had been a student of Alden and Rose Ann Blethen many years earlier at the Abbott Family School in Maine. He became a well-known comic actor and remained a family friend, always visiting the Blethens when he played Seattle. Harry Chadwick, in his ongoing newspaper feud with Blethen, often needled Blethen about his relationship to Goodwin, shown here in the autographed publicity for A Gilded Fool, *which premiered at Seattle's Grant Theatre.*

(#16642, Special Collections, University of Washington Libraries)

trying to restrain him. Goodwin, a successful comic actor, had gained a reputation as a great carouser, a heavy drinker, and a much-married man. After Blethen's arrival, Goodwin first came to Seattle in December 1896. *The Times* welcomed him as "the greatest living actor," and in a single issue gave him an illustrated article, an editorial, and a glowing review that anticipated "a great and brilliant" performance. Alden Blethen was a faithful friend, loyal to a fault. Once Blethen's paper puffed Goodwin, *The Argus* ridiculed him, and Blethen responded by exaggerating Goodwin's modest talents to Olympian heights.[41]

The feud had seized upon Nat Goodwin; it could have been anyone. Harry Chadwick's distaste for Alden Blethen was intense, personal, and went far beyond politics or journalism. Their mutual hatred was visceral. Blethen always went armed with a heavy-headed cane, loaded with lead-shot, but when both Chadwick and Blethen took to carrying revolvers, their friends wouldn't allow them to walk the streets of Seattle alone, to prevent bloodshed.[42]

At the height of their feud, Chadwick dipped his pen in vitriol to write of Blethen, "the animal which edits *The Times*":

> Hades could be skimmed for a thousand years, the offal thus accumulated being concentrated and molded into the image of a man and the result would be a man of honor and refined sensibilities when compared with this creature.... Seattle has harbored some queer things in her day. She will harbor others. But had she a brothel on every street corner, a gambling hell in every block, and a saloon in every school house, the lesson that would be taught the youths of the city would not be any worse than seeing this emblem of God's carelessness and man's depravity walking the streets of Seattle and breathing the free, pure air of heaven.[43]

Alden Blethen held violent forces in tension within himself, disciplined only by his fierce ambition and fear of failure. *The Seattle Times*—editorials to classifieds—became a grand screen on which to project his powerful and contentious personality. Vital, stubborn, pugnacious, he was a man of ordinary gifts who pursued greatness, a reformer plagued by vices, a relentless enemy and an indulgent friend. In 1897, Blethen continued a game of bluff for the highest stakes of his life against seasoned gamblers nearly as desperate as he. But, in Seattle, the pot was very lean.[44]

In a few weeks, all that changed. In July 1897, the steamer *Portland* docked in Elliott Bay carrying nearly seventy very ordinary men who reportedly had found a ton of gold—a million dollars' worth—along the streams of the Yukon River. It happened so quickly that *The Times* wasn't sure whether to typeset Clondyke, Klondyke, or Klondike, and used the three spellings at random. Seattle began a great ride and everybody went along. For years, hopeful editors ballyhooed even the smallest traces of gold in an Okanogan stream bed or a nice piece of quartz from Index. The Klondike wealth seemed unbelievable, and anybody could get rich.[45]

In the early flush of discovery, the wide-eyed *Times* ran an excited letter home from a Seattle boy prospector in Alaska:

> We have struck it pretty good and are taking out good money now.... The first day we got on the pay we got out of one bucket of dirt $282.25. Next day from three pans we got $90.25 and picked up $115 in nuggets. One nugget was $77, and it is a dandy.... We panned out in five days $1500 from fourteen pans. We have got it as good as anyone. Just above us here James McNamee found an $80 nugget and another worth $211, and just above him they got $500 in

one pan. This is the richest thing ever known. Everybody is crazy.[46]

The atmosphere was exhilarating and ten thousand Seattleites went north to strike it rich in the Canadian and Alaskan goldfields. Even Seattle's mayor resigned so he could try his luck. Over the next four years, hopeful argonauts poured into the city from all over the United States, preparing to jump-off to the Yukon. Among the tens of thousands of prospectors—the "floating population," as the city directory termed them—it proved hard to determine just who lived in Seattle. But the settled population of the city essentially doubled between 1890 and 1900. It

The "gold ship," the steamer Portland, *as it arrived in Seattle July 17, 1897, carrying miners who had struck it rich in the Klondike. Wild rumors flew through the city about how much gold was aboard. The* Seattle Times' *headline reported in tones of wonder and disbelief that the* Portland *carried* **Half a Ton of Gold**.

(The Seattle Times)

In a long-forgotten gold rush promotion, a wagon drawn by a team of dogs has pulled up in front of The Seattle Times' offices at Second and Columbia, in the Boston Block.
(The Seattle Times)

Crowds jammed Seattle's docks, headed for the Yukon gold fields. Through the efforts of the local newspapers and the chamber of commerce, Seattle became the West Coast portal to Klondike riches.
(The Seattle Times)

was a terrific time to own a newspaper and in August 1897, for the first time, *The Seattle Times* turned a profit.[47]

The gold wasn't found nearby but much of it returned to Seattle, passing through the portal of the Alaska steamship lines. The Chamber of Commerce hired former *Times* editor Erastus Brainerd to sell the little city as the world's gateway to the Klondike. As *The Times* noted, it wasn't so much the gold that boomed Seattle as the Klondike rush itself, "rolling its golden wave over Seattle and dropping its richness into [our] laps." Only the luckiest argonauts would return with gold, but every man needed information, outfitting, and relaxation. The denizens of Seattle's brothels, saloons, and gambling joints, the local guides and "geologists," the outfitters, the local bankers—and the local publishers—all set out to mine the miners, coming and going.[48]

Every newspaper in the city—daily, weekly, and monthly—published special guides to the Yukon, complete with maps, traveler's information, and lists of what the well-appointed gold seeker should bring. Seattle's two daily newspapers squabbled over who said what first and who had the best advice. *The Times* assigned reporter Joseph A. Costello to travel by steamer to Dawson City and make the trek to the Klondike, promising that his eyewitness accounts would contain "the earliest, most comprehensive, accurate and uncolored reports from the new diggings." Costello's dispatches would be particularly useful, claimed the paper, because he was headed north "to make his fortune, as thousands of others have done and are now doing."[49]

Within days of the *Portland*'s arrival, *The Times* pointed out that the gold rush offered Seattle the "opportunity of controlling the entire outfitting trade to Alaska and the

Northwest Territory." But the Klondike brought much more than a service economy to Seattle. *The Times'* reporting grew more and more frenzied as it became clear that the gold rush would bring prosperity to everyone, "the butcher, the baker, and the candlestick maker." Entire industries sprang up to meet the miners' needs as Seattle entrepreneurs developed prefabricated houses and collapsible boats, and figured out how to manufacture "crystallized eggs" and "concentrated potatoes." More significantly, local shipyards designed and built dozens of barges, river and ocean steamers, and tugs for the Yukon. The Pacific Coast and Alaska Steamship companies boomed, and both more than doubled their fleets of ocean-going steamers.[50]

Over the years of the gold rush, The Seattle Times *printed dozens of guides to the gold fields in special supplements and editions. The newspaper provided information on how to get to the Yukon, how to prospect for a good claim, what supplies to bring, and where to buy them.*

(The Seattle Times, August 21, 1897)

This July 1897 map was drawn exclusively for The Times *by a "Klondyke" prospector, and was one of the very first available. Shortly thereafter,* The Seattle Times *dispatched its own correspondents to the Yukon gold fields to provide the most accurate and timely information to readers.*

(The Seattle Times, July 24, 1897)

Between 1898 and 1902, $174 million in gold cleared the new federal assay office in Seattle. The city, flush and ambitious, began to confront its urban problems. The smelly tideflats, the mud or dust of unplanked roads, the hills which seemed to block the city's growth, inadequate wharfage for the new trade, and the lack of a welcoming railroad depot concerned status-conscious Seattleites. Seattle's newspapers fought to be the city's spokesman to newcomers and to represent contending points of view to long-time residents. As the city entered upon its new prosperity, *The Post-Intelligencer* and *The Times* renewed their struggle, this time for municipal leadership. Of Seattle's many issues, the contest for moral authority over vice proved most difficult to resolve.[51]

During the gold rush, Seattle never slept. The pace of the instant city was frantic. By day, men did business out of stables and tents; canvas signs flapped in the breeze. Goldseekers and sightseers thronged the docks and city sidewalks, and harried outfitters piled merchandise outside their doors. Horses and wagons clogged the streets; dog teams trotted by. Wiry newsboys chanted "Wuxtra! Wuxtra! Fifth Creek Pays Good!" Barkers stood out on the sidewalks and yelled their wares; hucksters grabbed passersby to sell them the best map, a sure thing, a good time.

By night, Seattle was a "hot town," as *The Times* put it, a great carnival of the senses. After the merchants closed their doors, the action moved downtown to the city's Tenderloin, accompanied by piano music, laughter, shouts, breaking glass, and the occasional pistol shot. The saloons and burlesque theaters were bright, warm, and welcoming; beer and whiskey—even champagne—flowed freely, and a few out-of-the-way places offered the less common thrills of opium and morphine. Most miners, the newspaper observed, got drunk both going to and returning from the Alaska goldfields, first in anticipation, and then in celebration or consolation. Women entertained the prospectors, performing as singers, dancers, and comediennes, serving drinks, or dealing cards. Seattle gambling was penny ante or high stakes, wide-open, come one, come all.[52]

The Tenderloin was that area where "the fallen women of the city shall reside" as *The Times* put it, bounded by Yesler Way—the Deadline—on the north, and by Jackson Street, Railroad Avenue, and Fifth Avenue. Newspaper reporters, fascinated by the city's "soiled doves," wrote with either scandalized dismay or mawkish pity. *The Times* ran stories nearly every week about the murder of a

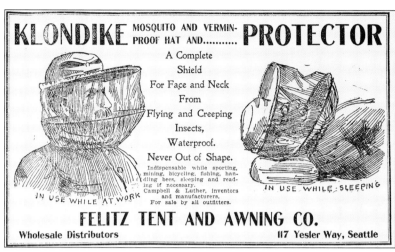

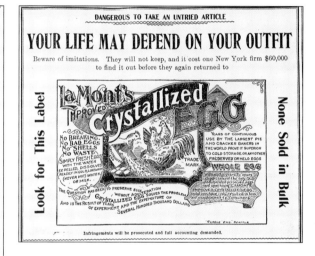

The gold rush also made fortunes for Seattle's merchants as they scrambled to outfit the hordes of eager prospectors and transport them to their dangerous adventure. After August 1897, a rapidly increasing number of advertisements in The Times ballyhooed local services and products, from mosquito-proof hats to bobsleds.

(The Seattle Times)

VICTIMS OF CHEAP OUTFITTERS

RESULT OF PROPER OUTFITTING

P-I ENG.

Blethen's Times *grew profitable during the gold rush as both circulation and advertising revenues soared. Here, a front-page cartoon warns readers of the dangers of heading to Alaska with poor equipment and provisions—the victims of cheap outfitters lie dead in the snow while those properly outfitted stride through the drifts. This cartoon specifically promotes the Seattle invention of crystallized eggs, a dried protein product which was frequently advertised in* The Seattle Times.

(The Seattle Times, March 10, 1898)

pimp or a prostitute's suicide, a miner being rolled or a gambler robbed. Yet Klondike vice was arguably as big a business in Seattle as Klondike outfitting. Testifying before a grand jury, John Considine, Seattle theater impresario, would admit that turn-of-the-century profits from his Standard Gambling House averaged more than $120,000 each year. Entrepreneurs built dozens of new saloons, restaurants, theaters, brothels, and gambling halls to "handle the crowds," as *The Times* delicately put it. Between 1897 and 1910, more ink and less sincerity were lavished on vice in Seattle than on any other issue—it became the touchstone of city politics. Extremists advocated either municipal prohibition or debauchery; cynics recognized vice as an inevitable and profitable business, and argued for regulation within a district. But restriction encouraged protection

rackets, by both police and hoodlums, outside public scrutiny.[53]

The Times used sensational Tenderloin stories to sell newspapers and initially reported with enthusiasm on the profits to be made from vice, but the Fusion newspaper opposed Republican mayor Thomas J. Humes. *The Times* argued that Humes had refused to suppress gambling or contain "the social evil" in Seattle—crime had broken out of the Tenderloin, and Seattle was no longer a family town. In 1898, Alden Blethen introduced *The Times'* Platform calling for municipal control of vice through saloon license fees of $1,000 (or "high license"), nighttime and Sunday saloon closings "enforced to a reasonable extent," and restriction of gambling and prostitution to a clearly defined district. Voters resoundingly defeated *The Times'* combination of Fusion and reform, and under the headline **OUR WATERLOO!—We Have Met The Enemy and We Are Theirs!**, the paper predicted Seattle would "be a hot old town tonight and every other night for the next two years." Blethen's *Times* believed—or affected to believe—that the Humes administration actively supported vice in the city. Indeed, when high license finally did pass in March 1902, *The Times* maintained that it did so despite the efforts of Mayor Humes' army of "besotted drunks."[54]

In this early period, prior to 1904, *The Times* was a reform newspaper. But contemporary rumor and—eventually—sworn testimony persistently linked Alden Blethen to Seattle investments in gambling and prostitution. Yet C.B. Blethen portrayed his father as a progressive reformer, a champion of independent journalism and the righteous city:

Almost single-handed *The Seattle Times* stopped gambling and regulated the saloons. Two of the boss gamblers, both armed, spilled a satchel of currency on Alden's desk

in an effort to bribe him. Their experience was identical with the one Jesse James experienced. In terror they fled Alden's office. While one of them, pistol in hand, mounted guard in the hallway outside, the other frantically picked scattered bills from the floor as they were ejected from the doorway, at the business end of an ordinary broom.[55]

A veteran Seattle newspaperman told a similar tale in his memoirs. In 1900, senatorial candidate Aaron Van de Vanter treated *Times* political reporter Joseph Smith to a drink in Seattle's Horseshoe Saloon. Smith was brand new in the job; *The Times* had just fired his predecessor for "grafting," as the newspaper's city editor put it. But many Washington politicians and newspapermen were cozy bedfellows, and Van de Vanter

confidently placed a thick roll of five and ten dollar bills on the bar between the two men. As the bartender and a few customers looked on with interest, Smith pushed the money away. Smiling, the candidate shoved it back. The embarrassed reporter finally grabbed the roll of bills, jammed it in his pocket, and ran back to the newsroom.

At his desk, he counted the money—it was nearly $1,000—and decided to write a memo describing the incident. He dropped the money and the note on Alden Blethen's desk. Reporter Smith related the outcome, illustrating Blethen's unique code of honor and vigilante justice:

> That afternoon Colonel Blethen sent for me. I found him boiling over with indignant profanity. He blankety-blanked

Seattle city streets took on a boomtown air, as hardware and grocery stores were transformed into outfitters for the Klondike gold rush. Here merchandise is piled on the sidewalk before a number of the city's supply houses, and delivery wagons are poised to carry a prospector's "outfit" to his Alaska steamer.

(The Seattle Times)

The intersection of Jefferson Street with Yesler Way, looking east from the Pioneer Square area. This early gold rush photo shows the Tyee Saloon on the Tenderloin side of the Yesler Way Deadline. Vice, whether or not confined to the Tenderloin's "restricted district," remained a hot topic in Seattle politics for twenty years.

(The Seattle Times)

Alden Blethen worked hard with many other Seattle boosters to convince the federal government to locate an assay office in the city. This photo shows Andrew Chilberg, president of Seattle's Scandinavian-American Bank, receiving deposits of Yukon gold dust and bars in 1900. The Klondike gold rush continued to bring wealth to the city well after the turn of the century.

(The Seattle Times)

Van de Vanter for several picturesque sentences, then passed me over a letter to Van de Vanter, reviling [him] and returning the money....

The Colonel then took up the bills, divided them into two equal piles, put half of them in the envellope [*sic*] and handed the other half to me with the remark:

"Just keep this half for yourself. It's a tax we are levying on Van de Vanter for trying to get gay with me. And if Van ever says anything to you about how we shortchanged him, tell him that if he has any complaint to see me about it."[56]

Once *The Times* became financially secure, Alden Blethen was better able to meet the journalistic standards of his day. His public voice, in *The Seattle Times*, spoke powerfully against vice and political corruption. And in private life, Alden Blethen was a family man with a sheltered wife and two pampered daughters. A faithful communicant at Seattle's Plymouth Congregational Church, he had sworn an oath never to drink in public. But local skeptics doubted this show of morality, and condemned Alden Blethen as a hypocrite.

The Times' endorsement of high license rather than prohibition was taken as evidence that Blethen had friends and interests in saloons, brothels, and gambling joints below the Deadline. *The Argus*, and later *The Post-Intelligencer*, published dozens of sly insinuations about Blethen's own nights on the town, carousing in gambling joints with the city's riffraff. His editorials on honesty and virtue, sneered an anonymous critic, were "the crowning glory of his entire career." How could this scoundrel, the same critic continued, "walk down Second Avenue with his head high in the air, acting as if he was king of Creation...[or] enter good brother Temple's church on Sunday morning, place

his hat under the seat, and listen intently to every word of the service?"[57]

When Seattle's Republican machine soundly defeated *The Times*' anti-Humes reform ticket in 1900, *The Argus* wrote with glee:

It was a landslide.... The mongrel ticket, sired by a jackass and damned by everybody with common sense, has been defeated. The people have declared that they had no confidence in reform, headed by Eugene Way, an ex-gambler, Alden J. Blethen, an all around sneak, and Rev. W.H.G. Temple, who has been annexed for the purpose of throwing the rather doubtful cloak of his respectability around the movement.[58]

However, in this period before 1904 Seattle writers who wanted to dish the dirt on Alden Blethen usually mined his Minneapolis years.

The four children of Rose Ann and Alden Blethen pose for a studio portrait in about 1900. Marion Blethen is to the left, and Florence Blethen is on the right. Joe Blethen stands center rear, and his younger brother, C.B., is seated center front, apparently dressed in the uniform of the University of Washington cadet corps.

(Courtesy of Joseph Mesdag)

The comfortably dim bar of The Oriental was a Seattle male bastion, built of mahogany, mirrors, and brass, complete with spittoons. Such establishments usually offered a free lunch of cheese, bread, and pickles to encourage beer-drinking customers.

(PEMCO Webster and Stevens Collection, Seattle Museum of History and Industry)

The searing 1899 exposé *Municipal Monopolies,* by respected political scientist Edward Bemis, described graft and corruption in American cities, and revived the old charges that Blethen had peddled the influence of *The Minneapolis Tribune* to Tom Lowry. *Municipal Monopolies* made its way onto reading lists at the University of Washington. But even the most casual Seattle newspaper reader was already familiar with the Bank of New England litigation and Blethen's lawsuit against Tom Lowry.[59]

Blethen's unique personality—his "violent unpredictable temper"—was also common knowledge in Seattle. Loud, vulgar, and arrogant, Alden Blethen strides "smoking hot" through the reminiscences of his contemporaries, fists clenched, his "face forbidding as a thunder cloud." Employees trembled before his wrath as he barreled across *The Times'* newsroom, bearing down on a miscreant's

desk. I can hear him now, remembered city editor James Wood,

"like the rumbling of a coming storm.... Something would go wrong, somewhere, it might be anywhere—in our own department, in the business office, downtown, back East or in Europe...but presently the Colonel would come swinging through in what appeared to be, and sometimes was, a towering rage.[60]

Described more than once as a human volcano, Alden Blethen's speech is always transcribed with exclamation marks; in memory, he always seems to be yelling.[61]

Harry Daniels, longtime composing room foreman, once had the temerity to question the headline **COMPARISONS ARE ODOROUS**, inquiring whether "odious" wasn't the word Blethen had in mind. Alden Blethen bellowed, "Damn it, Harry, follow copy!" And so it was printed, testimony to the Colonel's wrongheaded obstinacy. Percy Jefferson, an advertising salesman for the turn-of-the-century *Times,* had to deal with people whose accounts had brought Blethen's wrath down upon their heads for some offense, real or imagined. When an advertiser complained about his treatment, Jefferson had to relay Alden Blethen's edict, "Tell that son of a bitch he'll crawl on his hands and knees before he runs another inch of space in *The Seattle Times!*"[62]

Blethen was the overbearing paterfamilias of the extended family of *Times* employees. He seemed to know everything about everybody in the crowded building at Second and Columbia. The home of *The Times* from 1896 through 1902, the Boston Block became an increasingly busy place as the paper grew. From three o'clock on in the afternoon, the great press shook the floors and tipped calendars awry on the walls; the smell and

Entertainment in Seattle became big business. The Isis Theatre, photographed in 1914, was part of a lively new theater district in the city that featured moving pictures for a largely male audience, as shown here.

(PEMCO Webster and Stevens Collection, Seattle Museum of History and Industry)

This 1898 photograph of Joseph Blethen and C.B. Blethen shows them in the tiny office they shared in the Boston Block, at Second and Columbia. Nearly thirty, Joe was then managing editor of The Times. At eighteen, C.B. was a student at the University of Washington. After a brief stint in 1900 at the University of Chicago, he returned to The Seattle Times as news editor, and was soon promoted to managing editor.

(The Seattle Times)

These engravings in The Seattle Times' business annual, February 3, 1898, show the relationship between detailed base photographs and the simpler lines of newspaper illustrations. The artist "cleaned up" the images not only for dramatic effect but also because of the technology of creating metal engravings for printing.

(The Seattle Times, February 3, 1898)

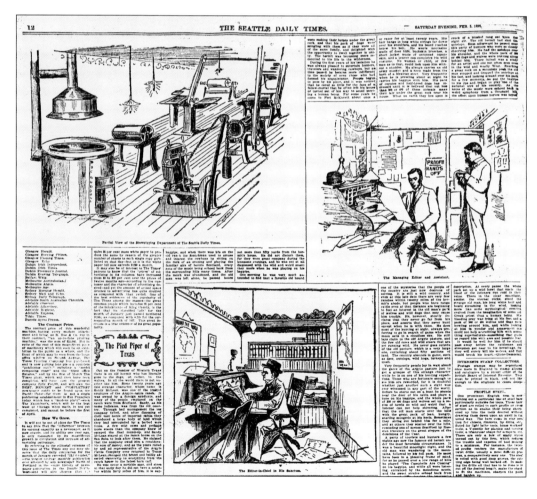

heat of the plate-casting permeated the building. Telephone wires draped over banisters and hung over the potbellied stoves. The entire news staff worked on a makeshift balcony, six by twenty feet, tacked along the building's long wall. Editors pinned sheaves of copy to cords, and dangled them down to composing. After C.B. Blethen left the University of Chicago, he and Joe shared a tiny sanctum just south of the city desk.[63]

Alden Blethen's own office was so small he had to "scooch his chair into the corner" to make room for his secretary Bessie Hammons to take dictation. *The Times'* machinist didn't like Blethen's temper, and took his revenge by hammering on his anvil when the boss tried to dictate an editorial or make a phone call. But as angry as Blethen got with his employees, he permitted no one else to yell at them. And, as ill-tempered as he was, he could also be indulgent and sentimental. He allowed no one else to feed the stray cat who lived in the Boston Block composing room, daily offering it raw liver and fresh milk. He worried about horses suffering on their pulls up Seattle's steep hills, and rerouted *Times* deliveries. Blethen, a methodical and hard-driving man, arrived at *The Times* in the early morning and worked until the late afternoon, went home for dinner, and then returned to the office in the evening. Yet he liked to sit down at odd times for an hour's chat, offered to pay for schooling his employees hadn't noticed they lacked, and led the annual "turkey march" to the meat market to buy a holiday bird for each married member of *The Times'* staff.[64]

Blethen's Thanksgiving dinners for *The Times'* newsboys were legendary. Mystified observers watched this volcanic man "flutter about" as he "brought more white meat for one boy, a piece of butter for another." All his life, Alden Blethen felt a special tie to lonely, unhappy boys. The kids who sold *The Times*

on Seattle's street corners claimed a special place in his newspaper. These "tireless little men," as *The Times* called them, were portrayed as heroes in a Horatio Alger novel—grubby and tough but honest and hardworking, supporting themselves and a widowed mother or consumptive father. *The Times* publicized the Seattle Newsboys' Union, organized in 1892, and openly sympathized with these street kids.[65]

In 1898, Joe Blethen wrote an article in an Irish/Scandinavian dialect about an upcoming "treat" that his father had arranged:

TIMES NEWSBOYS' FROLIC

"I done see dat man what's peekin' out der moon torkin' ter our boss, an' I done hear 'im, Mr. Blethen, sayin' ter him, says he, 'All right, dat's a go; I'm 'tickler pleased what you give me dis chance to give my little workers a jolly good time.... I hearn yer

The Seattle Newsboys' Union was founded in 1892, and this view was taken that same year. Alden Blethen took a special interest in these boys, and sponsored annual banquets and entertainments for them.
(*Washington State Historical Society*)

Pioneer Square, Seattle, 1900.
(The Seattle Times)

show is a very good one.' An' dey touched flippers an' quit."

Then a little ragged, smudgy-faced urchin, just tall enough to look over the counter in *The Times* office, inquired of the cashier, "Say, Mister, is *Der Times* gon' ter send all de kids w'at sells poipers ter de show?"

[Told yes, the urchin enthused], "I don't want ter trow up bookays at Mr. Blethen an' Der Times, but dey treats us kids a dern sight better'n some o' dese papers what keeps refrigerator news on ice."[66]

Even advertising the Newsboys Frolic, *The Times* couldn't resist a dig at *The P-I*. During

the gold rush, the city became a hot newspaper town and Seattle dailies competed hard and grew fast, with lots of turnover. In the early years on *The Times*, Blethen couldn't match offers made to his men by *The P-I*, and reporters remembered going into his office and saying, "I've had a better offer from *The P-I*. What can you do about it?" Blethen replied, "Not a damn thing. Pick up your check and go over there." But when things got better, *The Times* paid top dollar, and Percy Jefferson recalled that he only had to walk into Alden Blethen's office, twisting his cap nervously, and inquire, "Busy, sir?" to have Blethen, without saying a word, letter a piece of scrap paper "Give Percy $5 more each week" in his unmistakable scrawl.[67]

Turn-of-the-century reporters worked odd hours, driven by their deadlines and breaking stories. There were plenty of takers for the White Elephant gambling house's midnight lunch, offered free to newsmen. An informal lunch club of editors and writers met in the grill room of the Butler Hotel. Although *The Times* didn't publish a Sunday edition until 1902, three "good fellows" from *The Times*—Joe Blethen, E.L. Reber, and Bill Sheffield—used to get together with men from the other city newspapers on Saturday nights after *The P-I* Sunday paper was "put to bed." The "almost Press Club" met at a number of hospitable dives: the Horseshoe Saloon and the Nevada Saloon, the White House and the Double Stamp. The White House management lured the newsmen with a free buffet of herrings, cheese, hot dogs, pilot bread, popcorn, and clam broth. The thoughtful proprietor also set out lemon peel and cloves to chew afterward, to rid the drinker of beer or whiskey breath before his return to work. But on Saturday nights, the boozy celebrants took the "newspaper streetcars" at 4:00 a.m., riding home at dawn with the Sunday morning papers.[68]

By January 1898, in the heat of the gold rush, *The Times*' weekday circulation had more than doubled since Blethen's purchase, to nearly 12,000 daily readers, gained largely "among the common people of Washington." The newspaper emphasized hot news, sports, local crime and politics, humor, entertainment and the theater, with pages of beauty tips and society news to appeal to women readers—all beautifully illustrated. The Saturday edition—a lively and exciting mix of news, features, and fiction—had nearly tripled its circulation and outsold any other Saturday newspaper in the state. The

weekday newspaper ran five editions, with frequent extras, and the company ordered a new press to meet the growing demand. *The Times* included "German Notes" and "Normanna Heimen" for its readers who had recently immigrated; the "People's Forum" ran letters to the editor across a wide range of opinion, from trade unionism to prohibition. *The Times* built a new urban reading audience, just as *The Penny Press* had done in Minneapolis, but it caught the wave of Seattle's growth as *The Press* had not. *The Times* harped on circulation, a subject, Blethen recognized, "monotonous to the ordinary reader but never to the publisher nor the advertiser." And, of course, that was the real goal of the circulation war, to persuade advertisers that "there is no advertising medium published in Washington of equal value to THE TIMES."[69]

The Times openly challenged *The P-I*'s circulation claims:

$1000 REWARD!

The Post-Intelligencer of this city has kept at the head of its editorial columns for four years the following notice:

"The P-I hereby guarantees its advertisers a bona fide paid circulation Daily, Weekly and Sunday, DOUBLE that of any other newspaper published in the State of Washington. Advertising contracts will be made subject to this guarantee."

THE TIMES will pay any man ONE THOUSAND DOLLARS in cash for proof of the truth of the above statement.

THE TIMES will pay FIVE HUNDRED DOLLARS for proof that the statement quoted above is within 50 per cent of the truth.

THE TIMES will pay TWO HUNDRED AND FIFTY DOLLARS in cash for proof that the statement is within 25 per cent of the truth....

"OH, WHAT A DIFFERENCE IN THE MORNING."

COL. ALDEN J. BLETHEN,
The morning after election.

This Argus *cartoon caricatured Alden Blethen on "the morning after" the defeat of* The Times' *reform coalition ticket in the 1900 municipal election. Throughout his life, Blethen's antagonists often targeted his drunkenness. Here Chadwick's* Argus *satirizes the headache and thirst of Blethen's political hangover.*

(University of Washington Libraries)

Who will undertake to secure any one or all of these rewards?[70]

According to *The Times*, no one ever claimed any of these rewards, and *The P-I* soon capitulated and removed the statement from its masthead.[71]

In the ongoing game of moves and counter-moves, *The P-I* organized a boycott of *The Times*, arguing that Blethen was a "knocker" of Seattle. His retort demonstrates Alden Blethen's view of life as war, competition as conquest or defeat, success as a battle prize. And, it shows his fierce commitment to this city. He would never leave, and he intended that his sons wouldn't either:

The Times has cost its owners a great deal of money and hard labor. Its proprietors are citizens of Seattle. Everything they have on earth or expect to have is in this city. It is here that we expect to live and die and fight the battle of life.[72]

In 1896, *The Seattle Times* had been a militantly populist paper and considered itself "the backbone of the workingmen." It nearly went out of business. By 1901, the newspaper's circulation had climbed to nearly 25,000, sharing the Seattle market with two major dailies, *The P-I* and *The Star*. All three newspapers had prospered because of the gold rush and the Spanish-American War, that "splendid little war," only four months long, made to order for the new journalism. Though *The P-I* was most reluctant, all three Seattle daily papers had become more "yellow" to remain competitive—looking bolder and brighter, featuring lively copy, emphasizing scandal, fraud, and crime.[73]

With tongue firmly in cheek, Blethen reprinted on *The Times'* editorial page a serious criticism of the yellow journalism that boomed the American newspaper business:

THE NEW JOURNALISM

Ply your muck-rakes, thrust them in to the fetid bogs of sin;

Lift them dripping with the slime of the cesspools of our time;

Search through every social sewer, search for all that's most impure,

Hunt for every deed of shame and for deeds without a name

Let the eager public see all our moral leprosy.

For it is our daily stint the unprintable to print;

'Tis the glory of our clique the unspeakable to speak.

Run we through our printing-press myriad miles of nastiness;

Smear with slime its league-long rolls— Food, my masters, food for souls.[74]

War news worked just as well as "deeds of shame," disguising the lure of blood and guts with a patriotic glow. *The Times* beat the drums against Spain for months before the actual sinking of the battleship *Maine* off Cuba in February 1898. The Spanish committed daily atrocities against liberty and morality, *The Times* maintained, and President William McKinley allowed the honor of the United States to be insulted. Alden Blethen's *Times*—and Hearst's New York *Journal*—called for war with Spain from day one. War news was of vital interest to rich and poor, and broadened *The Times'* readership. Papers encouraged their readers to expect today's news today, but the temptation to be first with the most led to the over-eager invention of breaking stories. When the evening *Times* could beat its morning rival, Alden Blethen exulted, "the *P-I* was scooped out of its pajamas!"; when it couldn't, *The Times* sometimes stretched the truth.

Thriving on the sense of emergency, *The Seattle Times* published dozens of extras. It featured war bulletins in front-page boxes, and pasted them up in the Boston Block windows. Like the Civil War, the Spanish-American War accelerated information technology, and news artists sent to draw the battlefield in Cuba found themselves outnumbered by photographers sent to shoot pictures of it. The ability to print half-tones from stereos on rotary presses distinguished the most advanced coverage of the distant conflict, and *The Seattle Times* spent money to keep up.[75]

In that war year, Harry Chadwick and Alden Blethen buried the hatchet. Chadwick offered his grudging praise in *The Argus,* and it must have been sweet to Blethen ears: "Seattle has never had a better evening paper than *The Times* is just now...[o]ne must be forced to admit that after tearing the editorial page out of *The Times*, it is very readable." In hopes of securing a political ally, Chadwick moderated his stinging attacks from invective to satire, writing optimistically that Blethen was at best a reluctant Democrat, "[t]ied to a political party that he detests," and that he "has never been anything else than a republican at heart." Certainly, Seattle's Republican newspaper establishment was in complete disarray.[76]

When Spokane's George Turner sold his Rossland mine for a reputed $5 million, he purchased the state's leading Republican organ, *The Seattle Post-Intelligencer. The Argus* indignantly joined *The Times* in claiming that Turner had bought himself a newspaper simply to push his political hopes. Then, Hughes and Davies, former owners of *The Seattle Times,* launched their own Republican evening paper, but *The Journal* closed within a month, a poorly produced and uninteresting effort. Less than a year later, former

senator John L. Wilson bought *The P-I* from Turner. Already disheartened by *The Journal's* failure, the Republican *Argus* grew increasingly disgusted with *The P-I's* fawning articles about publisher Wilson. *The Argus* turned hard against *The P-I* as the paper frittered away its Republican political capital, swinging like a weathervane toward whomever currently held the purse strings. Chadwick of *The Argus* hoped to enlist Blethen as a newspaper ally for the beleaguered Republican Party in Washington state.[77]

But Blethen once again threw *The Times'* support to Fusion and Free Silver in the 1900 elections, writing passionate editorials on behalf of Democrat William Jennings Bryan and Populist John Rogers. In fact, Alden Blethen had attended the 1899 Chicago Fusion convention as the Washington state delegate. However, in the wake of the Spanish-American War, Blethen differed with Bryan over growing U.S. imperialism. Colonel Alden Blethen showed his patriotism—which one historian has termed "at best maudlin and at worst pathological"—by bedecking his newspaper, office, and building with slogans and flags. Blethen worried in print that Bryan would lose the election if he persisted in his misguided notions that "liberated" territory in Cuba and the Philippines should be returned. Blethen traveled east for a chat with William Jennings Bryan. On his return, he pronounced himself reassured, and reaffirmed his support for Bryan and the Fusion ticket.[78]

In that national election year, *The Times* published an ambitious book, *Seattle and the Orient*, to promote trade between Seattle and Asia. In the four years since the Klondike Gold Rush, Seattle had become the commercial center commanding the coast north of San Francisco. Blethen argued that Seattle was well on its way to becoming the

In 1900, Blethen's Times *supported William Jennings Bryan in his second unsuccessful bid for the presidency. This poster from Bryan's campaign literature announced his rejection of the gold standard, his eagerness to break up the octopus* TRUSTS, *and his clear stand against American imperialism among the territories conquered during the Spanish-American War. This last position greatly troubled Alden Blethen, and he traveled east to offer counsel to William Jennings Bryan.*

(The Seattle Times)

Both before and after publication of Seattle and the Orient, The Seattle Times *provided respectful coverage of Pacific Rim trading partners, including this 1905 trade and diplomatic delegation from China.*

(PEMCO Webster and Stevens Collection, Seattle Museum of History and Industry)

industrial center of the Pacific and the hub of a new Pacific Rim trading system. The Moran Shipyards alone employed more than five hundred men in the construction of the great battleship USS *Nebraska*, a contract that transformed the industrial face of Seattle.[79]

The Seattle Times had led the public campaign that raised more than $100,000 in an extraordinary effort to help Moran lower its bid to the U.S. Navy, and thereby win the *Nebraska* contract. *Seattle and the Orient* claimed that *The Times* spoke for the new industrial Pacific Northwest, and that Alden, Joe, and C.B. Blethen were the men who made the paper. Alden Blethen described *The Times* when he bought it in 1896, as "in no sense a newspaper," having little circulation or influence. But after four years of his management, Blethen claimed, *The Seattle Times* had grown to be "one of the most conspicuous successes in newspaper publishing in the West." Distributed nationally, *Seattle and the Orient* was a bold attempt to convince public opinion that *The Times* was the leading daily newspaper in Washington state, influential in economic and political matters.[80]

But Free Silver and Populism were dying issues and Bryan lost again to McKinley. *The*

Times had to choose a new course. Even had the Blethens wished it, *The Times* could not afford to become the evening Republican newspaper while *The P-I* remained the morning Republican paper. It would have been a suicidal business decision. Despite *The Times'* success, and its own frequent changes of ownership, *The P-I* maintained a commanding dominance among Washington Republicans. Boxed by necessity into supporting the minority Democrat and Fusion candidates, Blethen's *Times* had little effect on turn-of-the-century elections.

The *Seattle Times* proclaimed itself an independent newspaper—a new course, but one that did not significantly increase Alden Blethen's influence. In a predominately Republican town, political independence meant that the newspaper supported minority candidates, and that those candidates lost. But as Alden Blethen himself pointed out, if only working-class Democrats and Populists bought his paper, he would have been out of business. Nearly three-quarters of his readers were middle-class Republicans who purchased *The Times* because it was readable and provocative.[81]

Nevertheless, *The Times* carefully cultivated its political ambiguity, disingenuously justifying its own slippery position with Republican war hero Theodore Roosevelt's remark, "The party man who offers his allegiance to his party as an excuse for blindly following his party, right or wrong, and who fails to try to make that party in any way better, commits a crime against the country." But *The Seattle Times* might as well have been a Democratic newspaper, complained *The Argus*, which had hoped for a Republican ally. In 1902, *The Times* pushed the candidates of the Democratic Party statewide, including Alden Blethen's son, C.B., who ran for the House of Representatives in the 45th congressional district as a Democrat. C.B. Blethen, only twenty-two, lost handily, but he continued his active interest in the Washington state Democratic Party and the presidential candidacy of millionaire publisher William Randolph Hearst. Blethen was a member of the Executive Committee of the National Association of Democratic Clubs at the time when Hearst served as its head. In fact, C.B. maintained in *The Times* that rank-and-file Democrats, especially young men, preferred Hearst to other Democratic presidential candidates.[82]

The Seattle Times' continual waffling denials and coy protestations of independence were not convincing to contemporaries, as *The Argus* later summarized:

> *The Times* is supposed to be a—well, we don't know what kind of a paper it is supposed to be. When its editor first came to Seattle he was a republican and always had been. But he bought *The Times* right in the middle of the free silver fight, and found that the free silver people wanted an organ. He went to work at once to pump wind into that organ and has been at it ever since.... Since that time he has attempted to get on the popular side of every question which has come before the people. It mattered not to him whether the question was right or wrong, so long as it pleased his patrons.... He prostituted his energies for the almighty dollar.[83]

Observers could be forgiven their confusion about Alden Blethen's politics. When Seattle's Iroquois Democratic Club formed in 1902, the membership of more than three hundred *unanimously* elected Blethen their president.[84] He declined the club nomination with thanks:

> In order that the Times may stand in the position of an independent newspaper, published in behalf of good government,

no matter by what party administered, I feel that its Editor should refrain from all complications of an extreme partisan nature...which might tend to greatly reduce the influence of this publication.[85]

That influence was about to increase dramatically. In 1902 *The Times* moved into a brand new building at Second and Union, built to its specifications, and featured in the holiday issue of its old enemy, *The Argus. The Times* proudly described its "modern newspaper workshop," inviting readers to tour the offices, the mailing room, and the composing room, and then to watch the great presses put out the paper. *The Times* claimed it now had the best production machinery in the West.[86]

In 1902, The Seattle Times *moved to the Denny Building at Second Avenue and Union, and would remain at this location until The Times Square building was completed in 1916, after Alden Blethen's death. Although the Denny Building was built to* The Times' *specifications, the newspaper leased its office and production space, sharing the building with other tenants. Passersby read news bulletins and viewed the presses in the basement.* The Seattle Times *corner became an urban public space that attracted city people for election results and baseball scores.*

(The Seattle Times)

This view looks north up "the Second Avenue canyon," as contemporaries named it, bustling with Seattle's turn-of-the-century city life. The Times Denny Building is at the corner of Second and Union, next door to Sherman Clay, and The Bon Marché is across the street and to the north. Farther north, up Second Avenue, "Your Credit is Good" sign marks the location of the Standard Furniture Store, and the Moore Theatre stands at the northernmost end of the view.

(PEMCO Webster and Stevens Collection, Seattle Museum of History and Industry)

The Times needed these new facilities to carry out "its duty to its patrons," as Blethen put it, by offering a politically independent Sunday newspaper, beautifully produced. On February 9, 1902, *The Times* published the annual business review as the first Sunday edition, breaking *The P-I*'s monopoly on that day of reading and reflection. Alden Blethen's introductory editorial served notice that he would challenge Republican dominance of the Sunday morning press. Driving for increased advertising revenues, Blethen introduced *The Sunday Times* to subscribers for no additional charge—"Seven Days A Week All For the Same Price"—an inspired business strategy. In 1902, *The Times* sold nearly 30,000 copies daily, and distributed 31,000 copies each Sunday, with *The Times* selling 46,000 lines of display advertising to *The P-I*'s 38,000 in one month.[87]

Alden Blethen was a fierce and antagonistic competitor, never satisfied with a draw in the battle of life. For instance, in 1901, *The Times* refused to concede the Seattle city printing contract to the tiny rival *Bulletin*, which had underbid. Undaunted by two adverse court decisions, *The Times* harried *The Bulletin*'s parent company, the Puget Sound Publishing Company, until it gave up and sold out to *The Times*. It took three years and cost a small fortune, but Blethen finally won. In that same year, The Times Printing Company undertook its own small effort at a statewide newspaper chain, purchasing *The Reveille* and then *The Puget Sound American* in Bellingham, advancing against the terrain of rival publishers. Most significant was *The Seattle Times'* direct challenge in 1907 to *The Post-Intelligencer*'s morning turf. *The Morning Times* lasted through only seven months of bitter and expensive conflict, until the Blethens were forced to abandon the effort. Alden Blethen hated to lose.[88]

Blethen consolidated his Seattle success, turning his attention to his evening newspaper and to arranging the continuity of ownership within the family. Chastened by experience, he protected his own personal wealth from the threat of business failure. Blethen's attorneys separated The Times Printing Company, which owned the newspaper business, from the Times Investment Company, which owned the Blethen homes and personal property, as well as a great deal of real estate throughout Seattle and the Pacific Northwest. He arranged a living trust that issued stock in both corporations to the members of his immediate family. Alden Blethen and his two sons held three-fifths of the corporate stock, while his wife and two daughters divided the remaining two-fifths. *The Times* had become a valuable asset—as early as 1902, Blethen declined an offer of

Above left: The front page of the first Sunday edition of The Seattle Times, *February 9, 1902. The Sunday paper prominently featured photographs above the fold, and offered a provocative mix of national and international news—some datelined to* The Times' *Washington, D.C., bureau—with stories of human interest and scandal.*

(The Seattle Times)

Above: The Seattle Times *exhibited endless ingenuity in its self-promotion, including this graphic of February 8, 1903, which compares the five trainloads of white paper consumed by the daily and Sunday* Times *editions during 1902 with* The Times' *entire consumption in 1896 and 1897.*

(The Seattle Times)

Left: In 1911, The Bon Marché's delivery wagon was decorated in celebration of the twenty-first anniversary of the store's founding. Seattle's daily newspapers and great retail stores grew up together.

(The Seattle Times)

Above left: In 1907, The Seattle Times *mounted a direct challenge to* The Seattle Post-Intelligencer's *dominance of morning readers in the city. Although no issues of* The Morning Times *have survived, this front-page announcement in the evening edition boasts of the "interesting and perhaps novel" nature of the new morning paper.* The Morning Times' *first issue appeared just after April Fool's day, 1907, and was published for only seven months.*
(The Seattle Times, March 7, 1907)

Above right: On February 12, 1905, The Seattle Times *devoted a full page to a graphic celebration of "The Blethen Properties," including the three* Times *editions— daily, Sunday, and weekly—the business daily,* The Seattle Bulletin, *and the Bellingham Puget Sound American.*
(The Seattle Times)

one million dollars for the newspaper he bought in 1896 "on wind."[89]

Alden Blethen emerged as the single most powerful publisher and editor in Washington state, with his legacy apparently assured by the family succession. Achieving wealth and influence so late in his life, he had no intention of letting go, yet he had to transfer authority to his sons, who were both trapped and privileged by his accomplishments. Their peers considered Joe and C.B., "live newspaper men [to whom] much of the rapid advancement of their paper is due." "The boys"—as the family called them well into their thirties—could earn their colleagues' praise but never duplicate their father's success. They had to deal with his rivalry, as well as their own.[90]

Joe Blethen had gained a modest national reputation for his short stories and poetry. His wife, Genevieve, encouraged his literary ambitions, challenging him to write eight short stories during their first year of marriage. His play "The Chinook" toured Midwest theaters for many years. "The Alaskan,"

a musical comedy, would be a modest hit with local audiences. President of the Seattle Press Club, Joe Blethen devoted his attention increasingly to the business side of *The Times.* Both Joe and C.B. Blethen worked hard at the paper—Alden Blethen didn't tolerate slackers—but C.B. ascended with surprising speed to the position of *Times* managing editor in 1903. After 1904, *Times* staff reminiscences mention C.B., not Joe.[91]

As managing editor, C.B. Blethen had authority over *The Times'* wire services and news staff. A man in his early twenties with strong military interests, he managed a tough and cynical team of veteran newsmen who, later in life, remembered him with respect. The staff much coveted his "T-mat" award— given to *The Times* man whose work achieved national attention.[92]

C.B.'s particular interest lay in color printing and news photography. *The Times* began to use color in January 1902, purchasing its own four-color press in 1904—the first in the Pacific Northwest. C.B. Blethen owned a half dozen cameras and refined his own skills as a photographer, shooting hundreds of photos of wrecked cars and houses afire. He did not earn his first patent in photo technology for nearly two decades, but even in 1902 his excitement about today's PHOTOGRAPHS FROM EVERYWHERE mirrored his father's interest in THE NEWS THE DAY IT HAPPENS. The photo revolution had begun with halftones of the Spanish-American War; five years later, all good newspapers showed a photograph of breaking news above the fold. C.B. Blethen claimed that *The Times* was the first newspaper in the United States to publish a photo the day it was taken. In May 1904, *The Times* set a speed record by shooting a photo of a big downtown fire, making a half-tone engraving, and locking it into the frame for the

Above left: The Blethen family and friends on the steps of Alden Blethen's Queen Anne Hill home. From left to right, Joe Blethen and his wife Genevieve, Alden Blethen, Marion Blethen, Will Hammons, Rose Ann Blethen, Florence Blethen, and Fred Hammons.
(The Seattle Times)

Above: The craze of bicycling took Seattle by storm in the 1890s. Here is C.B. Blethen on his "wheel," as bikes were commonly termed, while a student at the University of Washington.
(The Seattle Times)

Left: A group of turn-of-the-century bicyclists rests at a rustic stop along Lake Washington Boulevard.
(The Seattle Times)

Alden and Rose Ann Blethen's Highland Drive home on Queen Anne Hill. Though thoroughly modern in its kitchen and bathroom conveniences, the spacious and comfortable home seemed "colonial" to many observers. Certainly its columns, dormers, porches, and widow's walk, looking to Elliott Bay, must have reminded the Blethens of the elegant homes of Bramhall Hill, in Portland, Maine.

(The Seattle Times)

evening front page, all in less than two hours. During the great San Francisco earthquake, C.B. promised to pay $50 sight unseen for each photograph of the devastation that ran in *The Times.*[93]

Truculent as ever, Alden Blethen remained both publisher and editor-in-chief of *The Seattle Times,* his tantrums, crusades, and personal journalism the pride and despair of his sons. He personified the paper and still ran it his way. He insisted, for instance, on absolute obedience by the news reporters to *The Times'* editorial positions. In 1902, Blethen was embarrassed and infuriated by an article that slipped past the city editor and into print. The simple interview with Seattle's city comptroller pointed out that high license had not decreased the number of saloons in the city. In fact, saloon keepers didn't seem to be having much difficulty at all ponying up the $1,000 fee. But for six years, *Times* editorials had promised that high license would decrease the number of Seattle saloons. Alden Blethen went through the roof.[94]

The inimitable *Argus* described the scene:

Just what happened to the reporter who wrote the interview no man knoweth, but the balance of the force speak his name in hushed tones. The city editor has been wiped off the map, the office cat has crawled into a hole and pulled the hole in after it.[95]

In his editorial, Blethen fumed that the city editor "is supposed to keep in touch with the editorial policy of the paper and never permit any antagonism to occur in the local [news] department toward that editorial policy." He considered the whole affair "a humiliating experience," and continued, "It is very seldom that a newspaper is called on to apologize for the stupidity of its own employees, but *The Times* has been caught at last and an apology is in order" to its readers, who had the right to expect complete consistency from their newspaper.[96]

Blethen had once again achieved business success and financial security; he gained some degree of respectability, too. Despite the death of his populist patron, Governor John Rogers, he continued his long term as regent at the state university into 1904. Alden Blethen was a thirty-third degree Mason and an honorary life member of the Seattle Press Club. He had joined the Plymouth Congregational Church, whose pastor, the Rev. W.H.G. Temple, counted him "an intimate personal friend." Throughout his adult life, he remained a trustee of the Kent's Hill Seminary, and contributed substantially to the renovation of Blethen Hall on campus. In Seattle, Colonel Blethen and his family lived for years in rented houses but in the spring of 1901, they moved into their final home on Queen Anne Hill. The house on Highland Drive was a splendid mansion, built to their design, comfortable and up-to-date in every detail. Joe and his wife had a new home

In 1903, Seattle turned out to welcome President Theodore Roosevelt. Residents crowded the city's waterfront for a better view.

(Seattle Museum of History and Industry)

This cartoon, originally published in The Tacoma Ledger and reprinted in Seattle's Argus, caricatured the pretensions of Blethen's Queen Anne Hill mansion and parodied the publisher's sorrow at missing President Roosevelt's visit.

(University of Washington Libraries)

The Times

Alden J. Blethen, Editor-in-Chief.

Joseph Blethen, Associate Editor.

C. B. Blethen, Managing Editor.

Kenneth C. Beaton, City Editor.

Published Every Day by

THE TIMES PRINTING COMPANY

Office....................1400 Second Avenue

EASTERN OFFICES:

No. 510-512 The Tribune Building, Chicago, and 43, 44, 45, 47, 48, 49 Tribune Building, New York City. The S. C. Beckwith Special Agency, Sole Eastern Agents.

TACOMA, WASH., OFFICE:

1121 Pacific Avenue. Telephone John 2441

PRICE OF DAILY AND SUNDAY:

One month, by carrier....................$ .50
One month, by mail......................... .50
Six months, by mail......................... 3.00
One year, by mail!......................... 6.00

THE SUNDAY TIMES.

One month, by mail...................... .20
One month, by carrier.................... .20
Six months, by mail or carrier......... 1.15
One year, by mail or carrier........... 2.25

THE WEEKLY TIMES, per annum.. 1.00

Make all remittances by check, post-office or express orders. Money or stamps will be at sender's risk.

Subscribers ordering their addresses changed should give the old as well as the new one.

In this February 8, 1903 Times *masthead, C.B. Blethen is newly identified as the newspaper's managing editor.*

(The Seattle Times)

nearby, too. The Highland Drive house, the boys in the business, the girls in school, the honor of the university regency—all symbolized Alden Blethen's wealth, influence, and respectability, lost in Minneapolis, reclaimed in Seattle.[97]

Fiercely proud of his achievements, Blethen confidently believed he had a right to advise statesmen and command national respect. He clearly expected that, had William Jennings Bryan won the presidency in 1900, he would have received a diplomatic appointment. When President Theodore Roosevelt visited town, TR asked that his party, on a pleasure drive in the city, stop by Colonel Blethen's home on Queen Anne Hill. However, the editor was working downtown and missed the president. Tortured by regret, Blethen explained and re-explained his absence.[98] *The Argus'* Chadwick, ever observant, needled the Colonel:

Owing to an unforeseen incident the visit of President Roosevelt to Seattle was a dismal failure. It is well, perhaps, that the President did not know what he missed, and so departed early Monday morning, perfectly satisfied, to all outward appearances, with his visit here. But to those Seattleites who have for a number of years witnessed the upbuilding of that great and noble edifice on Queen Anne Hill, fit for the abiding place of gods, it is indeed mortifying that the hand of fate decreed that its beauties and splendors should not be unveiled for the pleasure of one so great.... The next time that the president of the united states [*sic*] calls on the Editor of the Times it is to be hoped that he will have the good taste to wait for an invitation.[99]

Whether TR visited him or not, Alden Blethen, who had failed so spectacularly, who had considered suicide, who had seemed "a football of fortune" to his contemporaries, had decisively won what he called "the battle of life." *The Seattle Times* is a bit "yellow," judged a Seattle contemporary, but it is "a great newspaper. It has a circulation of which its publishers are justly proud [and] it has considerable influence in public affairs and would have more if its editor could appreciate the fact that he was not here like Mt. Rainier when Washington was first discovered.... Truly the *Times* is a great paper, but it is a little—just a little—Blethenesque." In 1905, at the top of his game, Alden Blethen was sixty years old. Still, he would not rest content with his success.[100]

MUTE EVIDENCE OF HORROR WHICH VISITED 'FRISCO

SOUTH SIDE OF MARKET FROM MASON, LOOKING WEST.

PALACE HOTEL, WHEN FIRE FIRST STARTED.

WORK OF THE EARTHQUAKE IN SANSOME STREET.

LOOKING DOWN MARKET FROM SEVENTH, THURSDAY.

RUINS OF EXAMINER (HEARST) BUILDING.

CITY HALL.

Special 4-Page Photographic Supplement of **The Seattle Daily Times**

SEATTLE, WASHINGTON, MONDAY EVENING, APRIL 23, 1906.

FIRST PHOTOGRAPHS OF FIRE AND EARTHQUAKE!

The Call Building on Fire

Eager to provide Times *readers with graphic images of the 1906 San Francisco earthquake, managing editor C.B. Blethen offered $50 for each photograph that reached Seattle by train from the stricken city. A four-page photo supplement featured these images—pictures heavily enhanced with an artist's brush.*

(The Seattle Times, April 23, 1906)

Second Avenue was Seattle's main downtown thoroughfare, and Alden
Blethen hurried along it daily to reach The Seattle Times' offices,
located at the corner of Second and Union. The Times Building can be
seen at the far right of this photograph, which looks north up Second.

(PEMCO Webster and Stevens Collection, Seattle Museum of History and Industry)

5 "Raise Hell and Sell Newspapers"

*I*n 1905 Alden Blethen could feel just pride in his accomplishments. *The Seattle Times* had become a great newspaper, his family had prospered, and he had attained undisputed power and prestige in the community. Seattle, a backwater when he arrived only eight years before, was rapidly growing into an urban metropolis. Blethen could look down from his comfortable Queen Anne Hill mansion to the sprawling city below and know that he had helped to promote, even shape, its growth. Seattle had been good to Alden Blethen; the city had no stronger civic booster.

The controversial Colonel also had become a local institution. Everyone recognized him, purposefully striding down Second Avenue, immediately identifiable by his burly figure, the wavy silver-gray hair curling around his high collar, and the familiar gold-headed cane clenched firmly in his hand. He lunched daily at the Butler Hotel grillroom along with many of Seattle's influential businessmen, and as he made the long walk back to the paper along the city's busiest thoroughfare, people constantly hailed him for a comment on some political matter or for support in a new fund-raising campaign. Blethen loved the attention, but when he reached *The Times* building at Union Street, he turned back to the serious business of overseeing a newspaper that now had over 150 employees and more than 30,000 Seattle area readers. Alden Blethen was at the top of his game.[1]

Yet Blethen had been at the top of his game before, in Minneapolis, only to see *The Tribune* fire, the disastrous economic downturn of 1893, and a few poor business decisions cause his own tower of debt to come tumbling down around him. His experiences in Minneapolis had chastened him, and Alden Blethen, on the surface still the brash and self-confident gambler, now moved more cautiously in his own financial dealings. Determined to build and stabilize the business, he also wanted to protect his personal fortune. Blethen enjoyed being a benefactor to others, but he would never countenance receiving family charity again.

Alden Blethen was among the most patriotic of men and quite fond of decorating The Times *building with flags and bunting for holidays and other special occasions.*

(Washington State Historical Society)

THE TATTOOED MAN

He Still Does Not Own the Very Clothes Needed to Hide His Shame. **See Below.**

The rival P-I *seized any opportunity it could to satirize* The Times' *outspoken editor. Blethen was depicted as the "Tattooed Man" when it became public that he had placed all his possessions, including wearing apparel, under the name of The Times Investment Company to avoid personal taxes.*

(The Seattle Post-Intelligencer, August 16, 1908)

He had taken the first step toward long-term financial stability back in October 1900, when he created The Times Investment Company, allowing only Joseph and Clarance to join him as trustees and placing general oversight in the hands of his attorney and trusted advisor, Daniel Kelleher. The Times Printing Company held the assets of the newspaper, but Blethen placed all his real estate, stocks, and other personal property in the new investment company. Alden Blethen had learned by bitter experience that the newspaper business was often precarious, so he chose to separate the family's assets, hoping in this way to protect them from potential disaster.[2]

When he chartered the investment company, its capitalization included stock in over twenty mining companies in Washington and Alaska. The Blethens were not immune from Klondike fever, but all of these properties were in Joseph Blethen's name, held in trust for his mother and siblings until transferred to the new corporation. The Colonel had put everything he owned into building up *The Times* during his early years in Seattle, and, with limited capital, he made few other investments. Blethen had speculated in real estate with fair success ever since his first ventures as a young lawyer in Portland, Maine, but in Seattle's topsy-turvy economy, he moved slowly. He thought first to provide for his family's needs. Not until his sons had settled into homes of their own did he begin to make other land acquisitions in anticipation of Seattle's continued growth.[3]

Through the years, The Times Investment Company became the main vehicle for Blethen purchases, which grew substantially as the paper prospered. The company also shielded the Colonel from personal taxes, as he explained to the county auditor, because it "owns all property in possession of the Blethen family, even including wearing apparel." Rival newspapers later gleefully pounced on the remark, parodying the editor who did not even own the clothes on his back; but for a man who had two highly publicized brushes with bankruptcy, it was a necessary insurance measure.[4]

Even at *The Times* during these early years, the Colonel carefully monitored every expenditure. When the paper quickly outgrew its facilities in the Boston Block, Blethen chose to lease a building in 1902 rather than become heavily indebted by new construction. He negotiated with one of Seattle's pioneer families, the Dennys, to design the proposed *Times* Building according to his specifications, so that without any personal investment, he could still boast that he had a state-of-the-art plant tailored to his newspaper's needs. Always a devotée of the latest technology, Blethen nonetheless held off purchasing new presses until the paper's growing circulation required them and until

he could pay up front and avoid debt. "No other publisher in the United States ever made such an order," he assured readers, "and accompanied the same with cash." Since his earliest days in the city when *The Times* was a hand-to-mouth proposition, Blethen conducted all of his financial affairs through the Scandinavian-American Bank. The bank gave him credit during those hard times, but now the Colonel could claim that he had not been forced to borrow for any business improvements since 1901.[5]

Fiscal conservatism aside, Alden Blethen knew that the best way to assure his family's security was by the continuing growth of the newspaper. The Colonel placed the burden of the future on *The Seattle Times;* the paper's success came because of his own ingenuity and hard-won experience. When other men his age contemplated retirement, Blethen continued to hold tight to the reins of his newspaper empire, giving increasing responsibility to his sons, but remaining the paper's

Above left: Throughout his newspaper career, Alden Blethen always insisted on state-of-the-art facilities. The Denny Building at Second and Union was constructed specifically for The Times. Here in the composing room, lines of type were locked into frames. (Washington State Historical Society)

Above right: In The Times' "local room," reporters and editors gather around a desk to review stories for a 1905 evening edition. (Washington State Historical Society)

Left: Two employees at the Denny Building prepare to pour molten metal into molds to make the half-round impressions or stereos used on the presses. This photograph and others of the newspaper process were taken by Asahel Curtis in approximately 1905. (Washington State Historical Society)

THIS ISSUE OF THE SUNDAY TIMES.

THE SEATTLE SUNDAY TIMES today consists of 66 pages, carrying 193 columns of advertising—22 inches to the column, or an aggregate of **4,246 inches.**

One hundred and ninety-three columns in **The Times** is equal to 212 columns in **"The P.-I.,"** The San Francisco Examiner, or the leading papers of New York City.

This advertising is all carried at the regular contract rates made by **The Times Printing Company** for its Sunday Edition, and without a cent's discount to any man.

Under such circumstances, and with no extraordinary effort on the part of the publishers, **this record** is one to which reference will be made in the future.

For more than two years the merchants of Seattle have **known**, and most of them **have admitted** that **The Daily and Sunday Times** are vastly superior to any other medium ever employed in the Pacific Northwest.

While the Seattle merchants are extraordinarily liberal and permit themselves sometimes to be **jobbed** by fake advertisers and therefore squander a good deal of money—nevertheless **all of them agree** that they **get their full value** of return from **The Times.**

Within a month the "morning organ," failing to obtain what it thought it ought to have, and what it really needed to **maintain its expense account**—made up its mind that **success was to be obtained only** through the employment of **colors** in its publication.

Starting out two years and a half ago to **damn The Times** for having adopted the use of **colors**—when the "organ" moved into its new quarters it failed to prepare for this **modern necessity** in the publication of newspapers.

It labored under the impression that if it occupied some portion of a **great building** up on Union Street, and had a countingroom big enough for half the banks in the city—**business would come.**

But business didn't come any better in the big office on Union Street than it had been coming in the little one on Cherry Street—and so a conference took place between Wilson and Uncle 'Rastus, the Rip Van Winkle editor of The "P.-I.,"—and Little Sammy Weston, the **spice and pickles** of the business end of that publication.

Uncle 'Rastus swore in the name of **Joe Jefferson's best Rip Van Winkle performance** that he would have **none of The Times damnable color!**

Sweet Pickle Sammy, however, told Wilson that Uncle 'Rastus didn't have to **scratch gravel** and **hustle for the spondulicks** with which the cashier must be supplied on every Wednesday afternoon to meet the yawning maw of the ladies and gentlemen who assemble weekly in the vast office on Union Street.

So Wilson told Uncle 'Rastus that he sympathized with the attitude of the editor—but that **sympathy** wouldn't meet **payrolls,** nor liquidate **white paper and ink accounts.**

Wilson told Uncle 'Rastus **more.** He said that he had **sworn a great oath fourteen stories higher than the Alaska Building** that **never,** while he continued to be a **candidate for the United States Senate,** should any **red,** or **yellow,** or **blue,** or **green,** or **purple ink** be used upon the sacred pages of The Post-Intelligencer ! ! !

But Wilson was obliged to confess to Uncle 'Rastus that, in spite of his **fearful oath,** the men who were compelled to **manage** the **financial department** of The "P.-I." were shouting for **colored ink ! ! !**

As a result, a contract was made with the pressmen of The Chicago Tribune, and a **patent outside,** which doesn't fit The "P.-I." any better than **John L. Sullivan's** overcoat would fit **John L. Wilson**—and with the **ferocious pictures of tigers and bobcats** which are appearing in that **patent outside,** the tart and vinegary business manager of The "P.-I." **descended upon the business public of the town!**

With a half dozen imported solicitors from **Tacoma** and **Renton,** an effort was made to secure more **advertising on a single Sunday** than **The Times** ordinarily carried.

By discounting **card rates 70 per cent,** and carrying **"Servants Wanted"** and "Situations Wanted" **without charge,** The Sunday "P.-I." of two weeks ago actually led **The Times** in advertising by the splendid sum of **eleven inches ! ! !**

An attempt to repeat that **scheme,** however, last Sunday left the **poor old organ** in the rear by more **than 200 inches**—and **The Times** made no effort whatever to secure **illegitimate business.**

Alden Blethen used "speckled editorials" filled with bold type to emphasize his positions on local, national, and even international issues. Often opinionated and brash, he also believed that raising hell would sell newspapers.

(The Seattle Times, May 21, 1905)

personality and guiding force. He dedicated the rest of his life to building the power and prosperity of *The Times* and establishing a family newspaper dynasty. He did whatever it took. In later years his son C.B. recalled his father's favorite saying, one that aptly expressed his personal and business philosophy: "The road to success in journalism is to raise hell and sell newspapers."[6]

And raising hell was Alden Blethen's specialty. He had an opinion on every issue from national monetary policy to international trade, but he saved his passionate crusades for local affairs. Whether lambasting a city official, lobbying against municipal ownership, or touting a new development project, *The Times'* editor always took a strong stand. A majority might not agree with him, but they certainly could not ignore him. Critics frequently portrayed the Colonel as a tool of the Seattle business interests, but his loyalties were more selective. Alden Blethen followed his own vision for the city—a vision consistent only in its desire for progress in Seattle's development. As Seattle grew, so did *The Times,* and with it the fortunes of Alden Joseph Blethen.

Yet it is too simple to suggest that only opportunism and self-aggrandizement motivated him. Alden Blethen obviously had developed a deep love for this Pacific Coast boomtown and took pride in the role he played in directing the city's destiny. "He was endowed with a strong feeling of local patriotism," a member of his staff once wrote, "and fought the battles for everything he conceived to be to the advantage of Seattle with relentless persistence." He also nourished a deep, decidedly visceral dislike for certain men whom he felt stood in the way of progress or whose vision for the city's future clashed with his own. All too frequently Alden Blethen's crusades turned into vendettas, honest differences of opinion into bitter feuds. When taken to extremes, the qualities of personality that had ultimately made him a success—drive, ambition, dogged determination—could occasionally become an embarrassment.[7]

Blistering editorials in *The Times* served as the primary vehicles for his hell-raising. He accented his so-called "speckled editorials" with words and phrases in bold, black type, their pattern suggesting the sputtering, staccato intensity of his speech. He did not write all the editorials featuring the black type, but according to his son Joseph, the speckled style indicated that he had personally edited the piece. His opinions also frequently spilled over into news stories with huge headlines, and provocative leads, often accompanied by photographs or cartoons further embellishing a position or lampooning a targeted individual. As the editor-in-chief, Alden Blethen supervised all aspects of the paper, and his stamp was visible throughout. But, as a rival newspaper editor later suggested, in those boldly highlighted editorials, "often of inordinate length and frequently reflecting grievances and fancied wrongs, his unique personality was revealed in every line."[8]

Through the years Alden Blethen waged many editorial battles over home-town or statewide issues, with politics and civic development most likely to arouse his attention. But his all-out wars with individuals elicited the most savage prose. There were many who momentarily drew the editor's ire and felt the sting of his disapproval, but three stand out because of the depth of the enmity they provoked, and the impact of their feuds on Blethen's own career as well as Seattle's growth. These men, Erastus Brainerd, former head of Seattle's Klondike Information Bureau who became editor of *The P-I*, city engineer R.H. Thomson, and the Reverend Mark Matthews of the First Presbyterian Church were all, like Blethen, strong and forceful personalities. Each sought the power to shape Seattle to his own standards. Whether the issue was the political, moral, or physical development of the city, these men stood their ground, colliding head on with Alden Blethen. No one came out unscathed. Their feuds became public and ugly, begun on the pages of *The Times*, but often continued in other venues—from the city hall to the pulpit to the courtroom.[9]

The most bitter dispute began with rival newspaperman Erastus Brainerd, and this ongoing slugfest provided the backdrop for the next decade of Blethen's career. Blethen

had sized up *The P-I* as his only major competition when he first came to town, and *The Times* had prodded and poked fun at the staid morning paper ever since. But the rivalry, largely circulation-driven, rarely took on a personal tone during those early years. Things changed when Brainerd became editor. He began to trade poisoned barbs with the Colonel as soon as he arrived at *The Post-Intelligencer* in January 1904. Thin-skinned and intemperate, he did not allow Blethen a wide berth. The two began a war of words that one contemporary likened to "the

In the intensifying battle with The P-I *for circulation, Blethen developed a lively, frequently sensationalistic, format to set* The Times *apart from its staid rival. In this unusual edition, nine full-line headlines were stacked at the top of the front page.*

(The Seattle Times, May 25, 1904)

scrapping of two eight year old school boys." But these were not boys. They were bull-headed men, each quite unwilling to concede an inch to the other.[10]

If Alden Blethen and Erastus Brainerd were alike in their volatility and willfulness, their backgrounds could not have been more dissimilar. Brainerd, the product of New England society, studied at Harvard and traveled widely in Europe before beginning a peripatetic career that ultimately led him through art and theatrical circles into journalism. He had gained a reputation as a highly literate writer and editor for newspapers in New York, Philadelphia, and Atlanta, but he had little success in business. Brainerd arrived in Seattle in the summer of 1890, on the rebound from two financial failures in running his own newspapers. He became the editor of *The Press-Times*, and was immediately thrown into the maelstrom of Seattle journalism where papers seemed to fail or change hands on a weekly basis. Brainerd tried gamely to make *The Press-Times* a lively alternative to the well-entrenched *P-I,* and he gained ground until the Panic of 1893 hit Seattle. The paper's precarious balance sheet showed increasing losses, and the owners let Brainerd go.[11]

Alden Blethen later claimed that the cause of Brainerd's animosity toward him was resentment over Blethen's success in transforming the "wreck" that Brainerd had left behind into a highly profitable newspaper. "For Brainerd," he commented editorially, "the success of the Editor of *The Times* was sufficient to incur his everlasting hatred and his desire for constant vengeance." Yet the two exchanged cordial letters during the years after Brainerd left *The Press-Times* and served first as a state land commissioner and then as Seattle's publicity agent during the Klondike rush, showing a distant but cooperative work-ing relationship. Only later, when they became head-to-head rivals, with money and prestige as well as egos on the line, did the ill-feelings rapidly escalate. The feud with Brainerd began in 1904 and lasted well after *The P-I* editor left his position in 1911. It became the impetus for many of Blethen's journalistic decisions during that period. Of all the men who challenged the Colonel, Brainerd in many respects threatened Blethen the most because of his connections in both politics and journalism.[12]

Former senator John L. Wilson, a career politician who had had been the new state of Washington's first representative in Congress and then served as its senator for one term, hired Brainerd as editor of *The Post Intelligencer.* Wilson was the acknowledged head of Washington's Republican Party machine, but in 1899 his days as a power broker seemed threatened by the loss of his Senate seat and rising Populist and Fusion sentiment in the state. The purchase of a newspaper offered him the chance to redeem that power and add to his political base. Wilson, it was widely rumored, planned to use *The P-I* to boost his own campaign to get back into the Senate. He needed an editor who could go after his opponents and "dish out the hot stuff unsparingly." The rabid Republican Erastus Brainerd could fill that role perfectly, and Wilson entrusted him with the additional tasks of loudly supporting Republican causes and, of course, advancing Wilson's own political career.[13]

The arrangement was not unusual. George Turner, *The P-I*'s former owner and also a politician, had frequently faced accusations that he had used the paper as his personal political organ. Despite the trend toward more independence in the press and an increasing emphasis on journalistic ethics, most newspapers in the rising young cities of the

West still remained heavily partisan. "It was a devotion and sometimes a frenzy," wrote one long-time Seattle political reporter. "It was commonly believed that newspaper support or opposition meant everything to a party and its candidate. Newspapers afforded the only means for diffusion of party doctrine and they diffused it plentifully." Certainly the role of party spokesman did not displease Erastus Brainerd, as he considered himself above all else a "statesman of the press."[14]

Yet Brainerd was not even-handed or diplomatic in the grand tradition of the statesman. "He dealt with everything, especially everything political, with no gloves," wrote one fellow journalist; another described him as an "egotistic dyspeptic who wielded a trenchant pen." His style made him enemies, and he seemed to relish the controversy.[15]

Alden Blethen, certainly no stranger to controversy himself, had made a career of attacking rival editors in Minneapolis. Yet no other opponent, not even Will Haskell, Blethen's *Minneapolis Tribune* nemesis, struck such a sensitive chord in the Colonel. Perhaps Brainerd's privileged background and more polished writing skills, or possibly his strident style, threatened *The Times'* editor. Blethen always maintained that Brainerd had started their war of words, and that he had merely followed in kind. Certainly there was never a honeymoon period between the two men. Brainerd had referred to *The Times* as *The P-I's* "comic contemporary" on his first day in the editorial chair. Blethen evidently interpreted that remark and other barbs as signals of the confrontational stance Brainerd planned to take. Both editors had "an explosive capacity for vituperation" and quickly embarked on a dangerous and destructive rivalry with politics and boosterism as their fodder.[16]

Politically, once silver Republicanism and Fusion had lost their local following, the

Study These Three Pictures!

HON. WILLIAM RANDOLPH HEARST

This is the man whom The New York Evening Post and Seattle Post-Intelligencer characterized as "the nameless candidate." Mr. Hearst is 41 years of age, was born in San Francisco, and became a newspaper publisher as soon as he graduated from college. He is the only child of the late Senator Hearst of California.

He inherited with his mother a fortune of about fifteen million dollars—and has invested in seven different newspapers nearly half that sum of money. He has made a phenomenal success of The San Francisco Examiner—the net profits of which exceeded $200,000 last year—an equal success of The Chicago American and Examiner, morning and evening and Sunday publications, whose net profits exceeded $400,000 in 1903.

Mr. Hearst also owns The New York Evening Journal, and with his mother, The New York American, whose net profits were greater than the profits of The Chicago publications—thus yielding an income of more than $1,000,000 from the publications in the three cities.

Mr. Hearst is a member of Congress from New York City, receiving the largest majority ever given a candidate from his district, and is recognized as one of the most aggressive and fearless editors and publishers living.

He is a candidate for the presidency on the Democratic ticket, to be determined in St. Louis in July of the present year. Mr. Hearst is a large man physically and shows himself to be an extraordinary manager and judge of men.

MR. ERASTUS BRAINERD
Editor of the Post-Intelligencer

The man who denounces Hearst as the "Nameless Candidate" and cartoons him as an idiot, characterizes his neighbors as "knockers" and pitches into most everything.

MR. ARTHUR BRISBANE
Chief Editorial Writer for the Hearst Newspapers

Mr. Arthur Brisbane, the chief editorial writer for the Hearst newspapers, was initiated by the late Charles A. Dana, fully developed by the late Mr. Joseph Pulitzer of the New York World, on a very high salary, and subsequently employed by Mr. Hearst at a still greater one.

Mr. Brisbane was educated abroad, chiefly in Germany and France, and speaks both languages fluently. He is acknowledged to be one of the ablest writers in the field of journalism today, and all-in-all perhaps has no equal among American editors. It was he that indited that splendid letter addressed to The New York Herald showing Mr. Hearst's capabilities and strength among the people.

It is a credit to Mr. Hearst that he had the good judgment as well as the financial ability to take such a man as Arthur Brisbane away from such a publisher as Joseph Pulitzer has proven himself to be. Mr. Hearst has received more personal encouragement from Mr. Brisbane as a presidential candidate than from all other sources combined. Even the men who despise Hearst most, are compelled to take their hats off in recognition of Arthur Brisbane's wonderful journalistic ability.

Colonel had returned to his claims that he ran an independent paper, beholden to no special interests. As Blethen editorialized, "*The Times* is a personal paper. It belongs solely to the Blethen family. It has no strings on it. It is rather independent in politics.... It has no axes to grind. It has no other ambition in the world than to publish the best possible newspaper." But to continue in business *The Times* had to stake out a territory differentiating it from its competitors. Since the leading Republican in the state owned *The P-I*, Alden Blethen had no choice but to make his "independent" position primarily a Democratic one.[17]

The feud between Alden Blethen and Erastus Brainerd began almost immediately after Brainerd became The P-I *editor in 1904. When* The P-I *ran an unflattering picture of William Randolph Hearst and belittled him as a presidential candidate, Blethen retaliated with his own uncomplimentary portrait of Brainerd.*

(The Seattle Times, April 17, 1904)

Political differences ignited a hostile exchange between the two papers within weeks after Brainerd began work at *The P-I*. *The Times* had boosted Blethen's favorite Democrat, William Randolph Hearst, as a presidential candidate since the previous spring, daily running lengthy articles on his campaign appearances and political philosophy. Brainerd, with Republican fervor, belittled the Hearst candidacy, calling him a comic "Katzenjammer kid" and publishing an unflattering portrait of the newspaper magnate labeled "the unspeakable candidate." Blethen, infuriated, replied with a front-page defense of Hearst and added his own equally unflattering depiction of Brainerd. *The Times* sandwiched a drawing of *The P-I* editor, looking dissipated and seedy, between statesmanlike portraits of Hearst and Arthur Brisbane, the chief editorial writer for the Hearst newspaper chain. The accompanying article instructed readers to study the three pictures and then draw their own conclusions, yet the writer offered his own gratuitous advice: "The contrast will show to what depths of infamy people claiming respectability may descend when politics be involved." The insulting feature caused a furor.[18]

At the same time the two editors paraded their political differences, they also sparred over Seattle boosterism. In April 1904, *The Times* published a front-page exposé on the government's neglect of the Puget Sound Naval Yard at Bremerton, claiming that the Republican Party diverted shipbuilding to California bases to encourage that state's support of Teddy Roosevelt in the upcoming presidential election. *The P-I* took exception to the charge and called *The Times* the "evening knocker," accusing the paper of undercutting the reputation of Seattle and the region by these false allegations. The Colonel regarded the term "knocker"—"one

Blethen admired newspaper magnate William Randolph Hearst as an editor and backed his run for the presidency so strongly that The P-I *insinuated Hearst owned an interest in* The Times.

(The Seattle Times)

who works against the interests of the city in which he lives"—as the ultimate criticism, for above all he prided himself on his contributions to the community's development. "A knocker is the most offensive term in the English language," he later wrote. "There never has been a cause of any name or nature presented for the benefit of Seattle that 'the Times' has not promptly, vigorously and freely aided with all its power."[19]

Feeling he had suffered a very personal affront, Blethen began to develop his own names for his rival editor. A few of the milder ones included "grandmother Brainerd," "the old woman of Cherry Street," and "John L. Wilson's hired man," but "imbecile," "pinhead" and "crooked and crack-brained whelp" soon followed. By June, Harry Chadwick over at *The Argus* commented that Brainerd had nothing left to be worried about, writing that "Alden J. Blethen has now thrown his entire printable vocabulary at his offending head." But Chadwick was wrong—the battle lines had been drawn, but the heavy artillery was not yet deployed.[20]

After two months of the name-calling, both Blethen and Brainerd apologized to their readers for the ongoing conflict, promising to refrain from such insults in the future. But the truce was short-lived, and by the fall of 1904, as election time approached, the attacks became increasingly vicious. Blethen expanded his targets to Senator Wilson, and delighted in exposing the "campaign of falsehood, slander and vilification" carried on by Wilson and his fellow Republicans. In contrast to the strong partisanship that Wilson required from his "hired man," *The Times* continued to proclaim its independence, although Blethen could do little but support rival Democratic candidates, developing a *Times* slate of candidates and promising to give all comers a forum.[21]

The Republican Party had retained power in Washington almost continuously since the Civil War, and it had warmly embraced business interests. Opponents accused the party of selling out to the railroad monopolies in general and James J. Hill, the owner of the Great Northern, in particular. A broad agitation for reform helped to elect a few Populist and Fusion candidates in the state, but when those movements lost momentum, Washington's Republicans had strongly reasserted themselves. In the notorious 1904 Republican state convention, the railroad interests resumed their domination of the party, ramming through the nomination of their own hand-picked gubernatorial candidate. Outside the state, rivals had taken to calling Washington "jimhillville."[22]

One of the big issues of the 1904 campaign was whether to institute a state railroad commission to monitor this powerful interest group. *The P-I* strongly opposed the commission because of John L. Wilson's corporate connections. Wilson staunchly advocated for James J. Hill's interests, having borrowed the money from him to buy *The P-I*. Ironically, his most vigorous opponent, Alden Blethen, also owed Hill a debt for keeping him in the newspaper business. Blethen carefully tiptoed around this landmine, favoring the railroad commission, but with a more subdued political voice than usual. He preferred, instead, to save his loudest blasts for other Republican enemies, most notably the political candidates favored by Brainerd and Wilson.

In particular, *The Times* bitterly denounced the Republican candidate for sheriff and accused a county clerk who supported him of graft and perjury. The clerk filed charges of criminal libel against *The Times* and the battle

In 1906, William Randolph Hearst ran as the Democratic candidate for governor of New York. On the night of the election, The Seattle Times *brashly proclaimed Hearst the winner. The day after the 1906 election, the headlines tell the true story—Hearst was defeated.*

(The Seattle Times, *November 6, 1906, November 7, 1906*)

was on. With headlines boldly splashed across almost half a page—**DESPERADOES SHOW THEIR HAND**—*The Times* accused John L. Wilson and Brainerd of engineering the lawsuit. *The Times* labeled Wilson a "political guttersnipe" and "a whelp of the most unscrupulous character," claiming he had attempted to make political capital on the eve of the election by having Blethen arrested. Alden Blethen had not been dragged to jail, as his paper's headlines implied. In fact, the prosecuting attorney brought the bond to his office and politely asked him to sign it. It was good copy, though, and *The Times* made the most of it.[23]

As Blethen focused on the lawsuit, Erastus Brainerd unleashed his most scathing and personal attacks yet. In an editorial simply titled "Blethen," Brainerd denied that anyone from *The P-I* had a hand in the libel suit, but blasted *The Times'* editor in his inimitable way, dredging up the Bank of New England as just one more example of a pattern of criminal activity. The Bank's collapse had become a public issue again only weeks before, when Blethen's former Minneapolis attorneys sued him, asking additional compensation for their role in the bankruptcy proceedings.[24]

Brainerd's brief discussion of the Colonel's past business practice became the basis for further accusations about his unspeakable behavior, in which he labeled *The Times'* editor a "debauched, half insane and mouthing savage who is almost nightly to be seen staggering crazy drunk in public resorts among decent people who fear the foul tongue and are disgusted by the conduct of this journalistic strumpet." Brainerd wound up with the most scathing epithet of all, calling Blethen a "paretic mattoid who should be deprived of the control of a daily paper and put under restraint." All of Seattle turned to their dictionaries to learn that one editor claimed the other had gone mad, attributing his condition to advanced stages of syphilis or acute alcoholism, and recommending that he be institutionalized. Alden Blethen, who "excelled in invective," had met his match, and

---

BLETHEN

That model of all the virtues, that pure-minded, clean-hearted person, Alden J. Blethen, has been arrested for criminal libel.

The suit is of record. It is open to all the world. It is as open as the record in the case of the Bank of New England of Minneapolis, in 1893. In that the reputation of Blethen was shown to be so crooked and so involved that even now he has to slink and sneak through Minneapolis on a Sunday in order to avoid arrest.

Dastardly and desperate, with failing fortune and mind, with only the rancid remains of a foul character, Blethen, a social pariah and outcast, seeks to drag down to his own abysm of degradation all who are engaged in the business which he disgraces and defiles.

No sooner is he arrested than he cries out that the controlling owner of *The Post-Intelligencer* is the cause of his being seized by the iron hand of the law.

His plea, if true, would not operate as a defense of his crime. The man who can put Blethen in the walls of a penitentiary or of an insane asylum will do the public a service.

There is now and has been no connection or arrangement of any description between anyone concerned in or connected with *The Post-Intelligencer* and the candidates on the county ticket, the county commissioners, or the young man against whom Blethen has committed his crime. There is no more such connection than there is between ocean and sky.

The Post-Intelligencer does not, at this moment, propose to waste further space on this debauched, half insane and mouthing savage, who is almost nightly to be seen staggering, crazy drunk, in public resorts among decent people, who fear the foul tongue and are disgusted by the conduct of this journalistic strumpet.

In justice to the public it is time that this paretic mattoid should be deprived of the control of a daily newspaper and put under restraint where he can no longer abuse, blackguard, and blackmail the public.

Erastus Brainerd, The Seattle Post-Intelligencer, November 6, 1904

Harry Chadwick of *The Argus,* in the past a bitter Blethen critic, called Brainerd's accusation "the vilest attack on a human being which had ever been made in the press of the state of Washington."[25]

Blethen waited until the following Sunday to make his reply, taking time to build up his own ammunition or, as *The Argus* suggested, to save his response for the Sunday edition in which advertising rates were highest. Blethen chose not to trade further insults, nor to address the personal references, but rather to defend himself, point by point, against the allegations of *The P-I* about his conduct in the Bank of New England litigation. Making a personal request of readers to compare his evidence to Brainerd's "lies," Blethen devoted a full page to the Bank of New England, reprinting testimonials from a number of his creditors and including a large portrait and letter from his old Kent's Hill roommate, William Pattee, who applauded Blethen's efforts to repay the Bank of New England debts. In days to come the editorial page continued to print articles and letters of support for Blethen's character and his philanthropy.[26]

The feud between Brainerd and Blethen had little effect on the 1904 elections. Voters followed their traditional patterns, sweeping Republicans into the governorship and almost every other major office in both Seattle and King County. But the exchange of editorial insults—ostensibly political—continued for many years, regularly intensifying at election time. And the bitter warfare did sell newspapers. "People liked the newspapers fighting each other," observed one long-time Seattle businessman, Joshua Green, who knew Blethen and Brainerd well. "A lot of the rivalry was put on because the newspapers knew it pleased people." Several editors also agreed. Harry Chadwick called the "paretic mattoid" exchange "a cold-blooded business proposition," while Brainerd received a complimentary letter from a fellow editor in Vancouver, British Columbia, about the tactic: "We are much interested in the little newspaper war going on in your town. It livens things up. Honors seem to be with you."[27]

If Blethen, in the eyes of some, had lost the first round to Brainerd in their battle of words, he was determined to win the more important circulation war. In 1905 and several years to follow, *The Times* was as bold, lively, and colorful as it ever had been. Blethen had long been labeled "Hearstesque," not only for his political allegiances to the newspaper magnate, but also his adoption of Hearst's notoriously sensationalistic style. Everything in *The Seattle Times* of that period seemed bigger than life, from the huge typefaces and lavish use of photographs to its overblown coverage of all sorts of murder or mayhem. Opponents repeatedly chided *The Times* for its "yellow" tinge, and yellow it was, but the paper also brought its readers the best of what the new technology and expanded wire service access could provide. *The Times,* as one of its editorial columnists wrote, "from cover to cover reveled in color," produced on its state-of-the-art presses. Its Sunday editions were jam-packed with fashion features, short stories, cartoons, and photographic essays supplied by several news agencies to which the paper subscribed.[28]

Blethen began to crow about his paper's technical superiority to *The P-I* as the Brainerd feud moved into its second round. Blethen, as had been his practice throughout his career, had consistently updated his equipment, gambling, in particular, on the new color technology. The more conservative *P-I* lagged behind, even condemning *The Times* editorially for its use of color.

In their war of words, Blethen and Brainerd battled not only for reputation, but also for advertising dollars. The "Seattle Philosophy" of this Times *want ad also seemed to mirror the editorial policy of both of these irascible newspapermen.*

(The Seattle Times, November 5, 1906)

According to Blethen's account, "John L. Wilson swore to a hundred men in this city that he would never publish a paper in colors," but the brilliant appearance of *The Times* and its popular appeal eventually forced him to concede. Blethen took particular delight in portraying Brainerd and Wilson as technological bumpkins. He continually expressed pity for "poor Uncle 'Rastus," so hopelessly behind *The Times,* writing: "The only trouble about Uncle 'Rastus is that...the old man has gotten rusty. We suppose he isn't to blame because one must get outside the frog ponds and the coon bushes of Puget Sound to keep in touch with the world."[29]

Ultimately, the numbers told the story as the two papers vied for the attention of Seattle's reading public and, of equal importance, its advertisers. For the year 1905, *The Times* claimed an average daily circulation of almost 38,000, nearly a third more than *The*

One of The Times' *early advertisers was Frederick and Nelson, which became a true department store when it expanded into the Rialto Building on Second Avenue between Madison and Spring Streets.*

P-I, and its *Sunday Times* had an even wider lead among readers. Advertising, too, if *The Times'* numbers can be believed, showed Blethen's paper far in the lead, boasting well over 135,000 more column inches of advertisements than *The P-I.* Blethen enjoyed flaunting *The Times'* advantage, even offering prizes of as much as $1,000 to anyone who could prove *The P-I* circulation figures were even lower than the paper claimed.[30]

During this time, *The Times* linked many of its promotional strategies to Seattle boosterism, as reflected in a number of popular home-grown features appearing most often in the Sunday edition. A long-running contest to select "The Most Beautiful Woman in Washington State" from photographs sent in by readers had given way in 1905 to several continuing features highlighting some of Seattle's most prominent male citizens. "Men Behind the Seattle Spirit" celebrated established business leaders who had spearheaded Seattle's development, while a series called "Reasons Why Seattle is a Young Man's Town" focused on up-and-coming newcomers who were also some of the city's most ardent boosters. Full-page portraits of these Seattle movers and shakers, frequently set in fanciful borders, vied for space in the Sunday magazine section with photographic essays of local scenery. *The Times* prominently featured the work of local photographer Edward Curtis, then gaining national attention for his images of North American Indians.[31]

The contents of *The Times* also indicated that women had become an increasingly important segment of its readership. The paper devoted eight pages of the Sunday edition to articles of feminine interest, and began a special series on independent Seattle women that included profiles of "girls" who held jobs as diverse as working in cigar factories and

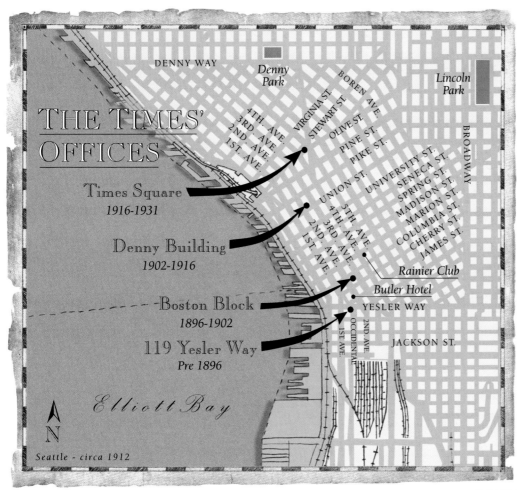

THE TIMES' OFFICES

DENNY WAY

Denny Park

Lincoln Park

BOREN AVE.

VIRGINIA ST.
STEWART ST.
OLIVE ST.
PINE ST.
PIKE ST.
UNION ST.
UNIVERSITY ST.
SENECA ST.
SPRING ST.
MADISON ST.
MARION ST.
COLUMBIA ST.
CHERRY ST.
JAMES ST.

BROADWAY

4TH. AVE.
3RD. AVE.
2ND. AVE.
1ST. AVE.

5TH. AVE.
4TH. AVE.
3RD. AVE.
2ND. AVE.
1ST. AVE.

Times Square
1916-1931

Denny Building
1902-1916

Boston Block
1896-1902

119 Yesler Way
Pre 1896

Rainier Club

Butler Hotel

YESLER WAY

OCCIDENTAL
1ST. AVE.
2ND. AVE.

JACKSON ST.

Elliott Bay

N

Seattle - circa 1912

(Bo Hok Cline)

lumber mills. One installment even focused on "The Girl in the Printing Office," describing capable women who had gone into the printing trade, despite the fact that "women engaged in mechanical pursuits are generally thought by the cold-blooded bosses to be a nuisance." However, Alden Blethen still had little use for women in the newspaper business. At this time a San Francisco newspaper quoted him as saying, "I have one woman on my paper—a society editor. I have no more because as a general proposition I have not found them equal to the work. I say this in all deference to the sex."[32]

If Blethen's policy toward women on *The Seattle Times* was not as open-minded as the features appearing in the paper would imply, he did take on some crusades that reflected the growing influence of progressive reform movements springing up around the country. An increasing number of Americans in the early twentieth century, outraged by the abuses and excesses that had resulted from the country's rapid industrialization and urbanization, chose to take action. Whether fighting for the underdog, breaking up corporate monopoly, advocating temperance, or exposing political graft and corruption, activists sought to promote change and renew the moral values of American society.[33]

Alden Blethen only selectively embraced progressive causes. What linked him most conspicuously to the reformers of his day seemed to be his desire to better the city, to make the urban environment attractive enough to promote further growth and development. Seattle was a young Western city, not yet facing the problems of the older, crowded urban centers of the East, but with concerns of its own caused by explosive, uncontrolled growth. Its population numbered barely 30,000 when Blethen arrived in 1896, but the Klondike boom raised that number to over 80,000 by the turn of the century. And Seattle had continued to grow steadily, doubling by 1905 and reaching well over 230,000, similar in size to Kansas City, by the end of the decade.[34]

Seattle's city fathers and its business leaders wanted to see this growth continue, but they could not ignore the complex problems it presented. Citizens clamored for better city services—water systems, streetcars, electric lights, sewers, and sidewalks—while they hotly debated whether local government or private enterprise could best provide them. And what about the social effects of such growth? How would the city handle the problems of poverty and vice? Did the government of the old-time politics and old-time allegiances really act in the public interest? Seattle was increasingly dominated by newcomers who demanded answers, forcing the city into a period of rigorous self-examination.

The Seattle Times, as the political outsider and vocal proponent of the city's interests, had a wonderful opportunity to establish itself as the pied piper of these eager reformers and do-gooders. And the paper did frequently embrace that role, eagerly campaigning for causes that would promote civic betterment. In 1905 *The Times* launched an investigation into the wretched conditions of Seattle's poor, finding that many got their food from the city's dump and found shelter in shacks made out of bits of refuse. Another series took on the so-called Italian garbage trust, blaming it for unsanitary conditions in the city and advocating reform of the municipal garbage ordinances. And despite lingering community prejudices, *The Times* even launched a highly publicized fund-raising effort to pay the legal expenses for Ah Sou, a young Chinese girl protesting an arranged marriage that would send her back to China as a virtual slave.[35]

Yet these crusades did not establish *The Times* as the champion of reform elements or stop the frequent rumors that Alden Blethen took payoffs from corporate interests or had a financial stake in the city's illicit gambling and liquor establishments. The Colonel's opposition to some progressive measures and his continuing criticisms of important community activists damaged his credibility as a reform leader.

Seattle city engineer R.H. Thomson became one of Blethen's most frequent targets and the personal feud between the two men escalated during the 1906 election campaigns. Alden Blethen and R.H. Thomson had much in common as avid Seattle boosters and energetic advocates of the city's continuing growth and development, yet the two clashed bitterly. Blethen seemed to blame all civic ills on Thomson, and throughout this period relentlessly attacked him on the pages of the paper. Thomson ignored the gibes for years, but ultimately retaliated by filing repeated libel suits against Blethen and *The Times*.[36]

Thomson had come to Seattle in 1881 as a young man of twenty-five and soon received an appointment as city surveyor. By 1892, after stints in railroad and mining engineering, he was named city engineer, a position he held until 1911. His duties included overseeing all original construction projects conducted for municipal benefit—from sewers, water mains, and sidewalks to streets, bridges and public buildings. Described as an intense and serious-minded Scotsman, a hardworking and competent engineer, Thomson was also a dreamer, with grand visions for what Seattle could become. A technical man with a streak of imagination, he let no natural obstacle keep him from the boring, tunneling, grading, and building necessary to complete the infrastructure for a great city. More than any other man, people said, R.H. Thomson had changed the face of Seattle.[37]

Thomson also made many enemies along the way. Tenacious and inflexible, he disdained those who did not share his particular visions. Some called him "arrogant and dictatorial" and others decried his insensitivity to the disruption and high costs of his elaborate schemes. "There are thousands of people in this city," wrote *The Argus*, "who don't believe that City Engineer Thomson is the proper man for the position he holds." No one in the city, however, proved more scathing in their criticisms of Thomson than Alden Blethen. To the Colonel, he seemed a despot and a czar, extravagant, nefarious, even criminal. And Blethen made his criticisms highly public, in literally hundreds of editorials and front-page exposés of Thomson's reportedly negligent and incompetent behavior.[38]

The feud apparently originated just before the turn of the century, when the city's burgeoning population had strained its existing water systems to the limit. Many residents thought development of private wells would meet the city's future water needs, while others, like *The Times'* editor, foresaw much

greater growth. Blethen initially supported Thomson's ambitious plan to gravity feed the water by pipeline from the Cedar River, a distance of nearly thirty miles. He also joined Thomson in advocating the city's purchase of the entire watershed when private power companies threatened to pollute its waters with generating plants.[39]

But construction delays and design problems slowed the completion of the system. Costs rose, and *The Times* soon voiced the complaints of Seattle citizens who questioned Thomson's efficiency. When the Cedar River pipeline finally opened in 1901 and water shortages continued, the paper blamed the city engineer. At that time Blethen's critiques of Thomson were still more joke than jab— "it is certainly evident that he doesn't belong to the Baptist persuasion," the Colonel wryly

Alden Blethen feuded continually with R.H. Thomson, the visionary Seattle city engineer whom Blethen regarded as arrogant and inflexible. In one of many front-page exposés of Thomson's alleged incompetence, The Times *accused him of wasting the taxpayers' money.*

(The Seattle Times, *October 4, 1907*)

commented, "or this water famine would never have taken place."[40]

Some observers have suggested that personal issues, not civic ones, may have pushed *The Times'* editor over the line with Thomson. Blethen indignantly protested the repeated fines levied on him by the city for illegally watering his lawn during rationing; he constantly battled to have the roads paved leading to his home. He was later accused of starting the feud over a disputed property survey made by one of the city engineer's deputies. But whatever the motivation, Blethen's criticisms began to lose their gentle edge as Thomson proceeded with other expensive and controversial projects around the city.[41]

During the city election campaigns in the spring of 1906, the attacks against Thomson in *The Times* grew particularly strong. Thomson strongly advocated municipal ownership, the popular progressive crusade to wrest control of public utilities from private hands. Just as he believed that the Cedar River water system must be owned and run "for the benefit of the people," so Thomson advocated municipally owned light and power companies as well as street railway systems. A Municipal Ownership Party, formed in late 1905, ran its own candidate for mayor, William Hickman Moore, who by just fifteen votes beat the conservative, business-backed Republican candidate in the city election. No Democrat ran, and *The Times* supported Moore, but claimed it backed the man, not the principle of municipal ownership. The paper applauded Moore's efforts to reform city government, but rumor had it that, behind the scenes, the candidate had made a deal, promising to get rid of Thomson as city engineer in exchange for Blethen's public support.[42]

But despite these rumors, Thomson retained his post during the Moore administration, just as he had through several previous political regimes. His relationship with Blethen only grew worse. During the summer of 1906, Thomson set the Colonel ablaze with his proposal for a bond issue to raise $8 million for a city-owned street railway system. In the fall voters would also be asked to pass two more municipal bond measures, one for funding a second Cedar River pipeline and the other for constructing a canal linking Lake Washington to Puget Sound. *The Times* joined business leaders in advocating the Lake Washington canal proposal, but Blethen fiercely opposed the other two measures, making it a hotly contested campaign.

The Times repeatedly attacked the "municipal ownership faddists" whose plans could jeopardize Seattle's credit with investors. On the editorial page, Blethen insisted that city control would make the streetcar system more costly and less efficient than it was under private ownership; other cities had been bankrupted by such experiments, he claimed. His arguments were not new—he had made them back in Minneapolis defending Thomas Lowry's street railway franchise. Blethen also had strong personal attachments in the Seattle fight. His old ally Jacob Furth was president of the Seattle Electric Company, the current operator of the city's transit system. Blethen felt indebted to Furth, affectionately known as "Uncle Jake," who had befriended him during his first days in the city.

The P-I jumped into the fight, and in a complex reversal of roles, came out for municipal ownership. Brainerd clearly believed that anyone who opposed the bonds must be a "pawn" of the Electric Company, and he accused Blethen of being a hired gun of Jacob Furth. In private letters to The *P-I*'s owner, Brainerd claimed to have convincing evidence that Furth "bought Blethen in the most glaring and flagrant manner." Some others in town had the same suspicions. The Seattle Electric Company was one of *The Times'* largest advertisers, and the paper had run numerous flattering stories about Furth.[43]

Despite the spotlight on the street railway issue, *The Times* had also made Thomson an issue in the fight against the Cedar River water bonds. Blethen favored expansion of the Cedar River system, but in a very direct slap at Thomson, urged voters to reject bonds for these improvements, arguing: "If the present system has been so improperly constructed that the city is not receiving more than 70% of the flow of water which it should get, then we are certainly against the expenditure of two and a quarter million dollars by the same force of men who demonstrated their incompetency in the first instance." To prove Thomson's incompetence, attacks against him in *The Times* grew feverish. Bold headlines charged **MORE OF THOMSON'S BLUNDERS!** News articles detailed his errors and extravagances. The evening after the election the top half of the front page blared the news—**THE TIMES WINS—Municipal Ownership Lost in a Blizzard of Votes—1436 Majority**. Careful readers found that the street railway bond proposal had been defeated by 1436 votes, but *The Times'* campaign against Thomson had failed as voters approved the water bonds.[44]

From that time forward, the attacks stepped up. Blethen obviously was galled by the power of the city engineer and his ability to make himself indispensable. A front-page story in May 1907 described the nearly unlimited authority given to the engineer by the wording of the city charter:

> Thomson can hinder and delay, if not prevent important public works such as street

improvements, sewer mains, water mains, lighting service, and the like in any section of the city. Likewise he can forward improvements of the character indicated.... He is absolute master of the specifications and assessment rolls...he can either make or unmake councilmen and other city officers, he can control committees and mold their reports to suit his own purpose, and he can even bring the mayor of this city on his knees, begging favors.[45]

The Thomson feud soon carried over into a campaign against the Moore administration. Blethen had quickly become dissatisfied with Mayor Moore who, after retaining Thomson, had added insult to injury by publicly acknowledging the important role the engineer played in city government. Moore had called Thomson "the brains of the administration," an unfortunate characterization that *The Times* parodied ceaselessly. Cartoons appeared daily, drawn by *The Times'* noted artist, Doc Hagar, which portrayed the top of the mayor's head swinging open and the small figure of Thomson popping out.[46]

Thomson rarely responded publicly to the Colonel's digs and insults, although in private he complained of the unfairness of Blethen's attacks. As he wrote to a friend, "I am not acquainted with anything more brutal and cowardly than the actions of an unprincipled editor who always has the opportunity of vilifying those who have no possible means of making full reply." Many local journalists had asked Blethen to tone down his rhetoric and back away. "City Engineer Thomson may be 'off' in some respects," *The Argus* wrote, "but he is certainly not as bad as he is painted by *The Seattle Times*."[47] H.C. Pigott, a Seattle journalist who ran a printing company and edited his own small newspaper, was most distressed by what the Thomson feud indicated about the Colonel's character:

Blethen strongly opposed the concept of municipal ownership and used The Times *to fight against two 1906 ballot measures. When voters turned down one of the proposals,* The Times *took credit, claiming victory with one of its most sensational, though misleading, headlines.*

(The Seattle Times, September 13, 1906)

Right: R.H. Thomson believed that the steep terrain of downtown Seattle hurt the city's potential to expand and began an ambitious program of regrading. Huge hillsides were cut away as seen in this 1907 photograph taken of Third Avenue at Marion Street.

(The Seattle Times)

Below left: As the cutting and filling proceeded during the regrade project, many large buildings had to be moved or torn down. The Fremont Hotel, shown here, was raised over 25 feet on pilings as work proceeded on Sixth Avenue South near Charles Street.

(The Seattle Times)

Below right: Alden Blethen supported the need for regrading, but loudly accused R.H. Thomson of mismanagement, favoritism, and even improper expenditures of funds. This view shows the work on Fourth Avenue north from Cherry Street with the Rainier Club in the distance.

(The Seattle Times)

You must fight! fight! fight! all the time.

And what has it availed you? How did you profit mentally, morally or financially in your discrediting, belittling war on the administration of Mayor W.H. Moore? You will say your fight was aimed at city engineer Thomson. Your own power in Seattle began to wane when you began that senseless fight. Your cartoons of the "brains of the administration" were laughed at for a while, and then the laughter switched to you when it became known that an understrapper in the city engineer's office had set your pegs wrong on Queen Anne Hill. As a result Moore's administration was heralded as a farce and Moore himself an ass; and you destroyed him. Must you destroy because you cannot dictate?[48]

Too frequently Alden Blethen allowed emotion to reign over reason, pursuing his feud with Thomson to absurd lengths. Even when his sons asked him to moderate his attacks against the city engineer, he refused to budge. Harry Chadwick of *The Argus* also believed that Blethen placed too much trust in the advice of "interested parties"—supposed friends—who may have provided him with false or misleading information about the city engineer's mistakes. Perhaps Blethen wanted to believe the worst, but he damaged his credibility by his lack of discrimination.[49]

This trait soon caused him to jeopardize not only his reputation, but also his entire career. He became embroiled in another controversial issue—the control of Seattle's growing vice and crime—which called into question both his temperament and his choice of friends. During this first decade of the twentieth century, Seattle's physical appearance had changed dramatically as Thomson shaped the boomtown into a true urban center. But the city also developed in other ways as the Klondike era came to a close. The number of gold ships dwindled,

but the city still remained the major shipping point for trade with Alaska, and profits from that region continued to pour into Seattle until the end of the decade. The population stabilized, leaving behind its transient, predominately male character.

Vice, gambling, and prostitution—part of the Klondike legacy—were anathema to many of the newcomers who saw the future of Seattle as a family town. Alden Blethen had long taken the position that gambling and prostitution were undesirable, but inevitable. Since vice could never be stamped out, he advocated a segregated area where such activity could be profitably confined. Although for years he had campaigned against an open city and in favor of Sunday saloon closures, he soon became identified as a supporter, if not a purveyor of vice.[50]

By 1910 parts of Seattle resembled a moonscape, as Thomson's regrading efforts changed the face of the city. The photographer was looking south from Bell Street between Third and Fourth Avenues.
(The Seattle Times)

My ardent admirer and worshiper, Hiram Gill Esq.

Alden Blethen's feud with R.H. Thomson spilled over into politics. Seattle Mayor William Hickman Moore refused to fire the city engineer as he had promised before his election, and then later praised him as "the brains of the administration." Blethen was infuriated, and The Times began to parody the relationship between the mayor and Thomson in a series of controversial cartoons.

(The Seattle Times, September 19, 1907)

The Reverend Mark Matthews was a tall and quite imposing figure who used his pulpit and public influence to promote reform in Seattle.

(The Seattle Times)

The Reverend Mark Matthews loudly accused Blethen of being connected to syndicate criminal elements and became his third bitter enemy. Matthews, pastor of the First Presbyterian Church in Seattle, took it upon himself to expose corruption wherever he could find it in the city. The lanky six-foot five-inch evangelist, called to Seattle in 1902 from Tennessee, had earned a reputation as a social reformer and civic activist. With his impressive height, long black mane of hair, and characteristic dark frock coat, Matthews was a striking figure made even more compelling by his unquestioned oratorical abilities. In his pulpit he was, as one observer recalled, "a master of smashing similes that stick and scald and burn." Matthews used this stinging rhetoric to preach a gospel of urban righteousness in which the church would lead the movement to reform the city by influencing public policy and molding the urban environment. Matthews sought the limelight as he pledged to lead the church in these reform efforts.[51]

The Times had cordially welcomed Matthews to the city, commenting that the young preacher was "taking his congregation by storm." *The Times* reprinted many of Matthews' weekly sermons in its Monday paper, and the progress edition of 1904 devoted a full page to the preacher's comments on the religious outlook for Seattle during the upcoming year. "Our city cannot be built on coin, out of gold, or by the hands of lecherous, licentious, avaricious men," wrote Matthews. "The year 1904 will find the moral forces of Seattle aligned with but one purpose, namely, to elevate the moral tone of the business circles."[52]

Initially, this crusade meshed neatly with Alden Blethen's efforts to make his paper the driving force in civic betterment, but soon *The Times'* editor found that he, too, was among the businessmen needing a more elevated moral tone. In this early stage of his career, however, Matthews welcomed Blethen's backing in his crusades, and *The Times* expressed wholehearted support for the efforts of the zealous Presbyterian minister in exposing what he termed the "symptoms of graftitis" on the Seattle city council and among other civic leaders. As the year 1904 closed, both men had eagerly joined forces to target Hiram Gill, the Republican president of the city council, whose main career was as a lawyer representing the interests of the Tenderloin's saloonkeepers and brothel owners.[53]

Matthews had accused Gill of graft, and Gill had responded with a rather unpleasant tirade about the "church cur" who made accusations without any foundation. Blethen jumped in to defend Matthews and launched a crusade for a grand jury investigation of graft in the city government, supporting as well a charter amendment that would allow citizens to recall elected city officials. *The Times* also published a series of cartoons entitled "Gill's Gang" that lampooned the members of the council allied with Gill, each with his own grafting occupation. *The P-I*, which had run its own campaigns for civic reform, remained uncharacteristically quiet, as Brainerd had strongly supported the Republican Gill in the previous election.[54]

The Colonel's bluster sounded fierce, but his campaigns of a political nature rarely had any effect, and this one was no different. For all the exposés of vice and corruption and Blethen's strenuous efforts to tie them to other Republican incumbents in city government, Seattle remained a thoroughly Republican town. The prosecuting attorney found insufficient evidence to call a grand jury to investigate Matthews' charges against the city council, and Hi Gill won reelection in 1906.

Voters, however, approved the recall provision and Gill would much later face the full force of their recriminations.[55]

Blethen and Matthews attacked the "graftitis" of the city council, but the mayor and his appointee, the city chief of police, primarily set the moral tone for the town. For three terms beginning in 1897, Mayor Thomas Humes had allowed the city's saloons and gambling halls to run all night and Sunday too. Subsequent mayors attempted to tame the Tenderloin by degrees, first outlawing gambling, then enforcing nightly and Sunday closing laws, and ultimately shutting down the district. But these approaches never fully succeeded, as the forces of vice remained strong.

The Times gave editorial support to only one of these mayors, William Hickman Moore. Blethen had supposedly backed Moore because of his promise to get rid of R.H. Thomson, but also praised his plans to shut down vice and appoint Charles W. Wappenstein as the city's chief of police. The editor held Wappenstein in the highest

Mark Matthews and Alden Blethen were both strong-willed and opinionated, and their once-cordial relationship deteriorated rapidly. Matthews' height and distinctive hairstyle made him the perfect subject for caricature, as evidenced in this 1908 article from The Seattle Times.

(The Seattle Times, January 19, 1908)

Early in his career, the Rev. Mark Matthews joined with Colonel Blethen and The Times *in attacking the city council for "graftitis." A series of cartoons ran in* The Times *lampooning "Gill's Gang" of corrupt councilmen. The target in this cartoon was Hiram Gill himself, the flamboyant president of the city council who also worked as an attorney defending many of the entrepreneurs of Seattle's vice district.*

(The Seattle Times, March 16, 1905)

GILL'S GANG—No. 3

THE PRESIDENT OF THE COUNCIL.

Hi Gill—You know where to find me, boys. Walk right into the council meeting any Monday night. The city can wait while I get your bonds.

regard, and gleefully editorialized after the election that "Seattle will be closed tight."[56]

Wappenstein, a former Midwestern police chief, worked for the Pinkerton detective agency before joining the Seattle police department during the Humes administration. While he helped to round up thieves and crooks during Seattle's Klondike days, accusations surfaced that detective Wappenstein also ran his own scams on the side, allowing various con men and "bunco" artists to take advantage of unsuspecting citizens in return for a kickback. After an investigation, the department asked for his resignation, but Mayor Humes soon reinstated him. William Pinkerton himself recommended Wappenstein to candidate Moore as Seattle's police chief. With unintentional irony, an official biography of Wappenstein published soon after his appointment best described his qualifications for the job: "Chief Wappenstein has the widest acquaintance with crooks of any peace officer in the West. He has also a very wide circle of friends and acquaintances among the business and professional men of Seattle."[57]

Alden Blethen proved to be one of his greatest friends among the Seattle elite. Perhaps, as one historian has suggested, the friendship grew because Wappenstein provided numerous favors for the Colonel, including the services of a burly police officer as a personal bodyguard. Otherwise, it is difficult to understand why Blethen became such a strong admirer of the police chief, remaining his defender throughout the rest of his life. Wappenstein's past transgressions apparently had no influence on *The Seattle Times'* editor, who, in fact, seemed to have been thoroughly convinced that any charges against his protégé were patently untrue, merely the lies of enemies. With Wappenstein, as with numerous others,

Blethen seemed to be a very poor judge of character, compounding his problem by a fierce loyalty that defied logic or judgment.[58]

Alden Blethen cultivated friendships that cast doubt on his own reputation. Blethen constantly sought respectability, but a part of him was attracted to disreputable, even vulgar or criminal companions. His own "school of hard knocks" career, and his intense need to succeed, to make money, or just to win, made him feel more comfortable with men whose own lives were as Horatio Alger-like as his own. Increasingly, the Colonel chose to take his lunch at the Italian-American Club, across the street from the posh Butler Grill, but a world away in character. He made friends with a number of men who ran businesses in the Tenderloin—restaurants, hotels, dance halls, and saloons. All of them maintained that their establishments were entirely above reproach, but only a few of them were telling the truth.[59]

Blethen's friends included Jack Barberis, the owner of the Maison Barberis and manager of the Italian-American Club. These two Seattle restaurants catered to Italian immigrants as well as to the saloon owners and barkeeps in the restricted district. A frequent patron of the Club was Charles Berryman, proprietor of the Northern, a local bar and grill which, it was rumored, ran gambling tables in the back. Blethen had befriended Berryman, even loaning him money when the bank threatened to take his home over a bad debt. Ludovic Dallagiovanna was a partner of Berryman's in various business enterprises, including a short-lived dance hall called the Arcade. Some reformers liked to call him "The King of the Maques," a popular term for one who procured the services of young women for prostitution. When Dallagiovanna had business in Alaska, Blethen provided him with a letter of

The Times' *editor conferred with Seattle police chief Charles Wappenstein, whom Blethen steadfastly defended despite charges of graft and corruption.*
(The Seattle Times)

introduction to newspaper associates there, prompting allegations that the Colonel himself was involved in the "white slave trade."[60]

Blethen became notorious for his unsavory companions, and Erastus Brainerd published rumors of his drunken binges on the editorial pages of *The P-I*. But Brainerd also carried his commentary on Blethen's character beyond the newspapers into Seattle society. He could not have chosen a means better calculated to hurt and humiliate Alden Blethen than to openly protest his admission to the Rainier Club, the city's most exclusive social organization. Both C.B. and Joe Blethen had been members for several years, but Brainerd kicked up a fuss when Alden Blethen's name was proposed in 1908. Furious that the nomination went through despite his objections, *The P-I* editor resigned in protest, writing:

> After nearly twenty years pleasant membership in the club, their action in admitting a man who has been driven out of two cities as a known blackmailer, whose daily associates in Seattle notoriously are the dregs of humanity, renders membership in the club no longer desireable to a person whose regards for common decency will not permit his acceptance of A.J. Blethen in such intimate relations as those of club membership usually are among gentlemen.[61]

The newspaper rivalry between the two ran red hot as *The P-I* made Wappenstein a target of editorial abuse in the 1908 mayoral campaign. Alden Blethen, who had not supported Mayor Moore for reelection in the primary because of the feud over R.H. Thomson, suddenly became a booster when Moore pledged to retain Wappenstein as police chief, while his Republican opponent, John Miller, would not. In response to *The P-I*'s charges that he was "flip-flopping," Blethen made a strong editorial defense of

CAFE BARBERIS
BILLIARD PARLORS

There is no more genteel or fascinating after-dinner game than billiards. Appreciating this fact, for the accommodation of our patrons and as an attraction to our place, we have completed during the past week and thrown open, the most luxurious billiard parlors in the Northwest. Our billiard parlors occupy all of the third floor on the James Street side. They are appointed with seven new Monarch cushion tables—as is shown in above illustration. One is an English billiard pool table, 6x12 feet, another is a ladies' billiard table, 3x7 feet, the others are all 4 1-2x9 feet. Each table can be arranged separate from the general parlors for the advantage of parties desiring private games. The rate for use of billiard or pool table is only 50c per hour. Teachers will be furnished on request of patrons.

During the eight years of our business career in Seattle, we have catered to the best trade. We take pride in the satisfaction expressed by many of our best known business and professional men, their wives and families, who are regular patrons of the Cafe Barberis.

We make a specialty of supplying banquet and wedding parties, either at our cafe or in private residences, as requested. *We furnish the best dinner in Seattle during the week or Sunday at 75c.* Beginning Monday we will serve a business men's lunch at 40c which will be the most complete for the price ever served in the city.

Second and James **CAFE BARBERIS** Second and James

Later in his life, Blethen's press rivals increasingly accused him of public drunkenness with unsavory companions. Blethen frequented the Italian-American Club, giving up his attachment to the Butler Grillroom. The club was located for a short time upstairs from the Cafe Barberis on Second Avenue near Yesler.

(PEMCO Webster and Stevens Collection, Seattle Museum of History and Industry)

Proprietor Jack Barberis, a long-time friend of Alden Blethen, advertised the billiard parlors he had installed at his Second Avenue restaurant. Although the Cafe Barberis sought an up-scale clientele, it was more frequently patronized by business owners and saloon-keepers from Seattle's Tenderloin.

(The Seattle Times, February 26, 1905)

THE REAL ISSUE

Wappenstein, also revealing his own role in the police chief's career:

It is now pretty well understood that Mayor Moore appointed Charles W. Wappenstein to be Chief of Police at the earnest request and solicitation of the Editor of the Times.... Thus it follows that if *The Times* were to stay behind the reform movements inaugurated by Moore—such as the closing of the saloons on Sunday and at midnight—and the suppression of gambling, all of which are to be credited to the mayor...and also to stay by the Chief of Police, whose appointment *The Times* had occasioned—then there was no possible choice left but to support Moore as against Miller....

Personally we like John F. Miller better than we like William Hickman Moore—and if that gentleman could have given any assurance that the present police regime would have continued, Miller would have received the support of this newspaper.[62]

Blethen's backhanded support did not help Moore. The Republican tide overwhelmed him and he was handily voted out of office. With him went Charles Wappenstein. Not one to abandon friends, Blethen made sure that Wappy, as both the newspapers and his

compatriots below the Deadline called him, soon had another job. The Alaska-Yukon-Pacific Exposition, the ambitious showcase for Seattle's renewed civic spirit and international trade hopes, was set to open in June 1909. Blethen, an ardent fund-raiser and booster for the fair, lobbied strenuously and finally succeeded in having Wappenstein named as chief of security. Brainerd battled the appointment all along the way.

All the feuding, name-calling, and guilt by association came to a dramatic climax in the election of 1910 and the events that followed. Hiram Gill, the old nemesis of Blethen and the Reverend Matthews back during the 1905 "graftitis" controversy, was now running for mayor, this time supported by the Colonel. Blethen had softened his position toward Gill, taking a "forgive and forget" approach and applauding the former city council chairman for his stance on vice.

Mayor Miller had shut down Seattle's notorious restricted district as promised during his term, but soon found that his efforts had merely diffused the problem, sending many of the illicit activities undercover and many of the city's more than four hundred prostitutes to boarding houses and hotels all over town. Gill's platform included a return to the restricted district, which had also been Alden Blethen's stated goal. Gill told a national magazine writer that he believed in a designated area for prostitution so that other parts of the city would not swarm with "vicious" women. "Would it not be wiser to quarantine them, like an infectious disease, so that they might contaminate only the people who voluntarily put themselves in the way of danger?" Gill had asked rhetorically.[63]

Hiram Gill won the election, and the announcement of his victory in *The Times* included a large portrait of the man Gill chose to be his chief of police. Wappy was back and so was the Tenderloin. The saloons and dance halls, gambling dens and hurdy gurdy joints all swept away the dust and unboarded the windows as the "lords of vice" once more opened for business. Soon horrified reformers found that, despite *The Times'* frequent articles describing Wappenstein's crackdowns and reforms, the chief did not maintain the limits of the so-called restricted district. Worse, the city teemed with new arrivals who, for twenty-four hours a day, seven days a week, engaged in every form of debauchery imaginable. The chief of police was said to preside over the district, quickly dubbed "Wappyville" by his opponents.[64]

Erastus Brainerd in *The P-I* spoke for the discontent building among the reform elements in the community. The paper had adopted a new, more independent stance after owner John L. Wilson withdrew from the Senate race in 1910. Growing anti-Gill sentiment gave Brainerd the opportunity to lead his first reform crusade.[65]

But the city council dramatically seized the moment in the fall of 1910, when both Gill and Wappenstein were out of town at the same time. An ambitious young councilman, Max Wardall, officially took over the mayor's functions in his absence, and as his first order of business began a crackdown in the Tenderloin. Wardall also made preparations to fire Wappy and replace him with a police chief more willing to keep vice in check.

Getting wind of the revolt, Blethen quickly arranged a meeting with the mayor's private secretary, Robert "Bobby" Boyce, an old newspaper colleague. The two men plotted to help out Gill and Wappy. While Boyce notified the mayor of the impending crisis, Blethen fired off a letter to the police chief warning him of the situation and advising him to keep out of the city. "Wardall will remove you and your enemies will do all in their power to keep you out after Gill returns," he wrote. "...I do not believe he can legally remove you during your absence. Now I have given you sufficient information to put you entirely on your guard and if you will keep in touch with me by long distance telephone until I give the word, you will very much oblige your personal friends."

The "Dear Wapp" letter—as it came to be known—also indicated that Tenderloin entrepreneur Charles Berryman had telephoned Blethen for advice when the acting mayor closed down his Arcade Dance Hall as a public nuisance. *The Times'* editor evidently advised him to obey the edict and settle the matter in court. Brainerd became active on behalf of Blethen's enemies, urging councilman Wardall to appoint a new chief of police immediately.[66]

Mayor Gill returned to town and faced strong pressure from Brainerd, among others, to fire Wappenstein himself and begin a real clean-up of the city, but Gill refused to take any action. Led by *The P-I*, a movement began to remove him from office. It gained

Despite Gill's promises to restrict vice, Seattle's shocked reformers soon found that the city teemed with more saloons, gambling, and prostitution than ever before. The Seattle Police Department kept busy rounding up the drunk and disorderly in a self-propelled paddy wagon called the Black Maria, but many of the city's policemen were thought to be involved in vice, including their chief, Charles Wappenstein.

(The Seattle Times)

ANOTHER COWHIDING COMING

Women, who were newly enfranchised, played a big role in the recall election of Mayor Gill. In this cartoon, The Times *claimed that the majority would not be easily swayed by Brainerd's rhetoric against Gill. During this campaign,* P-I *editor Brainerd reinforced his reputation for pedantic phrases, calling a local judge who tried to obstruct the recall "anile and caduke."*

(The Seattle Times, February 4, 1911)

momentum with the formation of a Public Welfare League that began circulating recall petitions in early October 1910. According to the petition, Mayor Gill was "a menace to the business enterprises and moral welfare of said city." By the end of December, petitioners had gathered enough signatures to force a recall election the following February and run a new candidate for mayor.[67]

The Seattle Times led Gill supporters, but Blethen was once more on the losing side. A majority of the voters selected Gill's opponent, George Dilling, a Republican with an "excellent reputation for business honor and clean living." Some observers attributed the success of the recall to women who had just gained the vote in Washington the previous November. Limousines carrying some of the city's nearly five hundred "ladies of the night" arrived at polling places to cast their vote for Gill, but the more respectable middle class women of Seattle, many sporting banners

that read "Dilling for Decency," carried the day for a family city. Estimates were that more than 22,000 of them voted to throw Gill out of office.[68]

The Reverend Mark Matthews headed the city's Ministerial Association, many of whose members had actively campaigned for the recall. The Presbyterian preacher, who generally loved the spotlight, remained uncharacteristically quiet about the recall efforts in both the pulpit and the papers. But behind the scenes, he had secretly hired the William J. Burns Detective Agency to investigate the conditions of vice and corruption in Seattle and particularly the activities of police chief Wappenstein.[69]

Later, Matthews offered an explanation to the public, claiming he had been driven to this desperate measure after several meetings with Gill. He had informed the mayor that the chief of police had betrayed his trust and "was permitting a condition of lawlessness to exist which would plunge the city into disgrace, financial and social sorrow." According to one source, Matthews had promised to use his influence to stop the recall if Gill dismissed Wappenstein and enforced the law. Gill refused, however, and thus Matthews commissioned the investigation by Burns, instructing him that he "wanted the city cleansed [and] those who had been guilty of graft and every form of viciousness discovered, arrested and punished."[70]

The Burns investigation began in November 1910, and the nationally known detective evidently had no trouble finding incriminating evidence against Wappenstein. "Never in my experience have I seen more of a cinch," Burns later told the press. "We've got the goods on Wappy. The case against him would not be any stronger were he to come in here before us and sign a statement admitting everything." Matthews, who chose to remain silent about his involvement until many months later, secretly took the detective's evidence to prosecuting attorney John Murphy, who immediately called for a grand jury investigation.[71]

The town was in turmoil. As one political watcher reported:

> The grand jury which convened Friday, and for which W.J. Burns has collected a mass of incriminating testimony, will probably give this old town a cleaning up such as it deserved for years. Wappenstein will probably be the goat and several others of the bright lights will have their fingers stained with graft before the thing is ended. The Times is bucking like a bronco and there is a story abroad that they have something on Clarence [sic] Blethen which may prove embarrassing."[72]

Alden Blethen would not accept the allegations against his protégé without a fight. When the grand jury indicted Wappenstein for suspected bribery and extortion, Blethen immediately started a campaign to restore Wappenstein's reputation. *The Times'* editor also took out after *The P-I,* Matthews, and others who had tarnished Seattle's image, resurrecting the term "knocker" to characterize the leaders of the anti-vice crusades. Yet Blethen's feverish efforts to defend Wappenstein's character and condemn his detractors stalled when, on the eve of the police chief's trial, the grand jury delivered a new series of indictments that included charges against the Colonel, as well as The Times Printing Company and its managing editor, C.B. Blethen.[73]

The Grand Jury, after hearing the testimony of numerous witnesses, brought indictments against Blethen for libeling a city councilman, conspiring to protect illegal gambling, prostitution and liquor sales, and helping to maintain a public nuisance, the

Arcade Dance Hall. Also listed as co-conspirators in the latter two indictments were Blethen's Italian-American Club friends, Tenderloin businessmen Charles Berryman and Ludovic Dallagiovanna, as well as former chief Wappenstein and deputy Mike Powers. The arresting officer allowed Blethen to finish putting out the paper, but the next morning he appeared in court, branded a criminal. He posted bond of $15,000, guaranteed by his long-time associates in the Scandinavian-American Bank as well as another old friend, Jacob Furth of the Seattle Electric Company.[74]

In his first public comments on the indictments, Blethen declared his innocence and bitterly blamed his enemies for the unjust accusations. "It is because *The Times* would not join this gang of marauders, headed by Dr. Matthews, an elder of whose church is foreman of this grand jury, that Matthews' friends have been determined to get an indictment," he told reporters. He also denounced John L. Wilson and Erastus Brainerd at *The P-I* for playing politics with the charges. But in a later editorial Blethen acknowledged that beyond these personal feuds, his own character had played a role:

> My fault consists in standing by men in official position so long as I believe them to be honest and faithful to duty—and if that be a crime then the whole gang of marauders and character assassins may make the worst of it.[75]

Blethen, infuriated by the situation, prepared to defend himself, no matter what it took. Characteristically, the Colonel seized the offensive, filing a $100,000 libel suit against *The P-I* for Brainerd's scathing editorial about the indictments in which he had called *The Times'* editor "a dishonor, a disgrace and degradation" to his profession. Blethen also monitored the unfolding

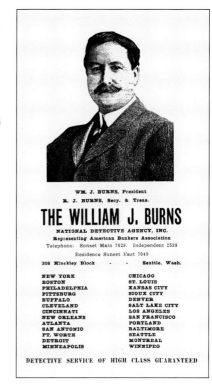

The Reverend Matthews secretly hired William Burns to conduct an undercover investigation of Seattle vice. A grand jury indicted police chief Wappenstein on charges of bribery and extortion, based on Burns' findings. Burns advertised his "high class" detective services in the Seattle Blue Book *of 1911.*

A. J. BLETHEN INDICTED!

Grand Jury Charges Criminal Libel and Conspiracy
Illegal Drawing of Grand Jury Charged by Wappy

INDICTED POLICE CHIEF DEMANDS CONTINUANCE!

Files Affidavits Showing Curious Methods by Which Grand Jury Was Selected and Pointing Out Unfairness of Compelling Trial While Inquisitorial Body Continues to Menace Witnesses for Defense.

The Seattle Daily Times

SEATTLE, WASHINGTON, TUESDAY EVENING, MAY 23, 1911.

22 PAGES.   Price 1 Cent   News Stands and Trains, 5 Cents.

Col. A. J. Blethen

PROSECUTING ATTORNEY REFUSES TO SIGN BILLS!

Murphy Declines to Append His Signature to Indictments Until Ordered to Do So by Judge Main—Technical Arrest of Times Editor Occurs Shortly After Noon But No Bail Is Required.

Grand jury indictments charging the publishing of libel and conspiracy were returned at noon today in Judge Main's court against Col. A. J. Blethen, editor, and C. B. Blethen, managing editor of The Times. An indictment for libel was also returned against Chauncey B. Rathbun, city editor of The Times, and an indictment for conspiracy against the Times Printing Company. It is not known at this time who the complaining witness is, but City Councilman J. Y. C. Kellogg is believed to be the person who asked for the indictments.

Four indictments were also returned against C. W. Wappenstein.

Deputy Sheriff John W. Roberts served warrants upon The Times editors at 1 o'clock, and under instructions from Prosecuting Attorney John F. Murphy, released the defendants upon their own recognizance.

From the proceeding in court it was evident that the prosecuting attorney declined to sign the indictments until ordered to do so by Judge Main. Murphy's reasons for refusing could be only that he did not believe the evidence warranted the indictments.

GRAND JURY WHICH INDICTED COLONEL BLETHEN

SUNDAY TIMES, MAY 28, 1911.

A Statement From Colonel Blethen

To the Readers of The Sunday Times:

I have been indicted on the following counts:

1. For publishing a libel against J. Y. C. Kellogg.
2. For conspiring to encourage vice and infractions of the law.
3. For maintaining a public nuisance (the Arcade Dance Hall).

Anything which The Times has said concerning Kellogg it is perfectly willing to take before the courts at the proper time.

The charge that I entered into a conspiracy to encourage vice or any other infraction of the law is absolutely false. This I will prove in court when opportunity be given.

The charge that I had any connection whatever with the Arcade Dance Hall is also false. This I will prove whenever required.

So much for the work of the Grand Jury. Just a word concerning The Post-Intelligencer. That newspaper last Wednesday morning printed very serious charges against me—calling me a criminal, a dishonor and a disgrace to my profession, an impenitent thief, a degenerate, etc.

I have sued The Post-Intelligencer Company for $100,000 for publishing these libels. Despite the busybodies who have been circulating reports to the effect that the suit was brought only for its temporary effect, I wish to say most emphatically that I shall prosecute this suit to a conclusion if it takes my last dollar and my last drop of blood.

Further than what I have here set forth I will say nothing regarding these charges—legal, libelous or both—until my day in court shall come, but at that time I and my attorneys will say enough to clear me of the silly and contemptible indictments, and will do enough to bring about the utter humiliation of the newspaper which has sought to cover me with slime!

Alden J. Blethen

The P-I *gleefully seized the opportunity to publicize Blethen's indictment and the editor of* The Times *responded by filing a $100,000 libel suit against the rival paper, promising to pursue the case even if it took his "last drop of blood." Blethen also proclaimed his innocence in a signed editorial statement published in* The Times.

(The Seattle Times, May 28, 1911)

Alden Blethen, another target of the Burns investigation, was indicted for criminal libel and conspiracy in May 1911. In addition, the grand jury also indicted Blethen's son, C.B., two Tenderloin business operators, and a police officer.

(The Seattle Times, May 23, 1911)

MATTHEWS BOSS

By "O——."

AN ACCOUNT OF MY STEWARDSHIP

By Rev. M. A. Matthews, D. D.

Blethen also blamed Mark Matthews for engineering the indictment, and The Times *portrayed the minister as the city's boss, manipulating behind the scenes to increase his own power.*

(The Seattle Times, May 28, 1911)

Colonel Blethen bitterly complained that the grand jury foreman was an elder of Matthews' church. Times cartoonist "Dok" Hager made fun of these religious zealots and the endless number of indictments in his daily weather cartoon.

(The Seattle Times, May 24, 1911)

THE WEATHER — Showers tonight and Thursday; moderate southwest winds. Temperature at 1 p. m. today, 58. Temperature during the last twenty-four hours: Maximum, 58; minimum, 45.

Wappenstein proceedings with great concern, obviously worried about his own upcoming trial. He may not have been aware that detectives, still bankrolled by Matthews, watched his every move. The Burns agency had assigned these men to protect the star witnesses in the Wappenstein case—two gambling hall operators who had agreed to testify about bribing the police chief and were "fearful of what Wappy was going to do to them." Much of the time, however, the operatives worked undercover in the Tenderloin, hunting for evidence against possible grafters, most notably Alden Blethen.[76]

The behind-the-scenes reports described the Colonel arriving at court recess to confer with Wappy and his attorneys; "storming around" the Italian-American Club, spouting profanities; or gathering "dope" on a potential witness against him. One detective warned of the Colonel's tenacity: "Before you go to trial with Blethen you must have enough evidence as he will fight you for all he's worth; the story around town is that a fund of $50,000 was raised for the entire set of trials."[77]

The detectives attempted to establish a direct link between Alden Blethen and several of the Tenderloin's more notorious business operators including Berryman and Dallagiovanna. A Burns investigator unsuccessfully searched public records in the auditor's office, trying to find if Blethen had any property transactions with either man. Another put pressure on Berryman to make a confession, to "show him he didn't have an out in the World unless he joined our forces." They also threatened that Matthews' supporters on the city council would revoke his license if he did not turn against his friends. Despite the pressure, Berryman did not crack, and the operatives looked elsewhere for leads.[78]

They next approached Blethen's most vocal enemy, Erastus Brainerd, believing that he would give them all the information they needed. "Brainerd will throw some light on this transaction when he returns," one wrote. *The P-I* editor was away from town, but when he came back he did cooperate fully, spending an entire afternoon with one of the detectives. Brainerd advised him to pursue the so-called Nome letter, a note of introduction written by Blethen for Ludovic Dallagiovanna in 1906. In the communication Blethen wrote that "Mr. 'Ludovic,' as we all call him in Seattle, desires to put in acquaintance with men on whose word he can depend, if he needs any advice, as he probably will, while in the North." With Dallagiovanna's widely suspected involvement in prostitution, the detectives considered the letter an important piece of evidence, possibly connecting Blethen to the notorious white slave trade.[79]

While the detectives pursued their leads on Blethen, the Wappenstein case continued. The police chief's first trial ended in a hung jury, so the prosecutors retried the case in July 1911, this time gaining a conviction. Wappy received a sentence of three to ten years in prison. Mark Matthews had won a great victory in his crusade for reform, but the verdict was a blow to Alden Blethen, who had continued to express his support for the discredited police chief throughout the proceedings. According to the story around town, Blethen felt so sure of Wappy's acquittal that *The Times* began to print hundreds of papers with the headlines—**WAPPY NOT GUILTY**—and the entire front page devoted to the officer's life. When word of the conviction reached Blethen, he directed his staff to burn all the copies.[80]

Alden Blethen's defense of his friends had made him notorious, not just in Seattle but nationwide. His name appeared prominently in articles about the affair, including a feature in popular *McClure's* magazine:

> Blethen, according to general reputation is a man of considerable wealth, and that he should have personally profited from Seattle conditions seems incredible. While the pending criminal proceedings against Blethen will determine whether there is any justification in these suspicions, and to what extent, if at all, he became involved, the fact is already evident that he was the confidential adviser as well as journalistic advocate of Wappenstein. And a Seattle jury has just branded Wappenstein as a grafter and a blackmailer.[81]

Because of all the public attention after the Wappenstein verdict, Blethen redoubled his efforts to strengthen his own case. Reports suggested that he was gathering information all over town, and had even sent Clarance and *The Times'* political reporter M.M. Mattison to canvass the local gambling establishments. His feverish concern reached such heights that when he heard rumors that the prosecuting attorney had a "doctored" picture of him in a compromising position, he decided to retaliate in kind—to prove how easily it could be done, he later claimed. He asked a local photographer to concoct a pornographic picture, placing the heads of the Reverend Matthews and prosecuting attorney Murphy atop two naked "human figures in indescribably loathsome relations" from a naughty French postcard.[82]

Veering wildly between impropriety and decorum, the Colonel tried his best to rally support and maintain a positive public front in the wake of the indictments. On August 11, 1911, in honor of the fifteenth anniversary of Blethen's purchase of *The Seattle Times*, he held a gala dinner at the Rainier Club, attended by over 160 of Seattle's leading citizens, politicians, and businessmen as well as a number of out-of-town guests. In addition to good food, wine, and music, the celebration included a number of toasts and some heartfelt remarks by the host. "The occasion gave Colonel Blethen a charming opportunity to tell the sad sweet story of his life since coming to Seattle," *The Argus* acidly reported. But without directly mentioning his current troubles, the Colonel also presented what he undoubtedly considered his vindication:

> I have endeavored, gentlemen, in spite of the adverse criticism that has been heaped upon me for a decade, to keep this newspaper on lines that I maintained at all times. It was not always easy to do it. You may find yourself in a corner without knowing it. Moreover, I have an extraordinary weakness. It doesn't belong to all men, but that weakness is this: If I ever associate myself with a man, or stand behind him for any cause, and I believe him to be right—all hell can't stop my following that man to the end.

His friends rose to their feet and honored him with prolonged applause.[83]

Blethen's actual trial seemed almost an anti-climax after all the furious behind-the-scenes preparations. During the two-day proceedings, fifty witnesses appeared, drawn from the highest and lowest ends of Seattle's business community. The Colonel's friends attested to his good character, and his enemies insisted on his greed and dissipation. But prosecutors failed to present any direct evidence that incriminated Blethen in illegal activities or proved that he had owned a share in any dance hall, gambling room, or house of prostitution. Ultimately, the case against Alden Blethen revolved around whether he had violated the law by offering advice to his friends. In the mind of the judge, Blethen's actions were not criminal, and he instructed

the jury to return a verdict of "not guilty." Once he was exonerated, the charges against Blethen's co-conspirators were also dropped.[84]

After Alden Blethen's struggles, there were other vindications. Only a few months before, *P-I* publisher John L. Wilson had accepted Erastus Brainerd's letter of resignation. Wilson made the official announcement with "the greatest reluctance," but rumor had it that his son-in law, the paper's manager, had finally wearied of the irascible editor's diatribes. Reginald Thomson, too, had left his position as city engineer, "tired of the fighting," he claimed, although he soon returned to public life as a Seattle port commissioner.[85]

But the fight was not over for Alden Blethen. More lawsuits loomed on the horizon from Thomson, detective Burns, and others who wanted to exact their pound of flesh from the Colonel's tough hide. Raising hell had cost him plenty both in his private life and public esteem. But raising hell also had its rewards. *The Times* grew stronger than ever. Daily circulation climbed over 64,000 and distribution of the Sunday edition reached nearly 84,000. And it was on *The Times* that Blethen based his family's future.

Wappenstein was convicted of the charges against him, but Alden Blethen was exonerated in his late November 1911 trial. Blethen would never forgive those whom he believed had damaged his reputation and continued to excoriate them in his paper. This front-page exposé of William Burns later resulted in a series of libel suits filed by the detective.

(The Seattle Times, November 3, 1912)

The Seattle Sunday Times

SECOND EDITION
ALL THE NEWS THAT'S FIT TO PRINT

SEVENTY-SIX PAGES.   SEATTLE, WASHINGTON, OCT. 23, 1910.   FIVE CENTS

WILSON'S DREAM

FIRST ONE—THEN THE OTHER

" * * * He that filches from me my good name
Robs me of that which not enriches him
And makes me poor indeed."—Shakespeare.

* * * * Things done relates, not done she feigns,
And mingles truth with lies.
Talk is her business, and her chief delight
To tell of prodigies and cause affright.
She fills the people's ears—"
—Virgil on Slander, Book IV., Æneis (Dryden's translation.)

FORMER SENATOR WILSON can not control Mayor Hiram C. Gill, nor can he control Chief of Police Charles W. Wappenstein. He can not issue orders to the Mayor to "do this" or "do that." He can not name Gill's appointees for municipal offices. He can not make Gill a contributing member of The Post-Intelligencer's news staff. He can not force Gill to construct a political machine for the newspaper proprietor's benefit.

Former Senator Wilson can not dictate the conduct of police affairs. He can not direct Chief Wappenstein to "do this" or "leave that." He can not control the tenderloin or its denizens by the aid of Wappenstein's police department. He can not make the policemen of Seattle reporters for his newspaper.

But all these things he has tried to do—and much more. But he has failed. Mayor Gill will not kneel in the dust. Chief Wappenstein will not kiss the royal feet.

This is crime. No punishment can be too great for such offenders. Moreover, Gill and Wappenstein are both poor—both in debt. Both occupy public office—therefore Wilson's newspaper, supplied with low, cunning and desperate craft by Brainerd, may be used to destroy them.

Nothing is wrong with either of them—*but Wilson must have revenge!*
Wappenstein must be deprived of reputation, friends, his living wage!
Gill's present and future must be blasted. His children must be disgraced!
Why? *BECAUSE THESE TWO MEN WILL NOT CALL SENATOR WILSON "MASTER!"*

The P-I *allied with reform groups to force a recall election when Mayor Gill refused their requests to fire Chief Wappenstein and clean up the Tenderloin.* The Times *accused John L. Wilson, The P-I owner, of trying to bludgeon Wappenstein with the power of his newspaper and dramatized the charges with this front-page illustration.*

(The Seattle Times, October 23, 1910)

Throughout his newspaper career, Alden Blethen always insisted on purchasing the most up-to-date production equipment. In 1903, Blethen added an attachment to one of his presses allowing him to print in color. Color first began to appear in comics and also highlighted special Sunday sections.

(The Seattle Times, November 22, 1903)

WHY SOME PEOPLE PREFER PUGET SOUND

Thanksgiving Day Down East

Thanksgiving Day Out West

Nationally syndicated articles filled most of the pages of the Sunday supplement, but The Seattle Times *also produced some of its own artwork and local features, often in color.*

(The Seattle Times, November 22, 1903)

Contests generated interest and attracted new readers to the paper. The search for "The Most Beautiful Woman in Washington State" lasted for many months. Each Sunday, The Times published lavishly illustrated pages displaying the portraits of entrants who were vying for the grand prize: a diamond bracelet.

(The Seattle Times, October 16, 1904)

A Curtis Poster

Reproduction
of a
Special
Indian Poster
Designed for
The Times'
Third
Anniversary
Number

Actual Two-Color Photograph

Copyrighted, 1905, by Edward S. Curtis

A Limited Number of the
Original Posters for Sale
See Advertisement.

*Edward Curtis, a well-known society
photographer in Seattle, gained much
wider fame for his portraits of Indian
people.* The Times *frequently featured
Curtis photographs, often in full-page
layouts, as part of its Sunday editions.*
(The Seattle Times, February 12, 1905)

After the installation of a new four-color press in 1904, The Times featured color more prominently in the paper, occasionally using it to accent front-page news. Blethen claimed to be a political independent—to separate his paper from the Republican P-I—but patriotically displayed his admiration for Teddy Roosevelt in this inauguration extra.

(The Seattle Times, March 4, 1905)

The comics were the most colorful and popular of the supplements to The Sunday Times. *Buster Brown's illustrator, Richard F. Outcault, had gained fame as the originator of the "Yellow Kid," a cartoon character whose name became synonymous with the sensationalism of the era.*

(The Seattle Times, April 2, 1905)

The Times *often promoted civic events in its Sunday features. A few of these gala activities, like the opening of the boating season, have continued until the present day.*

(The Seattle Times, April 9, 1905)

THE OPENING OF THE PUGET SOUND YACHTING SEASON

PHOTOGRAPH FOR COVER DESIGN
BY OLIVER P. ANDERSON

The Seattle Sunday Times

PART III
Magazine Section
Eight Pages

APRIL 9, 1905

THE OLYMPIC   COPYRIGHT BY OLIVER P. ANDERSON

The paper increasingly recognized the role of the "progressive" woman in the workplace and ran a feature on "Seattle Women Who Maintain Their Independence," highlighting a different occupation each week.

(The Seattle Times, May 7, 1905)

Large, bold headlines could create an even greater impact if printed in color. Rival editor Harry Chadwick of The Argus *once joked about the new sensationalism of* The Times: *"A great deal of it is yellow, and very little red."*

(The Seattle Times, May 9, 1905)

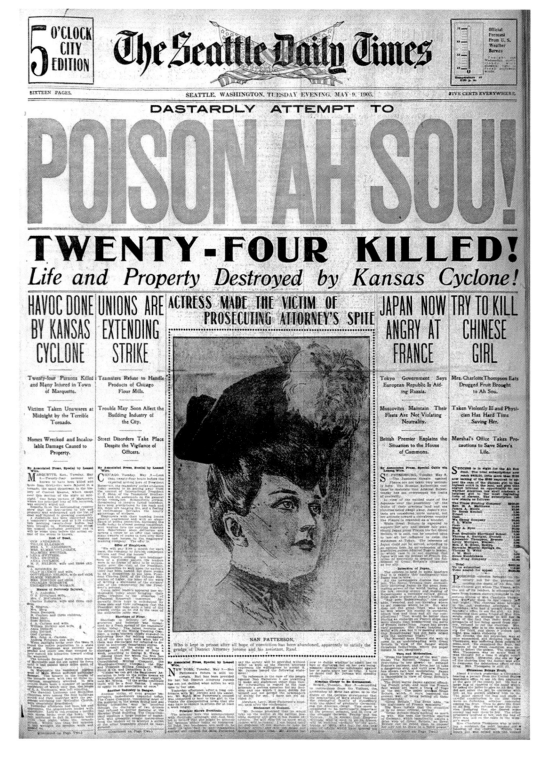

MOUNT RAINIER at SUNSET

FIRST COLOR PHOTOGRAPH OF SEATTLE'S GREAT LANDMARK EVER PRINTED

PHOTO COPYRIGHTED 1903 BY W.P. ROMANS

In 1905, The Times *continued its experimentation with color. The scenic wonders of Puget Sound offered perfect subject matter, and the paper boasted of its pioneering efforts to publish hand-tinted photographs of local landmarks.*

(The Seattle Times, May 21, 1905)

Alden Blethen loved patriotic displays and always ran an American flag on the paper's masthead. The Times *also published elaborate holiday commemorations, including this red, white, and blue tribute to the spirit of Memorial Day.*

(The Seattle Times, May 28, 1905)

REASONS WHY SEATTLE IS A YOUNG MAN'S TOWN

REASON NO 2:
WILL H. PARRY

PHOTO BY
JAMES & BUSHNELL
ARCADE BLDG.

Blethen was an ardent civic booster and initiated several weekly series to focus attention on business leaders who had helped Seattle grow.
(The Seattle Times, June 11, 1905)

Best known for his scathing editorials, Alden Blethen also occasionally wrote feature articles. This dramatic illustration accompanied Blethen's own reminiscences of the disastrous Minneapolis Tribune *fire.*

(The Seattle Times, January 7, 1906)

The Seattle Times *provided sensational coverage of the San Francisco earthquake. The first few days after the quake, the paper lured readers with huge headlines and tinted illustrations depicting the disaster. C.B. Blethen wanted* The Times *to be the first Northwest newspaper to run actual photographs of the devastation and offered to pay $50 a picture.*

(The Seattle Times, April 19, 1906)

To attract more female readers, The Sunday Times expanded its women's sections, including fashion, fiction, home-making tips, and society news. There were also special pages devoted entirely to the interests of children.

(The Seattle Times, November 4, 1906)

Seattle hosted the Alaska-Yukon-Pacific Exposition in 1909 to celebrate its phenomenal growth since the gold rush days as well as its expanding role in the Pacific Rim. Alden Blethen, a strong supporter of the exposition, was instrumental in raising money in the community and then publicizing the event through the pages of The Seattle Times. As a former regent, he also lobbied effectively for the AYPE to be held on the campus of the University of Washington.

(The Seattle Times, February 14, 1909)

The Alaska-Yukon-Pacific Exposition, a huge success, drew more than 3½ million visitors. Pay Streak, among the most popular areas of the fair, offered food, gambling, dancing girls, and other forms of exotic entertainment.

(The Seattle Times, February 14, 1909)

SEATTLE POTLATCH·1913

The AYPE had been such a remarkable attraction for visitors that many Seattle businessmen hoped to continue the spirit of the fair in a yearly civic celebration called the Potlatch. The Seattle Potlatch reflected not only the region's Indian heritage, but also its ties to the sea, with ships from the navy's Pacific fleet making an annual appearance. Joseph Blethen served as president and chief organizer of the Potlatch festivities in 1912 and The Times consistently provided publicity.

(The Seattle Times, June 8, 1913)

During Potlatch week in 1913 The Times was accused of inciting a riot between visiting sailors and members of the city's radical labor organizations. Seattle mayor George Cotterill, fearing further trouble, ordered local police to shut down the newspaper. After getting a temporary court injunction, a furious Alden Blethen ran this scathing denunciation of Cotterill.

(The Seattle Times, July 20, 1913)

Most of the lavish color features in The Seattle Sunday Times *portrayed the city in a positive light, emphasizing its scenic beauty or economic opportunities.*

(The Seattle Times, June 8, 1913)

As the number of women who read The Times *increased, the paper expanded its fashion sections. National syndicates supplied these pages, which seemed to reflect the tastes of society's elite.*

(The Seattle Times, October 13, 1912)

Often The Sunday Times *ran full pages devoted purely to natural scenes or romantic images that allowed the paper to show off its color capabilities.*

(The Seattle Times, May 26, 1912)

The depiction of women in many of the Sunday features seemed in marked contrast to the images that feminists of the day promoted.

(The Seattle Times, October 13, 1912)

The 1913 version of the "pin-up" often ran in The Times as a weekly series tied to a particular theme. The brightly colored Seaside Studies were hand-tinted.

(The Seattle Times, May 25, 1913)

Seattleites loved cars and The Times *ran numerous articles and special supplements featuring the automobile industry's latest designs and innovations.*

(The Seattle Times, February 8, 1914)

BUSINESS MEN AT THE WHEEL

JOSEPH BLETHEN

Automobile Club president who works for good roads.

Alden Blethen grew up in the horse and buggy age and never felt comfortable behind the wheel of a car. In contrast, both of his sons were avid motorists, purchasing the newest models and occasionally competing in long-distance driving competitions. A 1915 Times *series on local men and their cars prominently featured Joseph Blethen.*

(The Seattle Times, May 2, 1915)

This 1913 view of Seattle looks northeast from the King Street coal bunkers, across the docks and up toward the urbanizing cityscape. Here under construction, Smith Tower would long stand as the tallest building west of the Mississippi River.

(Seattle Museum of History and Industry)

6 An Open Life

*C*ontemporaries perceived the decade before World War One in Seattle as one of wrenching transition from a boom-town to a metropolis, marked by contests for community authority on every hand. The great events of the last five years of Alden Blethen's life involved him in these struggles among capitalists, socialists, anarchists, prohibitionists, and progressives. Blethen's life and work merged into one, so that the man became the newspaper and the newspaper the man, and he lived, as James J. Hill put it, "an open life," on daily newsstand display. He wove together his violent enthusiasms and hostilities, his need to "educate his two sons into the paper," his power and wealth, and his booster's love of the city.[1]

Blethen's *Times* worked hard for municipal goals. The paper strongly advocated annexation of Seattle's suburbs: South Park, West Seattle, Columbia City, and Georgetown, then Ballard, Ravenna, and Laurelhurst. Despite his personal dislike of R.H. Thomson, Blethen enthusiastically supported Seattle's ongoing dramatic self-sculpture, sluicing hills into the tideflats and the "regrade." Colossal public engineering projects like the Panama Canal—promoted in the Seattle press as the next Klondike bonanza—were the order of the day. In Seattle, the projects to create Harbor Island and to dig a ship canal from Elliott Bay to Lake Washington joined wilder schemes, to tunnel First Hill, to fill in lower Lake Union, and to bridge Lake Washington.[2]

Alden Blethen believed strongly in the common good and worked hard to boost Seattle, but he was also convinced that many community needs could be better met by private rather than public ownership and management. When Blethen wrote of "Some Things We Much Need"—a library, a respected university, a good theater, a railway depot, a first-class hotel, a spacious public meeting hall, a community market, a trade exposition, a summer carnival—he expected philanthropy to fill in where private enterprise could not make a profit. No institution so symbolized the merger of the interests of private business with the ideal of public progress in Seattle between 1910 and 1915 as the chamber of commerce. In October 1911, Alden Blethen joined the chamber and became chair of its bureau of publicity. For more than three years—until his death—the Colonel adopted each chamber community initiative as a personal crusade, and *The Seattle Times* vigorously promoted his agenda.[3] As he wrote:

> [A]ll *The Times* owns in the world is in the City of Seattle and therefore, whatever will benefit Seattle must benefit *The Times*.... Men who have built up a property like *The Times*—the taxes alone upon which will be $3000 this year, whose payroll averages $8500 a month—will not assume any attitude in this community which they do not believe to be absolutely for the best interests of all.[4]

Seattle's Pike Place market originated in 1907 as a site where farmers could sell their own produce, and has long been one of the city's most popular public spaces.
(The Seattle Times)

The ornate pergola in Seattle's Pioneer Square has been a city landmark since its construction in 1909. This photograph of the original glass structure, taken shortly thereafter, shows a lively street scene in the Square.
(The Seattle Times)

Blethen had lived through times so bad that wealthy families went bankrupt and poor families went hungry; he had lived through times so good that there were jobs for all. He believed that good times benefited everyone, rich and poor, and that no fundamental antagonisms existed between classes in the development of Seattle. His newspaper was a bully pulpit. *The Times'* annual business reviews presented galleries of successful businessmen whose lives offered models of self-help—their enterprise earned them wealth, built the cityscape, and created jobs. Many of Blethen's editorials have a school-teacherly air, homilies on the virtues of property and self-discipline, primers in the economics of investment. He believed uncritically, with many others of his generation, in Progress.

City critics were "knockers," in the slang of the day. Rhetoric during the Gill recall had portrayed Seattle as a wide-open town, filled with prostitutes, drunks, gamblers, and crooks. Blethen indignantly reprinted lurid stories from Eastern newspapers about Seattle's "infamous reputation," which would, he argued, discourage respectable newcomers and prospective investors. He angrily predicted it would "take years to blot out the stigma that has been cast upon [Seattle]" by the ballyhoo over vice, led by *The P-I* and *The Star*. Historian Eldon Coroch has argued that Blethen believed the city's normal growth was halted by Seattle's notorious reputation and did not resume until 1912.[5]

Although *The Times* increasingly promoted itself as the newspaper of Seattle's middle class, it had gained its early strength as a working-class paper. In the teens, *The Times* continued to insist that it was on the side of the honest union man, and the paper featured a department devoted to labor issues, emblazoned with the emblem of the Seattle Trades Council. On his own newspaper, facing his own unions, Alden Blethen acted paternally, doting on "his boys" one moment and furious with them the next. In 1905, Blethen anticipated a strike by the Typographical Union, and with typical vehemence told his friend Harry Chadwick, "the typographical union will soon want a *four* hour day, in order that they may have *eight* hours in which to raise hell!"[6]

In less impassioned moments, Blethen agreed that workingmen should organize to protect their own interests. But labor radicals like the Industrial Workers of the World [IWW] infuriated him. Founded in 1905, the Wobblies were committed to revolutionary class struggle and scornful of negotiation. The IWW was strong among the young, single wage-workers in the Northwest woods and mines who—from Alden Blethen's point of view—sabotaged machinery and made fun of their employers. They were just bums, Blethen wrote in horror, "too lazy to work and too cowardly to steal."[7]

Alden Blethen detested the Wobblies because of their irreverent disregard for every

Blethen's Seattle Times *honored Labor Day in 1907 with this front-page editorial cartoon, in which Uncle Sam and organized labor join in the defense of the traditional American values of law, justice, and mercy.*
(The Seattle Times)

Seattle's Press Club organized formally in 1905 as a social and professional fraternity for city newsmen, putting on annual shows and publishing the Wuxtra! *yearbooks. Joe Blethen was twice president of the Club, and Alden and C.B. Blethen were longtime members. Here we see a Seattle Press Club contingent, visiting Portland for the Rose Festival parade.*

(PEMCO Webster and Stevens Collection, Seattle Museum of History and Industry)

value that mattered to him: achievement, patriotism, and "the upbuilding of Seattle." He was convinced that, "If these dirty, ragged, loafing whelps had their way, there wouldn't be one brick upon another in Seattle today!" In the name of Seattle's Progress, Blethen expected local newspapermen to suppress bad news and ministers to ignore gambling and prostitution; he certainly had no patience with labor radicals whose antics embarrassed the Pacific Northwest.[8]

In his sixties, publisher Blethen remained tough, smart, ambitious, vulgar, and senti-mental, but he finally developed a sense of humor about himself, at least among his friends. The men in the bureau of publicity of the Seattle chamber of commerce threw him a combined Christmas and birthday party with some concern—his capricious and violent temper was well-known. But a brave soul had brought a prank gift, and soon the party turned into a roast. It happened that Blethen loved sarcastic humor at his expense, at least among friends.[9]

Once, on a chamber of commerce junket to tour the penitentiary at Walla Walla, in the wake of the indictments and libel suits, Blethen joked:

Gentlemen...I have just been of my own free will where a number of the people of Seattle have been trying to put me for several years—the penitentiary. And...I must say that I enjoyed it very much.[10]

But, even in his sixties, Blethen was no pushover. In the dead of an August night, a burglar jimmied a window at Blethen's High-land Drive mansion. He expected an easy time of it, quickly sneaking around and walk-ing away with a rich haul. He didn't reckon with the ferocious Blethen temperament. Roused from sleep by the burglar's misstep, Alden Blethen woke the household with tremendous whoops and hollers, and the entire family chased the miscreant from the house. They raced after him down the hill— Rose Ann and C.B. "hot in the chase, the Colonel in the lead, shouting and trying to discharge a revolver." The burglar outran the Blethens and escaped.[11]

Blethen continued to work long hours at the Second and Union office, wearing his old "blue office coat" with the elbows out.[12] He loved to show off *The Times*, and city editor James Wood recounted a typical session of Alden Blethen's banter with visitors touring the building:

> Here's the local room. This is where they write the news of the town—when they get it, which is not often. There's Parish, assistant city editor; look at him: gettin' fat for lack of work. Where's C.B.? Oh, making up, eh? We'll see him when we get to the composing room. Hello, Wood. This is Jim Wood, city editor, loafing as usual. Fellow over there with his feet on the desk—Shorty Hughes—best sportin' editor in the West—in the world, maybe, I don't know. Matt's out on politics, I guess....[13]

Some evenings he hung around cheap clubs with "low friends"; others he played billiards at the Arctic Club. He liked plain "New England food" and plain-spoken people. He had vowed never to be drunk in public again. But Blethen, resourceful and not above a little trickery, always carried an apple in his pocket. If he wanted a drink, his bartending friends poured him a teacup of brandy and he inconspicuously dipped the apple in the cup, nibbling away until he finished the liquor. Appearances were as important as reality to Alden Blethen, who claimed the honorary title of "Colonel" with unbecoming eagerness. An earthy man, he wished to be perceived as an American aristocrat.[14]

Blethen, proud of his deep roots in the East, generously supported Seattle's New England Club whose members celebrated New England Puritan stock as "one of the great civilizing forces of the modern world." In 1911, he privately published a genealogi-cal history of his family. He used it to establish a pedigree, an extraordinary European and American heritage of Welsh nobility, Quaker iconoclasts, and Revolutionary patriots. This little book, combined with a brief personal history composed for obituary purposes, comprise a skewed and sanitized autobiography, which his own son regarded as untrustworthy.[15]

In 1910, with the manuscript of the genealogy nearly complete, he returned home on "a grand triumphal tour," as Harry Chadwick described it. Himself an Eastern transplant, Chadwick spoke for many Western men when he teased Blethen for his "burning desire to show the old folks back in Pembroke, Maine, or some other little joint, that he was the real candy." On his visit to Kent's Hill, Blethen unfolded "the sad, sweet story of his life" to a reporter from *The Boston Globe*. It was an American saga, as he told it, the hardworking boy who struggled against all odds, and succeeded by pluck and determination.[16]

A wealthy man now, Blethen had more than once been a poor one. He'd had good breaks and bad in his life, and he was drawn to men and women down on their luck. At times, his philanthropy was flamboyant, and Harry Chadwick's gibe—"If Alden Blethen ever does an action worthy of praise that he does not air in his paper, it must be when he is asleep"—rang true. However, at other times, Blethen practiced a self-effacing benevolence; at his death, many kindnesses came to light for the first time. His most spectacular public embarrassments in Seattle had begun with quiet private favors—to Berryman, to Dallagiovanna, to Wappenstein. From his younger son's point of view, he handed out "enormous" amounts of money to petitioners, many of whom were "unworthy."[17]

Charity from Alden Blethen usually came with counsel and expectations. He believed that he had learned how to live, and he had no hesitation about sharing his advice along with his money. In these years before disability or social security insurance, Blethen established a pension fund for men and women who were injured at work or retired from *The Times* after many years of service.

Late one night, it was said, he stormed into *The Times* "smoking hot," his face purple with anger over some outrage. A charwoman was scrubbing the floor, and Blethen stopped short, "What are you doing?! How old are you?!," he demanded of the terrified woman. "You're too old to work for me!" he declared with an emphatic thump of his cane. "You're fired! Go home! You'll get your wages each week, in full, as long as you live!"[18]

But he expected these pension recipients to lead frugal and respectable lives; he wished to help only the "worthy poor."

As an example, Charles Williams had survived *The Tribune* fire, but suffered for many years from the scars in his throat and lungs. After his old friend's death, Blethen supported Williams' widow and children. However, in Blethen's judgment, she did not conduct "an economical life," and her son had ungratefully turned down a chance to work on *The Times*. Blethen eventually withdrew his financial support.[19]

Blethen, a prominent resident of Queen Anne Hill, contributed materially to the community's beauty and convenience. As a member of the Queen Anne Hill Improvement League, he took responsibility for lighting and paving much of Highland Drive, and contributed $500—a substantial sum—toward the construction of a library on Queen Anne Hill. It had pleased him twenty-five years before to return to Kent's Hill as a benefactor; in his later life, philanthropy for civic improvement continued to appeal to this man, not strictly out of the top drawer, who so eagerly sought respectability and prominence.[20]

Alden Blethen had achieved national stature as a newspaperman. A ranking and influential member of the Associated Press, Blethen became chairman of its Western Advisory Board in 1912. In 1913, he and Scott Bone of *The Post-Intelligencer* succeeded in bringing the AP's Northwest bureau office to Seattle, stealing it from Portland.[21]

He attended the annual meetings of the Associated Press for thirty-five years, and was proud to be one of the select group of publishers who also edited their newspapers. Scott Bone recalled his charm at these gatherings, where he was a "most hospitable, even prodigal, entertainer, and a most companionable man." He enjoyed the company of these "famous newspaper men, who 'are the paper,'" including William Randolph Hearst.[22]

Alden Blethen offered lavish Thanksgiving dinners for The Seattle Times *newsboys each year. Observers familiar with his volcanic temper were startled by his warm affection for the kids who sold the newspaper, some of them homeless, others their families' chief breadwinners.*

(The Seattle Times)

Alden Blethen's admiration for Hearst continued into the new century. *The Times*, more staid contemporaries charged, imitated Hearst's yellow papers. When Hearst visited Seattle, Blethen hosted him at the Rainier Club and led a toast to his guest's vast publishing empire. Blethen concluded with a wry little joke: "[Hearst] has been able to accomplish all of these things without running up against the antitrust laws and without being called on the carpet by President Wilson—as yet. He is a creator and a builder."[23]

Blethen's ongoing efforts to impress Hearst occasionally misfired. Harry Chadwick related "a good story going the rounds on Col. Alden J. Blethen...[who] has one subject of conversation which is old but always new and that is the circulation of *The Times*." On his trip east to the AP meetings, his friends wearied of Blethen blowing his newspaper's horn, and decided to play a practical joke on him. They gathered some 1898 copies of *The Times* from its New York agency and hired a newsboy to pretend he was selling them as today's news:

> The Colonel was in conversation with Willie Hearst and a number of others who are counted among the big boys in journalism.
>
> "Yes, sir," said *The Times* man, "our circulation is going up in a manner that is surprising, even to me. Why *The Times* is on sale everywhere. We have the longest leased wire in the world, and our news is always fresh."
>
> Just then the sonorous tones of a newsboy were heard in front of the hotel.
>
> "*Seattle Daily Times*! All about Dewey's victory at Manila!" The Colonel began to splutter and stammer.
>
> "I see that your paper is being pushed, even in New York," said Hearst.
>
> "Oh, yes," replied the Colonel, with a sickly smile, for he knew that something was wrong.

> "*Seattle Daily Times*! All about the sinking of the battleship MAINE!"
>
> "Your news does seem a trifle fresh," observed another member of the party.
>
> "Excuse me while I get a copy," said the Colonel, rushing out of the hotel.[24]

But business *was* good at *The Times*. The paper's growth mirrored that of the city. Seattle's population had doubled between 1890 and 1900; it tripled in the following decade, and then leveled off. Likewise, newspaper circulation grew magnificently in the thirteen years following 1897, but would moderate its growth between 1910 and 1915. Daily circulation had tripled to about 60,000 copies between 1900 and 1910; however, in the five years that followed, it increased only to about 70,000. *Times* circulation remained steady through World War I and into 1920, when it stumbled and declined in response to the Hearst acquisition of *The P-I.* [25]

The most extraordinary event of 1911 in the Seattle newspaper business was Erastus Brainerd's departure from *The P-I*, and the subsequent reconciliation between Alden Blethen and *P-I* publisher John L. Wilson to "promote the best interests of the city." Blethen secured a position for Wilson on the board of the chamber of commerce; Wilson, in turn, directed that his newspaper downplay coverage of Blethen's grand jury difficulties. In an editorial, Blethen identified Brainerd as the "discordant element," responsible for the newspaper warfare of the previous seven years that had been so destructive to cooperation toward civic progress.[26]

When Wilson and Blethen shook hands at the fall 1911 chamber of commerce dinner, symbolizing their new "spirit of harmony," the crowded room burst out with "a yell which fairly raised the roof." Wilson chose Scott Bone as *The P-I*'s next editor, and he

This view of the University of Washington looks east toward Laurelhurst, and was taken in about 1905, four years before the Alaska-Yukon-Pacific Exposition was held on campus. Denny Hall—then the administration building—is most prominent in the photo, and the newly opened Science Hall—later renamed Parrington Hall—can be seen to the right. Alden Blethen began his tenure as university regent in 1897 and concluded it in 1905.

(PEMCO Webster and Stevens Collection, Seattle Museum of History and Industry)

worked well with Blethen on chamber and AP matters. *The Argus* celebrated an end to the bitter antagonism between the town's two leading dailies by running front-page portraits of Bone and Blethen.[27]

In 1912, Seattle had three strong dailies. *The P-I* was Seattle's elite newspaper, *The Times* appealed to the middle class, and *The Star* to the working class. As historian Roger Sale has pointed out, in comparison with *The P-I*, *The Times* was "generally a splashy and vulgar paper," constantly defending itself against charges of "yellow journalism." However, *The Star,* a Scripps chain paper, delighted in the tawdry scandals, gruesome murders, and anti-corruption crusades that were the yellow press' stock in trade. As *The Argus* remarked snidely of the changing situation, "*The Times* can no longer be unique by

being yellow. The semi-respectable field is all that is now left open to it."[28]

Nevertheless, contemporary journalists considered *The Times* in "an enviable position," freed by its financial independence. *The Times* could afford to print whatever its publisher and editors wished. If it made errors in taste or judgment, they were not made because of outside influence.[29] A contemporary remarked:

> *The Times* is...one of the few big dailies of the country which is not absolutely tied up to some big corporation or other. To be true the Blethens owe allegiance to Jim Hill—but Hill does not own them. And they must jump through a hoop when Hearst says so, or Willie Boy may take his [feature] service away from them.... But taken as a whole it is in a position to be pretty independent...[30]

In March 1912, *The Seattle Times* crowned its success with the announcement of its purchase of a wedge of land north of "downtown" between Fifth and Fourth Avenues, at Stewart and Olive, almost in the suburbs. After a decade, the Second and Union building was bursting at the seams, and it was time to build a "new home."[31] Blethen noted:

> It has been the ambition of the present owners of *The Seattle Daily and Sunday Times* from that moment, in the boom following the discovery of the Klondike, when it became evident that Seattle had a splendid present and a magnificent future, in which *The Times*, along with thousands of other business institutions, would prosper, to erect from its own earnings an adequate and permanent home.[32]

In his editorial he predicted that "Times Square would be the center of the City of Seattle of ten years hence," and promised "the newspaper's leadership in creating a new business district of shops, offices, and public spaces.

As a University of Washington regent, Alden Blethen combined this active civic boosterism with his roles of philanthropist, dominant state publisher, and newspaperman of national stature. When he began his tenure in 1897, the university included two buildings and two hundred and fifty students; when he left in 1905, there were six buildings and just under one thousand students. Blethen more than once called the University of Washington "the pride of my life."[33]

In 1901, Blethen presided at the laying of the cornerstone for the school's new Science Hall, and he gave a visionary and inspiring speech:

> Where you stand today will be reared one of the greatest universities of the nation. I have called your attention to the men who have

wrought out great results in life without the aid of the college or the university more for the purpose of impressing upon your minds the contrast between your lives, your opportunities, and those of the men who practically had none, and yet have builded so well.... Do you appreciate this difference? Do you recognize that the God of the Universe has been extraordinarily partial to the youth of this generation by permitting them to be born at the close of the nineteenth century?[34]

According to Blethen's son, his greatest contribution as regent—and it is not clear to what extent he shared the responsibility—was to insist that the university retain the ten-acre metropolitan tract. Once a forest, then a pasture, this enormous piece of land bounded by Third and Sixth Avenues and Union and Seneca Streets seemed too far north of "real downtown Seattle" to be of much value. *Times* newsman "Matt" Mattison emphasized

Science Hall at the University of Washington is pictured shortly after its dedication. Meteorology equipment is visible on the roof, and the entire natural history collection, which would one day form the core of the Burke Museum, was held in the three floors of the wing on the right. At the hall's cornerstone ceremony in 1901, Alden Blethen predicted that here would be "reared one of the great universities of the nation."

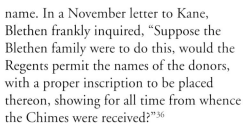

In 1908, advance planning for the Alaska-Yukon-Pacific Exposition ground to a halt, as legislative funding proved inadequate to complete the ambitious project. Blethen's Seattle Times of October 16, 1908, boldly featured this provocative headline, daring Seattle's Rich Men to return to the community a Little of the Wealth gained there. Leading the campaign with substantial contributions, the Blethens restored the AYPE's momentum.

(The Seattle Times)

Blethen's role in the early development of the metropolitan tract, writing that he "devised the plan to make the old university campus a profitable holding...and to prevent it from being sold for...a trifling sum."[35]

During the summer of 1911, university regent John Rea approached Blethen about contributing a major gift to the school. Rea had attended Cornell University, and fondly remembered the music of its bells drifting over the campus. He thought that a set of such chimes would make the UW seem more established, less raw and Western. Blethen agreed, and gave John Rea general encouragement that the family would be interested in making such a gift.

However, Alden Blethen approached this donation cautiously, apprehensive of negative public feeling. Within weeks, he was due to appear before the grand jury, indicted in a conspiracy to further vice in the city. Writing with uncharacteristic delicacy, he repeatedly sought assurance from Rea and from UW President Thomas F. Kane that if he were to donate the bells, he would be able to have them inscribed with the family name. In a November letter to Kane, Blethen frankly inquired, "Suppose the Blethen family were to do this, would the Regents permit the names of the donors, with a proper inscription to be placed thereon, showing for all time from whence the Chimes were received?"[36]

Kane reassured him that the university wouldn't dream of accepting such a donation without a proper inscription. On the strength of this encouragement, Blethen wrote to John Rea, telling him that Kane felt the bells could be inscribed, and asked that Rea "discuss this matter quietly with [the regents] and sort of feel them out as to what they would consent to."[37]

Meanwhile, on December 1, after weeks of sensational testimony, Judge James T. Ronald instructed the grand jury to acquit Alden Blethen of connections to gambling and vice. Three weeks later, during Christmas break, the university publicly announced the Blethen family's gift of the chimes.[38]

It seems certain that Rea and Kane kept the name of the donor to themselves as long as possible, trying to build enthusiasm for the chimes rather than unmask the mysterious philanthropist. As late as December 19, 1911, the regents' meeting minutes indicate their general interest in a chime of bells from "an unnamed donor," also referred to as "a person or persons." However, toward the conclusion of this meeting, the regents demanded the donor's identity, and Rea finally named Alden Blethen. After spirited discussion, the regents voted four to two to accept the Blethen Chimes.[39]

At first, there was little public fuss. *The Argus* reported Blethen's gift of the Chimes, and joked that "they will probably be tuned to play 'Hot Times in the Old Town To-night.'" On January 5, *The Daily*, the student newspaper at the University of Washington,

In 1909, silver-tongued orator William Jennings Bryan visited Seattle's Alaska-Yukon-Pacific Exposition and spoke to a huge crowd in an open-air amphitheater on the fairgrounds. In this photograph, Bryan's longtime political supporter Alden Blethen is seated, cane in hand, on the speakers' platform just behind Bryan. Other local politicos include former state senators Josiah Collins and Charles Heifner, as well as governor Marion Hay.

(The Seattle Times)

The AYPE was enormously successful, focusing international attention on Seattle and encouraging nearly four million visitors to see the fair on campus and spend time in the city itself. Here, we see the great WELCOME sign erected during the fair at Columbia Street over Second Avenue. The achievements of the Alaska-Yukon-Pacific Exposition encouraged local boosters in the Seattle Chamber of Commerce and the Seattle Commercial Club to plan the annual summer festival that would become Seattle's Potlatch.

(The Seattle Times)

Opposite lower: This bird's-eye view of the 1909 Alaska-Yukon-Pacific Exposition at the university was shot from a tethered balloon. Looking up Rainier Vista, the cluster of fair buildings leads north from Geyser Basin—today's Frosh Pond—toward Science and Denny halls. The AYPE left a campus legacy of Olmsted design and landscaping, paved roads, and many structures that were later adapted to student use.

(The Seattle Times)

Looking west from the city across the docks and piers, and out to Elliott Bay. Built to meet demand for steam passage to Alaska and the Yukon, Seattle's busy waterfront also thrived on the new opportunities offered by Asian trade. This photo was shot a year after Alden Blethen's ill-fated campaign to pressure Seattle's new port commission into acceptance of a New York syndicate's plan to build terminals on Harbor Island.

(The Seattle Times)

published a letter which acknowledged the gift as "handsome," but warned that it must not be accepted "at the price of intellectual freedom." *The Daily* letter writer explained his disquiet with vague reference to "the things for which the donor stands." An eccentric Seattle weekly, *The Patriarch,* had been a constant Blethen critic, and protested at once in December 1911 that "The chimes of triumphant perfidy...will cause modest women to blush and virtuous men to curse." But, in general, the Seattle community received news of the Colonel's gift in silence. The calm would not last.[40]

Though tainted by malice, testimony against Blethen before the grand jury had been shocking. *The P-I* had muted its coverage and, under instruction, the grand jury

had excused Alden Blethen. But he was not exonerated at the bar of public opinion. Privately, he hoped that the generosity of his gift would silence his critics; however, he soon became involved in an ambitious scheme for waterfront development that would run afoul of Washington progressives, on campus and off. His role in the Harbor Island controversy would provoke bitter opposition to his "purchase of a character" by buying a chime of bells with "tainted money."

In September 1911, Seattle elected its first set of port commissioners, dedicated to public ownership and development of the waterfront. The commissioners' ideas ran counter to those of established Seattle business interests, represented by the chamber of commerce. There had been general agreement within the chamber that Seattle needed major harbor construction to take successful advantage of the Panama Canal's opening. Blethen initiated a spectacular scheme. In December, he announced to the chamber trustees that Joe Blethen, on business for *The Times* in New York, was deeply involved in negotiations with investors interested in developing Harbor Island in Seattle's Elliott Bay. If the port would build $3 million in new facilities, the New York syndicate would lease and maintain those facilities for thirty years, and then return them to the port's ownership. It was daring and ambitious; the chamber was stunned. They at once appointed Blethen chairman of the special committee on the Harbor Island Terminal Project.[41]

He had great plans for Seattle and its port commission. First, the city had to place a bond issue on the ballot. Once voters approved that bond, the port had to acquire title to a hundred additional acres on Harbor Island, to construct two huge piers at once, and four more within the year. The terminal project on Harbor Island was to be developed along the "general lines of the famous Bush terminals of New York." Blethen pressed the issue hard in *The Times*: there was no time to waste, he urged, because a "rival city"—likely Tacoma—was bidding against Seattle for the New York investment.[42]

The port bonds came before the voters in March 1912 and included not just the money for the Harbor Island development but for other projects as well. The bonds totaled $5 million, an astronomical sum for the day. Blethen pledged his newspaper's efforts to try to convince "the mechanic and artisan that [the bonds' passage] means employment, the real estate owner that it means an increase of 20% in the value of his lot, the wharf owner that it means his business."[43]

The Sunday Seattle Times, on the weekend before the election, published its huge annual business review. The newspaper could not have pushed harder for "yes" votes on the port bonds, running alarmist headlines, like, **Loss of Terminals Would Drive Away Great Industrials—Citizens Should Know What Defeat Entails**. The Colonel instructed the voters to Vote YES because the terminal was key to general prosperity. Opponents—like port commissioners Robert Bridges and Hiram Chittenden and new port engineer R.H. Thomson—were "vicious knockers" who sought "to strike down the greatest improvement ever offered the people."[44]

The port bond issues did pass, and *The Times* crowed **TERMINALS WIN!** applauding the triumph of the "New Seattle Spirit" over the "vindictive opposition of...certain malcontents." But Alden Blethen had not reckoned with the port commission's

Alden Blethen firmly believed that public ownership of utilities—municipal ownership—would lead to mismanagement and waste. Here, a Times *political cartoon during the March 1912 campaign shows a City Light construction crew, managed by corrupt-looking bosses, over-manned and under-worked, with plenty of time to smoke, to watch the clock, and to lean on their shovels. Although* The Times *pressed hard for public passage of the port bonds, Alden Blethen became bitterly disappointed by the commissioners' lack of cooperation with his plans.*

(The Seattle Times, March 5, 1912)

MUNICIPAL OWNERSHIP

The Construction Gang.

The Seattle Sunday T[imes]

EIGHTY PAGES.   SEATTLE, WASHINGTON, MARCH 31, 1912.

Another Prometheus Bound

By the end of March 1912, Alden Blethen had become convinced that the port commissioners and their engineer, longtime adversary R.H. Thomson, were dragging their heels on the Harbor Island construction. Here, on the front page of The Seattle Times, *a political cartoonist relates the long-standing Seattle-Tacoma rivalry to the Greek myth of Prometheus, as the vulture Tacoma is poised to tear out the entrails of the heroic Seattle, bound and chained to the rock by its own port commissioners.*

(The Seattle Times, March 13, 1912)

resistance. Elected to administer a public port, the commissioners found themselves railroaded into developing a Harbor Island facility for private use. Blethen seemed a high-handed meddler with suspect motives who had cooked up his "great deal" virtually without the port's knowledge.[45]

The commission remained fundamentally hostile to his proposal and declined to deal with the New York investors, wishing to develop its own improvement plans. At the end of March 1912, *The Times* ran a fantastic front-page illustration of Seattle as the mythic Prometheus chained to a rock by the port commission, attacked by the vulture of Tacoma about to gorge on its vitals. Alden Blethen had spent a lot of his own time and money on the New York deal, and the cham-

ber of commerce honored his "earnest and unselfish desire for the good of Seattle." Yet almost certainly, the New York syndicate was inexperienced and undercapitalized. The port chose to proceed with the terminals without Blethen's outside investors. *The Times* never forgave the port for ignoring this beneficent offer, and for questioning the integrity of chamber boosters. The port had, Blethen wrote bitterly, squandered the people's money.[46]

Hulet Wells did not agree. A prominent Seattle Socialist, Wells saw the Harbor Island deal engineered by Alden Blethen as "an elaborate plan to take our new public port facilities out of the hands of our Port Commission and turn the operation over to a private profit-making concern." Wells condemned *The Times* for using a newspaper campaign "to bludgeon the people into submission."[47]

Many politically active University of Washington students who had paid little attention to the regents' decision to accept the Blethen Chimes shared Wells' sympathies for municipal ownership. One student remembered a common campus notion that the so-called New York investors were "a dummy outfit," a cover-up for potential harbor investments by Alden Blethen and other moneyed interests. A university group invited Blethen to attend a meeting in the spring of 1912. Unsuspecting, he agreed. In their political science classes, the students had read Edward Bemis' *Municipal Monopolies*, which matter-of-factly discussed Blethen's sale of *The Tribune*'s influence to Thomas Lowry. The students quizzed Blethen about Bemis' allegations. They asked about his preference for private ownership of utilities, and his efforts to "ruin City Light." They asked about the port deal. Confronted by insolent questions, an infuriated Blethen stormed out. These students became the core of a protest movement against the Blethen Chimes.[48]

Moving to the right himself, Alden Blethen had become obsessed with Seattle's leftward drift, from the docks to city government. In March 1912, George Cotterill, a prohibitionist and urban progressive, had been elected Seattle's mayor in its first nonpartisan election. He favored municipal ownership of public utilities and transportation services, and his tolerant politics and inflexible moral code alarmed pragmatists like Blethen. Chadwick of *The Argus*, equally distressed, wrote that "no greater calamity could possibly befall Seattle" than to elect "this puritanical egotist" mayor. Another bad omen in the mayor's race: Socialist Hulet Wells ran a strong third to Cotterill.[49]

One historian has argued that the results of the 1912 election sent Blethen "into a tailspin," horrified at the increasing strength of radical Socialists like Wells. On May Day 1912, Seattle leftists marched past *The Times* Building, carrying the red flag and the United States flag at the head of their procession. A group of men rushed out of the alley and the U.S. flag was torn and muddied in the ensuing scuffle, photographed by a suspiciously handy *Times* staffer. The photo ran on the front page of the paper, accompanied by accusations that Wells, "local leader of the direct action faction of the Socialist party," had called the flag "a dirty rag." Hulet Wells sued *The Times* for libel, and Mayor Cotterill defended the Socialists' right to parade and speak in the city streets.[50]

Under Cotterill's administration Seattle reformers also stepped up their efforts to cleanse the city. A band of police officers known as the purity squad aggressively rooted out vice, accosting single women on the street and bursting into hotel rooms. *The Times* often took the bumbling "pew-rity" squad to

Seeing Seattle - - - By Dok

"On the left, the Female Cop!"

By 1912, vice had been the touchstone of Seattle politics for nearly a decade. When the restricted district was closed, respectable city residents found that prostitution, gambling, and after-hours drinking spread through the city. The city's vice squad—popularly known as the purity squad—was organized specifically to track down and arrest offenders against community morals. As a member of the squad, the Seattle Police Department hired its first woman detective, here portrayed as a homely busybody by Times *cartoonist "Dok" Hager on the paper's October 4, 1912 front page.*

(The Seattle Times)

The Seattle Times *parodied the purity squad as the pew-rity squad, and antagonized its supporters among the moral progressives who sought to cleanse the city. In this October 8, 1912 editorial cartoon, the squad accosts a man and his wife walking home from an evening visit with friends and mistakenly hauls them into court on vice charges.*

(The Seattle Times)

THE SEATTLE DAILY TIMES, TUESDAY EVENING, OCT. 8, 1912.

Well, Do You Blame Him? By Jenner

This 1912 photo shows some of the twelve bronze bells of the Blethen Chimes, still on their shipping pallets on the University of Washington campus.

task. For instance, in the middle of the night, the Squad raided the room of a registered nurse who had just moved to Seattle to look for work. Half-asleep, in her nightgown, she refused to open the door and the purity squad broke it down to make sure she was sleeping alone. During the summer of 1912, *The Times* defended the honor of more than a hundred women who had been "treated as if they were street walkers by a lot of [police] women who ought to be horsewhipped for the insults which they perpetrate."[51]

Blethen's *Times* made a lot of enemies in the spring and summer of 1912. Meanwhile, the foundry cast the twelve great bronze bells of the Blethen Chimes, destined to be "the most perfect chimes ever manufactured in the United States," according to their donor. *The Times* termed them "a magnificent donation" that surpassed anything Regent John Rea had ever anticipated. As the bells were shipped, hung, and then tested, *The Times* published photographs and glowing reviews of their

music. "The beautiful, clear, and mellow notes from the Blethen Chimes" reached throughout the University District, up the north slope of Capitol Hill, out along the east side of Queen Anne Hill, and out toward Meridian.[52]

On the evening of the formal dedication, *The Times* hoped for "a vast outpouring of students, faculty members, regents and friends of the University of Washington," despite the threat of rain.[53] *The Times* printed thousands of programs, which included a portrait of Alden Blethen captioned "The Donor," and the following inscription from the bells:

These Chimes were presented to the
University of Washington by
Col. Alden J. Blethen
of Seattle
to commemorate his services as a member
and
President of the Board of Regents and
also to commemorate the participation of
the
Blethen Family
in the work of this University.[54]

But only a small crowd turned out. In public, Alden Blethen bravely editorialized that "but for the fact that a cold rain with frequent gusts of wind made the night unusually inclement, there would have been an audience of several thousand." In private anguish, he wrote to President Kane that the whole chimes affair had been "a very severe disappointment to me, as such a thing can occur only once in a lifetime and it seemed as if the Devil himself had conspired to make everything disagreeable." Blethen sent his chauffeur to Kane's office to pick up the unopened packages of chimes programs, requiring the president's secretary to sign a receipt agreeing that the reason there were any left over "was owing to the horrible weather which kept thousands of people away." It *was* a chilly, rainy night, but that was not why the event was poorly attended.[55]

University students had organized a protest against the acceptance of the Blethen Chimes because of the notorious character of the donor. They were opposed to Blethen's past, his recent "effort to bulldoze the Seattle Port commission into leasing Harbor Island to a dummy corporation," and his current campaigns of red-baiting and zealot-baiting. It seemed to them that Blethen believed he could buy his way out of everything. They did not want him to "purchase a character" on the university campus, and they wanted to embarrass him.[56]

The students circulated a petition of protest and gathered fifty-one signatures. They requested that the editor of *The University of Washington Daily* publish the document, and he agreed to place it on the front page. Apprehensive, the paper's faculty advisor telephoned President Kane, who ordered him to remove the letter. *The Daily* editor refused to print the paper unless the letter ran, and Kane ordered the presses stopped. *The Daily* suspended publication for two days.[57]

Students took their protest letter from *The Daily* office to a local print shop, and turned it into the leaflet *SUPPRESSION!* Included was a poem:

Clang the Chimes—clang the Chimes,
Help to glorify *The Times*...
Rear them high, and let them swing
For the Open City Ring;
Let them clang, clang, clang,
For the glory of the Gang.
Every hour of night and day
Let the college chorus say,
"Praise to all that get the dollars;
"Learning talks, but money hollers";
Hear us tell, every bell,
All is well; all—is—well.[58]

The open protest letter, also published in the pamphlet, attacked Alden Blethen's career in Minnesota and Washington, as well as his Seattle association with Ludovic Dallagiovanna and Charles Berryman. The pamphlet reprinted Blethen's "Dear Wapp" letter to his protégé Charles Wappenstein and lengthy editorial quotes from Erastus Brainerd concerning Blethen's "betrayal of public trust and debauchery of public and private morals." The chimes, the students protested, would every day ring out "the triumph of the dishonest dollar [because] each peal of its bells will testify that money can purchase respectability for any man no matter how sordid his character."[59]

The students decided to organize a protest at the dedication ceremony, and distributed a four-page leaflet to everyone entering the auditorium. On that cold and rainy night, few braved the student gauntlet; few proved willing to stand up and be counted as Alden Blethen's friend.

After the chimes were hung, numerous civic and fraternal organizations joined the Seattle Commercial Club in passing

The University of Washington Daily *intended to publish a letter of protest signed by fifty-one students against the Blethen Chimes on October 22, 1913, the day that the bells were to be dedicated. UW President Kane forbade the campus newspaper to publish the material and shut down the presses when* The Daily's *editor refused to cooperate. The letter was republished, along with other materials, in the leaflet* SUPPRESSION!, *which was widely distributed in the days prior to the chimes' dedication.*

(Special Collections, University of Washington Libraries)

SUPPRESSION!
Free Discussion of Chimes Question Denied by President Kane

There will be no "Daily" tonight. Presses at the Printing Department ordered stopped by President Kane at 3 o'clock after daily had gone to press. He demanded that the open letter submitted as a protest against the acceptance of the Blethen chimes, and signed by 51 students, be torn from the forms. The editor of the daily, contending that the columns of the student publication shall be open to any and all students desiring to express their opinions, refused to comply with President Kane's demand. The administration then ordered the presses stopped; the "Daily" will not be printed tonight.

Washington: "What Next"

Political progressives at the University of Washington were offended by the campus prominence of the statue of James J. Hill, the railroad magnate often accused of ruthless business practices. Here, in a 1912 protest circular, Hill's bust is coupled with the Blethen Chimes as affronts to the dignity and ethics of the man for whom the University was named, made here to inquire solemnly, "What next?"

(Lister Papers, Washington State Historical Society)

resolutions of support for the student protest. A coalition began a statewide drive to raise enough money to refund the chimes' purchase price to Blethen, and then remove the offending inscription. The drive collected thousands of names, from Bellingham to Pullman.[60] Blethen ridiculed the petition organizers in one of his "speckled" editorials:

> [A] few old women, deprived of the privilege of domesticity, decided to reform the world and began by holding real **old cackling bees** in a down town restaurant.... [S]uch **old hens** and a few **hot air pumpers** who have disgraced the Commercial Club in the last few years [combine] to put forth **any sort of slander**—provided they can **borrow money** enough of **somebody** to **pay their bills!!**[61]

In the fall of 1912, Alden Blethen believed himself beset by enemies of all sorts. When the regents denied Socialist Emma Goldman the right to speak on the UW campus, a local radical vowed "destruction of property in retaliation." Concerned that Seattle anarchists—"who seem to be the protégés of George F. Cotterill"—would attack his chimes, Blethen insured them for $10,000 against destruction or damage by the "I.W.W. torch or the Dynamic Socialist bomb." He renewed this policy annually until his death.[62]

The Federation of Ministers organized a boycott of *The Times* in response to Blethen's long-standing campaign against the purity squad. Blethen called the squad nothing more than "a gang of highwaymen, paid by the City Council, who nightly break into private homes... without even a semblance of a complaint and absolutely without any warrant of law." He continued to condemn the "ministerial-detective combine" of zealots who wished "to run the City of Seattle according to a new set of religious rules." Blethen wrote angrily to the Federation,

"You call on your people to boycott *The Times*—and so did the I.W.W.'s and the socialistic anarchists who belong to that gang of defamers of the flag."[63]

Alden Blethen ferociously attacked his community antagonists. The chimes—a well-intentioned gift—had become the catalyst for a joint campaign of all his 1912 adversaries: religious zealots, Socialists, and reformers. But Blethen himself wouldn't allow the chimes incident to fade from view, raising it time and again. In *The Times* he responded compulsively to the familiar charges against his conduct and character, repeating his own well-worn explanations. And his attacks on his enemies became increasingly reckless. Blethen continued to insist that Mayor George Cotterill had masterminded the student protests, and that the university had become "a hotbed of dynamic socialism."[64]

In print *The Times* mildly suggested that the students should be "soundly spanked," but privately, Blethen wanted much stronger action. He wrote later that President Kane pussy-footed with the protesters and "did not use the male fist when he should have done it. If [he] had taken that gang of rowdies that Cotterill set going at the University against the Chimes and broken their damn necks as any good old-fashioned school master would have done, there would have been no trouble." However, the university expelled no students, though twenty received disciplinary action ranging from probation to reprimand.[65]

Alden Blethen was angry, embarrassed, and deeply saddened. *The Daily* had reprinted correspondence from a Bowdoin student who claimed that in response to the scandal, the school's president said he "was extremely sorry that such a man could make any claim on Bowdoin at all." All his life, Blethen had been proud of his honorary Bowdoin degree. Scott

Bone, editor of *The P-I,* later wrote that the chimes incident "cut him to the quick—filled his heart and soul with anguish." Blethen offered to take down the chimes, store them until the Times Square Building was complete, and then "put them on top of that building to the edification of our friends and the disappointment of our enemies." Rose Ann Blethen never forgave the University of Washington, and until her death, the school received little assistance from the Blethen family. The whole episode was a disaster. Alden Blethen finally turned away from the chimes, and back to his newspaper.[66]

Alden Blethen had been preoccupied by the chimes controversy for more than six months and his sons had taken on new responsibilities at the paper. The only diplomat in the family, Joe Blethen managed the business affairs of *The Times.* He had turned his literary talent to copy writing, his winning ways to public relations, and became a remarkable combination of solid businessman, raffish bohemian, and civic booster. Joe had once been his father's indispensable right-hand man, jack of all newspaper trades. But when his younger brother returned from college, the two men shared the work that their father did not do himself.

Joseph Blethen probably did not want to be publisher of *The Times,* but C.B. Blethen unquestionably did. As Joe became increasingly involved with civic activities, C.B. became his father's "closest friend and most intimate confidant." In fact, C.B. later claimed that he and his father had designed the Times Square Building together. Alden Blethen and his younger son were kindred spirits. Blethen was very proud of his family's tradition of military service, and C.B. had been ranking cadet officer at the University of Washington. Though C.B. attended both the UW and the University of

The Blethen Chimes were originally meant to hang in the cupola of Denny Hall, but proved too heavy for the structure. An unused water tower was hastily remodeled to accommodate the chime of bells, and is here shown a few years later. The Chimes Tower was destroyed by fire in 1949.

(The Seattle Times)

Chicago, he never took a degree, impatient to work on *The Times*. Polished in manner and of refined tastes, C.B. had nevertheless rejected the academic world for his father's world of action.[67]

Newsman Christy Thomas, in his reminiscence of *The Times*, remembered that C.B. Blethen "impressed [him] immediately as a capable executive of tremendous vitality." Intense and hard-driving, as headstrong as his father, he willingly made the newspaper his life. A son after Alden Blethen's own heart, C.B. "directed many of the paper's red-hot crusades and made them a big success." After 1912, his influence became pronounced in *The Times'* growing emphasis on red-baiting, super-patriotism, and militarism.[68]

Joe Blethen had no such interests. Easygoing, tall and handsome, a bit of a carouser, he

This photograph of C.B. Blethen, at the steering wheel, includes his first wife, Frances Hall Blethen, seated on the right in the back seat. The child is most likely their first son, Frank Blethen. C.B. Blethen and his brother were avid motorists, and The Argus' *Harry Chadwick teased that both young men were speed demons who spent lavishly on these wonderful new toys. The car is parked in front of C.B. Blethen's home on Queen Anne Hill.*

(The Seattle Times)

served as the glad-handing president of the Advertising Club, the Seattle Press Club, and the Automobile Club. He had been *The Seattle Times'* ambassador to Seattle's journalists when his brother was in college and his father was a blustering renegade. After 1910, he became *The Times'* delegate to the community. As longtime chair of the chamber's city affairs committee, Joe was a natural to be chosen in 1912 as president of the city's Potlatch, an entertainment extravaganza with only the loosest connections to the traditional Indian ceremony.[69]

Joe described the Potlatch as a summer carnival for the city's benefit to encourage tourism in this "immense playground" of the Pacific Northwest. Seattle's Advertising Club, long an informal group, organized specifically to work on the 1912 Potlatch. To Joe Blethen, the Potlatch was, "an advertising stunt" that "chased the village pessi-

mist out into the never-never and established a perennial parade of optimists on Second Avenue."[70]

In the great July celebration, "the city came out to frolic in the sunshine with the whole wide world for playmate." In 1912, under Joe's direction, the Potlatch entertained and educated, weaving together a complex mesh of themes. The great gold ship *Portland* returned once again, and the Pacific fleet of the U.S. Navy gathered in Elliott Bay. A parade of giant totem poles marched through the city streets, and bright-eyed Seattle car salesmen pretended to be tyees and tillikums, Chinook jargon for chiefs and friends. The Potlatch emblem was "a grotesque from a totem pole of the tribe of the Tlinkit [that] grins and grins and grins, yet always with good nature." Called the Potlatch bug, the "microbe of optimism" sprouted on lapel pins, banners, and lamp standards.[71]

Many believed the 1913 Potlatch would be bigger and better than ever. But that year the Potlatch became contested ground in the struggle for moral authority in the city. What did this celebration mean? Whose vision of the city would it express? Driven by the unhappy experiences of 1912—the Harbor Island failure, the grand jury, the chimes' protests, the ministers' boycott, Seattle's leftward drift—Alden and C.B. Blethen would turn the 1913 Potlatch into a mad parody of a celebration, a riot instead of a festival.

Blethen's *Times* had continued to antagonize Seattle's leftists and religious zealots. *The Seattle Sun*, a brand new evening daily that debuted with 50,000 paid subscribers, threw down the gauntlet at the Blethen family's feet with its first issue in February 1913. *The Sun* was the self-proclaimed response to "an overwhelming public demand for a clean family newspaper." C.B. Blethen wrote that *The Sun* was "largely backed by churchgoers, with the announced object of upsetting the domination of … [The] Seattle Times." His father agreed, calling *The Sun* "an alleged reform newspaper" whose sole purpose was "to put *The Times* out of business." *The Sun* spoke for the forces of the righteous city, alienated by *The Times*.[72]

Baiting the left, *The Times* carefully drew a distinction between "good" union men or "good" Socialists and the direct action Socialists "who advocate sabotage and the firebrand." But *The Times* itself encouraged direct action by "patriots" to deliver vigilante justice to the "anarchists." On February 9, *The Times* threatened Seattle radicals, writing that local veterans had not forgotten how the American flag was carried lower than the red flag, how it was ripped from its standard and muddied in the street on May Day 1912. Mayor Cotterill had been **HELPLESS**, wrote *The Times*, but the old

Joseph Blethen was president of Seattle's Potlatch in 1912. A longtime member of the Seattle Chamber of Commerce, he also involved friends from the advertising and press communities in the celebration. Shown here at his Times *desk with the Potlatch "bug," Joe's easy charm, hard work, and emphasis on good public relations made the 1912 Potlatch a triumph for city boosters.*

(Seattle Public Library)

soldiers would remember how to respond if it happened again. *The Times* worried that the "I.W.W. Horde" planned a general strike in Washington's lumber industry for May Day 1913.[73]

Four days later, an early morning fire struck *The Times* Building. At dawn, newsboys sleeping on the stairs of *The Times* Building were awakened by smoke and rushed out to turn in the alarm. The fire destroyed newspaper files back to 1881 and thirty years of Alden Blethen's correspondence; it burned *The Times'* library, its photo archive, and ruined its physical plant. Two thousand Potlatch lapel pins melted in Joe Blethen's desk. Seattle's newspapers pulled together, and *The P-I's* presses printed the February 13 *Times*. Insurance covered the damages, and no one was injured. Compared to the nightmare fire at *The Minneapolis Tribune, The Times'* blaze was inconsequential.[74]

However, C.B. Blethen had been out of town during the fire. When he hastily returned "to resume charge of the news departments," the next issue's front page asked provocatively:

Was *The Times* fire of last Thursday of incendiary origin or was it not? If it was incendiary, was the torch applied by representatives of that vicious, lawless element which through anonymous letters and posters, time and again threatened to destroy *The Times*?...[T]wo newsboys who were resting on *The Times* doorstep the morning of the disaster...today declared that before they discovered smoke...a stranger dashed past them, down the front steps and out on the street.[75]

The story described how an intruder had earlier tacked an anonymous letter threatening to blow up *The Times* Building on the third-floor city room door. *The Times'* fire served as the peg for a provocative campaign of red-baiting patriotism, almost certainly masterminded by C.B. Blethen. Posters turned up all over town showing a huge American flag flying over the burning building. Lettered **THE FLAG THAT STANDS FOR PRINCIPLE**, they reminded the public that "miraculously" *The Times'* flag had flown throughout the fire. "Neither death nor jealous attack," boasted the posters, "can injure *The Times* standard." In the aftermath of the fire, the upcoming Potlatch fought for newspaper space with an increasingly belligerent crusade against the left.[76]

Throughout the spring of 1913, *The Times* continued a steady barrage against anarchists, direct action Socialists, and IWWs—calling them "I Won't Work's" who believed that the world owed them a living. According to the paper, Wobblies pretended to be radical thinkers, but were merely criminals who "proposed the entire overthrow of the Government of the United States and to establish an industrial republic wherein all present-day political functions will become extinct." Not only that, they were not even "real Americans," according to *The Times,* editorializing on the IWW's appeal to "the worthless element among the foreign born population." After *The Times'* long heritage of encouragement to recent immigrants, this nativism was a radical departure.[77]

However, militarism was not a new theme for *The Seattle Times*, which had encouraged U.S. overseas adventurism, glorified the American fighting man, and portrayed local veterans as a posse of patriots. But starting with this Potlatch summer of 1913, *The Times'* militarism became identified with C.B. Blethen's personal experiences. In June he joined the Mounted Scouts of the Second Washington Infantry, a company of the Washington National Guard. He became interested in the state's coastal defenses and transferred to the Guard's Coast Artillery Corps as a sergeant, making first lieutenant and then captain. *The Times* covered every detail of his military career.[78]

C.B. Blethen went to his first National Guard encampment July 1913, and he took along his camera. Daily, *The Times* ran three or four photos of the "citizen soldiers" in camp. When he returned to Seattle, the Potlatch had gathered six warships, a tender, and a submarine for naval maneuvers in Elliott Bay. The ships would light up the night sky with searchlights and fire a salute in honor of Secretary of the Navy Josephus Daniels, Seattle's most distinguished Potlatch guest. On Thursday, Daniels would view the military parade of Washington's National Guardsmen, members of fraternal orders from throughout the state, and more than four thousand uniformed sailors and soldiers. The 1913 Potlatch had a distinctly martial air.[79]

Seattle's Potlatch Week had glorious Northwest weather—bright, warm days and cool, clear evenings, with a freshening breeze off the bay. Visitors ready for fun mobbed the city. Along the parade routes, Potlatch work-

ers had transformed each lamp post into a mock totem pole surmounted by a cluster of American flags. Over each block, an immense American flag hung, combined with the Potlatch bug emblem. Joe Blethen was a member of the General Reception Committee of Tillikums, "friends" of all visitors to the Potlatch, and one of only four official Klosh Klahowyas, or handshakers for the city. An official greeter, with a dozen responsibilities, he hardly slept during Potlatch Week, dashing from luncheon to reception to grandstand to dinner. A year's planning had come down to these seven days.[80]

The Times wrote that the Spirit of the Potlatch presided over Seattle like a "great golden Colossus," awaiting the arrival of the Great Tyee on Wednesday night, led by a blazing comet to celebrate the anniversary of Klondike prosperity in July 1897. The organizers planned a huge nighttime "electrical parade" with floats that wove together Native American motifs, booster mania, and sheer whimsy. A great motorized Indian canoe bearing the smiling Potlatch nobility, and floats covered with pretty girls wearing headdresses like daisies highlighted the parade. *The Seattle Times* had entered a float that

Opposite top: The February 1913 fire at The Seattle Times, *in the Denny Building at Second and Union, began very early in the morning. Discovered by newsboys sleeping in the hallway, the fire is here shown shooting flames through the roof, backlighting the newspaper's sign.*
(The Seattle Times)

Opposite lower: The fire caused heavy destruction, burning the newspaper's photo archives, Alden Blethen's correspondence, and more than thirty years of the The Times' *bound copies. The charred rubble in the basement—which had been newsroom desks and files —still smoldered when this photograph was taken.*
(The Seattle Times)

After C.B. Blethen's return to town, The Times' *coverage of the February fire took a distinctly provocative turn. The paper strongly suggested that the fire had been set by Wobblies and radical Socialists, a "vicious, lawless element" who had made frequent threats against* The Times. *Here is one of the giant posters that the newspaper printed and posted all over town, boasting that the American flag had flown bravely over the newspaper building throughout the destructive blaze.*
(The Seattle Times)

In a cartoon, "Dok" Hager's Umbrella Man tosses an anarchist into Elliott Bay, reminded by a duck to take his red flag along. For years, The Times *had ridiculed unreliable forecasts of Seattle's capricious weather, and eventually offered its own best estimates in daily panels that featured the Umbrella Man and his Pet Duck.* Times *artist Hager modeled the Umbrella Man on Robert Patten, a Civil War veteran. Known as the "human barometer," Patten was famous for the accuracy of his folk weather forecasts; his long white beard and silken umbrella hat had become familiar sights in downtown Seattle. Here, Patten is shown as he looked in about 1910.*

(photo: The Seattle Times; cartoon: The Seattle Times, May 2, 1912)

depicted a miniature newspaper plant, with a telegraph operator receiving news, a reporter working at a typewriter, a trio of photographers, and a miniature press. Two hundred Tillikums dressed in distinctive white suits roved the city, to answer tourist questions.[81]

Josephus Daniels had agreed to visit Seattle, *The Times* wrote, at the joint urging of Alden Blethen and Scott Bone. What a grand opportunity, editorialized Blethen, to show him that the Puget Sound Navy Yard at Bremerton was the best location for a West Coast repair facility. As Daniels said, "After the opening of the Panama Canal...the fleet will be in Puget Sound just as often as heretofore it has been in Boston and New York. The real purpose of my visit here is to ascertain...what are the requirements and improvements of the Bremerton yard to accommodate the enlarged fleet so that I can make recommendations to Congress." The chamber of commerce hosted a glittering dinner at the Rainier Club in the navy secretary's honor.[82]

That night, after the parade, lots of folks strolled the city's streets, carrying their picnic hampers and folding camp chairs, just enjoying the warm July evening. It would be

the last tranquil night of the 1913 Potlatch because of two unrelated events occurring only blocks apart, but in different worlds. At the Rainier Club, Daniels made an after-dinner speech to Seattle's elite, and a street-corner shouting match ended in a fistfight. The newspaper would bring these two incidents together.[83]

Next afternoon, *The Times* ran the banner headline **DANIELS DENOUNCES TOLERANCE OF RED FLAG**, reporting on its front page that Daniels condemned "Un-American Mayors" who would permit red flag demonstrations in the city streets. *The Times* wrote that Daniels gestured to the American flag on the Club wall and said, "This country has no place for the red flag and it has no place for the believers in the red flag!" A wildly enthusiastic audience rose to its feet again and again, "frantic with delight over the secretary's bitter denunciation of the conditions which have so long disgraced Seattle."[84]

At the same time, a few blocks away, the newspaper reported that "a gang of red flag worshipers and anarchists were brutally beating two sailors and three soldiers who had dared protest against the insults heaped on the American flag at a soapbox meeting." *The Times* claimed that the soapbox speaker had sneered, "Don't be a soldier, be a man!" amid Wobbly taunts. Yelling "Kill them! To hell with the flag!" the mob of several hundred attacked the soldiers and sailors and beat them severely. *The Times* described a lawless city where Wobblies thumbed their noses at law and order.[85]

Most outspoken in their indignation were Spanish-American War veterans who, *The Times* pointed out with heavy emphasis, "will lead tonight's Potlatch parade...past the scene of the attack." The paper quoted one of the veterans as saying, "If they start anything with us, they will meet something they never did before. Our men will be armed with everything from bolos to head axes and we will be ready for them." That Friday night, the city got ready for trouble. Five hundred white-suited Tillikums, supposed to be tourist guides, were instead pressed into service, and "the boosters were possessed of police powers, two fists, and a nightstick to every man." On its front page, *The Seattle Times* predicted "The result tonight will be interesting."[86]

After *The Times* came out that evening, rumors of impending trouble cleared the streets of soapbox orators, except for a brave Christian bearing the placard, "Jesus Loves All." By 7:30, *The Sun* reported that hundreds of sailors, soldiers, and "hoodlums" lined Washington Street, between Occidental and First. That Friday night, a mob of several hundred, swelling at times to many thousand, rioted in Seattle. They first burned the IWW office on Occidental Avenue, then, carrying hundreds of little American flags, danced a serpentine to the Socialist Party headquarters on Fifth Avenue and wrecked the place.[87]

Early Saturday morning, Mayor Cotterill surveyed the smoldering Potlatch city. Fearing repetition of the previous night's rioting, he declared a state of emergency and assumed control of Seattle's police force. Cotterill issued proclamations to close the saloons, outlaw street speaking, and shut down *The Seattle Times* to prevent further "incitement to disorder." The mayor charged that *The Times* had deliberately instigated Friday night's riot, and he suspended publication of the newspaper for the next two days unless it furnished him with complete advance proofs.[88]

Chief of police Claude Bannick served the mayor's order to Alden Blethen, in his third

A view of some of the military units in the 1913 Golden Potlatch parade, marching north from Pioneer Square. The city is gaily decorated and spectators came from miles around to line the sidewalks and enjoy the marchers, bands, floats, and clowns.
(Seattle Museum of History and Industry)

The Seattle Times *entered this float, described as a "miniature newspaper plant," in the July 1913 Potlatch parade competition. The telegraph operator, seated at his desk, took down news "from all parts of the world," and next to him a reporter typed up a story. Three photographers—two with tripod cameras and one "with a swiftly operating graflex"—shot photos of the crowd, while a miniature printing press turned out copies of the newspaper to be distributed to spectators along the parade route.*
(The Seattle Times, July 20, 1913)

The Potlatch mob wrecked the Square Deal Store in the early morning hours of Saturday, July 19, 1913. That evening, this photo ran in The Times *after Alden Blethen's lawyers had forestalled Mayor Cotterill's order to shut down the newspaper. The caption ran, "I.W.W. joint on Washington Street, near Occidental Avenue, which was sacked by sailors last night." A patriotic locomotive engineer had climbed to the top of the building at 2:00 a.m. to place the American flag over the "I Won't Work" headquarters, as* The Times *put it.*
(PEMCO Webster and Stevens Collection, Seattle Museum of History and Industry)

George F. Cotterill, mayor of Seattle during the Potlatch riots, was best known politically for his equally strong advocacy of prohibition and municipal ownership. Alden Blethen had not actively pitted The Times *against Cotterill's mayoral run in 1912, but the two men were soon at sword's points when the mayor upheld the rights of Socialists, suffragettes, and Wobblies to speak freely from their soapboxes on Seattle's street corners.*
(The Seattle Times)

floor office at Second and Union. Enraged, the publisher telephoned his lawyers; then he stormed downstairs. The Seattle policemen stationed at the *Times* Building halted the distribution of an "extra" to the newsboys. *The Sun* reported that "Col. Blethen made several dashes into the alley in the rear of *The Times* Building...[and] gesticulating wildly, unburdened his opinions of the police department to the police stationed there to enforce the mayor's order." He tried to make a speech to the crowd, milling outside the *Times* Building.[89]

Just after lunch, Judge John E. Humphries issued a temporary injunction restraining Cotterill from prohibiting circulation of *The Times*. Based on Joe Blethen's affidavit that the police had occupied the Denny Building, *The Times'* lawyers also asked Humphries for warrants for the arrest of Cotterill and Bannick. The attorney argued: "Is this man, the mayor, a czar that he can say to the press of the city when you shall print or when you shall not? Are we to submit our articles to him for the nicety of his censorship before we, in this free American country, print our paper?" From the bench, Judge Humphries agreed, issuing warrants for contempt of court to Cotterill and Bannick. The violence was the radicals' fault, Humphries declared, and if the Wobblies didn't leave town, they would "be hanged at the lamp posts," and justly so. By late afternoon, *The Seattle Times* was for sale in the city streets.[90]

The Times portrayed the Potlatch riot as the just vengeance of patriotic soldiers, sailors, veterans, and civilians fed up with Seattle's Red shame. The rioters were not a mob. They had passed the hat to collect money for a bugle and a flag, and as they marched and burned, they "cheered...[because] it was almost more joy than they could stand." Defiant, *The Times* again threatened that "if anarchists were looking for trouble they would get all they wanted," because the soldiers and sailors had stayed in town, "ready to repeat the lesson if need should arise."[91]

These events completely bewildered Secretary Daniels. On Thursday, at the Rainier Club, his generic after-dinner speech had sent the audience into a frenzy of delight. On Saturday, praised by Seattle's patriots and condemned by Seattle's Socialists, he protested that his remarks had absolutely nothing to do with the local situation. He had not meant to insult Mayor Cotterill, recall May Day's flag incident, or incite a vigilante riot; in fact, he had just given the identical speech in Erie, Pennsylvania. Embarrassed, the presidents of the chamber of commerce, the Arctic Club, and the Rainier Club joined together to apologize to Daniels for their city.[92]

On Sunday morning, Alden and C.B. Blethen published vicious attacks on Mayor Cotterill. Alden Blethen unburdened himself in a characteristic speckled editorial:

> The Times Printing Company will bring a **DAMAGE SUIT** against this **LOATHSOME WHELP** who sits in the office of the **MAYOR**.... *The Times* calls on the businessmen of this city to join with it immediately to establish headquarters—to formulate charges and inaugurate a canvass that will secure not only the **LEGAL NUMBER OF NAMES FOR RECALL** of this wretch, but *The Times* will subscribe $1,000 to help put the **CAMPAIGN THROUGH**....
> Let the law abiding citizens of Seattle, who have been **HANDICAPPED** for more than two years by a most wretched condition of affairs, **GET RID OF THIS OBSTACLE OF PROGRESS AND GET RID OF HIM FORTHWITH!!!**[93]

The Sunday Times published a similar fire-breathing article, signed by C.B. Blethen.

In The Times, *Alden and C.B. Blethen insisted that Mayor Cotterill had no one to blame but himself for the Potlatch riots. He had coddled the Wobblies, they argued, and their behavior had grown increasingly outrageous and militant, insulting all good American citizens. The Blethens maintained that patriots had been forced to take matters into their own hands. After the mayor's effort to suppress* The Times, *the newspaper undertook a recall campaign against Czar Cotterill. Here we see* The Times' *front page published on July 19, 1913, the night following the Potlatch riot.*
(The Seattle Times)

C.B. labeled Cotterill a "foreign-born American Mayor" who tried "to suppress an American newspaper for its defense of the American flag." Since May Day 1912, "the struggle between *The Times* on one side and the Mayor and his Reds on the other has gone on night and day." Friday night, Blethen wrote, the sailors had come on shore for revenge against the Wobblies because the mayor could not ensure an orderly city.[94]

On Monday, *The Sun* deplored the "incendiary articles" by "the wild frothing outfit which edit that newspaper [*The Times*]" as clear incitement to violence. Under the headline **Made Grave Charges Against A.J. Blethen**, *The Sun* published a lengthy statement by Cotterill that named *The Seattle Times* the "most evil and dangerous influence in Seattle."[95]

Cotterill claimed *The Times* had perverted love of country to advertising purposes, wrapping in the folds of the American flag its efforts to reinstate "wide-open vice" and foster "private monopoly." Radical street speakers, said the mayor, may have at times abused the right of free speech, but *The Seattle Times* daily abused the right of a free press. The last straw was the deliberate distortion of Daniels' remarks, and the escalation of a drunken fistfight between a few sailors and passersby into the first battle of an anarchist revolution. *The Times* fully intended to incite a riot, wrote Cotterill.[96]

Vicious name-calling among powerful spokesmen for the city, outshouting one another to portray Seattle as either vice-ridden and dangerous, or a haven for bomb-throwing Reds, crowded the fun of the Potlatch off the front pages. The 1913 Potlatch was a nightmare for its planners, including Joe Blethen. Horrified by Cotterill's panicky suppression of the press, *The P-I* wrote that "The mayor made a mountain out of a

molehill...proclaiming a sort of martial law when there was absolutely no occasion for it," and continued, mournfully:

> What was bad enough Friday night, told on every telegraph wire the country over and perhaps cabled cross the ocean, was made many times worse Saturday morning by the mayor's proclamation.... To the outside world, Seattle was under martial law.... Then there is the matter of the many visitors from near and far.... Many left the city Saturday afternoon. Some...suspected that the Potlatch fun was done for. And who could blame them.... There is now but one thing for us to do: Forget it. The incident is over, the blunder made, the damage done.[97]

But *The Times'* men were determined to stay the course, as they would have put it. On July 21, the Coast Artillery Reserve went into its own encampment, and Lieutenant C.B. Blethen corresponded to *The Times* from Fort Worden as "military observer and aide de camp to the adjutant general." He wrote, too, that "the recent red flag incidents and Mayor Cotterill's attempt to muzzle *The Times'* fearless exposé" were the main topics of discussion at meals.[98]

Next evening, *The Times* ran a front-page headline about an army sergeant **Stabbed By I.W.W. Dies of Wounds at Fort Flagler!** claiming that one of the soldiers beaten on Thursday night had died. But that soldier had not succumbed to wounds from his Potlatch beating; in fact, he was very much alive. *The Seattle Times* had reported as headline news an unconfirmed camp rumor that C.B. Blethen phoned in from Fort Worden. In the super-heated Seattle atmosphere, it proved a foolish act at best. Under the scathing headline, **Times Simply Made It All Up**, next day's *Sun* maintained Alden Blethen's "mendacity" knew no limits; he understood full well, a *Sun* editorial argued, that the report was a lie, but he simply wanted to incite more disturbances. If anyone knew the tale of the soldier's death to be an irresponsible lie, it was C.B., who casually retracted the story in the next issue.[99]

The Sun attacked Alden Blethen, suggesting in an editorial illustrated with four Jolly Rogers that *The Times* should replace the American flag on its editorial page with the skull and crossbones, because Blethen was a buccaneer of journalism. A cartoon on *The Sun*'s front page depicted a raging Blethen wrapped in the American flag under the caption **Whom the Gods Would Destroy They First Make Mad**. Rolled indictments and grinning demons danced about his feet.[100]

No one who knew Alden Blethen doubted his allegiance to his country, his city, or his newspaper, but he betrayed all three loyalties in the Potlatch riot. A man of many powerful convictions, he was also a man of violent temper and high passion. In 1913, he could have become an elder statesman, widely respected, honored for his principles, courted for his influence, and consulted for his measured opinions. Instead, circumstances conspired against him and in the "pressure cooker of his head," Blethen became trapped by his own personality. Defensive, self-dramatizing, stubborn, he could not admit his mistake and express regret, but simply cast about for new enemies.[101]

A natural target was Socialist Hulet Wells, who had first sued *The Times* for libel after the paper asserted he called "the Stars and Stripes a dirty rag" during the May Day 1912 incident. Wells believed Alden Blethen to be "a malevolent man" who had it in for him—an attorney who did not practice, an intellectual who wished to be a laboring man. In June 1913 while his libel case moved slowly through the courts, delayed time and again by *The Times*' legal maneuvers, he joined

other Socialists in bringing a criminal libel suit against both Alden and C.B. Blethen on behalf of colleague Joseph Jarvis. The *Times* had reported that Jarvis—a "rabid Hulet M. Wells follower"—stole $1,000 from a 1912 fund-raiser for Eugene Debs, Socialist candidate for president.[102]

The trial of Joseph Jarvis in Judge John E. Humphries' courtroom, Wells later wrote, "was like something out of Gilbert and Sullivan." From his point of view, the proceedings had virtually nothing to do with the plaintiff's good name; rather, the defense, the prosecution, and the judge had agreed beforehand on the trial's outcome. In retaliation, Wells hit upon the idea of writing a three-act

The Sun's front-page political cartoon of Alden Blethen was published a week following the Potlatch riot.

(The Seattle Sun)

This handbill for Hulet Wells' satire "The Colonel and His Friends" includes the cast of characters and a sketch of the play's action. The Red News Wagon, at Fourth and Pike, was one of the major downtown sources of Socialist newspapers, magazines, and books. During the Potlatch riot, the mob destroyed the wagon, which was covered with posters advertising the upcoming production of Wells' play at the Moore Theatre.

(Ault Papers, Manuscripts and University Archives, University of Washington Libraries)

farce that would parody the judicial proceedings and hold Alden Blethen up to "public ridicule."[103]

The play, "The Colonel and His Friends," was scheduled to be presented just after the Potlatch in Seattle's Moore Theater. Wells told a reporter from *The Sun* that "a realistic interpretation of the exact facts and words of the trial would make the best burlesque possible"; the entire third act was taken verbatim from the trial transcript. Wells promised a hilarious script. Judge Humphries—Judge Humpty-Dumpty—was to be played by the owner of the Seattle Red News Wagon, a Socialist newsstand; Alden Blethen—Colonel Blather—was to be played by a notorious drunk; Fulton Walters, Blethen's attorney,

was to be played by one of the UW students who had organized the chimes protest.[104]

Blethen's sense of humor did not include mockery by a crowd of "long-haired men and short-haired women." *The Times* reported that a committee of Spanish-American War veterans had appealed to Mayor Cotterill to cancel the upcoming performance of "The Colonel and His Friends." They could not restrain, they feared, the honest anger of American patriots. Cotterill ignored their thinly veiled threat, but the Moore Theater's manager canceled the contract two days before the performance. The promoters next tried the Seattle Theater and a performance hall at the University of Washington, but found all city theaters closed to "The Colonel and His Friends." Nor could they rent a hall in Everett or Tacoma. The Blethen family had shut down the play.[105]

As parodied in "The Colonel and His Friends," John Humphries had indeed become a doddering and compliant judge, susceptible to "the extravagant praise" that *The Times* lavished on him. During its first month of publication, *The Sun* had trumpeted **Testimony to Show Connection of Col. A.J. Blethen Is Stricken from the Record.** Humphries had halted testimony in the trial of a wiretapping "detective-reporter" for *The Times* that threatened to confirm the rumor that he was on Alden Blethen's private payroll. That summer, Humphries also agreed to expunge all testimony about Blethen's involvement with the Italian-American club from the records of the 1911 grand jury.[106]

The Colonel defended Humphries, claiming the judge had edited the transcript from the "infamous Grand Jury" because it contained defamatory and inaccurate testimony. If the grand jury had evidence to convict him, he reasoned, they would have done so; instead, they did their best to blacken his name. In 1913, Alden Blethen wanted to revise and justify the past, control the present, and shape the future. He wanted to cleanse the record, "to set it straight," and be known as Citizen, Patriot, Editor.[107]

Blethen's friends on the chamber of commerce's publicity bureau stood behind him in this endeavor. In a special ceremony that summer, they presented him an engraved silver loving cup. The frank presentation acknowledged him fully, his strengths and weaknesses, his vices and virtues:

> The credit in life belongs to the man who is actually in the arena; whose face is marred by sweat and dust and blood; who strives valiantly; who errs and comes short again and again; for there is no effort without error and shortcoming. Fortunately, in his community, we have an editor [who] is a man of action; his face is marred by the conflicts of life. He is more than an editor: he is a part of the community in which he lives.... We know his public spirit; we know his generosity and how his name has headed and set the pace for public subscriptions from the day of his arrival in this city.... We, the members of this bureau, know how this strong-willed, opinionated man has merged his views with those of his associates.... Here's a toast to our loved Chairman.... We love him for the good that is in him, and we forget his faults because we know his virtues outshine them.[108]

This tribute, like every one he ever received, served for him as his vindication by men of good judgment and good will. His reply did not predict any mellowing in this man of sixty-six:

> It is impossible for any man to conduct a great newspaper like *The Times*...without making enemies.... When that miserable indictment was returned against me through the malice of an incompetent Foreman of a Grand Jury, I offered to retire from this Bureau and the Chamber of Commerce.... The promptness with which the suggestion was repudiated gave me my first proper conception of my standing with this Bureau.... Gentlemen, the words you have spoken and this beautiful evidence of your esteem and affection are received as the best evidence of your approval of my conduct as the Chairman of this Bureau, my acts as a public citizen, and my work as a publisher—for all of which you have my sincerest thanks.[109]

Alden Blethen had worked hard to suppress student protests over the chimes, to prevent performance of "The Colonel and His Friends," and to purge the grand jury testimony; he was content to bask in the approval of his peers. He was, then, understandably infuriated when Washington state congressman J.W. Bryan read Cotterill's Potlatch riot statement attacking him into the

Here, members of the chamber of commerce's bureau of publicity pose for the camera at one of their Christmas parties, which doubled as a celebration of Alden Blethen's birthday. Blethen truly enjoyed these festive occasions, which turned into hilarious roasts of the truculent editor. In the last decade of his life, the Colonel began shaving a year off his age. At this party, in December 1914, the bureau ought to have celebrated Blethen's sixty-ninth birthday.

(The Seattle Times)

In early 1915, while Alden Blethen took his long journey through the Southern states, Joseph and C.B. Blethen settled James Bryan's lawsuits, printing a retraction on the advice of Times *attorneys. As this* Town Crier *satirical poem makes clear, the apology received far less attention in the pages of* The Seattle Times *than the original libels, which had charac- terized "Popcorn" Bryan as an anarchist, a crook, and a cur.*

(Bryan Papers, Manuscripts and University Archives, University of Washington Libraries)

Left: A view of the corner of Second Avenue and Union Street as the Seattle Fire Department battles the destructive Times *fire at the Denny Building in October 1913. The two women standing on the front seat of the automobile are almost certainly Rachael Kingsley Blethen, C.B. Blethen's second wife, and either Genevieve Swadley Blethen, Joe's wife, or one of Alden Blethen's daughters, Marion Blethen Mesdag or Florence Blethen Duffy.* **Below left:** *A curious crowd has gathered to watch the second* Times *fire in one year.* **Below right:** *Joe, C.B., Alden Blethen, and a fourth unidentified man anxiously watch the progress of the "Wobbly Fire," as* Times *employees always referred to this blaze.*

(The Seattle Times)

Congressional Record of the United States. *The Sun* jeered that Alden Blethen had "finally secured a place in the imperishable Record made for posterity in the Halls of Congress." Representative Bryan read every word of Cotterill's lengthy document, including the mayor's description of the notorious pornographic photo that Blethen had concocted for his vice trial. In fact, Bryan dwelt on the image, "that dirty, filthy picture manufactured by this 'patriot' [that] exhibits an awful crime against nature."[110]

The Sun wondered in its editorials how Alden Blethen would go about getting the *Congressional Record* altered. In the fall of 1913, Bryan made political hay out of Blethen's errors in judgment, mailing copies of his oration to fifty thousand Washington residents. The Blethens struck back at "Popcorn" Bryan, also calling him, "a renegade, a cur and a vagabond," a "fee-seeking...legal

Above, Alden Blethen, holding his cane, stands with sons C.B., center, and Joseph at the Times Square groundbreaking in 1914. C.B. Blethen is shown carrying a camera and likely recorded the photo of his father on the right with shovel in hand, digging with enthusiasm, and locking eyes with one of the workmen hired to begin digging the foundations. This project was delayed and not resumed until after Alden Blethen's death.

(The Seattle Times)

parasite," and so forth. J.W. Bryan filed five libel suits against *The Times*, and eventually the paper would be forced to apologize. And the *Congressional Record* stood.[111]

That fall, *The Times* burned again. As great clouds of smoke billowed from the building, Alden Blethen's black limousine pulled up amid the fire trucks. Newsman Christy Thomas remembered Blethen as he dashed back and forth, from police to firemen to newsboys, "wild with anger and excitement," brandishing his cane to force a path through the crowd. The goddamn Wobblies did it, he shouted; they said they would do it, and they did, damn it! *The Times'* newsroom always referred to the conflagration as "the Wobbly Fire." The fire raised suspicions, but police and fire department investigators could not conclusively prove arson.[112]

In 1914, two years after *The Times'* land purchase, "Colonel Blethen armed himself with a shovel and began to dig for the foundation for the new Times building." In photos of the event, he appears rugged and vigorous. Alden Blethen got his hands dirty; he did not treat this ground breaking as an empty corporate gesture. He intended the Times Square building to be the greatest material expression of his years of competition and achievement, the monument to his life's work.[113]

In 1914, four daily newspapers competed in Seattle. Suffering from lack of advertising, *The Sun* went out of business and resurfaced as a struggling employee cooperative in December 1914. Alden Blethen could not restrain his glee at the death of his antagonist. Since its founding in February 1912, *The Sun* had hounded Alden Blethen and his family. All his life, Blethen had personalized business rivalries into business feuds, and he regarded *The Sun*—and its editor—as bitter personal enemies. Although *The Sun* did not officially

breathe its last until August 1915, the business failure of "this gang of character assassins" was one of the great delights of Alden Blethen's last few months of life.[114]

By Christmas 1914, he had been ill for months. He had tried to fight his illness with willpower, but fatigue, fevers, and a series of stubborn colds plagued him. The strain began to show; Blethen did not look well. In December, the chamber's bureau of publicity staged its annual Blethen birthday roast and Christmas party. In 1914, it responded to 25,000 letters of inquiry from tourists, settlers, and investors, distributed half a million fliers, sent out promotional packages of photographs to hundreds of libraries, developed and distributed a lantern slide show about the city, and planned a book "of full-page pictures" and a movie about the city. The volunteers had worked hard to boost Seattle, and the year had been a success. There was a great deal to celebrate, but Alden Blethen felt little energy or enthusiasm.[115]

In February, Blethen requested a ten weeks' leave of absence from his duties as bureau chair "compelled, under advice of his physician, to relinquish his work and leave the city." He held the final meeting of his chamber committee on February 16, the day before he left town. James Wood remembered that Blethen seemed depressed and uncertain about the future; he "talked frankly of his condition and his need of change and rest." His lingering illness stymied physicians. C.B. Blethen wrote that his father suffered from a general infection that had spread from untreated, abscessed teeth; his daughter, Florence Blethen Duffy, also referred to an abscess, but caused by influenza, that spread its infection throughout his body. He refused, she said, to undergo surgery.[116]

Uncomfortable and out of sorts, gloomy over local business conditions, Alden Blethen

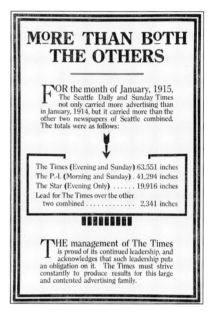

MORE THAN BOTH THE OTHERS

FOR the month of January, 1915, The Seattle Daily and Sunday Times not only carried more advertising than in January, 1914, but it carried more than the other two newspapers of Seattle combined. The totals were as follows:

The Times (Evening and Sunday) 63,551 inches
The P.-I. (Morning and Sunday) . 41,294 inches
The Star (Evening Only) . . . . . . 19,916 inches
Lead for The Times over the other
   two combined . . . . 2,341 inches

THE management of The Times is proud of its continued leadership, and acknowledges that such leadership puts an obligation on it. The Times must strive constantly to produce results for this large and contented advertising family.

The best-selling newspaper in the state by 1915, The Seattle Times *did not rest on its laurels. Here is a typical volley in the endless war of words over circulation and advertising among* The Times, The Post-Intelligencer, *and* The Star.
(The Seattle Times, February 2, 1915)

A portrait of Alden Blethen at home with his first two grandsons, the sons of C.B. and Frances Hall Blethen. The eldest, Frank Blethen, father of The Times' *current publisher, stands at the right, and Clarance Brettun Blethen II sits on his grandfather's lap.*

(The Seattle Times)

painfully revealing journal of a losing battle against a consuming illness.

Blethen's chamber committee sponsored a booth at the Panama-Pacific-International Exposition in San Francisco, and he wired an article to *The Seattle Times* describing the fair's opening day. The weather, he wrote, was cool and rainy; the crowds sparse. He enthusiastically reviewed the exhibit from Japan, but noted that the war had prevented many European nations from participating. He found business conditions in California very like those he had left in Seattle—with everything over-built, those who had been most optimistic suffered the worst consequences. Clearly, Blethen worried about the Times Square Building, as he noticed no new construction and declining rents and prices all over California.[117]

Horrible weather also pursued him. After shivering in California, Blethen would find snow in Arizona and New Mexico. He and Rose Ann endured a disagreeable ride to New Orleans only to find that beautiful city so chilly that they moved on to Jacksonville, Florida. They then encountered a record cold wave in the Sunshine State. Shaking his head, Alden Blethen wrote with a flash of wit:

> Any man who left the Pacific Coast with the idea of finding warmer weather in the Gulf states—even way down in Florida—has lived to be exceedingly disappointed in what he sought.... We are about to start for Havana. If we do not find the inhabitants engaged in the cutting of ice from the native rivers and ponds, we shall undoubtedly remain for a week.... [If] it be no good there, we will take a flying machine for Seattle.[118]

But Havana "was disappointing." Blethen couldn't sleep, and wrote restlessly of "the dead hours of night" and "a despondency that amounts to thick gloom." Alden Blethen encountered an old Seattle friend in

did not prepare a *Times* annual business edition in 1915 for the first time since his arrival in Seattle. Long accustomed to attending the annual meetings of the Associated Press and the American Newspaper Publishers Association, he headed south early with Rose Ann, hunting for sun, warmth, and healing. He meant to keep working, and prepared a series of reflective essays on the stops along his journey. The observations of a man interested in politics and business, the articles are also a

Miami—the only bright spot in an otherwise dismal trip. He had taken this vacation against his better judgment; it wasn't working and he hated the enforced inactivity. He headed north to New York, hoping to renew his well-being among his cronies at the Associated Press annual meeting, to find his health again as an active and vital newspaperman, talking politics, making plans, hatching deals.[119]

Blethen delighted in these annual meetings, spending time with a "group of famous newspaper men, who 'are their papers,'" as editor James Wood put it. These old-time publishers and editors had the custom of gathering early, before the business meeting began, for a couple days of good food and conversation. He hoped that the conviviality among these familiar friends would restore him, but he found himself—once more—disappointed and depressed. The group had been thinned by death.[120]

Blethen could bear only one day of New York, and then boarded a train for home. He left the train in Chicago, desperately ill, and cabled Seattle from his hotel. C.B. Blethen hastened east to meet his father. Together the men traveled home. Alden Blethen received bad news along the way, and *The Times* published his characteristic retort:

> I arrived at Havre, Montana, yesterday, advised of the verdict in the libel suit of R.H. Thomson against *The Times*. I was prepared for an adverse verdict when I saw that the jury was so largely composed of women, who are naturally unacquainted with public affairs.
>
> I have instructed our attorneys to leave nothing undone to set aside this verdict. We will carry the case to the Supreme Court if necessary. Not one cent of actual damages was or could be proven. Therefore *The Times* will exhaust, if necessary, its last resource in its efforts to reverse this verdict.[121]

Alden Blethen's family doctor traveled to Spokane to meet his train and accompany the ailing editor. The party arrived in Seattle on May 1, met by the rest of the family. Thin and weak, Blethen asked to visit the old Second and Union offices. Going "through the building...with his customary cheer, [he] greeted the old employees with whom he had associated intimately for years." It would be the last time.[122]

Confined to bed, he sent brave weekly messages to the publicity bureau: "Getting on fine.... May be hung up here for a few more weeks, but will be down for work and lunch just as soon as these doctors will stand for it." He was so convincing that *The Times* publicly discouraged calls and visits to the Queen Anne house, including a brief notice that described him as only "somewhat better."[123]

During Alden Blethen's long absence in the spring of 1915, The Times *continued to campaign against Wobblies and other political radicals. In February, the newspaper provided extensive print and photo coverage of a local rental house, occupied and then looted and abandoned by "I.W.W. Fanatics."*

(The Seattle Times, February 14, 1915)

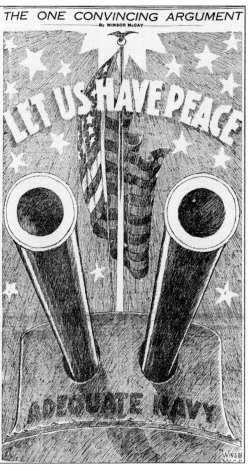

As he lay in bed, a series of physicians came and went, trying to keep him comfortable but unable to reverse his decline. When he could still think and speak, he composed the lengthy "Advice and Recommendations," a substitute for a will that offered direction to his family for the next five years. He asked that the newspaper headlines be read to him morning and evening, and when he was no longer able to speak, he gestured to hear entire articles in which he remained interested. With great effort, he sometimes made "facetious comments" about old enemies and friends, or offered brief directions on how *The Times* might pursue a story. It was a hard time for him to sit idly by. The nation was

sliding into war. A week after his return to the city, the *Lusitania* was torpedoed and sunk with terrible loss of life. The general *Times* coverage of the worsening situation bore the clear stamp of Alden Blethen's thinking, but his last signed piece of work appears to be the editorial of May 12, calling for German apologies and reparations under a doctrine of "strict accountability."[124]

The Times ran front-page bulletins on Alden Blethen's condition, signed by Joseph and C.B. Blethen. In the hushed and darkened house, he sank deeper and deeper, his voice stilled. On Sunday, he appeared "brighter and apparently stronger," but that night was very hard. The family gathered on Monday, July 12, and spent the day together, waiting. In the late afternoon, time ran out for this dogged fighter, this most vital and determined of men.[125]

Telegrams and notes of condolence streamed into *The Times*. The Queen Anne Hill home filled with flowers as friends and employees came to pay their respects and extend their sympathy. The family held a brief service at home, without music or any fuss, just as he had wanted it. Reverend William Temple spoke quietly and candidly, as though chatting with a group of friends, remembering Alden Blethen in his congregation in 1896, on the edge of despair, the first night he came to Seattle. When he finished, the pallbearers carried the casket to the car, and the mourners drove to the cemetery.[126]

On the day following his death, Seattle's presses stopped for him. On July 15, work came to a standstill at *The Times*, the chamber of commerce, and many businesses throughout the city, honoring Alden Blethen's memory. And the Blethen Chimes tolled for ten minutes, the strokes of the bells tolling the years of a life, then filling the campus with music.[127]

*Edward Curtis shot this revealing portrait
of Alden Blethen for a series sponsored by
the Rainier Club. Curtis has captured
Blethen's flair and elegance, as well as his
disciplined violence, his toughness, and his
determination and forcefulness.*

(Courtesy Gilbert Duffy)

Afterword

Alden Blethen did not die an old man; in many ways, he died in the prime of life. His greatest achievements were recent; his greatest opportunities lay before him. At sixty-nine, he stood secure, proud of his splendid financial success, but still eager to work and ever alert to new possibilities. He lived an open life, his noble virtues and his glaring faults candidly displayed each day in his newspaper.

When he died, old friends and enemies across the nation set pen to paper in reminiscence, trying to understand this forceful and commanding man. Death always calls for judgment, for balancing the books, but Alden Blethen's distinctive words and deeds had been judged throughout his life. Since boyhood, Blethen's singular personality made him unforgettable to many who had crossed his path from Maine, west to Missouri, to Minnesota, and finally to Seattle.

William Henry Eustis, who had snared the Republican mayoral nomination that Blethen worked so hard to gain in Minneapolis, struggled to describe his old opponent. Eustis remembered Alden Blethen as "the most interesting man I ever knew...intense about everything.... He was approachable, affable, voluble, energetic, and above all optimistic... that type of man that can do a good piece of work, build up something for himself, but who finds it difficult to keep it.... His life story might be used as a text for a sermon to the fainthearted of the world."[1]

Eustis was acquainted with Blethen for only a few years, but Otis Moore, Blethen's brother-in-law, had known the editor for half a century, since the days of *The Phillips Phonograph* in Maine. Moore admitted that Blethen's quarrels "stood out in his life," but did not consider them paramount in judging his character or achievement. Above all, wrote Moore, Alden Blethen "moved in a practical, work-a-day world," leading an active life. Blethen was not a poet or visionary, his brother-in-law wrote, but an old-fashioned man who distrusted new ideas and believed in tried and true virtues. He ruefully referred to Alden Blethen's "turbulent spirit," but also noted his loyalty to his friends, his phenomenal success, and his extraordinary determination.[2]

Always in a hurry, Alden Blethen never wanted to take the time to reflect or to rest. Moore wrote that Blethen ought to have "worked himself to his grave many years ago." Few young men were willing to put in the long, hard days he had during the last twenty years of his life; he "died in the harness," still pulling. Blethen had started from scratch in Seattle at an age when most men would be taking things easy; instead, he had thrown himself into *The Times*, belligerent and uncompromising, delighting in controversy, inviting arson, mayhem, and lawsuits. Along with Moore, the newspapermen who worked for him may have questioned his common sense, but they never doubted his passion and dedication.[3]

The Blethen family commissioned a memorial to Alden Joseph Blethen and placed it in the lobby of the Times Square Building shortly after the September 1916 dedication. The confusion about Alden Blethen's year of birth, which he himself fostered, resulted in his memorial incorrectly noting his birth date as 1846 rather than 1845.

(The Seattle Times)

Working men in Seattle mourned Alden Blethen. At the time of his death, *The Sun* remembered that "in times of sickness and other troubles, employees of Col. Blethen found him their friend, [one] who was quick and generous with the assistance he gave." *The Seattle Union Record*, the city's labor paper, noted that union men at *The Times* "sincerely regretted the passing of Col. Alden J. Blethen...for death has robbed them of a real friend." One of Blethen's own reporters wrote that, "no one ever heard an unkind word about him from any man who ever worked for him." A printer who started with Alden Blethen on *The Minneapolis Tribune*

and *The Penny Press* wrote that any one of his employees "stood ready to take off his coat and fight, if necessary, for the good name of Col. Blethen."[4]

Blethen's comrade-in-arms, *Times* reporter "Matt" Mattison, wrote a loving memorial to set the record straight about his boss, and to settle a few old political scores. He described a man whose door was never closed to any visitor, whose intense campaigns were always waged to advance Seattle's best interests. In his view, Alden Blethen had become a master statesman, a civic benefactor, and a superb newspaperman, and Mattison accused anyone who thought otherwise of political malice. Likewise, Seattle newsman Paul Lovering considered Blethen to be "the last of the great editors of his time." And there were dozens of such testimonials of affection, gratitude, and respect, from friends far and near, famous and humble, rich and poor.[5]

Other reminiscences were more reserved. Former *Times* city editor James Wood acknowledged that he had frequently disagreed with Alden Blethen's judgments, with his "strong likes and dislikes," but added that Blethen never allowed differences of opinion to affect their friendship. Alden Blethen was "not a type," Wood concluded, "he was distinctive, unique." Likewise, Harry Chadwick, *The Argus* publisher, wrote of him with characteristic bite, "Col. Alden J. Blethen is dead. And I am sorry. And I would not have said so a few years ago because it would not have been true." Chadwick, an inveterate cynic who had known Blethen for twenty years, acknowledged the editor's difficult personality but nevertheless found much to admire in his life. However, the family chose not to include Scott Bone's penetrating character study in the scrapbook of obituaries. And Bone knew Blethen very well indeed—the two men worked side by side for years in

Seattle's chamber of commerce and had developed as cordial a newspaper rivalry as Alden Blethen could manage. In his reminiscence, Bone pitied Blethen as a deeply unhappy man—a "troubled soul," "quarrelsome and vindictive," who had practiced standards of journalism that could not be "copied with profit or perpetuated with safety."[6]

Despite the bewildering variety of these personal recollections, they have the ring of sincerity and first-hand knowledge. One wishes for more of them, but Alden Blethen had outlived many of his best friends and worst enemies. Tom Lowry was dead, as was William Henry Smith. And no one asked those men with whom he had feuded so publicly—Will Haskell, Erastus Brainerd, George Cotterill, R.H. Thomson, or Hulet Wells—what they thought of Blethen, at least not for publication. So, after the fashion of obituaries, many writers across the nation fell back on phrases and sentiments that seem shopworn. Blethen did not suffer fools willingly, he would give a friend the shirt off his back, he had a heart of gold, he was a lion of a man. But nearly everyone agreed that his was a quintessential American tale.[7]

Born and reared in Maine, Alden Blethen spent his whole life westering, riding booms and busts, chasing opportunities toward the sunset. A few of his eulogists saw him as a latter-day Western man. A Bellingham newspaper described him as "a picturesque character of the Great West"; a New Orleans paper wrote that he had "heard the call of the great, throbbing, undeveloped West." But Blethen had been an urban entrepreneur of the metropolitan West, a tenderfooted newcomer in a series of boomtown cityscapes. The panoramic sweep of his life and his edgy violence seemed uniquely Western to some. Alden Blethen's life "read like a romance" to one writer, like "a book of adventure" to another;

he was a veritable "mountain man in journalism," a two-fisted battling editor.[8]

As Alden Blethen matured, he increasingly personified his newspapers, from *The Journal* in Kansas City, to *The Tribune* and *The Penny Press* in Minneapolis. Blethen and *The Seattle Times* had grown virtually indistinguishable. According to his children, he himself wanted to be remembered as "a fighting editor," and many agreed that "he was an editor of the old school which believed that a newspaper should be run from the editorial rooms rather than the business office." But Blethen had worked most of his life to gather all the reins of the newspaper into his own hands—as publisher, editor, and manager—and he was a canny businessman. While raising hell, he had invariably sold newspapers. Still, he seemed to represent a passing age, "when the editor was the newspaper and the newspaper, the editor." By 1915, the distinctive personality of one man rarely stamped a metropolitan newspaper from the boardroom to the newsroom to the pressroom.[9]

Alden Blethen had come of age in the newspaper world of the 1880s, when the new journalism transformed the American daily press. The field's increasing sophistication encouraged a new professionalism among writers and editors, and the rising profits of the information business encouraged a new opportunism among publishers and managers. Professional journalism organizations, like the Missouri Press Association, and business associations, like the American Newspaper Publishers Association, were founded in the eighties, and developed and sharpened the division between the news side and the revenue side of a newspaper. As publisher and editor-in-chief, Blethen bridged that division and more than once chose to favor his newspaper's profits over its integrity. Alden Blethen was fully aware of the ethics and principles of the field of journalism—his editorials often took others to task for flouting them—but his own practice did not always measure up to these standards.[10]

In his editorials, Alden Blethen valued the ideals of journalistic independence: objective reporting and responsible editorial stands, support of the best man or the best idea, and pursuit of the greatest public good. And, after 1905, *The Seattle Times* achieved the financial security to conduct the newspaper according to these high-minded principles. However, after the paper had succeeded far beyond its competitors' reach, Blethen continued to use *The Times'* pages to pursue private vendettas and to further causes in which he had a personal stake. He loved the exercise of power and he did not always use good judgment in the men and causes he chose to support or to oppose. Easily hurt, quick to anger, Alden Blethen—and his son C.B.—were not just opinionated and outspoken, but at times idiosyncratic and outrageous. Alden Blethen's distinction as a newspaperman depended as much on his character as his convictions, and *The Seattle Times* often reflected this dualism.

Driven by his personality, Alden Blethen was nevertheless the ultimate self-made man who refashioned himself time and again. He had come from a stern tradition of back-breaking labor on harsh and unproductive land where just getting by took the full measure of men and women. Blethen's boyhood world had been lit by oil lamps and candles, heated with firewood, powered by muscles or water wheels. Drinking water came from the well; most food came from the kitchen garden, or from cows, pigs, and chickens. Human lives responded to the needs of the land and the seasons—to shear sheep, to harvest potatoes and apples, to tap the maple trees for sap—a rhythm that was, to Blethen, mind-numbing tedium.

During Alden Blethen's youth, his grandfather became obsessed with millions in unclaimed treasure in England, and his mother ran away from her children, broken by the demands of raising a family alone on the farm. In his boy's world, it was either fevered talk of unearned wealth beyond one's wildest dreams or endless, sweating toil on poor land. Fantasy or misery, nothing in between. When Blethen was in his sixties, a successful publisher, his cousins were still hard at work in the fields of Maine, but he had decisively broken the pattern: first, he ran away, and then he went to school, studied law, and entered business. He was a daring, yet practical, man.

He believed that he had learned how to live. He had earned every penny of his fortune and created a magnificent legacy for his family. Fiercely driven, he was a bold and decisive opportunist, a ruthless competitor, and a stern taskmaster. In his final "Advice and Recommendations," prepared in lieu of a will, Blethen reminded the family from his grave that he had "originated...these great properties" that he passed on to them, defeating "the misfortunes which overtook [him]" in Minneapolis. To his grieving sons, he seemed heroic. Joseph and C.B. called him the "best of fathers," but it would prove difficult—eventually impossible—for them to follow in his footsteps.[11]

Alden Blethen's "Advice and Recommendations," signed with a shaky hand, is a remarkable and revealing document. The old man was dying when he dictated "Advice," but he had tried to continue to think of every possibility, to protect everyone, to guard everything. For example, fearing the outbreak of war with Japan, he left detailed instructions for the family to gather cash from his safe deposit box and flee Seattle for the safety of the mountains of Maine. "Advice" was

RECENT BLETHEN FAMILY GENEALOGY

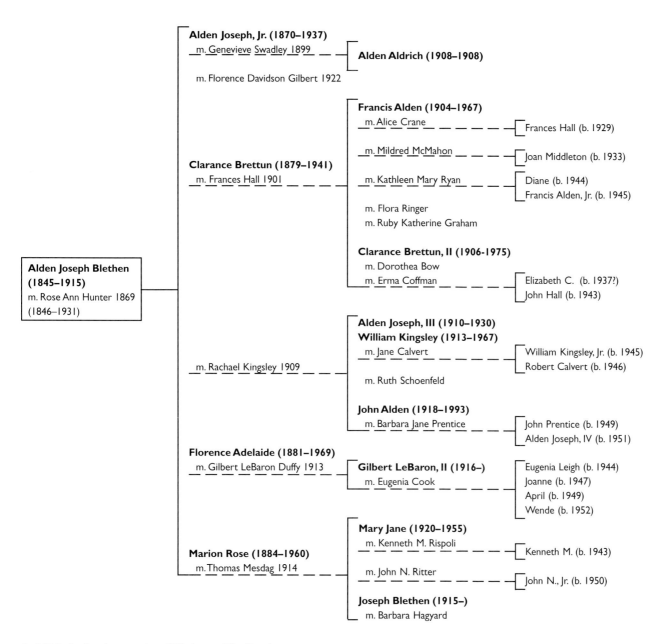

Alden Joseph, Jr. (1870–1937)
m. Genevieve Swadley 1899 — **Alden Aldrich (1908–1908)**

m. Florence Davidson Gilbert 1922

Francis Alden (1904–1967)
m. Alice Crane — — — — — Frances Hall (b. 1929)

m. Mildred McMahon — — — — Joan Middleton (b. 1933)

m. Kathleen Mary Ryan — — — Diane (b. 1944)
Francis Alden, Jr. (b. 1945)

m. Flora Ringer
m. Ruby Katherine Graham

Clarance Brettun (1879–1941)
m. Frances Hall 1901 — — — —

Clarance Brettun, II (1906-1975)
m. Dorothea Bow
m. Erma Coffman — — — — — Elizabeth C. (b. 1937?)
John Hall (b. 1943)

**Alden Joseph Blethen
(1845–1915)**
m. Rose Ann Hunter 1869
(1846–1931)

Alden Joseph, III (1910–1930)
William Kingsley (1913–1967)
m. Jane Calvert — — — — William Kingsley, Jr. (b. 1945)
Robert Calvert (b. 1946)

m. Rachael Kingsley 1909 — — —
m. Ruth Schoenfeld

John Alden (1918–1993)
m. Barbara Jane Prentice — — — John Prentice (b. 1949)
Alden Joseph, IV (b. 1951)

Florence Adelaide (1881–1969)
m. Gilbert LeBaron Duffy 1913 — — **Gilbert LeBaron, II (1916–)**
m. Eugenia Cook — Eugenia Leigh (b. 1944)
Joanne (b. 1947)
April (b. 1949)
Wende (b. 1952)

Mary Jane (1920–1955)
m. Kenneth M. Rispoli
— — — — — — Kenneth M. (b. 1943)

Marion Rose (1884–1960)
m. Thomas Mesdag 1914 — — —
m. John N. Ritter — — — — — John N., Jr. (b. 1950)

Joseph Blethen (1915–)
m. Barbara Hagyard

In 1996, the fourth generation of Blethens at The Seattle
Times *included Frank A. Blethen, Jr., publisher, chair of
the board, and chief executive officer; William Kingsley
Blethen, Jr., treasurer; and Robert Calvert Blethen,
corporate marketing director.*

characteristic of him in its compulsive attention to detail, its emphasis on self-discipline and frugality, and in its protective commitment to his own family and to the larger circle of family, friends, and dependents. Since the organization of the two family companies, Alden Blethen owned no private property but had transferred everything—automobiles to apparel—to corporate ownership. There was, then, no estate, no will, and no inheritance outside of shares in the Times Printing and Investment Companies.

"Advice" restated the long-planned division of stock within the family, and encouraged cooperation between the brothers and also with their sisters and brothers-in-law. Blethen reminded his sons of their duty to their mother, and of their obligations to distant family members and longtime friends who had become Blethen family retainers. Alden Blethen examined his charitable responsibilities, and recommended that some be continued and others be at his children's discretion.

As an example, Alden Blethen matter-of-factly considered the situation of John Cragwell, who had owned a barbershop in the Seattle Hotel. A prominent African American businessman, Cragwell was active in Republican politics and an amateur photographer. For many years, Cragwell had given Blethen his monthly haircut and a daily shave; the men had talked and struck up a friendship. As Cragwell grew older, he faced increasing difficulties meeting the monthly mortgage payments on his lot in the Rainier Valley, and Blethen had bought the property for him. Now, among his last requests to his survivors, he asked that *The Times* pay for the construction of a bungalow for John Cragwell "just as if it were being done for a white man instead of a black one."

Blethen prided himself on his paternal management of *The Times'* "family" of editors, reporters, ad men, typographers, pressmen, and newsboys. From turkeys at Thanksgiving to gold pieces at Christmas, Alden Blethen had distributed generous and well-publicized gifts among the *Times* staff. He hoped his sons would continue the holiday traditions, but he also encouraged the more private kind of long-term wage support for ailing or injured *Times* employees. In 1915, Washington state's recently enacted Insurance Compensatory Law provided injured employees with 40 percent of their wages during recuperation. However, for many years Blethen's *Times* had kept such employees on its payroll until their return to work and continued to do so after the law's passage, making up the shortfall in wages. Alden Blethen requested that, if his sons saw fit to discontinue this policy, that they do so "long after I have been forgotten by the present employees."

In "Advice," Blethen also paid his respects to his deep roots in Maine, reviewing his long history of philanthropy as trustee of Kent's Hill School. Through his generosity, the school built Blethen Hall in 1883 and remodeled it in 1910; the academy had benefited from his substantial annual gifts. In 1911, it came to the Colonel's attention that the school had charged the headmaster and his family for the rental of their living quarters in Blethen Hall. Showing a flash of his tart wit, Blethen remarked that such a method of raising money could have been conceived by "no one but a narrow-minded Methodist of Maine." He offered to pay the annual rental of $300 and did so for years, but he could easily see that his sons might wish to discontinue this contribution. He gave them permission to do so.

Turning to family charities, Blethen wryly observed that "it apparently was the fate of the Blethen family to be born poor and to stick to that condition throughout life." But, he counseled, "blood was thicker than water," so he surveyed the numerous requests for aid that his brothers and sister, nieces and nephews had mailed his way, and summed up his responses to date. Finally, he asked his sons and daughters to review appeals from the Blethen family with fairness and an open heart, and "to render such assistance as [they] deemed right." He felt sorry for "those poor devils," he wrote, and he encouraged his heirs to courtesy, if not generosity.

In 1915, Blethen cautiously valued *The Seattle Times* and its holdings at just under $2 million, but he discouraged extravagance among his children. Throughout his lifetime, Alden Blethen had occasionally indulged an expensive taste for ostentation. He crammed the family's grand mansion on Queen Anne Hill with first editions and ornate furniture, with marble baths, fountains, and elaborate gardens. Blethen, proud of his wealth, had boasted of it all in *The Times*. However, in his daily life, as a matter of habit, he was a frugal man, preferring simple food and comfortable old clothes. During his last years, Blethen had grown increasingly cautious with money. In "Advice" he counseled his children to avoid imprudent spending, sounding a familiar theme to these sons and daughters of wealth and privilege who chafed at his restraint.

When Blethen died, six years remained in the twenty-year trust of the Times Printing and Investment companies. Joe, C.B., and Alden Blethen had each received 20 percent of the companies' stock, while the three Blethen women equally shared the remaining 40 percent. Blethen had placed the trust in attorney Daniel Kelleher's care until 1921, and stipulated that family members sell no shares during that time. At his death, Alden's stock was divided equally between C.B. and Joe Blethen; at Rose Ann's death, her stock

would be equally divided between her daughters. "Advice" explicitly discouraged borrowing any money, despite the demands of the new building, forecasting a subdued business climate. Alden Blethen reminded his sons that he was leaving them two corporations that "owe nobody a dollar." He advised them to keep it that way.

There were some points of friction within the family. C.B.'s first wife, Frances Hall Blethen, had died in 1908, leaving him with two young sons, Frank and Clarance Brettun Blethen II. In 1909 he married Rachael Kingsley, the beautiful daughter of a prominent architect. C.B. and his patrician bride had extravagant tastes, and wanted only the best for their family of five boys. C.B. Blethen had grown ever closer to his father, as a son, a colleague, and a kindred spirit, and *The Times* reflected his increasing dominance. Joe Blethen had grown away from both his father and his brother; his "Manager's Corner" column had long since disappeared from *The Times* editorial page. Though he continued active in Seattle civic affairs, Joe Blethen was a restless and wealthy man; he traveled frequently and found friends away from Seattle. Florence Blethen had married Gilbert Duffy and Marion Blethen had married Tom Mesdag; "the girls" and their families initially stayed close to home.[12]

In his "Advice and Recommendations," Alden Blethen openly speculated about combinations of stock that would permit one faction of the family to wrest control of either corporation from another. Confident there was "little likelihood" that Joseph would act against the interests of his mother and sisters, he also doubted that C.B. would do so "after a full and careful discussion of all matters in a family conference." Alden Blethen saw himself in his willful and impetuous son. But C.B.'s arrogant manner and prodigal

The Times Square Building reached this stage of construction in June 1916. Although Alden Blethen had delayed the building, waiting for business conditions to improve, his "Advice and Recommendations" clearly indicates that he hoped the family would proceed with the new plant. After his death, his heirs voted to begin immediate construction of Times Square as a monument to his life.

(The Seattle Times)

spending made for hard feelings in the family. Blethen had repeatedly cautioned his younger son to moderate his expenses, and had often soothed his daughters' hurt feelings after a slight by C.B. or his wife.[13]

On his death bed, Alden Blethen made his final judgments about his sons, and requested that Joseph succeed him as president and general manager of both corporations, and that C.B. act as vice-president. He hoped that this arrangement would last for at least three years, and cautioned that "five years would be better." Joseph Blethen was a man of forty-five at his father's death and C.B. was thirty-six; they entered their responsibilities at *The*

Times in earnest "to prove worthy sons of [their] father." They had been "educated into the business" for more than twenty years and, at his death, Alden Blethen asked his sons to extend the responsibilities they already held by dividing his over-arching role as publisher and editor-in-chief. Two days after his death, Alden Blethen's name was removed from *The Times'* masthead, which then listed Joseph Blethen as president and general manager of The Times Printing Company, and C.B. Blethen as the newspaper's editor.[14]

Joseph Blethen spent less time at the elegant family compound on Queen Anne Hill, and lived for extended periods at his

The Times *moved from its Second Avenue and Union plant to the Times Square Building in September 1916, and horse-drawn drays carried most of the equipment. Here, workmen move a linotype machine along the north side of the building.*

(The Seattle Times)

rustic cabin on Three Tree Point, a lovely isolated spot on Puget Sound south of Seattle. It is tempting to see a thwarted poet in him, dominated by his father's business ambitions and perhaps embarrassed by his flamboyance. However, Joe Blethen spoke with apparently genuine enthusiasm of his role in the newspaper's business offices, managing the marketing effort that generated *Times* advertising revenue, fully 80 percent of the newspaper's income. In 1915, Joe also succeeded his father as chair of the chamber of commerce publicity and industrial bureau, and was soon elected to a three-year term as chamber trustee.[15]

Just after his father's death, a friend encouraged Joe as "the man to whom the entire Pacific Coast is looking with a friendly pat on the shoulder, and the exhortation, 'Go to it, Joe, the field is yours; all the best qualities of the Blethen blood flow in your veins; step in and win and we will help.'" But it would not appear that Joseph Blethen wanted to "win"—he did not seem to have realized he was in a race with his brother, or he did not wish to compete.[16]

For a time, the brothers worked well side by side, jointly signing editorials as "The Publishers," throwing themselves into construction of the Times Square Building. A week after Alden Blethen's death, the Blethen family—principal officers of The Times Printing Company—voted to begin immediate construction of the building. In his last months, Blethen had grown apprehensive of the sluggish business climate and delayed the undertaking, but his heirs decided to go ahead, dedicating the building to his memory.[17]

Alden Blethen produced newspapers in half a dozen buildings during his lifetime and two of them had burned down; he knew precisely what he wanted in "a model newspaper office." Before his death, Alden, Joe, and C.B. Blethen had spent many nights discussing the functional design of a modern production plant and had built cardboard models of the different layouts for their novel triangular newspaper building. Alden Blethen particularly envisioned a modern structure surrounded by light and air, a place where readers felt at home and visitors would tour,

Tom Thurlby, one of The Seattle Times *artists, drew this cartoon about* Times *cartoonist "Dok" Hager, as the entire work force packed up the tools of their trade, from pens and ink to typewriters to presses.*

(The Seattle Times, September 24, 1915)

sance," the Times Square Building's walls of rose buff terra cotta slowly rose above their granite bases. The structure was heavily ornamented with twelve great eagles, insignia of the publishing company, and emblems that twined with the letters "S" with "T" representing *The Seattle Times.* The building's southern entrance brought employees and passersby into the vestibule, with a great brass compass set into the marble floor. A deep relief sculpture of a telegrapher, linotypist, pressman, and newsboy—the men who made the newspaper—decorated the Olive Street doorway.

On September 25, 1916, *The Seattle Times* devoted the entire edition to the newspaper's great move into the magnificent new building. The old Denny Building had grown so crowded that the standing joke was that reporters had to be skinny to write for *The Times*; writers shared desks and editors shared filing cabinets. As the staff packed up and left the old building behind, they scrawled graffiti and cartoons on the walls of the newsroom, regaling one another with old stories and nostalgic jokes about missed deadlines and demanding editors. They also remembered Colonel Blethen.[19]

In their editorial "Home At Last," both Joseph and C.B. Blethen expressed pride that after "living for years in other people's houses," they were at last in their father's home. They lamented that they stood alone as the new building opened, in the absence of that "kindly far-seeing father." This issue featured warm articles about both brothers. An old newshand reminisced that Joe Blethen had helped to haul the press from the Yesler Way print shop to the Boston Block during the young man's first week in the city, back in 1896. Times Square was Joe's fourth newspaper move in Seattle, the old-timer recalled. And Joe surprised C.B. by slipping an article into the newspaper in praise of his brother,

with a full gallery along one pressroom wall and a newsroom open to view on three sides.

The Times Square Building was to be constructed on a triangular piece of land, its narrow point sloping up west toward Fourth Avenue. At its broad end, the building would soar six stories above Fifth Avenue, commanding the great urban plaza of Times Square. Alden Blethen had envisioned the Square as an emblem of metropolitan Seattle, a West Coast rejoinder to New York's Times Square—just as *The Seattle Times* echoed a response to *The New York Times*' "All the News That's Fit to Print." By night, the building would glitter above the city, its cornice outlined with hundreds of white lights.[18]

Construction began in September 1915, and continued for a year. Designed in a style reported by *The Times* as "Italian Renais-

In 1916, the entire staff of The Seattle Times *posed for a photograph at the Fifth Avenue entrance of their new building, overlooking Times Square. After fourteen years in the cramped Denny Building,* The Times *crew was proud to move to this model newspaper facility.*

(The Seattle Times)

Seattle turned out in force to view election returns in the great urban plaza that Alden Blethen designed on the Fifth Avenue side of the Times Square Building.

(The Seattle Times)

A group of newsboys outside the new Times Square Building.

(The Seattle Times)

Joseph and C.B.—identified as "The Publishers" of *The Seattle Times*—celebrated the move with a "twenty-one bomb" salute, along with a nighttime band concert and fireworks display set off from the roof. Among other selections, the band played "Puget Sound," a 1904 march dedicated to Alden Blethen, as well as the "Totem Pole March" from Joe Blethen's "The Alaskan," written in 1909. The flag that had flown, unscathed, over the Denny Building throughout the first "Wobbly Fire" of February 1913 flew over the Times Square Building for twenty-four hours, in great honor, illuminated by searchlights. Then, it was folded and saved in a glass case in *The Times'* trophy room.[22]

Seattle residents customarily gathered at *The Times* building to read Klondike, murder trial, or war bulletins pasted up in the windows of *The Times*. In these decades before radio, city people thought of the newpaper offices as their source of breaking news, and the paper encouraged this allegiance by printing frequent extra editions and by projecting election returns on the facade into the wee hours of the morning. *The Seattle Times* continued these traditions and the plaza at the foot of the Times Square Building became a great urban park where people congregated for information and entertainment. During World War One, Seattle citizenry became accustomed to decoding a series of blasts on *The Times'* siren and hastening to the building to learn of the latest military developments. In the summer, the World Series or the playoffs of the Pacific Coast League drew thousands to watch the play-by-play on the mechanical scoreboard facing Times Square. At noon each day, a huge red ball descended the flagstaff to mark the hour. The building itself was often decorated, swathed in flags and bunting, or draped with banners and festive

"the Editor as commanding officer," comparing C.B.'s precise organization of this move to a military operation. A sense of brotherly harmony and good fellowship permeated *The Times'* coverage of the grand opening of the Times Square Building.[20]

But the day belonged to Alden Blethen. His heirs intended the building as "a monument to his keen mind and wondrous genius," the direct result of his "long-cherished plan." The entire structure became a secular shrine to the patriarch, housing the family's last tribute to Alden Blethen, a huge bronze plaque, set into the wall at the building's main entrance:

COLONEL ALDEN J. BLETHEN
Born Knox, Maine, December 27, 1846
Schoolmaster, Lawyer, Journalist
Owner, Editor and Publisher
THE SEATTLE TIMES
from its establishment August 10, 1896
until his death July 12, 1915
The Times Building
erected by his family as a tribute to his
memory.[21]

ornaments. Fireworks displays, shot off from the roof, celebrated holidays and victories.[23]

In 1916, after the Times Square Building opened, C.B. took firm and immediate control of the public face of the newspaper business, initiating "a major shake-up of the staff," firing some newsroom old-timers and hiring new men. At his initiative, too, the newspaper established the Times Information Bureau, an instant hit with Seattle folks. From 7:00 a.m. until 9:00 at night, callers could dial Main 300 and ask questions of *The Times*, anything from who won a 1905 boxing match to what time the last ferry left each night. C.B.'s photographs (bylined D—x) remained conspicuous in the newspaper, but he also began writing a great deal more

for publication in *The Times*. C.B. Blethen competed with his brother's literary reputation, mailing off his fiction and non-fiction pieces to national magazines. *The Times* covered C.B. Blethen's activities to an embarrassing extent as he sought to displace the public memory of his father and become a larger-than-life editor in the tradition of personal journalism.[24]

With the world at war, the community engaged in spirited debate as to whether the U.S. had any business becoming involved in World War One. But *The Times* continued its strong emphasis on militarism and preparedness, consistently featuring C.B.'s own experiences. At his father's death, C.B. held the position of commanding officer of the First

Left: Joseph Blethen, photographed outside the Times Square Building at age forty-six, served as president and general manager of The Times Printing and Investment companies. This photo was printed in the newspaper on September 25, 1916.
(The Seattle Times)

Right: C.B. Blethen, in the composing room of the Times Square Building, in his rather military moving-day outfit. He made rapid changes in the newspaper after his father's death, and his hardheaded ambition and newspaper savvy created both admirers and detractors. Nine years younger than his brother Joseph, C.B. would eventually eclipse the older man on The Times.
(The Seattle Times)

Company, Coast Artillery of the National Guard of Washington, and the newspaper encouraged everyone's participation in the Guard, from the unemployed to entrepreneurs. The following summer, *The Times* published a front-page registration blank for the Guard's Business Men's Camp, asking applicants to mail their responses directly to "Captain C.B. Blethen, Editor, *The Times*."[25]

C.B. Blethen became a major in May 1916, assigned to reorganize the state's coast artillery companies into a regiment. Promoted to lieutenant colonel of that regiment five months later, he became a full colonel in 1917. In July 1918, his regiment was mustered into service and remained on active duty throughout World War One. Through the early fall of 1918, C.B. served as Coast Defense commander in the North Pacific Coast Artillery District and then reported to Washington, D.C., "as officer in charge of interior liaison," remaining on the staff of Chief of Coast artillery until his discharge in November 1918, at the end of the war.[26]

While busy in the Guard and on active duty, C.B. continued to manage the newspaper by phone and telegram, shaking up the rest of the paper as he had shaken up the newsroom. He resented employees who believed that their association with his father entitled them to their jobs. C.B. ordered his mother's brother, David Hunter, to leave *The Times* because Hunter "refused to obey [his] orders regarding mechanical affairs." Hunter had worked with Alden Blethen for decades, and had invented the paper conveyor in the Times Square Building, as well as the pneumatic tube system used in the Second and Columbia building. For years, C.B. Blethen also pressured business manager Fred Hammons to either shape up or quit; the Hammons family had been associated with Alden Blethen for thirty years as friends and employees. C.B. was also responsible for discharging the firm of Bausman and Kelleher as attorneys for *The Times*, and hiring Elmer D. Todd, of the firm Donworth and Todd. The terms of Alden Blethen's trust required that Daniel Kelleher remain as trustee for the stock in both the Times Printing and Times Investment companies through 1921, and the longtime Blethen family friend and attorney did so. But C.B.'s decisions caused hard feelings.[27]

As to business, C.B. Blethen had a widespread reputation for "disregard for expense in gathering the news of major developments." He spent with abandon while cutting reliable sources of income. Under Alden Blethen, *The Times* had grown conspicuous for the number and nature of the advertisements it accepted for "medical cures," suspicious personal liaisons, and spirit mediums. On the day of Alden Blethen's death, *The Times* ran nearly an entire column of classified ads for palm readers and clairvoyants. Within a few months, C.B. radically changed this policy, and barred from the newspaper "advertisements of a fraudulent or misleading character," including "matrimonial advertising, massages and baths, spirit mediums and clairvoyants, 'cures,' and many others." Advertising revenues fell, but *The Times* became a better paper.[28]

Alden Blethen had wanted Joe and C.B. to share *The Seattle Times*. As C.B. remembered, "Father's plan was for his two sons to work together dividing the paper down the middle—calling one side of it Business and the other side News and Editorial." Alden Blethen had not stipulated who should be publisher, but from C.B. Blethen's point of view he had become editor and publisher, "even before Joe left." C.B. Blethen resigned his commission as brigadier general of Washington's National Guard in December

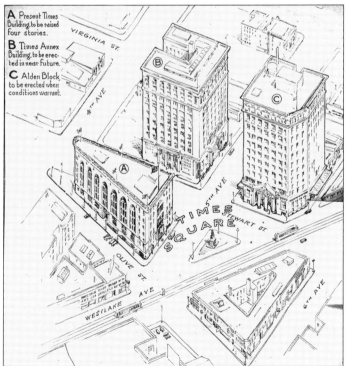

A Present Times Building, to be raised four stories.

B Times Annex Building, to be erected in near future.

C Alden Block to be erected when conditions warrant.

Alden Blethen's Times *moved steadily north over the years, beginning on Yesler Way, moving to Second Avenue and Columbia Street, then up the Avenue to Union Street, and finally to Fourth and Stewart. Occupying an entire wedge-shaped block, Blethen hoped that his Times Square Building would be the heart of a new business district, a site considerably north and east of "downtown." Here we see how visionary Blethen's plan was, as* The Times' *flatiron building rises above a district of two-story retail, warehouse, and office structures, just blocks away from a residential neighborhood.*
(The Seattle Times)

This drawing, prepared by a Seattle Times *artist, shows C.B. Blethen's grandiose plans prior to William Randolph Hearst's acquisition of* The Post-Intelligencer. *Conditions never warranted proceeding with the Times Annex or the Alden Block, and the newspaper would soon move even farther away from downtown. But big dreams ran in the family, and Alden Blethen would have approved his son's ambitious plans for Times Square.*
(The Seattle Times)

A general view of The Seattle Times *composing room in 1920. The typographers worked at long lines of linotype machines, setting the day's stories into type. Alden Blethen had dreamed of a modern newspaper building surrounded by air and light, and here we see the beautiful windows of the Times Square Building open to the sky.*

(The Seattle Times)

1921 because of the requirements of his newspaper business. He needed to devote his full attention to the paper because William Randolph Hearst had finally arrived in Seattle.

After all the years that *The Argus* had teased *The Times* about being the tail of Hearst's lion, when the great man finally did buy a newspaper in Seattle, it was *The Post-Intelligencer.* In April 1921, now publisher and editor-in-chief C.B. Blethen publicly welcomed "a greatly changed and truly vitalized morning paper," arguing that *The Times*

could not "retain its present greatness nor attain the fullness of its tremendous future when the second paper in the community is a failure." But the Hearst invasion would hurt *The Times.* Fighting hard, *The Times* held 1921 daily circulation at 56,460, and Sunday circulation at 83,703, but the effort proved costly. Revenues and dividends fell precipitously, and debts rose dramatically as *The Times* frantically spent money to compete head-to-head with the local representative of the most sophisticated newspaper chain in the country.[29] As C.B. Blethen put it:

In 1913, *The Seattle Times* had arrived at a position where its dominance of the Seattle field required very little expenditure to maintain, and this condition continued until 1921 when Mr. Hearst purchased *The Seattle Post-Intelligencer.* So expensive was his competition that *The Times* made a net loss in that year of more than sixty four thousand dollars, and we found ourselves fighting for our business lives. From that time forward we were compelled to readjust all of our ideas and expend enormous sums of money annually to maintain our circulation and prestige.[30]

At this moment, Joseph Blethen left the embattled *Times.* By 1921, six years after his father's death, he was ready to put Seattle and the newspaper behind him. On May 12, 1921, without public explanation, his name disappeared from the masthead of *The Seattle Times.* That summer, he formally separated from his wife and conveyed some of his stock to her; in that same month, it became public knowledge that, at the age of fifty-one, he was selling his interest in *The Times* and retiring. Seven months later, Joe Blethen sold all his remaining shares in the Times Printing

The composing room at Times Square is shown during the early 1920s as compositors lock the type and engravings for each page into frames, or "chases," which were rolled through the building on carts, often called "turtles." The flare of the long room is clearly visible here, as we look north toward the broad Fifth Avenue side of Times Square.

(The Seattle Times)

and Times Investment companies to family members. In early 1922, he remarried and moved to San Francisco to join the public relations and advertising firm of Evans and Barnhill. Letters between the brothers in the early 1920s seem affectionate, but the men would eventually grow cool and distant, seldom writing. After Joe's death in 1937, C.B. would characterize his brother as "a most lovable person, badly misled," and minimize his role in building up *The Seattle Times*.[31]

The substance of their disagreement is not known. Joe Blethen may have been bored, or he may have been overwhelmed by *The P-I's* new challenge. Joe may have had a relatively free hand on *The Times* during C.B.'s lengthy absences between 1916 and 1918, and resented his brother's expectation of complete control and absolute obedience after his wartime service. Or, perhaps, when C.B. returned to *The Times* and the competition with Hearst, he didn't think Joe was up for the fight—that Joe's heart wasn't really in it—and told him so.[32]

However it happened, by summer, 1922, C.B. Blethen was alone, editor-in-chief and publisher of *The Seattle Times*, his authority uncontested, just as his father's had been. He would hold the reins at *The Times* for nearly twenty more years. His five sons—Frank

Alden Blethen, Clarance Brettun Blethen II, Alden Joseph Blethen III, William Kingsley Blethen, and John Alden Blethen—ranged in age from four to eighteen, and C.B. hoped to bring them all into the newspaper. He resumed his rank as brigadier general in the National Guard, his military demeanor so striking that on meeting him, Washington's governor blurted out, "What the hell is this? Another war?!" Within the newspaper, there was "a soldierly snap to things, a parade-ground atmosphere," and C.B. expected the newsroom staff "to rise and stand at attention" when their editor entered the room, "as men in barracks must do when their commanding officer appears."[33]

But C.B. Blethen was not a mere martinet. A driving, vigorous personality, he protected the heritage of his family and his newspaper as he perceived them, infuriated by the 1919 accusations of Upton Sinclair's *The Brass Check*, that his father's *Seattle Times* had been "a railroad tool." Though he frequently ridiculed his father's published family history as futile and inaccurate, he took time to research and write a biography of Alden Blethen which he hoped to publish. Like his father, C.B. Blethen was a visionary. He continued his interest in color photography, and filed for his first patent in the field in 1921.

Likewise, he looked into the future of changing information technologies, dashing off a 1924 note to his business manager, "No question in my mind—we have to go into radio!" Like his father, C.B. Blethen was inspiring as a publisher, full of hard work and good ideas, willing to spend money freely on staff and equipment for *The Times*, eager to acknowledge and reward excellent reporting.[34] And *The Times* PLATFORM of 1921, printed each day on the editorial page, would have been familiar and reassuring to Alden Blethen:

1. Americanism—government "of the people, by the people" for the good of the greatest number, which means cooperation by the majority to prevent domination of this country by any class.

2. A square deal for labor and capital, which means protection for capital, organized and unorganized—and for labor, organized and unorganized.

3. Anti-Bolshevism and anti-anarchism, repudiation of the Red Flag whenever, wherever, and however displayed.

4. A new policy for Seattle's publicly-owned utilities, specifically its street railway system, that will prevent bankruptcy of the city.

5. Lower taxes through a reduction in the cost of government, state, county, and city, and through greater departmental efficiency.

6. The best schools and the best teachers the community can afford.

7. More industries and greater support for those already established.

8. More commerce, achieved by removing every handicap on trade through this port.

9. An American fleet second to none and an American army adequate for all defense needs.[35]

C.B. and Rachael Kingsley Blethen raised their five sons in this home on Queen Anne Hill. They lived well and loved beautiful things. C.B. ordered a succession of large and elegant yachts, and he delighted in presenting his wife with extravagant gifts from New York and San Francisco jewelry stores.

(PEMCO Webster and Stevens Collection, Seattle Museum of History and Industry)

These photos show the Times Square Building in two public uses. First, the building is outlined with bright white lights and crowned with fireworks as election returns declare Warren G. Harding the victor of the 1920 presidential election. In these years before radio, thousands turned out to watch and hear the election results posted in Times Square. Second, in 1931, just after The Times *had moved once again to its present home at Fairview and John, the Times Square Building was festively decorated as the headquarters for a national convention of Shriners in the city.*

(The Seattle Times)

But C.B. Blethen also differed from his father. When he grew more comfortable as *The Times'* editor and publisher, he moved away from Alden Blethen's distinctive "personal journalism" to became a modern editor. Though C.B.'s editorial positions could be as wrongheaded and stubborn as his father's, C.B. generally apologized if events proved him mistaken. In almost every case he willingly allowed his reporters and editors to do their jobs without interference. Gradually, *The Times* devoted less time and space to breathlessly relating the weekend experiences of the Blethen family, from National Guard camp to charity ball. It lost its old-fashioned, personal appeal, in which readers believed they knew the publisher, but it gained a more objective, metropolitan, and professional polish.

James Wood, Alden Blethen's old city editor, was still writing for *The Town Crier* when Joseph Blethen left *The Times.* He knew all three men, and characterized them with shrewd insight:

> [T]hose who had worked with him had long realized that there was another newspaper genius [besides Alden Blethen] in the Blethen family. C.B. Blethen was managing editor under his father and even then no small part of the paper's success was due to his ability. [C.B.'s] elder brother, Joseph, is likewise a newspaper man of ability. Colonel Blethen gave to each their full share of credit for the growth and success of their newspaper. But Joseph Blethen confined his attention almost altogether to the business administration of the paper and it was only a question of time when sole control and direction should be placed in the hands of his brother, which came about a few months ago, when Joseph Blethen retired from active concern with the publication of *The Times* and as an officer of The Times Printing Company.

In about 1925, Rose Ann Blethen—widowed for ten years—gathers her eight grandchildren together on the lawn of the Queen Anne Hill home. The front row, from the left, included Mary Jane Mesdag, John A. Blethen, Joseph B. Mesdag, and Gilbert L. Duffy II. Standing behind from the left are William K. Blethen, Francis A. Blethen, Clarance B. Blethen II, Rose Ann Blethen, and Alden J. Blethen II.

(Courtesy of Joseph Mesdag)

C.B. Blethen's methods and policies deviate from those of his father. But they are modern methods and policies. He is of the newer generation.... Personal journalism is a thing of the past. Times have changed. C.B. Blethen has inherited his father's genius, though it may run in somewhat different lines. He has preserved and observed the best traditions of the paper.[36]

In 1922, *The Seattle Times* and the Times Square Building were memorials to the spirit of Alden Blethen, as his son continued to mount crusades for men and ideas, to produce a lively and readable newspaper, and to fight the good fight against the Hearst-owned *Post-Intelligencer.* Clarance Brettun Blethen had become the guardian of his father's extraordinary heritage of determination and achievement.

Alden Joseph Blethen's life in journalism spanned a technological transition from hand-powered presses to telegraphy and telephones, to steam and electricity, to color photography. He joined other American publishers who built a huge urban reading audience for colorful, lively, cheap newspapers; his crusades were legendary and his papers salty and entertaining, filled with the latest news, the best features, and the finest illustrations. In Seattle, he created a newspaper that he hoped would endure for a hundred years, to be read daily by five million people. His driving ambition powered his life; his great vision and extraordinary personality powered his newspapers. Alden Joseph Blethen, flawed and imperfect, was nevertheless one of the great American newspapermen of his age.[37]

NOTES

Notes for Preface

1. For Alden Blethen's telegrammed birthday greetings to C.B. Blethen, see *The Seattle Times,* 26 September 1915.

2. For circulation, see 1995 *ABC Audit Report* (Audit Bureau of Circulations, Sept. 30, 1995). For the few other evening newspapers with metropolitan circulation, see *The Editor and Publisher International Year Book, 1995,* p. I-427.

Notes for Chapter 1

1. For background on Waldo County settlement, see J.W. Lang, *A Survey of Waldo County, Maine: Historical, Physical, Agricultural* (Augusta: Sprague, Owens, and Nash, 1873) and Frank E. Claes, *Waldo County: The Way It Was* (Camden: Down East Books, 1985) which includes, township by township, sections of an 1859 map of Waldo County noting property ownership. For general agricultural history, see Clarence Albert Day, *A History of Maine Agriculture* (Orono: University Press, 1954). Day includes numerous references to "wild lands," as does *The Biographical Review of Leading Citizens of Sagadahoc, Lincoln, Knox, and Waldo Counties* (Boston: Biographical Review Publishing Company, 1897). For Unity and general local history, see especially James Berry Vickery, III, *A History of the Town of Unity, Maine* (Manchester: Falmouth Publishing, 1954); see also Edmund Murch, *A Brief History of the Town of Unity* (Belfast: Burgess, 1895) and James R. Taber, *History of Unity, Maine* (Augusta: Maine Farmer Press, 1916). For basic family history, see Alden Blethen, *Genealogy of the Blethen Family* (Seattle: Merchants Printing Company, 1911). The Durham referred to was in the present state of Maine; however, in the 1780s, Maine had not yet become a state but was part of Massachusetts. For Blethen settlement in Thorndike, see C.A. Ferguson, et al., *A Brief History of the Town of Thorndike, Maine* (Thorndike: Newell White, 1919) or *Sesqui-Centennial Celebration of Town of Thorndike* (Augusta: Maine State Library, 1969); for Thorndike and Blethen homesteads, see "Plan of the Town of Thorndike, Maine," 10 May 1842, transcribed from Peter Moulton's original calfskin rendering, as well as 1859 map of Waldo County. For Blethen sheep and cattle earmarks, entered 1816, 1817, and 1823, see Thorndike Town Records, available on microfilm (LDS film #0011265) and extracted and transcribed by Elizabeth Mosher, as *Vital Records of Thorndike Prior to 1892* (Camden: Picton Press, 1993). Also see Clarance Brettun (C.B.) Blethen, "Alden," an unpublished manuscript biography for an account of Alden Blethen's life and the Blethen family history, including the lost fortune. The second family biographical account is Joseph Blethen, "Colonel Alden Joseph Blethen," *The Argus,* 29 January 1916. Both biographies are available in *The Seattle Times* Historical Archives.

2. For Joseph Blethen, religious beliefs, and the fortune, see his letters, transcribed in Blethen, *Genealogy,* pp. 52-57. Also,

see Clarance Brettun Blethen, "Alden," an unpublished manuscript biography, for an account of Alden Blethen's life and the Blethen family history, including the lost family fortune.

3. For Alden Blethen as justice of the peace, see microfilmed Thorndike Town Records, for instance, p. 195. See estate inventory in Alden Blethen probate packet for jointly owned store in Freedom, microfilmed as LDS microfilm #0012416. For James Lamson biography, see *Biographical Review of Leading Citizens,* pp. 162-164.

4. For his "last sickness," see claims against the estate in Alden Blethen probate packet, Waldo County records, Volumes 17, 20, 21, and 22, specifically the Administrator's petition and bond, Vol. 21, pp. 28, 248, the Administrator's appointment, Vol. 20, p. 544, the letters of Administration, Vol. 21, p. 589, Abigail Lamson Blethen's petitions for allowance and subsequent orders of notice, Vol. 17, p. 326, Vol. 20, p. 680, Vol. 21 p. 561, and Vol. 22, p. 32. Claims against the estate are enumerated in the First Account, provided by James D. Lamson, Administrator, and include Blethen's gravestone charges, commissions, travel allowances, and other claims, including Abigail Blethen's first allowance. The estate inventory itself is found in Vol. 21, pp. 273-274, and refers to a mortgage held on the store jointly operated by Alden Blethen and James Lamson in Freedom, as well as listing the contents of the home and barn.

5. See Alden Blethen's death notice in *Belfast Republican Journal,* 15 December 1848, noting Knox, 24 November 1848 as the place and date of death; see also published notices of James Lamson's appointment as administrator, 12 October 1849 and 26 October 1849, and of Abigail Blethen's petitions for allowance, 16 November 1849, all in *Belfast Republican Journal*; for contents of home and barn, see inventory in Alden Blethen probate packet; for 1849 drought, see Day, *History of Maine Agriculture.*

6. For quotes about sworn-off children, see microfilmed Thorndike town records, for instance, pp. 12, 13, 14. See *The Revised Statutes of the State of Maine* (Augusta: William R. Smith and Company, 1841), Chapter 32, "Of Paupers, Their Settlement and Support," specifically Sections 9, 13-20, for the system of binding out impoverished minor children.

7. See the United States Census, 1850. In Thorndike, Philip Blethen and his family were sharing the Thorndike homestead with Job Blethen, the old man, and none of Alden's children were with them. (Roll M432/270, p. 5A). Instead, Frances Blethen was living with James and Jane Blethen Lamson in Thorndike (Roll M432/270, pp. 2B-3A), Allen Blethen was living with Henry Whitney in Freedom (Roll M432/270, p. 269A), Charles Blethen was living with Ephraim Hall in Montville (Roll M432/271, p. 268), James Blethen was living with James Lamson (Abigail's father) in Freedom (Roll M432/270, p. 267B), Alden Blethen was liv-

ing with Eli and Joanna Blethen Philbrick in Thorndike (Roll M432/270, p. 7B), and Arabel Blethen was living with Elisha Mosier in Unity (Roll M432/270, p. 250A). For Alden Blethen's story of these years, as retold by his sons, see C.B. Blethen's "Alden" as well as Joseph Blethen's 1916 account in *The Argus,* "Colonel Alden J. Blethen." For Joanna Blethen Philbrick's death, see Blethen, *Genealogy,* p. 50. For Alden Blethen's own perspective on his boyhood, as recorded by family and friends, see also his lengthy obituary in *The Seattle Times,* 13 July 1915, contained in an extensive scrapbook of obituaries compiled at his death. Also, Alden Blethen wrote a brief description of his "school of hardship" for *The Kent's Hill Breeze,* Vol. XXVII, No. 9 (February 1910), pp. 11-12. This description was reprinted from *The Seattle Times,* and contains the quote concerning his auction.

8. In general, see Day, *A History of Maine Agriculture;* specifically for weather, see tables pp. 34, 37; for "low farming," see pp. 43-46, 56, 74-75. Also, see Lang, *Survey of Waldo County* for a contemporary indictment of primitive subsistence farming.

9. For traffic on country roads, see Vickery, *History of the Town of Unity* and Ferguson, *Brief History of the Town of Thorndike;* for fleece-buyers, see *Belfast Republican Journal,* 11 June 1847 or 9 July 1847. *The Belfast Republican Journal,* 1845-1855, provides a general sense of Waldo County during Alden Blethen's boyhood, though it was more interested in Belfast than the upcountry farmers.

10. Both C.B. Blethen's "Alden" and Joseph Blethen's "Col. Alden J. Blethen" refer to his running away, and substantially include the woods camp and the hat factory. Neither of them mention his return home.

11. The 1860 federal census shows Reuben H. Gould (34), Abby L. Gould (40), Chas. E. Blethen (18), Alden Blethen (14), Arabel Blethen (12), and little Samuel Gould (3) all living together on a farm south of Unity. The census indicated that all three Blethen children had attended school within the previous year (Roll m653/453, p. 253). The 1859 Waldo County map notes the Gould farm in the southern part of the township, near Washington Schoolhouse. C.B. Blethen's "Alden" refers angrily to Reuben Gould, "a swain younger than herself," who pursued Abigail because of her beauty, but refused to take care of her dead husband's "brat, Alden, then nine years of age," pp. 4-5. Although Alden Blethen's *Genealogy* skirted the issue, merely remarking that Blethen had been "orphaned" at 3, "Alden" was quite frank about the estrangement between Alden Blethen and his mother, Abigail Gould, which persisted until after Reuben Gould's death. According to this account, pp. 19-20, in her last years Mrs. Gould contacted Alden Blethen in Seattle, visited him, reconciled, and was financially supported by him at her home in New Hampshire until her death. In his "Advice and Recommendations," prepared by Alden Blethen for his family just prior to his

death in 1915, he referred under the heading of "Family Charities" to a group of Blethen relatives as "poor devils," dependent to a greater or lesser degree on his benevolence. Reuben Gould appears in Unity's town records for the first time in 1860, receiving payment for working as a laborer on the town road, and providing a portion of district school moneys between 1865 and 1870. See *Minutes*, pp. 71, 230, 248, 272, 296, 316, 317, 342, Town of Unity, at the Unity Historical Society, Depot Street, Unity, Maine.

12. For country schools, see Vickery, pp. 80-81; see also *Public Documents of Maine: Annual Reports of Public Officers and Institutions* (Augusta: Sprague, Owen & Nash), for the years 1865-1870, for a general discussion of country schools, teachers, and terms, plus quote, p. 115. See also Richard P. Mallett, *Two Centuries of Farmington Schools* (Wilton: Wilson Printed Products, 1992), p. 1, for description of such rural school agents. *The Belfast Republican Journal* in the 1840s and 1850s lists many advertisements for cheap teachers, placed by the Waldo County agents.

13. The *Catalogue of the Officers and Students of the Maine Wesleyan Seminary and Female Collegiate Institute, 1864-1865* (Portland: Bailey and Noyes, 1865) shows Blethen as a student for the first time, and is hereafter cited as *Kent's Hill, 1865 Catalogue*. For tuition and board payments, see ledger entries August 29, 1864, May 26, 1865, November 10, 1865, March 12, 1866, June 1, 1866, and March 16, 1868. For enrollment, see *Seminar College, Kent's Hill, Journal*, Fall 1864, Spring 1865, Fall 1865, Spring 1866, Fall 1866, Spring 1867, Fall 1867. In the spring of 1866, when he was twenty-one, Alden Blethen no longer listed his mother, Mrs. Reuben Gould of Unity, as his guardian. For Civil War experience of Blethen's brothers, see Alden Blethen, *Genealogy*, and his obituary, *Seattle Times*, 13 July 1915; see also Alden Blethen's biography in *A Volume of Memoirs and Genealogy of Representative Citizens of Seattle and King County* (New York and Chicago: Lewis Publishing Company, 1903), pp. 294-297, for interesting discussion of Alden Blethen's brother's war experience, and a dubious tale of his own enlistment and his bowing to his mother's plea that he remain at home. The account terms her "a widow," and does not mention her remarriage. The story is repeated virtually word for word in Clarence Bagley, *History of Seattle from the Earliest Settlement to the Present Time* (Chicago: Clarke Publishing Company, 1916), Volume III, pp. 11-12.

14. For Kent's Hill, see E.R. French, *History of the Maine Wesleyan Seminary* (Portland: Smith and Sale, 1919); John O. Newton and Oscar E. Young, *Kent's Hill and Its Makers* (Farmington: Knowlton & McLeary, 1947); and Robert E. Warrington, *Kent's Hill, 1824-1974: A Sesquicentennial*, (Kent's Hill, 1974). Also, the archives of the Maine Wesleyan Seminary and Female College have yielded the alumni magazine, *The Kent's Hill Breeze*, school catalogues, the minutes of organizations of which Alden Blethen was a member, and numerous ledgers to track his enrollment.

15. See *Kent's Hill, 1865 Catalogue* for entrance requirements and moral standards, and quote. Winter-term "teaching out" was common for Kent's Hill students. See Newton/Young, pp. 92, 202 for this custom, and pp. 193-196 for religious life at Kent's Hill. For visitor's quote, see *Libel Refuted: A Reply to Greene's Pamphlet* (Lewiston: The Journal, 1868) p. 91.

16. For general Kent's Hill description, see Newton/Young, *Kent's Hill*, pp. 38-9, 57, 194-196, and *Kent's Hill, 1865 Catalogue*; see also Warrington, *Sesquicentennial History*, p. 3. See Kent's Hill, 1864-1865 Boarding and Tuition ledgers for Blethen's payments and his student status.

17. An 1898 alumnus of Kent's Hill remarked, "the stu-

dent body...was largely from rural Maine, many diamonds in the rough, [and] we needed much grinding and polishing," p. 203, in Newton/Young, *Kent's Hill*.

18. A "seminary course" did not imply that a student was preparing for the ministry, just that he (and infrequently she) was not intending to transfer to another college at completion. See Newton/Young, *Kent's Hill*, pp. 56-57. For course of study and roommate William Pattee, see 1864-1865 catalogue, and "Alden," p. 9. For Edwin Haskell and Stilson Hutchins, see Newton/Young, *Kent's Hill,* p. 136. Alden Blethen was acquainted with either or both Davis and Drummond long before his graduation. Although not a Kent's Hill trustee, Drummond was a trustee of nearby Colby College and had been principal at China and Vassalboro Academies prior to his practice of law; Davis appears to have been related to two students in Alden Blethen's class. See Henry Chase, ed., *Representative Men of Maine* (Portland: Lakeside Press, 1893) for biography. After teaching in country schools for nearly ten years, Daniel G. Harriman entered Kent's Hill, and graduated in 1864. He remained active in the Calliopean Society, and taught both mental and moral science—psychology and philosophy—during Blethen's time at Kent's Hill, and left in 1866 to enter Davis and Drummond's law office in Portland. He passed the bar in 1867, and moved to New York City to practice. We cannot prove a clear connection with Alden Blethen, but their lives run parallel for nearly a decade and Blethen seems often to have followed Harriman's path. See *The Kent's Hill Breeze,* Vol. I, No. 3 (February 17, 1883) for Daniel Harriman's biography.

19. See *Kent's Hill, 1865 Catalogue*, and also Warrington, *Sesquicentennial History*, p. 18. See also the minutes and essays of the Calliopean Society for frequent mention of Alden Blethen. The only printed issue of *The Calliopean*, Vol. I, No. 1 (June 1865), listed "Joseph A. Blethen, Unity" as a member, and Blethen often appeared in Kent's Hill records as "J.A. Blethen" rather than "A.J. Blethen" or "Alden Joseph Blethen." In that same issue, Blethen was scheduled in the program for the upcoming Prize Declamation Competition to read "Pericles to the People." He was listed as "Editor" for *The Calliopean*, Vol. 55, No. 2 (1866) and was also noted in April 1865 as upholding the negative in a debate to resolve whether the country had sustained a greater loss in the murder of Lincoln than it would have in the defeat of the Army of the Potomac, Secretary's *Record*, Calliopean Society, 1859-1865, p. 247. See meetings described on pp. 250, 258, and 260 for Blethen's meteoric rise through the offices of the Calliopean Society.

20. For Louise Greene's suicide, see Jonas Greene, *The Crown Won But Not Worn, or M. Louise Greene, A Student of Five Years at Kent's Hill, Maine* (Boston: 1867). Jonas Greene was Louise Greene's father, and his book is a bitterly unhappy diatribe against Henry Torsey, president of Kent's Hill, whom Greene considered responsible for his daughter's death. The trustees of Kent's Hill responded with the book, *Libel Refuted*. The activities of the student committee, including Alden Blethen, are described in *Crown Won But Not Worn*, pp. 127-128.

21. For quotes, see Greene, *Crown Won But Not Worn*, pp. 127-8.

22. See historical development and significance of legal training in Alfred Zantzinger Reed, *Training for the Public Profession of the Law* (Boston: Merrymount, 1921) and Lawrence M. Friedman, *A History of American Law* (New York: Simon & Schuster, 1985). Quote from Joseph Blethen, "Colonel Alden J. Blethen." See also William Emerson Morris, *Biographical Catalogue of Western Maine Lawyers*

(Manuscript, 1877?). Held only at the Maine State Historical Society, this is an autographed list of attorneys in eastern Maine—largely in Portland—and provides a sketchy biography for each. It has proven impossible to find two accounts of Alden Blethen's life which agree entirely as to dates and events, and the *Catalogue* has some surprising deviations from published accounts and public records. Whenever possible, this account has relied on public documents in preference to personal narratives or accounts based on privately supplied information.

23. See *Phillips Phonograph*, February 14, 1880, for news items concerning Alden and Rose Ann Blethen, noting their connection to the village school at Phillips. For narrative accounts, see C.B. Blethen, "Alden," and Joseph Blethen, "Colonel Alden J. Blethen." However, Alden Blethen may have been acquainted with Rose Ann Hunter through school and family connections, prior to teaching together. Sarah Fossett Hunter was listed as a student in the *Kent's Hill, 1865-1866 Catalogue*; her home was given as Strong, and she married William H. Blethen, of Phillips. See Blethen, *Genealogy*, p. 71. For Alden Blethen and Rose Ann Hunter's brief marriage announcement, see *The Farmington Chronicle*, 18 March 1869.

24. For family, see for instance the "Family Charities—Blood is Thicker Than Water and I Have Always Recognized That Fact" in Alden J. Blethen, "Advice and Recommendations"; likewise, in Blethen, *Genealogy*, p. 90, Alden Blethen wrote "I believe a man's first duty is always to his family." Joseph Blethen, "Colonel Alden J. Blethen" and C.B. Blethen, "Alden," both refer to his deprived childhood and his subsequent love of physical comfort; "Alden" specifically refers to his reluctance to meet with his mother as late as 1882 and notes their reconciliation at her initiative after Gould's 1890 death. The 1870 life insurance policy was mentioned in "Advice and Recommendations." For Rose Ann Blethen's family, see notices in brother-in-law Otis Moore's *Phillips Phonograph*, referring to Alden and Rose visiting with friends and family in the area, 6 September 1879, 8 May 1880, 22 May 1880.

25. For general Portland, see Edward H. Elwell, *Portland and Vicinity* (Portland: Jones, Short and Harmon, 1876, reprinted Greater Portland Landmarks, 1975). This is an account of the city by Blethen's contemporary, including neighborhood tours, graphics, and considerable political and social history. See also Lydia B. Summers, ed., *Portland* (Portland: Greater Portland Landmarks, 1986). For the North School, see *Portland Annual Reports, 1868* (Portland: Portland Daily Press Printing, 1869), pp. 4-5, 10. The North School is mentioned in Alden Blethen's brief biographies in both the Blethen, *Genealogy*, p. 102, and in Charles H. Farnam, *History of Descendants of John Whitman of Weymouth, Mass.* (New Haven: Tuttle, Morehouse, & Taylor, 1889), pp. 200-201. Also see *The Portland Directory and Reference Book for 1869* (Portland: Thurston, 1869) which lists Josiah Drummond as a member of the Portland School Board, and provides additional details about the North School.

26. For Torsey reference, see C.B. Blethen, "Alden," p. 9.

27. For general Farmington, see Francis Gould Butler, *A History of Farmington, 1776-1885* (Farmington: Knowlton, McLeary, 1885). Also see Richard Mallett, *The Early Years of Farmington, 1781-1860* (Wilton: Wilton Printed Products, 1994) and Mallett, *The Last 100 Years: A Glimpse of the Farmington We Have Known* (Wilton: Wilton Printed Products, 1991). For education, see Mallett, *Two Centuries of Farmington Schools*. See also *The Farmington Chronicle* and listings of Farmington professionals, merchants, and factories

in *Maine State Year-Book* (Portland: Hoyt, Fogg & Breed, 1872), pp. 213-214.

28. See Gould's *History of Farmington*, pp 103-104; for grounds, see *The Farmington Chronicle*, 27 May 1869; for 1870 reunion, see *The Farmington Chronicle*, 29 September 1870, 6 October 1870.

29. For family and friends, see students listed in Abbott Family School catalog for period ending 30 June 1872. For the extended family group and their occupations at Abbott Family School, see the United States Census, 1870, Roll 593/543, p. 55.

30. *The Farmington Chronicle*, 12 January 1871 noted that Alden Blethen had taken up the school's lease. On borrowing, see Joseph Blethen's "Colonel Alden J. Blethen" which noted that Alden Blethen "borrowed, through his father-in-law,...sufficient money to commence that venture" at Farmington, and also noted that the young man paid back his father-in-law. See the Abbott Family School catalog for year ending 1 April 1871 and 28 March 1872 for courses of study and Blethen's teaching responsibilities. The first catalog is held in Bowdoin College, Special Collections; the second in the Abbott Family School collection at the Farmington Public Library. The long testimonial quote is from the Abbott Family School catalog for the period ending 1 April 1871.

31. For boys staying over Christmas, see *Farmington Chronicle*, 7 January 1869. The boys in residence at Abbott Family School were noted by the federal census recorder in 1870, including their ages and places of birth. For newsboys, see Alden Blethen obituary and James Wood reminiscence, *The Seattle Times*, 17 July 1915. Discipline quote from Abbott Family School catalog for period ending 30 June 1872.

32. Expulsion quote from Abbott Family School catalog for period ending 28 March 1872. This story is most fully told in C.B. Blethen's "Alden," which is the source of the long quote. See also Nat C. Goodwin, *Nat Goodwin's Book* (Boston: The Gorham Press, 1914), pp 17-19.

33. HOME and family quotes from *Farmington Chronicle*, 26 September 1872. Discipline quotes from Abbott Family School catalog for period ending 30 June 1872. Two reassurances from *Farmington Chronicle*, 3 August 1871 and 26 September 1872.

34. Quote from Abbott Family School catalog for period ending 1 April 1871. For *Farmington Chronicle* description of graduation exercises at Little Blue, including considerable description of "declamation" exhibition, see 3 July 1873.

35. For descriptions of library, gymnasium, personal accommodations, and other facilities, see *Farmington Chronicle*, 12 January 1871, and Gould, *History of Farmington*, pp 103-105.

36. For Blethen as guest editor, see *Farmington Chronicle*, 2 December 1869. For election to Kent's Hill Board of Trustees, see Newton/Young, *Kent's Hill*, p. 97. For honorary M.A., see *General Catalog of Bowdoin College* (Brunswick: The College, 1912), p. 434. Every Alden Blethen biography, reminiscence, and obituary mentions the Bowdoin honor. The Abbott Family School advertisements were signed, "Alden J. Blethen, A.M," for instance, 11 September 1873.

37. For Oddfellowship in Farmington, see "Franklin Lodge," in Newell R. Knowlton, *A History of Odd Fellowship in the Tenth District of Maine* (Farmington: Knowlton, McLeary & Co., 1898), especially pp. 50-53, and *Farmington Chronicle*, 5 December 1872 and 19 December 1872. For cornet band, see *Farmington Chronicle*, 10 April 1873 and also see Republican caucus in *Farmington Chronicle*, 28 August 1873.

38. Quote from *Farmington Chronicle*, 9 January 1873.

39. For nighttime law study at Little Blue, see C.B. Blethen, "Alden," p. 11. For description of graduation, see *Farmington Chronicle*, 3 July 1873. See Abbott Family School ads in *Farmington Chronicle*, 11 September 1873 and in *Portland Press*, 13 August 1873.

40. For story, see *Portland Press*, 26 September 1873, and see *Farmington Chronicle*, 11 December 1873 for quote and additional narrative about the move.

41. This letter is the earliest extant example of Alden Joseph Blethen's correspondence, and was written on his letterhead, "Office of Alden J. Blethen, Attorney and Counselor at Law," dated 24 November 1873, to Joshua Chamberlain. It is from the Joshua Lawrence Chamberlain papers at Bowdoin College.

42. See the city directories for Portland, 1875, 1877, and 1879 for maps and for listings of the three Blethen homes on Bramhall Street as well as his two business addresses on Exchange. Edward Elwell's 1876 *Portland and Vicinity* details the social geography of the city and its suburbs. See pp. 22-23, 64-68 for Bramhall Hill neighborhood and gardens; pp. 47-50 for North School.

43. See Blethen business ad in *Portland Press*, 23 December 1873.

44. For a biography of Blaine, see David S. Muzzey, *James G. Blaine* (Port Washington, NY: Kennikat Press, 1963), and of Reed, see William A. Robinson, *Thomas B. Reed, Parliamentarian* (New York: Dodd, Mead, & Co., 1930). For Blaine's benefactions to Kent's Hill, see, for instance, the presentation of Bearce Hall bell, in Warrington, *Sesquicentennial History*, p. 8. For brief overview Portland political atmosphere in 1870s, see Summers, *Portland*, pp. 73-77.

45. For survey of Portland commerce, see Summers, *Portland*, pp. 65-73. However, the confidence which infuses Elwell's contemporary 1876 account of the city offers a first-hand sense of the civic pride, exuberance, and sense of limitless possibility.

46. For description of Exchange, Middle, and Congress streets, see Elwell, *Portland and Vicinity*, pp. 75-79, quote p. 75.

47. For Blethen legal ads, see *Portland Press*, 23 December 1873 or 3 January 1874 and also *Phillips Phonograph* 21 September 1878 in which he promised special attention would be paid to Franklin County cases brought to the Portland state and federal courts. For Blethen's partnership with William Motley, see *Portland Press* ads, for instance 4 March 1874 and the Superior Court case account 27 November 1875.

48. For financial details leaving Farmington and coming to Portland, see Joseph Blethen, "Colonel Alden J. Blethen." Rose Ann Hunter Blethen's ownership of the Bramhall Street homes and Alden Blethen's speculation in houses on Congress Street can be traced in the ledger books labeled, *Valuation, City of Portland* for each year between 1874 and 1880. These volumes are held in the Portland Room of the Portland Public Library. Soranus Brettun had emigrated to Illinois from Maine in the late 1830s, and became wealthy as a shopkeeper in a region booming on the discovery of coal deposits. He would offer a helping hand to his niece, Rose Ann Hunter Blethen, and her husband on more than one occasion. His namesake, Clarance Brettun Blethen, described his uncle "Thomas" Brettun in the biography, "Alden," as "moderately well-to-do," and open to Alden Blethen's persuasion. Joseph Blethen, in "Colonel Alden J. Blethen," recalled him as Captain Brettun, "a rich coal miner in Illinois." Blethen placed advertisements renting city homes in *Portland Advertiser*, 5 April 1879 and 16 December 1879, for example. He placed an ad to sell a house on 24 September 1879 in *Advertiser*.

49. In general, see Elton H. Fales, *History of Odd Fellowship in Maine* (Portland: Grand Lodge of Maine, 1983). Also see frequent mentions in *Portland Press* of Oddfellows activities, for instance, 25 December 1873 for Christmas celebrations or 7 June 1875 for summer picnic and excursion. For the fifty-sixth anniversary, see *Portland Press*, 24 and 27 April 1875. Blethen was referred to as "Past Grand Blethen." For the Portland Provident Association, see Blethen's election to the Board of Managers, *Portland Advertiser*, 10 October 1879.

50. His position in Republican politics was discussed in the lengthy *Portland Press* obituary, 18 July 1915, which is the source of the "political orator" quote. The *Phillips Phonograph*, 6 September 1879, describing a holiday visit the Blethen family was making to the area, remarked on his penchant for "political speeches." The 1876 nighttime Republican parade is described in *Portland Press*, 8 September 1876. Blethen's interest in newspapers during the Portland period is mentioned in *The Belfast Republican Journal*, 13 May 1915.

51. See Blethen, *Genealogy*, quote p. 102 and Farnam, *Descendants of John Whitman*, quote, pp. 200-201. For rivalry with Reed, see "Alden," p. 11. Alden Blethen's obituary in *The Portland Press*, 18 July 1915 refers to a criminal case in which Blethen was said to have defended an unnamed young woman accused of murdering her newborn child. This may be a confusion of memory on the part of the 1915 informant with a strikingly similar 1880 case tried by Charles Mattocks or with the Witham case itself.

52. See C.B. Blethen, "Alden," and Joseph Blethen, "Colonel Alden J. Blethen." Also, nearly every obituary published at Alden Blethen's death in 1915 echoed the general sense that he was a successful attorney, and *The Portland Press*, 18 July 1915, went into some detail, including this dog story.

53. See *Portland Advertiser*, 13 and 14 May 1879 for the arraignment and early discussions of this case.

54. See daily coverage under this heading in the *Portland Advertiser*, May 20 through May 27, 1879. For the reference to Blethen's selection, see *Portland Advertiser*, 23 May 1879.

55. For Blethen's quote, see *Portland Advertiser*, 24 May 1879

56. Annie Small was described as weak-minded in the *Portland Advertiser*, 13 May 1879, and as pleasant on 21 May 1879. The general description of Charles Witham is from the *Advertiser*, 20 May 1879. See the *Advertiser*, 24 May 1879, for the prosecuting attorney's quote.

57. For "very able" judgment, see *Portland Advertiser*, 24 May 1879. For definition of fornication as "criminal intimacy," see *Advertiser*, 24 May 1879. In testimony during this trial, the boarding house in which Dr. Witham administered the ergot to Annie Small and where she gave birth, was repeatedly characterized as a place commonly used by young women "in trouble" to receive abortions. The defense even argued that the boarding house owner, Mrs. Smith, knew very well that an abortion was to take place in her home since Dr. Witham had quite frankly made the arrangements with her. The house was said to be notorious. Later in the summer, the *Portland Advertiser* referred to another boarding house which was operated as a place for unwed young women to give birth or receive abortions as "an infamous den where infanticide and abortion have been several times committed" (29 August 1879). Yet Mrs. Smith testified that she protested against Dr. Witham's behavior as "wicked," and that she protested, "No, it is not" (20 May 1879). For the prosecuting attorney's comment about Witham's way of life, see *The Portland Advertiser*, 24 May 1879.

58. For Solon Chase's quote, see *Portland Advertiser*, 11

January 1879. See Walter Nugent, *The Money Question During Reconstruction* (New York: Norton, 1967) and Irwin Unger, *The Greenback Era: A Social and Political History of American Finance* (Princeton, NJ: Princeton University Press, 1964) for general discussions of the United States Greenback Party.

59. For Lamson's party switch, see *Portland Advertiser*, 25 August 1879. For Blethen's speeches in Franklin County, see *Advertiser*, 29 August 1879 and 2 September 1879. For his prominence in the Greenback Party and his identification as a leading attorney who had joined the Greenbacker ranks, see *Portland Advertiser*, 27 August 1879.

60. For mockery, see *The Farmington Chronicle*'s jibes at the "Demo-Greeno" hicks and rubes from the back country, or *The Portland Press* reporting on Greenbackers. For Motley's bankruptcy, see *Portland Advertiser* 2 September 1879, but the toll of business failure in the city is consistent. Nevertheless, the Greenback Party never had much strength in Portland.

61. See *Phillips Phonograph*, 6 September 1879, for brief note on the Blethen family visit to Strong. See *Portland Advertiser*, 7 September 1879, for mention of Alden Blethen's return to the city, and description of his and his friends' overnight creation of the "straight Greenback ticket" on 8 September 1879.

62. For the level of violence, see *Portland Advertiser*, January 7 through 24, 1880. The fuse to Blaine's barn is mentioned 7 January 1880.

63. See *Portland Advertiser*, 24 December 1879 for an account of the indignation meeting, and of Blethen's remarks.

64. For the ongoing violence in Augusta, see *Portland Advertiser*, 7 January 1880, 13 January 1880, or 19 January 1880. James D. Lamson's focal role is described in *Advertiser* 12 and 13 January 1880, and throughout January. Lamson's letter to General Chamberlain, reprinted in *Portland Advertiser* 14 January 1880, called the Republican-dominated legislature "an illegal revolutionary assembly of persons." Maine State Judicial Court decision reported in *Portland Advertiser* 17 and 19 January 1880, and the military situation reported 24 January 1880. Blethen's departure for Kansas City is noted in *Portland Advertiser* 12 January 1880 and his return to Portland 31 January 1879.

65. For announcement and quotes concerning Alden and Rose Ann Blethen's plans to leave Maine, see *Phillips Phonograph*, 14 February 1880 and 15 May 1880, as well as *Portland Advertiser* 25 February 1880. See advertisement for the Blethen home at 14 Bramhall street, beginning 6 March 1880. The home is described as containing "hall, parlor, sitting room, dining room, kitchen, pantry and storeroom all on the first floor, and five pleasant sleeping rooms on the second floor; also Sebago (water), gas, bathroom, cemented cellar, basement kitchen and sleeping rooms in ell, heated by hot water. Lots laid out in lawn, fence built and grapery planted." He wrote that he had paid $4,750 for the house but was willing to sell for $1,000 or $1,500, with the balance secured by a mortgage. Papers owned by the Mesdag family include correspondence between Alden Blethen and William Carlile in the winter and spring of 1880, tracking their business partnership. There is no indication that Blethen was ailing.

66. See Joseph Blethen, "Colonel Alden J. Blethen," for hemorrhage of lungs; see C.B. Blethen, "Alden," for general story. Bronchial trouble quote from Alden Blethen obituary, in *Los Angeles Times*, 13 July 1915, and throughout obituary scrapbook.

67. For the collections professional ad, see *Portland Advertiser*, 7 February 1879. Anonymous comment is from Frank Carlos Griffith, "Maine Hall of Fame" scrapbook, including a biography of Blethen, *Portland Evening Express*, 26 October 1929, which includes the quoted assessment of his career. For the course of Alden Blethen's legal career before Maine Supreme Judicial Court, see *Maine Reports* (Portland: Dresser, McLellan, 1875 through 1881), for instance, Volume LXIV (1876), pp. 518-521 for the Motley/Blethen case. See *Maine Reports*, Volume LXVII (1878), pp. 140-144, pp 213-215; Volume LXXI (1881), pp. 172-175.

68. For notice of Superior Court and Municipal Court cases in which Alden Blethen represented clients, see *The Portland Press* 4 January 1877, 13 and 14 February 1877, 2 March 1877, 18 and 19 April 1877, 9 October 1877, 31 October 1877, 9 November 1877, 25 December 1878, 29 March 1879, 31 March 1879, 8 January 1880, or *The Portland Advertiser*, 25 April 1879, 18 December 1879, 14 February 1880, 5 April 1880, 20 May, 1880. "Great pleader" reference and general courtroom manner is from Alden Blethen obituary, *Portland Press*, 18 July 1915.

69. For "the Western fever," quote, see both *Farmington Chronicle*, 23 April 1868 and chapter entitled "The Call of the West," in Vickery, *Brief History of the Town of Unity*, pp. 177-185. See Yankee and adherence quotes in Lang, *Survey of Waldo County*, p. 98, and pp. 116-117 for population. Every newspaper surveyed for this chapter has published letters home to Maine from the West, advertisements for cheap railroad land, and articles about the opportunities offered by Western industries, agriculture, and urban growth.

70. The decision was rendered in Blethen's last case before the Maine Supreme Judicial Court on May 7, 1880, *Maine Reports*, Volume LXXI (1881), pp. 172-175.

71. For Blethen's departure, see *Portland Advertiser*, 27 May 1880. For Rose Ann Hunter Blethen, and Joseph and Clarance Blethen in Kansas City, see U.S. Federal Census, 1880 (Roll T9/693, p. 46), where they were listed as "Newcomers." For Coates House in Kansas City, see C.B. Blethen, "Alden."

Notes for Chapter 2

1. See W.H. Miller, *The History of Kansas City* (Kansas City: Birdsall and Miller, 1881), for general history and pp. 244-247 for discussion of the effect of railroads, as well as Roy Ellis, *A Civic History of Kansas City, Missouri* (Springfield, MO: Elkins-Swyers, 1930), pp. 36-48 for additional discussion of rail yards. For an excellent urban history study of Kansas City, see A. Theodore Brown and Lyle W. Dorsett, *K.C.: A History of Kansas City Missouri* (Boulder, CO: Pruett Publishing, 1978). Also, S. Ferdinand Howe, *The Commerce of Kansas City in 1886* (Kansas City: S.F. Howe, 1886) is an enthusiastic review of Kansas City's present and potential success, contemporary to Blethen's stay.

2. Alden Blethen's brother-in-law, Otis Moore, visited Kansas City in 1881, and his perspective on mud, dust, building, and the Western twang of his nephews is interestingly reported in *The Phillips Phonograph*, see especially 22 October 1881. Also, for tales of the grading, see Ellis, *Civic History*, pp. 69-70.

3. For the single best business history of Kansas City, see Miller, *The History of Kansas City*. For Sodom on the Kaw, or Kansas River, see *The Leavenworth Commercial*, quoted p. 12, in Ellis' *Civic History*. For city population, see Miller, *History of Kansas City*, p. 202.

4. In Portland, Maine, Alden Blethen had once confided to a friend that he was interested in "the newspaper business." See *Belfast Republican Journal*, 13 May 1915. See listings for Alden Blethen, for William Carlile, and for the Carlile and Blethen partnership in the 1880 Kansas City directory. In 1881, Carlile was practicing alone, and had his law offices in *The Journal* Building.

5. For discussion of legal codes in the United States and comparison with the common law, see Bernard Schwartz, *Main Currents in American Legal Thought* (Durham, NC: Carolina Academic Press, 1993), pp. 215-224 and Lawrence M. Friedman, *A History of American Law* (New York: Simon and Schuster, 1985), pp. 403-406. For Blethen's revulsion to the code and his subsequent indecision about a law career, see his obituary in *Los Angeles Times*, 13 July 1915, as well as a brief, undated "authorized" biography—which has all the appearance of an autobiography—in the Biography File, Alden Joseph Blethen, *The Seattle Times* Historical Archive. William D. Carlile was born and raised in West Virginia, of a distinguished Virginia family. Born in 1851, he was admitted to the West Virginia bar in 1872, and was elected to the West Virginia legislature the following year. He married and then practiced in Chicago for two years, then went to Colorado and California, and moved to Kansas City in December 1878. His biography in *The Bench and Bar of Missouri Cities* (St. Louis: 1881) indicated that he was still practicing in Kansas City in 1884, and that although he was "an erudite and profound lawyer, in all branches of the profession," his was principally a commercial business. In family papers owned by the Mesdag family, the relationship between Carlile and Blethen is sketchily chronicled. Pertinent documents have been photocopied and are held in *The Seattle Times* Historical Archives. The "tempting offer" quote is from Joseph Blethen, "Colonel Alden J. Blethen," *The Argus*, 29 January 1916.

6. For history of journalism in Kansas City, see "Journalism in Kansas City from 1865 to 1890," in William Griffiths, *History of Kansas City* (Kansas City: Hudson-Kimberly Publishing Company, 1900), and pp. 365-397 in *Kansas City, Missouri—Its History and People, 1808-1908*, Volume I (Chicago: S.J. Clarke: 1908), or Theodore Case, *History of Kansas City, Missouri* (Kansas City, 1888), pp. 122-138. All three sources provide business and mechanical information about *The Kansas City Journal*, but *Kansas City: An Illustrated Review of its Progress and Importance* (Kansas City: Enterprise Publishing Company, 1886) has an especially fulsome review of *The Kansas City Journal*, pp. 51-53. Henry C. Haskell, Jr. and Richard B. Fowler, *City of the Future: A Narrative History of Kansas City, 1850-1950* (Kansas City: Frank Glenn, 1950) is a good popular study of journalism and politics in Kansas City. For the family story of this encounter, see C.B. Blethen, "Alden," an unpublished manuscript biography available in *The Seattle Times* Historical Archives, and Joseph Blethen, "Colonel Alden J. Blethen."

7. For general history of the changing journalism of the late nineteenth century and development of the "new journalism," see the appropriate sections of seminal journalism histories like Edwin Emery, *The Press and America: An Interpretive History of the Mass Media* (Englewood Cliffs, NJ: Prentice-Hall, 1972); Alfred McClung Lee, *The Daily Newspaper in America: The Evolution of A Social Instrument* (New York: Macmillan, 1937), or Lee, *History of American Journalism* (New York: Garden City Publishing, 1923), or the newer general work of Michael Schudson, *Discovering the News: A Social History of American Newspapers* (New York: Basic Books, 1978). "Metropolitan Press," from Gunther Barth, *City People: The Rise of Modern City Culture in Nineteenth-Century America* (New York: Oxford University Press, 1980), is a rich and insightful survey of the role of newspapers in American urban life. Also, for newer, more specialized approaches, see Hazel Dicken-Garcia, *Journalistic Standards in*

Nineteenth Century America (Madison: University of Wisconsin Press, 1989), Gerald J. Baldasty, *The Commercialization of News in the Nineteenth Century* (Madison: University of Wisconsin Press, 1992). Gerald J. Baldasty and Jeffrey B. Rutenbeck, "Money, Politics and Newspapers: The Business Environment of Press Partisanship in the Late 19th Century," *Journalism History*, vol. 15, no. 2-3 (Summer/Autumn 1988), pp. 60-69 is a quantitative study of the emerging new journalism, which correlates the decline in blatant newspaper partisanship with changing business methods, specifically the need to attract advertising.

8. For management and dress quote, see reprint of testimonial by *St. Joseph Gazette*, in *The Journal*, 27 January 1881. In the Mesdag papers, there is an 8 March 1881 agreement between Soranus Brettun and Alden Brettun and his partner John Lawrence for $8,750 collateralized by Journal stock and repaid in 1883. This is considerably less than the figure claimed by C.B. Blethen, but may not represent all contracts between the men. See C.B. Blethen's "Alden" for the narrative of The Journal purchase. Quote welcoming Blethen and Lawrence from *The Kansas City Journal*, reprinted in *The Phillips Phonograph*, 22 January 1881. For Blethen's purchase, see *The History of Jackson County* (Kansas City: Birdsall, Williams and Company, 1881), pp. 573-4. *The Journal* also reprinted a greeting to Blethen on his arrival in Missouri taken from *The Topeka Journal*, welcoming this "lawyer of high standing" who had been "at the very head of the educational interests of the state of Maine."

9. For business activities of *The Kansas City Journal*, see brief surveys in *The History of Jackson Country*, pp. 573-574, Griffith's *History of Kansas City*, p. 82, and Case, *History of Kansas City, Missouri*, pp. 123-124.

10. Joseph B. McCullagh, editor of *The St. Louis Globe Democrat*, quoted p. 134 in William H. Taft, *Missouri Newspapers* (Columbia: University of Missouri Press, 1964), described this new journalism simply as "that which succeeds in interesting the largest number of intelligent people in the contents of a daily newspaper."

11. See *Kansas City Weekly Journal*, 27 January 1881, for full front-page description of the new press and the method of production. Quote about mechanical press from that article. Production figures are based on circulation claims, see *The Journal*, 16 December 1880.

12. See *The Kansas City Journal*, 27 January 1881, for this quote.

13. For Blethen's role, see *The Phillips Phonograph*, 28 May 1881, and *The Kansas City Journal*, 13 October 1881. For the pocket watch premium, see *The Kansas City Journal*, 5 April 1883. The supplement was introduced and described in *The Journal*, 21 April 1884. For name change of weekly newsmagazine and supplement from *The Weekly Journal* to *The Kansas City Weekly Journal and Agriculturalist*, see *The Kansas City Journal* on 15 November 1883, and "Cheapest Paper" quote, 22 November 1883. For Great New West promotion, see *The Kansas City Journal*, 1 December 1881. Blethen's promotions were quite innovative for the times; see Frank Luther Mott, *American Journalism* (New York: Macmillan, 1941), p. 439, for an interesting account of Pulitzer's similar promotions at the same time.

14. This block quote is from Clarance Brettun Blethen, "Alden," p. 19, and has been slightly edited for style and sense.

15. The "died like a dog" quote is from *The Kansas City Journal*, reprinted in *The Phillips Phonograph*, 15 April 1882. See "The Ballad of Jesse James," in Irwin Silber, ed., *Songs of the Great American West* (New York: Macmillan Company,

1967), pp. 254-255, for the romanticized image of the "boy rogue."

16. The cost of the morning newspapers in Kansas City is from Mott, *American Journalism*, p. 469. In the Kansas City newspaper rivalry, Mott characterized the two morning papers: *The Journal* was a "strong respectable paper, [standing] for the development of business interests, good morals, and the Republican party. The *Times*, ten years younger, was more lively." See pp. 468-471. There is an abundant literature on *Star* publisher William Rockhill Nelson, including Mott's *American Journalism*, John Tebbel, *The Compact History of the American Newspaper* (New York: Hawthorn, 1963), and especially Willard Bleyer, *Main Currents in the History of American Journalism*, pp. 307-321. Candidates quote p. 311. See also Icie F. Johnson, *William Rockhill Nelson and The Kansas City Star* (Kansas City: Burton Publishing, 1935), and the fine dissertation by William Littleton McCorkle, "Nelson's *Star* and Kansas City, 1880-1898" (unpublished Ph.D. dissertation, University of Texas at Austin, 1968).

17. Otis Moore traveled to Kansas City in the fall of 1881, combining the pleasure of a family visit with a job search. He wrote extensively in *The Phillips Phonograph* about his general impressions of *The Journal* and about his brother-in-law's responsibilities. See *The Phillips Phonograph*, 8 October 1881, for instance. The horses are described in *The Phonograph*, 22 October 1881. Tireless reporters quote from *The Kansas City Journal*, 27 January 1881. Also, see that issue for general description of how the newspaper was organized. The business of publishing newspapers became clearly distinguished from the practice of journalism during the very years and in the very places Blethen was becoming a newspaperman—in Missouri and Minnesota from 1880 through 1890. The Missouri Press Association, organized in 1867, pioneered in professional journalism, defining and upholding the reporting and editorial standards of "an absolutely independent press." For the development of journalism standards in Missouri, see William H. Taft, *Missouri Newspapers and the Missouri Press Association: 125 Years of Service, 1867-1992* (Marceline, MO: Heritage House Publishing, 1992), and Floyd C. Shoemaker, "History of the First Fifty Years of the Missouri Press Association," unpublished, undated manuscript, Missouri State Historical Society. This study is indebted to Stephen A. Banning, whose thesis "Unearthing the Origin of Journalistic Professionalization in the Mid-Nineteenth Century" (unpublished master's thesis, University of Missouri-Columbia, 1993) is a thoughtful reevaluation of the accepted wisdom that journalism did not develop professional standards until the Progressive Era. See Banning, p. 133, for quote from the Missouri Press Association. For an interesting discussion of reporters' workplace culture in this period, see Ted Curtis Smythe "The Reporter, 1880-1900: Working Conditions and Their Influence on the News," *Journalism History*, vol. 7, no.1 (Spring 1980), pp. 1-10.

18. See Richard Schwarzlose, *The Nation's Newsbrokers, Volume 2, The Rush to Institution, 1865-1920* (Evanston: Northwestern University Press, 1990), pp. 1-14, 39 for summary history New York Associated Press, Western Union, and the regional affiliates.

19. The telegraphed news details are from *The Kansas City Journal*, 2 August 1883. The figures are an estimate based on the Kansas and Missouri Associated Press 1883 contract with the Western Associated Press, referred to in January 1878 contract, *Charter and By-Laws*, William Henry Smith papers, Indiana Historical Society.

20. Kansas and Missouri Associated Press, *Charter and By-Laws of the Kansas and Missouri Associated Press* (Topeka, KS:

Commonwealth Printing House, 1883), which includes *Proceedings* and WAP contract, signed 7 July 1882. This KMAP pamphlet is held among the William Henry Smith papers, Indiana Historical Society. For Smith, see Schwarzlose, *The Nation's Newsbrokers*, Volume 2, throughout, but for the conflict involving Blethen, see Chapter 5, "Reaction and War."

21. Alden Blethen *may* have attended the Associated Press meeting in 1880. This is based on the firm claim by his obituary in *The Seattle Times*, 14 July 1915, that he had attended every Associated Press annual gathering for thirty-five years. It has proven impossible to verify his attendance in 1880, and—if he did attend—he did so after his visits to family in Erie, Pennsylvania, and before or after attending the Republican National Convention in Chicago. For full entrance in Western Associated Press, see *The Kansas City Journal*, 2 August 1883. For Blethen as vice president of *The Journal*, see Kansas City Directory, 1883. For an example of Alden Blethen's annual business trips, see *The Kansas City Journal*, 17 June 1883, for a trip that included Chicago, New York City, Brooklyn, and Portland, Maine.

22. See Lee, *The Daily Newspaper in America*, for his chapter "Labor," pp. 133-164, specifically pp. 145-146, and pp. 362-363 for the general labor situation, and for Kansas City in particular.

23. For a summary of this conflict, see David M. Huckett, "Characters in a Booming Western Town," *Program*, 122nd Convention, International Typographical Union, Kansas City, Missouri, 25-29 August 1980, in Collection 208, Western Historical Manuscripts Collection, University of Missouri at Kansas City. This collection also contains the minute books of Local 80, Kansas City, Typographical Union, dating from 1883. The minutes for 7 February 1886 contain a history of the conflict with *The Kansas City Journal* from the union's perspective. This interpretation of events depends entirely on these meeting minutes, which do not name Alden Blethen but rather repeatedly refer to speech and actions of an unnamed "business manager of *The Journal*." We have assumed the identity of the business manager referred to in the minutes was Blethen because of his position with the newspaper during this time period.

24. For the unfair designation, see for instance the minutes of 3 August 1884, in which *The Leavenworth Times* was termed "unfair," barring union men from working on that newspaper and identifying "rodents" who continued to work there. See minutes for 21 August 1884 for declaration of *The Kansas City Times* as unfair. *The Kansas City Journal* had been declared unfair before the minute books began in 1883, and continued to be so considered. See minutes for 4 October 1885 for an account of interview between Local 80's Executive Committee and Blethen's successor as *Journal* business manager, James A. Mann. Mann told the delegation, "he could not and would not discharge the men who had faithfully stood by him in the past and had pledged themselves to stand by him in the future." After a lengthy boycott of *Journal* advertisers by union families and their sympathizers, a contract was finally signed between *The Journal* and the typographers in 1892.

25. For the Fraternity in Kansas City, see Lee, *The Daily Newspaper in America*, pp. 133-146, which describes the organization's growth from its inception in Kansas City. For punishment or expulsion of ratted members, see Local 80 minutes, 18 November 1883, 1 December 1883, 6 January 1884. Also, the International Typographers Union Collection at the University of Colorado at Boulder contains lists of Kansas City Local 80 members who were "Expelled for Ratting," published in the national *Proceedings* for 1882, 1883, and 1884. For Blethen's refusal to meet, see 1 December

1883. See also retrospective look in Local 80 minutes, 3 January 1886. The chapter "Journalism in Hobnail Boots," in John Edward Hicks, *Adventures of a Tramp Printer* (Kansas City: Midamericana Press, 1950) provides rich general information on the Kansas City conflict between the newspaper management and the organized printers. The chapter describes forming a "reception committee" to run a scab printer out of town who had been encouraged to come to work for *The Journal*. In Hicks' chapter, "Going Hob and Nob With Death," he specifically refers to the Printers Protective Fraternity, and the rivalry between the two labor organizations in Kansas City and elsewhere. On p. 157, Hicks describes the technique ITU men used to identify themselves. See meeting minutes, 4 October 1885, for Report of Executive Committee, concerning visit with *The Kansas City Journal* business manager, who denied that *The Journal* had spent $500, but admitted that *The Journal* would not knowingly employ any union printers. The delegation did not believe his denial, but recommended that Local 80 boycott *The Journal* and its advertisers. For cradle and schemers quotes, see 6 March 1892.

26. These resolutions are dated 31 January 1883, *Proceedings of Kansas and Missouri Associated Press*, p. 26. They are not directly referred to in the meeting minutes of Local 80, International Typographical Union, but the minutes often mention the unfair practices of newspaper management in Kansas City.

27. For disagreement among partners over Blethen's handling of printer's strike, see Alden Joseph Blethen obituary, *The Minneapolis Tribune*, 13 July 1915. For Blethen selling out his stock, see Case, *History of Kansas City*, p. 124, or *Kansas City: An Illustrated Review*, p. 53. Scott Bone, in his rather acid obituary for Alden Blethen, is the only source for the possibility that Blethen left *The Journal* because of a disagreement over the wire service franchise and ensuing litigation. There is no record of this litigation, and contemporary newspapers made no mention of this dispute. See Bone's article in *The Seattle Post-Intelligencer*, 14 July 1915. For Blethen's departure, see editorial in *The Kansas City Journal*, 20 April 1884. For share prices and other details, see *The Kansas City Times*, 20 and 24 April 1884. Throughout the spring of 1884, *The Star* had made much of *The Journal's* recycling of stories from Chicago newspapers, and a growing carelessness with accuracy and attributions. See, for instance, front-page stories in *The Star*, 23 February 1884 and 29 February 1884. *The Kansas City Star* briefly noticed Blethen's leaving on 21 April 1884.

28. For an article on Blethen's "retirement," and the interview with him, see *The Kansas City Times*, 20 and 21 April 1884.

29. See Ellis, *Civic History*, pp. 45-48 for boom. Blethen's salary was published in *The Phillips Phonograph*, 15 January 1881. There are some suggestions that Kansas City's boom hit a peak at this time, and that prices went into a temporary decline, and it is possible that Blethen sold at precisely the right moment. His older son, Joseph, hinted that his profitable experience in the Kansas City boom encouraged him to speculate too boldly later in Minneapolis.

30. Alden Blethen's prominence and activities are made clear by the biographical articles written at this departure from Kansas City in 1884. For Quality Hill, see Clifford Naysmith, *Quality Hill: The History of a Neighbor-hood* (Kansas City: Kansas City Public Library, Missouri Valley Series No. 1, 1962). Naysmith describes Quality Hill as an enclave of New Englanders, who "came to Kansas City to invest their capital and make money, [living] in the city as if it were a foreign country and making Quality Hill an outpost of New England culture." For Blethen's prominence on boards and committees, see *The Kansas City Times*, 20 and 21 April 1884. Also, for Quality Hill, see Sherry Lamb Schirmer and Richard D. McKinzie, At the River's Bend: An Illustrated History of Kansas City (Kansas City: Jackson County Historical Society, 1982), pp. 99-100, and Ellis, *Civic History*, p. 70. For Joseph Blethen's schooling, see his Biographical File, Joseph Blethen, *The Seattle Times* Historical Archive. See *The Phillips Phonograph*, for visits of Alden Blethen to Maine, 18 June 1881, 29 July 1882, 26 August 1882, and Otis Moore's description of Quality Hill and the Blethen residence, 12 November 1881. Trustee Alden Blethen's suggestion that Kent's Hill alumni raise funds to build a home for the headmaster was printed in *The Kent's Hill Breeze*, 30 December 1882, and refers to his anticipated visit east for the annual trustees' meeting. The groundbreaking for Blethen Hall was described in *The Breeze*, 16 June 1883

31. For quote concerning Mrs. Gould, see Clarance Brettun Blethen, "Alden." For the general visit, see *The Phillips Phonograph*, 3 August 1883 and 10 August 1883.

32. For family money and argument quotes, see Joseph Blethen, "Colonel Alden J. Blethen," *The Argus*, 29 January 1916.

33. For the malaria story, see Clarance Blethen, "Alden." For quotes about Alden Blethen's ambition, see Joseph Blethen, "Colonel Alden J. Blethen."

34. Clarance Blethen remembrance from "Alden," p. 21. See William Pattee's biography in Horace Hudson, *A Half Century of Minneapolis* (Minneapolis: Hudson Publishing, 1908), p. 162, and William Watts Folwell, *A History of Minnesota*, Vol. IV (St. Paul: Minnesota Historical Society, 1926), pp. 444-448. Pattee would become first dean of the law school at the University of Minnesota. For prominence of Maine men see, for example, *The Minneapolis Times*, 8 February 1890. After Alden Blethen's death, *The Port Angeles Herald* claimed in a knowledgeable obituary, dated 14 July 1915, that Blethen had been "editor and proprietor of The Goodhue County Republican," in Red Wing, Minnesota, after leaving Kansas City and before moving to Minneapolis. We have investigated this claim at great length and can find no corroborating evidence.

35. Sons of Maine dinner described in *The St. Paul Pioneer Press*, 3 December 1884 and *The Minneapolis Tribune*, 3 December 1884. Son Joseph Blethen remembers his father's decision to enter Minneapolis journalism in *The Argus*, 27 January 1915. The new ownership formally took over the management of *The Tribune* on 1 December 1884, but evidently had a hand in publishing the Sunday edition of 30 November 1884. See *The Minneapolis Tribune*, 30 November and 1 December 1884.

36. William Haskell biography in *Who Was Who in America*, Vol. 1 (Chicago: A.N. Marquis Co., 1943), p. 532. For Kansas City cowboys, see Ted Curtis Smythe, "A History of the Minneapolis Journal, 1878-1939" (unpublished Ph.D. dissertation, University of Minnesota, 1967), p. 46. See also the Minneapolis journalism section in Horace Hudson, A Half Century of Minneapolis (Minneapolis: Hudson Publishing 1908), pp. 217-224. Names of at least five of the eleven cowboys and several mentions of their reputation in Minneapolis are in Press Club of Minneapolis, *Souvenir and Entertainment* (Minneapolis: 1904), pp. 23-24, 101.

37. Quote is from a letter written to long-time Minneapolis journalist Arthur Russell by an unnamed correspondent who was evidently one of the Kansas City cowboys. R.B. to Arthur Russell, 5 August 1917, in Arthur Russell papers, Minnesota Historical Society collection.

38. For a general history of *The Tribune* see *The Story of the Tribune, 1867-1939* (Minneapolis: Minneapolis Tribune, 1939) and Bradley L. Morison, *Sunlight on Your Doorstep: The Minneapolis Tribune's First Hundred Years, 1867-1967* (Minneapolis: Ross & Haines, 1967). The newspaper's first twenty years were characterized by many changes among owners, editors, and managers, but the high percentage of Maine men is striking. General Nettleton and his influence over the tenor of the paper was described in the daily journal of a cub reporter, Smith B. Hall, published in *The St. Paul Globe*, 2 April and 5 April 1884.

39. The description of the type of paper planned by the new ownership is in *The Minneapolis Tribune*, 30 November 1884. For the addition of syndicated stories, see, for example, *The Minneapolis Tribune*, 15 February 1885.

40. Blethen's hiring policies are discussed in a letter written by one reporter to a friend trying to land a job at one of Blethen's newspapers. William Lasley to HV (presumably Herschel V. Jones), 24 December 1884 in the collection of the Hennepin County Historical Museum, Minneapolis, Minnesota. Herschel Jones quickly became a respected newspaperman and later purchased *The Minneapolis Journal* himself. For premium schemes, *The Minneapolis Tribune*, 26 December 1884.

41. For descriptions of *The Tribune* Building, *The Minneapolis Tribune*, 18 January 1884 and 19 July 1885. The influence of architect Leroy Buffington on the growth of Minneapolis during this era and his design of *The Tribune* Building is described in Muriel B. Christison, "Leroy S. Buffington and the Minneapolis Boom of the 1880's" *Minnesota History* (September 1942), pp. 219-232 and particularly p. 226. *The Tribune* Building is also discussed in Larry Millett, *Lost Twin Cities* (St. Paul: Minnesota Historical Society, 1992), pp. 176-177.

42. For a solid history of *The Minneapolis Journal*, see Smythe, "A History of the Minneapolis *Journal*," especially pp. 43-45; 64-66. Farewell announcement of the paper's former owners, the Nimocks brothers, is in *The Minneapolis Journal*, 6 November 1885.

43. Hudson, *A Half Century of Minneapolis*, pp. 223-224; also Press Club of Minneapolis, *Souvenir and Entertainment*, p. 104. The circulation figures for *The Journal* are contained in Smythe, "A History of the Minneapolis *Journal*," p. 66.

44. Figures on the rise of the evening press and the new philosophy of "today's news today" are included in Emery, *The Press in America*, p. 355, and Lee, *History of American Journalism*, p. 352. For increase in circulation 1870 to 1890, see Mott, *American Journalism*, p. 507. Between 1880 and 1890, America's urban population (defined by the Census Bureau as all persons living in incorporated places of 2,500 or more) grew from 14,130,000 to 30,160,000. See Department of Commerce, *Historical Statistics of the United States*, Part 1 (Washington, D.C.: Government Printing Office, 1975) Series A 57-72, pp. 11-12. Additional discussions of this new newspaper constituency are found in Baldasty, *Commercialization of the News in the Nineteenth Century*, pp. 48-50, and Barth, *City People*, pp. 58-109.

45. Minneapolis as a New England town quotation from Lincoln Steffens, *The Shame of the Cities* (New York: McClure, Phillips, 1904), p. 64. Figures from R.I. Holcombe and William H. Bingham, *A Compendium of History and Biography of Minneapolis and Hennepin County, Minnesota* (Chicago: Henry Taylor, 1914), pp. 142-145. A description of the growth of the city during this period is also included in Hudson, A Half Century of Minneapolis, pp. 59-68.

46. Rising bank clearings were constantly cited as impor-

tant indicators of economic growth. See, for example, the special progress edition of *The Minneapolis Tribune,* 1 January 1891. Similar figures and other signs of growth were cited in Holcombe and Bingham, *Compendium*, pp. 138-149.

47. The quotation is from Charles King, "The Twin Cities of the Northwest," *New England Magazine* (1890), pp. 752-753.

48. Millett, *Lost Twin Cities*, pp. 108-109, reviews some of the problems with municipal services faced by both St. Paul and Minneapolis.

49. For the contrast between the two cities, see King, "The Twin Cities of the Northwest," pp. 752-753.

50. For background on *The Pioneer Press*, Richard B. Endes, "The Influence of Editorship and Other Forces on the Growth of the *St. Paul Pioneer Press, 1845-1909*" (unpublished Ph.D. dissertation, University of Missouri, 1939). For history of *The Tribune* during this period see Marlyn Evander Aycock, "A Study of the News Coverage and Editorial Policies of the *Minneapolis Tribune* during the 1890s" (unpublished master's thesis, University of Minnesota, 1956).

51. For circulation claims, see, for example, *The Minneapolis Tribune*, 19 February 1885, 2 April 1885, 4 April 1885, and 12 April 1885.

52. The William Henry Smith letter concerning wire service rights was published in *The Minneapolis Tribune*, 12 April 1885. Mention that protest was filed in *Proceedings of the Western Associated Press*, 21st Annual Meeting, 30 September 1885 (Detroit: WAP Executive Committee, 1886), p. 7.

53. For the insults and counter-insults, see *The Minneapolis Tribune*, 3 January 1885, and *The Pioneer Press,* 2 January 1885, 4 January 1885, and 6 March 1885. For the "cowboy manager" jibe, *The Pioneer Press*, 13 July 1885, although these themes are constant throughout this period.

54. The breaking news story of the Lake Minnetonka drownings, including some information provided by Alden Blethen, is included in *The Minneapolis Tribune,* 13 and 14 July 1885. The accusations about Blethen's behavior at the accident scene were first made in *The Pioneer Press,* 19 July 1885. The *Tribune* made a strong editorial reply, calling *The Pioneer Press* story "dastardly falsehood" and including letters of support for Blethen, *The Minneapolis Tribune,* 21 July 1885. The quote is taken from the backhanded apology of *The Pioneer Press,* reprinted in another editorial in *The Minneapolis Tribune,* 23 July 1885.

55. For mutual insults, see *The Pioneer Press,* 14 February 1885 and *The Minneapolis Tribune,* 2 April 1885 and 12 April 1885. Bully O'Blethen epithet in *The Minneapolis Tribune,* 17 May 1885.

56. The "skunk batteries" insult, originally published in *The Minneapolis Newsletter*, was reprinted in *The Minneapolis Times,* 17 February 1890.

57. For discussion of the Exposition, see Holcombe and Bingham, *Compendium*, pp. 142-143; Hudson, *A Half Century of Minneapolis*, pp. 60-61. Also, *The Minneapolis Tribune,* 1 March 1886; 1 September 1887.

58. See Haskell and Fowler, *City of the Future*, for the Clevelands' visit to Kansas City. Mott, *American Journalism*, pp. 510-512, for press hounding of Grover and Frances Cleveland throughout presidential campaign and on their honeymoon.

59. The remarks about the Clevelands are on the editorial page of *The Pioneer Press,* 12 October 1887. The crowd reaction to the Clevelands is from *The Minneapolis Tribune,* 12 October 1887.

60. The "Mr. and Mrs. Cleveland as Mere People" editorial appears in *The Minneapolis Tribune,* 14 October 1887.

61. Summary of general press remarks was published in *The Pioneer Press*, 13 December 1887.

62. Description of the effigy-burning in *The Minneapolis Tribune*, 15 October 1887.

63. *The Minneapolis Tribune*, 16 October 1887, for cartoon and letter to the editor.

64. *The Pioneer Press*, 16 October 1887, 17 October 1887, 19 October 1887.

65. *The Minneapolis Tribune*, 20 October 1887.

66. The interview with Blethen is from *The Pioneer Press*, 20 October 1887.

67. Clarance Blethen, "Alden," pp. 22-26; Albert Shaw to "My dear Capehart," dated 1 December 1899, letter marked "Not Sent," in which Shaw reminisced about the "old controversy between Mr. Blethen and Mr. Haskell," which had once again been revived by their requests for his version of events. Shaw recalled that Haskell had demanded and received the Cleveland editorial of him and that Shaw, disapproving of it, "took the liberty to advise strongly against it." Shaw wrote that he "personally went to Mr. B," and advised him to be sure to read the editorial before going home that night. Shaw did not know whether Blethen had done so, and concluded his unsent letter, "[There is only controversy about] the question whether Blethen should be considered as sharing with Haskell the responsibility." See also *The Los Angeles Times*, 15 July 1915, for an obituary perspective on these events.

68. *The Minneapolis Tribune*, 20 May 1888, for Blethen's vow not to leave Minneapolis. His family's trip to Maine is reported in *The Minneapolis Tribune*, 8 July 1888. The first notice of Blethen's of his *Journal* stock appeared in *The Minneapolis Tribune*, 11 August 1888. Blethen's comments on the sale ran in *The Minneapolis Tribune*, 14 August 1888.

69. *The Minneapolis Tribune*, 26 August 1888. He had made an earlier mention of his political ambition in *The Minneapolis Tribune*, 14 August 1888.

70. For a list of Republican governors of the state see *Collier's Encyclopedia*, Vol. 16 (New York: Macmillan Education Company, 1981), p. 326. A complete discussion of the various administrations is contained in Folwell, *A History of Minnesota*. For brief background on Minneapolis politics, see Hudson, *A Half Century of Minneapolis*, pp. 480-481.

71. Blethen's quote is from *The Minneapolis Tribune*, 8 September 1888.

72. Coverage of Blethen's address at the opening of the Exposition in *The Minneapolis Tribune*, 23 August 1888. His attendance at the Republican rally was noted in *The Minneapolis Tribune*, 4 September 1888. The Henry Villard reception received attention in *The Pioneer Press*, 11 October 1888. His banquet for former employees of *The Tribune* and *The Journal* was described in detail in *The Minneapolis Tribune*, 8 September 1888 and a notice of the event also appeared in *The Pioneer Press*, 9 September 1888.

73. *The Minneapolis Tribune*, 20 May 1888, for Blethen's statement of principles.

74. Quote about Ames administration from *The Pioneer Press*, 21 September 1888. For a somewhat later perspective on Minneapolis machine politics, see Lincoln Steffens, "The Shame of Minneapolis," *McClure's Magazine*, vol. 20, no. 3 (Jan. 1903), pp. 229-231.

75. For momentum of candidacy, see *The Pioneer Press*, 15, 16, and 22 September 1888. "Doc" Ames thought Blethen was the frontrunner, but refused to run against him. See *The Pioneer Press*, 28 September 1888.

76. For description of convention and quote from Alden Blethen concerning Babb's candidacy, see *The Pioneer Press*, 5 October 1888.

77. For conclusion to campaign for mayoral nomination and summaries of candidates' positions and post-convention sentiments, see *The Minneapolis Times*, 4 October 1888 and *The Pioneer Press*, 5 October 1888.

78. For examples of Blethen's efforts on Babb's behalf, see *The Pioneer Press*, 12, 14, 15, 17, and 18 October 1888. Among the numerous Republican rallies he attended was one for his old Maine acquaintance Thomas Brackett Reed. Blethen introduced Reed at this event, reported in *The Pioneer Press*, 18 October 1888. Mention is made of Blethen's efforts in the national campaign in his obituary in *The Portland Press*, 18 July 1915.

79. *The Pioneer Press*, 16 October 1888.

80. Letter William Henry Smith to Delavan Smith, 6 June 1888; Smith had apparently talked to Blethen about his possible participation as noted in William Henry Smith to Delavan Smith, 16 August 1888, Delavan Smith papers, M255, Indiana Historical Society.

81. For a detailed examination of Smith's career see Edgar L. Gray. "The Career of William Henry Smith, Politician-Journalist" (unpublished Ph.D. dissertation, Ohio State University, 1951).

82. For some details of the negotiations between Smith and *Washington Post* publisher Stilson Hutchins, see the Delavan Smith papers, Indiana Historical Society and particularly WHS to DS, 6 and 9 June 1888; Delavan Smith to Emeline Reynolds Smith, 7 July 1888; WHS to DS, 16 August, 25 September, 1 October, 10 November 1888. By November, Blethen seems to have become an integral part of the deal.

83. WHS to DS, 15 November 1888, for note that Blethen was coming to Washington to help with negotiations. Continuing options are mentioned in WHS to DS, 15 December 1888. All letters from the Delavan Smith papers Indiana Historical Society. For whereabouts of Blethen and his city editor see *The Pioneer Press*, 2 and 6 January 1889. The Minneapolis papers indicate that Blethen returned on January 5 from Washington, but it is unclear whether he had made more than one trip or whether he had remained in Washington since mid-November. For background on *The Washington Post* sale, see Chalmers M. Roberts, *The Washington Post, The First Hundred Years* (Boston: Houghton Mifflin, 1977), pp. 40-43.

84. Blethen's return to Minneapolis was reported in *The Pioneer Press*, 6 January 1889. His attendance at Board of Trade meetings was noted in *The Pioneer Press*, 8, 22 and 29 January, 5 February 1889. The family left for Washington on the evening of February 6 according to *The Pioneer Press*, 7 February 1888. Joseph's activities in Minneapolis during his parents' absence, particularly as a member of the University's Phi Delta Theta fraternity, were frequently described in the local papers. See, for example, *The Pioneer Press*, 5, 10, and 14 March 1889.

85. Smith's European trip is documented in letters to his son, Delavan Smith, in December, January and February. See for example WHS to DS, 15 December 1888. Delavan Smith collection, Indiana Historical Society. Smith gave his son authority to proceed, suggesting he consult Blethen, but Delavan Smith did not seem inclined to act. Rumors in *The Pioneer Press*, 14 March 1889.

86. Deposition of William Henry Smith, December, 1895, in *Alden J. Blethen v. Thomas Lowry*, Hennepin County District Court, Case #67059, Minnesota Historical Society. Smith's initial recollection was that he had met Lowry in Chicago, but under cross-examination was reminded that the first meeting was in New York.

87. *Ibid.*

88. Details of the purchase and Smith's withdrawal are in the Smith deposition, Hennepin County District Court case #67059. Announcement of the purchase is in *The Minneapolis Tribune*, June 1889.

89. *The Minneapolis Tribune*, 20 May 1889.

Notes for Chapter 3

1. Description of *The Tribune* Building as "fireproof" comes from *The Minneapolis Tribune*, 18 January 1884. *The Minneapolis Tribune*, 1 December 1889 described the night of the fire. Also, *The St. Paul Daily Globe,* 1 December 1889, carried *The Tribune's* story.

2. All the newspapers of the Twin Cities carried extensive coverage of the fire, 1, 2 and 3 December 1889. For *The Tribune's* in-house version, see, for example, 2 December 1889. Charles Alf. Williams' experience was related in his testimony before the coroner's inquest board, reported in *The Minneapolis Tribune*, 5 December 1889, and also described at his death, *The Seattle Times*, 10 April 1911. His career, including his fire experiences, were related in a *Seattle Times'* editorial written by Alden Blethen at Williams' death, *The Seattle Times*, 11 April 1911. In Blethen's "Advice and Recommendations," his personal form of a will dated 1915, he suggests that he had been supporting his old friend's family after Williams died. Alden Blethen later published his account of the fire in *The Seattle Times*, 7 January 1906.

3. *The Minneapolis Times*, 2 December 1889 for "Who's to Blame?" front-page story. The various problems with the building were discussed in coverage of the coroner's inquest, reported in *The Minneapolis Tribune*, 4-6 December 1889. The verdict of the hearing was a "mild censure" for the building's owners and for *The Tribune* management, see *The Tribune*, 6 December 1889. Blethen's own story of the fire focused on his personal losses. See, for example, a signed editorial in *The Minneapolis Tribune*, 15 March 1891.

4. Aside from the coverage of the fire's aftermath in *The Minneapolis Times, The Pioneer Press,* and other local papers of the period, Blethen later reminisced about the fire and his own experiences in *The Seattle Times*, 7 January 1906. The extent of the insurance coverage for *The Tribune* losses is never consistently reported. Blethen is quoted in *The St. Paul Daily Globe,* 1 December 1889, that *The Tribune* had a blanket policy of $25,000. *The Minneapolis Tribune*, 2 December 1889, claims that *The Tribune's* coverage for its plant was $23,000, but that the replacement value was $65,000. C.B. Blethen in "Alden," a manuscript biography in *The Seattle Times* Historical Archives, p. 28, blames the neglect of a business manager for insufficient insurance protection, and says that on "technicalities," the insurance company escaped from having to pay for much of the damage.

5. Details of Blethen's financial arrangements with Lowry are contained in the "Summons and Complaint," 12 October 1895, in *Alden J. Blethen v. Thomas Lowry*, Hennepin County District Court, Case #67059, in Minnesota Historical Society collections.

6. The annual Progress Edition of *The Minneapolis Tribune*, 1 January 1891, described the paper's new building in minute detail. Blethen's cost estimates are contained in "Summons and Complaint" in Hennepin County District Court, case #67059. Lowry's figures conflict with Blethen's. In their later court battle, Lowry maintained that the building costs were approximately $75,000, thus undercutting Blethen's estimates of his own personal investments in *The Tribune*. See "Answer," 25 October 1895, in case file #67059, Minnesota Historical Society collections.

7. See, for example, *The Minneapolis Times*, 13 December 1889.

8. The complimentary words were reprinted in *The Minneapolis Tribune*, 26 December 1889; Levi M. Stewart was the Blethen critic who "extended the olive branch" after the fire. *The Tribune* printed Stewarts' letter to Blethen and Blethen's reply in their entirety in *The Minneapolis Tribune*, 8 December 1889. The "diseased mind" quote is from *The Minneapolis Times*, 17 February 1890.

9. Clarance Blethen's description of his father's drinking is in "Alden," p. 12. For Alden Blethen's drinking habits and health problems, see his letter to J.T. Thurman, 11 February 1893, sent as an enclosure to Albert Shaw, 11 February 1893, Albert Shaw papers, New York Public Library, Box 2.

10. Quotation from *The Minneapolis Times*, 9 February 1890.

11. *The Minneapolis Times*, 1 May 1890, has early rumors of the impending sale and they continue until late May.

12. *The Pioneer Press* printed a sarcastic article about the loan that was reprinted in *The Minneapolis Times*, 24 May 1890. Some of Blethen's campaign speeches were reported in *The Minneapolis Times*, 30 September; 10, 23, 24, and 27 October 1890. News of the Democratic victory was in *The Minneapolis Times*, 9 November 1890. Blethen's vote tallies were reprinted in *The Minneapolis Times*, 13 August 1892.

13. Blethen's attendance at the WAP meetings is documented in the *Annual Proceedings of the Western Associated Press*. His committee service is seen, for example, in *Annual Proceedings of the Western Associated Press*, Detroit, 30 September 1885; 17 July 1889; 5 August 1890. An overview of the secret relationship between WAP and UP is provided in Richard A. Schwarzlose, *The Nation's Newsbrokers*, vol. 2 (Evanston: Northwestern University Press, 1990), pp. 140-155. Blethen's committee is discussed on pp. 153-154. Lawson must have considered Blethen an enemy as a result of his role on the committee. During the 1892 board meeting, Lawson raised the issue that Blethen was no longer a newspaper publisher and thus not entitled to sit on the Western Associated Press board. As a result, Blethen was forced to leave. See *Annual Proceedings of the Western Associated Press*, 18 August 1891.

14. Blethen's story of his financial "embarrassment" is contained in his "Summons and Complaint" in Hennepin County District Court case #67059. Thomas Lowry, in rebuttal, later claimed that the problems were due to mismanagement and extravagance. See "Answer," 25 October 1895 in case file #67059, Hennepin County District Court, Minnesota Historical Society collections.

15. Horace Hudson, *A Half Century of Minneapolis* (Minneapolis: Hudson Publishing, 1908), pp. 62-64; 68; 544-545.

16. Minneapolis Directory Company, *Minneapolis City Directory 1892-1893* (Minneapolis: Harrison and Smith, 1892), pp. 78-80. R.I. Holcombe and William H. Bingham, ed., *Compendium of History and Biography of Minneapolis and Hennepin County, Minnesota* (Chicago: Henry Taylor and Company, 1914), p. 145. Alden Blethen remained interested in bank clearances and editorialized about them frequently in his first few years as editor of *The Seattle Times*. In a column of 2 February 1898, on the editorial page, he responds to a reader's request to define and discuss the importance of bank clearings.

17. See *Minneapolis City Directory 1893-1894*, p. 1462, for Guaranty Loan building location. *The Minneapolis Times*, 20 January 1892, discusses the incorporation of the Bank of New England and lists the initial shareholders and the board of directors.

18. The choice of banking mentioned in Clarance Blethen, "Alden," p. 28.

19. An authorized biography of Alden Blethen, possibly written or edited by him, mentions the influence of friends on his banking decisions. See "Alden Joseph Blethen," vertical file, *The Seattle Times'* library. Joseph Blethen's quote in *The Argus*, 27 January 1916. Sources vary on the amount the Blethens had invested in the Bank of New England. *The Minneapolis Times*, 16 September 1897, lists his investment at $21,000, although charging he had withdrawn that amount and more in loans. One example of Alden Blethen's much higher estimates of his investments is included in *The Seattle Times*, 13 November 1904.

20. Advertisements for the Bank of New England appear in *City Directory of Minneapolis 1892-1893*, p. 1462. Description of Bank of New England's focus on laborers and children in *The Minneapolis Times*, 7 August 1892. Snide comments about the bank come from *The Minneapolis Times*, 16 September 1897. Other similar swipes at Blethen are found in *The Minneapolis Journal*, 15 and 26 April 1897 and *The Minneapolis Times*, 5 August 1897. Blethen had by this time purchased *The Seattle Times* and his competitors in Seattle republished these stories with their own commentary. See, for example, *The Argus*, 26 April, 8 and 22 May, 14 August 1897.

21. Accounts of the delegation's Washington, D.C., visit were published in *The Minneapolis Times*, 24 November 1891. A history of Minneapolis' effort to bring the Republican National Convention to the city were in *The Minneapolis Times*, 22 May 1892. Another account of the Minneapolis lobbying efforts is contained in William Henry Eustis, *The Autobiography of William Henry Eustis* (New York: James T, White and Company, 1936), pp. 112-116.

22. The story of the Blaine visit is in *The Minneapolis Journal*, 20 January 1892. William Henry Eustis had a slight variation on the exchange between Blethen and Blaine. According to Eustis: "Secretary Blaine asked us what date had been set for the convention. Someone of the hilarious crowd said, 'June the 7th.' Mr. Blaine humorously replied: 'I presume you will be thawed out up there by that time.' A.J. Blethen immediately replied: 'There is no freezing temperature in Minneapolis for you Mr. Blaine. The air is like the tropics.' To which the Secretary said: 'I know and I appreciate that fact.'" Eustis, *Autobiography of William Henry Eustis,* p.116.

23. Blethen as Blaine supporter in *The Minneapolis Times,* 4 June 1892. The same edition has article on Maine headquarters.

24. Comment on the "semi-political" atmosphere of the bank is in *The Minneapolis Journal*, 13 July 1915.

25. Blethen's announcement of his interest in the mayoral nomination is reported in *The St. Paul Pioneer Press*, 31 July 1897. For Blethen's stance on high license during the campaign see, for example, *The St. Paul Pioneer Press*, 10 August 1892. A discussion of Blethen's "liberalism" on the saloon issue as opposed to other candidates is in *The Minneapolis Times*, 3 September 1892. The other candidates are described in *The St. Paul Pioneer Press*, 31 July, 5 August 1892. The term "Brass band methods" comes from *The Pioneer Press*, 8 September 1892.

26. For convention descriptions see *The St. Paul Pioneer Press*, 25 August 1892; 9 September 1892; Eustis, *Autobiography of William Henry Eustis,* pp. 127-128.

27. *The Minneapolis Journal*, 13 July 1915; Eustis, *Autobiography of William Henry Eustis,* pp. 127-128; *The St. Paul Pioneer Press*, 9 September 1892.

28. All the Minneapolis and St. Paul papers cover the convention, although *The Pioneer Press* offers more details. See *The St. Paul Pioneer Press*, 9 September 1892.

29. The "disappointed man" quote also comes from *The Pioneer Press*, 9 September 1892. Blethen's intensity and bitterness about his political campaigns in *The Penny Press*, 25 November 1893 and also *The Minneapolis Journal*, 13 July 1915. The Knute Nelson papers in the Minnesota Government files at the Minnesota State Historical Society contain letters endorsing the selection of Blethen to the governor's military staff. His most prominent supporter was S.E. Olson, who was the commandant of the staff and a close Blethen friend. See also *The Penny Press*, 31 May 1895, and 27 June 1895 for descriptions of some of the duties of the military staff. *The St. Paul Pioneer Press*, 9 September 1892; *The Minneapolis Journal*, 13 July 1915.

30. For general description of collapse of 1893 see Mary Beth Norton, et al., *A People and A Nation* (Boston: Houghton-Mifflin, 1986), p. 575; Hudson, *A Half Century of Minneapolis*, p. 551.

31. *The Penny Press*, 13 December 1894, 14 November 1895, 15 November 1895.

32. The lawsuit which the state files after the bank's closure lays out its indebtedness and some of the companies whose notes are held by the bank. *State of Minnesota vs. Bank of New England*, 15 July 1893, Hennepin County District Court, Case #56604 in Minnesota Historical Society collections. Many of Alden Blethen's personal records of some of these transactions are contained in a box of his business papers and other effects held in the private collection of Joseph Mesdag. Charges of improper loans to the two Blethen land companies are made in *The Minneapolis Times*, 16 September 1897. An editorial explaining the Briar Bluff investments and defending their worth is in *The Penny Press*, 16 November 1895.

33. Brief explanations of the Chicago bank failures are in *The Penny Press*, 16 November and 13 December 1895. See also a later discussion of these bank failures in *The Seattle Times*, 28 August 1897. The term "rotten institutions" as it was applied to other Minneapolis banks which were declared insolvent comes from an article in *The Minneapolis Journal*, 6 April 1897.

34. Original quote about the pony comes from *The Minneapolis Journal*, 26 April 1897 and was reprinted in Seattle by *The Argus*, 26 April 1897 and again 8 May 1897. Blethen continues to defend his conduct in the Bank of New England failure throughout the rest of his career. See, for example, *The Penny Press*, 13 December 1894, *The Seattle Times*, 28 August 1897, and *The Seattle Times*, 13 November, 1904. Joseph Blethen's assessment of his father's banking career in *The Argus*, 29 January 1916.

35. The Blethen's Minneapolis addresses are listed in *Minneapolis City Directory, 1886-1887* and succeeding years. Also useful in tracking their moves are Minneapolis Inspector of Buildings, Property Card, beginning 26 March 1887 in Minnesota Public Library collections. Mortgages and other original property documents are contained in the Joseph Mesdag collection of Alden Blethen's personal papers. Photographs of Blethen homes and various portraits of the children taken in Minneapolis are in the personal collection of Gilbert Duffy, while the photograph of the Blethen and Pillsbury children riding bicycles is in *The Seattle Times* Historical Archives.

36. Only rare mentions of Rose Ann Blethen are found in the society pages of the Minneapolis press, and no listings have been found that show her participating in women's charitable events or civic organizations. Her devotion to her family is noted in interviews with two grandsons, Joseph

Mesdag, 26 August 1993; Gilbert Duffy, 19 August 1994, held in *The Seattle Times* Historical Archives.

37. References to Alden Blethen's daughters come from interviews with their sons. See Joseph Mesdag interview, 26 August 1993, and Gilbert Duffy, 19 August 1994, in *The Seattle Times* Historical Archives. For Joe Blethen's literary career, see *The Kansas City Star*, 26 October 1902, which refers to short stories written during his college days in Minneapolis "not one of which was accepted." His first play, "The War of the Roses," and three others were written in Minneapolis before his first success, "The Chinook," was sold for $150. See *The Star*, as well as *The Seattle Times*, 29 August 1896. After two years at the Minneapolis Academy and a year in the preparatory department of the University of Minnesota, Blethen matriculated at the university in 1887 and graduated with his class in 1891. He was very active in his fraternity as well as in literary and dramatic activities. He was on the editorial staff of the 1890 University of Minnesota *Gopher*, traditionally published by the junior class. For his student career, see *The Gopher*, 1888-1891, held at the Minnesota Historical Society. The class graduation was described in *The Minneapolis Tribune*, 3 June 1891, and featured an engraving of Blethen, the class poet. The poem surprised the reporter because it "was not particularly humorous," but nevertheless "ingeniously contrived and very creditable as a literary production." On his 1896 arrival in Seattle, *The Times* mentioned that he had given two tours as a comedian on the local circuit in Minneapolis, had been drama critic for three years at an unspecified "Minneapolis daily," as well as a lyricist for popular songs. See *The Seattle Times*, 29 August 1896. For C.B. Blethen see his biography in *Sketches of Washingtonians* (Seattle: Wellington C. Wolfe and Company, 1906), p. 115, which indicates that "he began his newspaper career in 1893," and worked "in various capacities" on Minneapolis newspapers. Also see the Seattle Press Club "Second WUXTRA" (Seattle, n.d.), probably published in 1911, for comment that "He [C.B.] has been around a newspaper office all his life, starting from the basement up—the mailing room." Likewise, the Blethen genealogy indicates that C.B. Blethen "was taught as a boy to understand the mechanical principles of newspaper work." For additional biographical information, see the Alden Joseph Blethen and Clarance Brettun Blethen Biographical Files in *The Seattle Times* Historical Archives, as well as Alden Joseph Blethen, ed., *Genealogy of the Blethen Family* (Seattle, 1911).

38. Clarance B. Blethen, "Alden," p. 29.

39. For background on the penny press see, for example, Andie Tucher, *Froth and Scum—Truth, Beauty, Goodness, and the Axe Murder in America's First Mass Medium* (Chapel Hill: University of North Carolina Press, 1994), pp. 7-17; 108-115; 191-195.

40. For Blethen's goals see *The Penny Press*, 21 October 1893.

41. The complicated relationships between the Associated Press and the United Press are discussed in detail in Schwarzlose, *The Nation's Newsbrokers*, vol. II, pp. 166-176; also see *The Penny Press*, 31 July 1895.

42. Schwarzlose, *The Nation's Newsbrokers*, vol. II, pp. 21-28; 153. "Such is war" quote is in *The Penny Press*, 21 October 1893

43. Descriptions of *The Penny Press* facilities are in *The Penny Press*, 30 January 1895; *The Penny Press*, 30 December 1895. Other papers continued to chide *The Penny Press* for its "low rent" operation. See, for example, *The Minneapolis Journal*, 24 December 1895.

44. The first issue of *The Penny Press* was published 21 October 1893. The paper was laid out in a seven-column format,

with only two display advertisements on the front page. From the beginning, large one-word headlines introduced stories— SCHIEG, about the disappearance of bank teller Phil Schieg; GOTHAM, a long story about New York day at the Chicago World's Fair; and SILVER! dealing with the congressional compromise over the silver debate—all appeared in the inaugural issue. See also *The Penny Press*, 25 October 1893.

45. New Year's message in *The Penny Press*, 1 January 1894.

46. From the editorial page on the first day he published the paper, Alden Blethen maintained an independent stance, *The Penny Press*, 21 October 1993. He consistently repeated that claim editorially, in advertisements as well as in his public actions. See, for example, ads in *The Penny Press*, 24 October 1893, and articles in *The Penny Press*, 18 and 20 January 1894 and *The Penny Press*, 23 April 1894. "Pro bono publico" motto explained in *The Penny Press*, 24 April 1894.

47. The letters exchanged between Ames and Blethen are reprinted together in *The Penny Press*, 27 October 1893.

48. Discussion of rapidly rising circulation figures is frequent; see, for example, *The Penny Press*, 13 and 18 November, 28 December 1893. For editorials lambasting premium schemes see *The Penny Press*, 16 March 1894.

49. Late February circulation figures are reported in *The Penny Press*, 6 March 1894. Attitude toward purchase of new typesetting machines in *The Penny Press*, 10 and 17 March 1894. Some testimonials to the paper's working class support in *The Penny Press*, 24 October and 12 December 1893. *The Penny Press* saluted by Populist candidate Sidney Owen, 19 October 1894. *The Penny Press* covered the Great Northern dispute daily throughout late April and early May, 1894. Editorials on *The Penny Press* position advocating arbitration can be found, for example, in *The Penny Press*, 23 and 24 April; 2, 5, and 31 May 1894. *The Penny Press* covered the Great Northern dispute daily throughout late April and early May. The reference to "scabs" was made in an editorial of 23 April 1894. See also *The Penny Press*, 31 May 1894; 5 May 1894; for circulation figures during the strike see *The Penny Press*, 19 April 1894.

50. The paper's focus on urban people and problems can be seen, for example, in *The Penny Press*, 19 May 1894; 21 June 1894. See *The Penny Press*, 16 November 1894, for paper's role in investigation of police corruption. The paper had also printed numerous articles examining the Minneapolis street railway system, some highly critical of Thomas Lowry's company and its treatment of workers. Examples include *The Penny Press*, 28 and 30 October 1893.

51. *The Penny Press* political endorsements are found in *The Penny Press*, 18 and 25 October 1894. *The Penny Press* published its "independent" ticket in 1894 which included 70 candidates for various local, state and national offices. The paper endorsed 22 Democrats, 38 Republicans, and 10 members of the People's Party. Election results and commentary are published in *The Penny Press*, 7 November 1894.

52. Editorials describing newspaper competition and circulation promotions are found in *The Penny Press*, 16 March and 14 April 1894. A later editorial reviews the price reductions by other newspapers as competition intensified, *The Penny Press*, 9 October 1895.

53. Haskell's original "kite" cartoon of Blethen in *The Minneapolis Times*, 16 October 1894. Blethen's cartoon reply and editorial in *The Penny Press*, 20 October 1894.

54. *The Penny Press*, 3 November 1894, describes his stereopticon experiment; Blethen reserved special seats in the newsroom for invited guests to watch the spectacle. Later in *The Penny Press*, 7 April 1895, he explained his rationale for the Sunday edition.

55. Announcements of the paper's progress in installing new equipment are frequent including *The Penny Press,* 24 March 1895; 19 April 1895; 1 May 1895. The special 18-month anniversary edition is included in *The Penny Press,* 19 April 1895.

56. The announcement of new investors and the formation of *The Penny Press* Publishing Company are made in *The Penny Press,* 11 and 13 May 1895. See *The Penny Press,* 25 May 1895, for awarding of the city printing contract.

57. Circulation figures are discussed in *The Penny Press,* 20 June 1895; national survey results and "put that in your pipe" quote are in *The Penny Press,* 22 June 1895.

58. Advertising lies circulated by competitors of *The Penny Press* are condemned in *The Penny Press,* 20 and 22 June 1895. *The Penny Press* published numerous charges against other papers. See, for example, *The Penny Press,* 15 November 1895.

59. *The Penny Press* first published news of the receivership 28 December 1895. *The Minneapolis Times* responded with its own report, 28 December 1895, and added more details, 30 December 1895. Blethen issued a front-page challenge on circulation figures in *The Penny Press,* 6 January 1896. The circulation examiner idea was adopted by other Minneapolis papers in early January, 1896, and four agreed to participate. *The Penny Press* is not represented, even though Blethen claimed he would participate. See, for example, *The Minneapolis Tribune,* 9 January 1896; *The Minneapolis Times,* 10, 11, and 18 January 1896. Blethen's initial response and intention to participate is in *The Penny Press,* 10 and 11 January 1896.

60. Blethen first filed suit against Lowry 23 February 1895. After legal maneuverings, the case of *Alden Blethen v. Thomas Lowry* first came to trial in September, 1895, but was dismissed on a technicality and refiled in October, 1895. Case file in Hennepin County District Court, Case #67059, at Minnesota State Historical Society. Newspaper accounts of pre-trial activity include *The Penny Press,* 13 March, 4 September, 15 October, and 27 November 1895.

61. The first lengthy explanation of the Lowry suit appeared in *The Penny Press,* 13 March 1895. When the trial began, local newspapers covered it extensively. See, for example, *The Minneapolis Times,* 5 February 1896 to 20 February 1896, for the most detailed treatment. Also, *The Minneapolis Tribune,* same dates. *The Penny Press* coverage is less extensive.

62. Coverage of the verdict is in *The Minneapolis Times,* 21 February 1896; *The Pioneer Press,* 21 February 1896; *The Penny Press,* 21 February 1896.

63. "Diabolical schemes" charged in *The Penny Press,* 21 April 1896. Blethen responded to criticisms of his actions after the bankruptcy in *The Penny Press,* 14, 16, and 23 March; 9 April 1896.

64. Announcement of Blethen's withdrawal in *The Penny Press,* 11 April 1896.

65. The bill for the auction of some of the family possessions and a letter from Alden Blethen to Joseph Blethen, 13 June 1896, providing details of the moving arrangements and attempts to close affairs in Minneapolis are in *The Seattle Times* Historical Archives.

66. A stock purchase between Blethen and Lansing Warren was drawn up and signed on 2 June 1896, but because Blethen evidently did not meet its terms, it was never executed. The contract is in *The Seattle Times* Historical Archives.

67. The letters between Blethen and his potential backer, Delavan Smith of Chicago, are in *The Seattle Times* Historical Archives. There are no letters pertaining to the matter in the Delavan Smith papers at the Indiana Historical Society.

68. For the last gamble, see Clarance Blethen, "Alden," pp. 29-30.

69. Quote from letter R.B. to Arthur Russell, 6 August 1917, in Arthur Russell papers, Minnesota Historical Society collections.

Notes for Chapter 4

1. For auction, see undated six-page receipt for furniture and tools, and for storage and fire; see Minneapolis receipt, dated 13 June 1896, for stored boxes, barrels, and a piano, and a handwritten notation that the fire occurred 10 July 1896. Both documents are in *The Seattle Times* Historical Archives. See spring 1896 letters and telegrams to and from WAP General Manager William Henry Smith's son, Delavan Smith, for his mounting exasperation with Blethen's desperate appeals and schemes, in William Henry Smith papers, Indiana Historical Society. In general, for Alden Joseph Blethen in Seattle, see Joseph Blethen's reminiscence of his father, "Colonel Alden Joseph Blethen," *The Argus,* 29 January 1916, and obituaries in *The Seattle Times* and in *The Aberdeen World,* by brother-in-law O.M. Moore, on 13 and 14 July 1915. Also, Clarance Brettun Blethen's manuscript biography of his father, entitled "Alden," in *The Seattle Times* Historical Archives. For existence quote, see "Alden," p. 29. Eldon Nick Coroch's biography, "Colonel Alden J. Blethen and The Seattle Daily Times" (unpublished master's thesis, University of Washington, 1966) is a thorough study of Blethen's Seattle years, with particular emphasis on his political positions.

2. See Clarence Bagley, *History of Seattle From the Earliest Settlement to the Present Time* (Chicago: S.J. Clarke Publishing Company, 1916) and Bagley's *History of King County* (Chicago: S.J. Clarke Publishing Company, 1929) Volume I, pp. 433, 440, 620. In general, also see Roger Sale, *Seattle Past To Present* (Seattle: University of Washington Press, 1976), Norbert MacDonald, *Distant Neighbors: A Comparative History of Seattle and Vancouver* (Lincoln: University of Nebraska Press, 1987), and Richard C. Berner, *Seattle 1900-1920: From Boomtown, Urban Turbulence to Restoration* (Seattle: Charles Press, 1991), p. 38, for Seattle population decline in mid-decade. Janice L. Reiff, "Urbanization and the Social Structure: Seattle, Washington, 1852-1910" (unpublished Ph.D. dissertation, University of Washington, 1981), is an excellent narrative and interpretive discussion of the city's history during this period.

3. MacDonald, *Comparative History,* pp. 34-35, 44-45. MacDonald and Berner, on the one hand, and Sale, on the other, differ somewhat concerning the depth of the 1893-1896 recession in Seattle, but all three agree that the Klondike gold rush gave tremendous impetus to Seattle's growth. Sale argued that Seattle's ongoing boom after the gold rush demonstrated the city's fundamental economic strengths. See also C.A. Rohrabacher, *The Seattle Spirit,* (Seattle: 1904), pp. 71ff, for a detailed chronology of city growth, written from the heart of the booster spirit.

4. Sale, *Seattle: Past to Present,* pp. 50-63 is an interesting discussion of Seattle as a walking city at this time. See Berner, *Boomtown,* and MacDonald, *Comparative History,* for discussions of Seattle as a "commercial city," not a manufacturing one.

5. For Seattle's Tenderloin, Murray Morgan's *Skid Road: Seattle, Her First Hundred Years* (New York: Ballantine, 1951) remains an excellent survey of vice and politics. See also Cornelius Hanford, *Seattle and Environs, 1852-1924,* Volumes I-III (Chicago and Seattle: Pioneer Historical Press, 1924), pp. 228-230.

6. See Joseph Blethen's reminiscence, *The Argus,* 29 January 1916 for these impressions of Seattle. For the association's annual meetings, see Otis Moore, ed., *Annual Proceedings of the Washington Press Association* (Hoquiam: 1891-1895). The 1895 *Proceedings* list both Blethen boys and their affiliation. Joe Blethen's articles appeared in Minneapolis, in *The Penny Press,* 17 August 1895 and 24 August 1895.

7. Seattle was said to be "a great newspaper town" by Polk's *Seattle City Directory,* 1895-96 but few publishers had made much money with their papers. An interesting blow-by-blow account of Washington State newspaper business failures and successes can be found in the annual Washington Press Association Proceedings. For battledore quote, see *The Argus,* 15 August 1896. For general *Times* history, see Coroch, "Colonel Alden J. Blethen," pp. 28-31, as well as *The Times'* Silver Jubilee Number, 25 February 1906 and "The First Fifty Years," 11 August 1946. Also see "From Village Weekly to City Daily," in Welford Beaton, *The City That Made Itself* (Seattle: Terminal Publishing, 1914). Davies and Hughes had purchased *The Press-Times* and renamed it *The Seattle Daily Times.* That was the paper's name when Alden Blethen bought his share, although he very soon renamed it *The Seattle Evening Times.*

8. Frequent changes in publication titles and inflated circulation figures complicate the business history of Seattle's newspapers. At various times and for various purposes, Alden Blethen or Clarance Blethen set the old *Seattle Times'* circulation as high as 5,000 or as low as 3,000. Blethen often simply characterized the circulation as "insignificant," and let it go at that. In *Seattle and the Orient* (Seattle: The Seattle Times, 1900), Alden Blethen provided the summer 1896 figure of 5,000, p. 168. *The Argus,* and Hughes and Davies themselves, gave higher figures. See, for instance, *The Argus,* 26 February 1898 or 16 April 1898. There seems no doubt that Hughes and Davies had built the newspaper's circulation, and that—when they sold to Fishback and Blethen—they did not realize what a valuable property *The Times* had become and had no concept of its potential.

9. For a brief account of Alden Blethen's arrival in Seattle, characterizing him as the "Penny Press man," see *The Times,* 27 July 1896. This account indicates that Alden Blethen arrived in Seattle July 26, 1896, coming to Seattle from Denver via San Francisco, and arriving on the steamship *Walla Walla.* See also Clarance B. Blethen, "Alden," for the newspaper quote. In his account, C.B. referred to "*The Press-Times,*" which was incorrect and is here edited for ease of reading. See also *The Times'* 1906 Silver Jubilee edition, for history of the newspaper back to *The Chronicle* in 1881.

10. Quoted interview and notices of Blethen's "visit" to Seattle in *The Seattle Post-Intelligencer,* 28 July 1896 and *The Times,* 27 July 1896.

11. Blethen's belief in the evening newspaper as the working man's paper was developed in Minneapolis and refined in Seattle. The goal of an evening edition was "to place the newspaper more largely in the hands of the 'common people,'" according to a *Times* editorial, 29 August 1896. There is frequent commentary on the phenomenon of evening newspapers in the West, for instance, *The Times,* 8 April 1897. Looking back, Blethen wrote in 1902, "With the growth in education of the wage-earning classes, there came a demand for the Evening Newspaper which should print 'Today's News Today' and deliver it after the day's work was over to the homes of the working men when their only opportunity for reading occurred" (*The Times,* 9 February 1902). For Florence Blethen Duffy's reminiscences, see her oral history as cited by Eldon Coroch, "Colonel Alden J. Blethen." The actual sale was announced in *The Times,* 10

August 1896. According to *The Argus*, 28 September 1907, "He [Alden Blethen] bought a paper on wind, and succeeded, by advocating any old thing that was popular, in working up a circulation." The original telegram to Joseph Blethen is in *The Seattle Times* Historical Archives.

12. The editorial "To the Public," signed by C.A. Hughes and T.A. Davies, is from *The Times*, 10 August 1896 as well as "Col. Fishback's Announcement," from which the bimetallism quote was taken. For "two colonels," see the snide story in *The P-I*, 4 September 1896. The first masthead which lists both men, Charles F. Fishback as president and Alden J. Blethen as editor-in-chief, was 25 August 1896. For Populism in general, including silver coinage, see Lawrence Goodwyn, *The Populist Moment: A Short History of the Agrarian Revolt in America* (New York: Oxford University Press, 1978), which makes clear the Greenback roots of the Populist movement. For silver coinage and Fusion in the west see Paul F. Gerhard, *The Silver Issue and Political Fusion in Colorado, 1896* (Wichita: University of Wichita, 1960), or Robert Larson, *Populism in the Mountain West* (Albuquerque: University of New Mexico Press, 1985). Also at the state level, see David Burke Griffiths, "Populism in the Far West, 1890-1900" (unpublished Ph.D. dissertation, University of Washington, 1967). Also see Thomas W. Riddle, *The Old Radicalism: John R. Rogers and the Populist Movement in Washington* (New York: Garland Press, 1991). There is a voluminous literature on Free Silver, Fusion, and the 1896 presidential election. Two useful starting points that tie these strands together in William Jennings Bryan's presidential bid, are Robert Franklin Durden, *The Climax of Populism: The Election of 1896* (Lexington: University of Kentucky Press, 1955) or Stanley L. Jones, *The Presidential Election of 1896* (Madison: University of Wisconsin Press, 1964).

13. For Reed, see account of his speech in *The Seattle Times*, 29 October 1896, in which Blethen argued that Reed did not speak to huge crowds back east because of his hard money beliefs but because of his popularity as a politician. Reed, in fact, was interested in bimetallism *if* the United States did not undertake the experiment alone, but was joined by the European nations. In 1898, Blethen declared, "I have never been anything else in politics but a Bimetallist from a Republican standpoint." *The Times*, 19 March 1898. For contortions to claim consistency, see editorial "The Times Not A Democratic Newspaper," *The Times*, 14 October 1906, a "history" of Alden Blethen's political views. This editorial was "speckled" with words and phrases set in bold type, indicative of his vehemence on the subject. Blethen maintained that he had been "a Blaine Republican" from his first presidential vote in 1868 until 1896, three years after Blaine's death. He considered Blaine the greatest leader the party produced in his lifetime. Blethen argued that the Republican Party had abandoned *him* in 1896, following McKinley and Hanna's hard money policies. As a Silver Republican, he remained consistent, working with Populists and Democrats for a "Fusion" that would address the money issue, which Blethen considered the most fundamental domestic concern of the 1890s. Fusion was the only way for the minority party and splinter groups to achieve political victory in a country which had habitually voted Republican, electing every Republican nominee to the presidency since 1860, except for Democrat Grover Cleveland in 1884 and 1892.

14. References to silk-stockinged gentlemen or silk-stocking brigades were frequent in *The Times* throughout the fall, 1896. See, for instance, editorial following the election, 8 November 1896. Charles Fishback's speech at the Seattle Armory, reported in *The Times*, 15 October 1896, set out the fundamental issue of the election of 1896 as, "Shall the people of this great country rule the country and themselves, or delegate that power to a few men to rule according to their own selfish interests?" Fishback opposed the interests of "the laboring man" to those of "the wealthy classes." For examples of the threatened violence of Goliath against David and *Times* dealers in Tacoma supposedly afraid to openly sell the newspapers, see *The Times*, 6 October 1896, and "A Warning," 29 October 1896, for fears of street violence during the campaign.

15. For move to Boston Block, see *The Times*, 18 August 1896, 24 August 1896, and 20 September 1896. For original Yesler Way offices of *The Times*, see *Seattle and the Orient*, p. 169. For "hole in the wall," see *The Times*, 18 December 1897, and for a good general history of facilities, *The Times*, 4 January 1902. Coroch's "Colonel Alden J. Blethen" is an excellent source for this entire period. See also Berner, *Boomtown*, and Richard Evans Fisch, "A History of the Democratic Party in the State of Washington, 1854-1956" (unpublished Ph.D. dissertation, University of Oregon, 1975), especially chapter 2. For lowering of subscription and street price, and common people quote, see *The Times*, 29 August 1896. James Wood, *The Times*, 11 August 1946, for his reminiscence of the Denny Building at Second and Columbia where the "whole plant was installed in one large ground-floor room, meant for a retail store, where small business office fronted on Second Avenue, with a separate entrance on one side into the larger ground floor composing room." Wood described the precarious balcony that housed the editorial and news room as "a mezzanine." For the editorial announcing lowered prices and intentions, see *The Times*, 29 August 1896.

16. For most popular newspaper in Washington quote, see *Times*, 18 September 1896. Blethen was a devoted fan of William Randolph Hearst, and wrote of his career often. For Hearst in this early period of *The Times*, see 14 November 1896 or 14 May 1897. Blethen would eventually support Hearst's Democratic political aspirations, and would incur suspicions that *The Times* was owned by Hearst. See, for instance, *The Times*, 8 May 1903, for endorsement of candidate Hearst. For discussion of the rivalry between Hearst and Pulitzer, see Willard Bleyer, *Main Currents in the History of American Journalism* (New York: Houghton Mifflin, 1927), pp. 354-388, and for circulation of *The Journal*, see pp. 358-59. The literature on yellow journalism is extensive. See Edwin Emery, *The Press and America* (New York: Prentice-Hall, 1972), pp. 414-446, for a brief overview. The newest edition of this classic journalism history is Michael and Edwin Emery, *The Press and America: An Interpretive History of the Mass Media* (Englewood Cliffs: Prentice-Hall, 1988).

17. For the first *Times* printing of circulation figures, see 16 September 1896; for the counter, see *The Times*, 26 September 1896; it was still in place 23 August 1897. Blethen's *Times* challenged *The P-I* advertising claims early on. See, for instance, *The Times*, 24 December 1896.

18. See the regional press columns in *The Times*, 25 August and 3 September 1896, for quoted reactions by Washington state newspapers to the Populist changeover. *The Fairhaven News* expected *The Times* to be "a power in the coming campaign," and *The Colfax Commoner* was delighted that "the friends of silver may rest assured that *The Times* will be in the forefront of the fight...for the people's cause." The People's Party ticket appeared on *The Times'* editorial page for the first time 17 August 1896 and "Fusion" among the Democrats, Populists, and Free Silver Republicans in Washington state was announced by *The Times*, 16 September 1896. For Fishback as silver-tongued orator, see *The Times* 18 August 1896.

19. For Masonic Hall meetings, see *The Times*, 8 October 1896. For the second meeting, at Germania Hall, see *The Times*, 29 October 1896. Blethen addressed an October meeting in Fremont at which he spoke for two hours, making "an exhaustive argument on behalf of free coinage." This was reported on the front page of *The Times*, 6 October 1896. Customarily, Blethen set his defense of free silver into a deep historical context but his arguments seem to have lacked sophistication. The conclusion of his Germania Hall speech ran, "More money means a higher civilization for it gives the means to acquire it!"

20. Block quote from last page, *The Times*, 23 October 1896. This quote is slightly edited for sense and style.

21. *The Times* covered the Republican "goldbug parade" on 23 October 1896 and Fusion rally for candidate Rogers on 27 October 1896.

22. Block quote from front page, *The Times*, 27 October 1896.

23. For *The Times'* goading of *The P-I*, see, for instance, 21 September 1896 or 29 September 1896. However, on Blethen's side, the jibes were virtually daily. For quote on gross misstatements, see *The Times*, 28 September 1896, and for discussion and quotes on general journalism standards, see *The Times*, 9 September 1896. This story of James Hoge is earliest told by Bagley, in his *History of Seattle*, Volume I, p. 194. "The Truthful Times" appeared in *The P-I*, 24 October 1896. For an example of the unnamed "Populist evening paper," see, for instance, *The P-I*, 16 March 1897.

24. The first editorial page mention of *The Times'* circulation was 16 September 1896.

25. For the Moore, Hammons, and Blethen families living together, see Polk's *Seattle City Directory*, 1898, which reflects the situation of the previous year. Also, see *The Argus*, 20 April 1901, for history of the Blethen rentals. For C.B.'s memories of this Christmas, see C.B. Blethen to his son, Frank Blethen, 25 December 1938, File #427, *The Seattle Times* Historical Archives. In the letter, C.B. refers to the "Christmas of 1897," but he was almost certainly mis-remembering, and referring to the Christmas of 1896. Things would be looking up for the Blethen family one year later.

26. For miserable failure quote, and discussion of gloomy business conditions see Blethen's editorial, *Times,* 3 January 1897, and for reference to general losses, see *Times,* 18 December 1897. Blethen would later refer to his losses and mention "as wretched a business condition...as ever had been known since the beginning," in *The Seattle Times,* 25 February 1906. See C.B. Blethen, "Alden," for AJB's telegram to James J. Hill "for assistance with his payroll"; for friends and family assistance, see Joseph Blethen and C.B. Blethen's Biographical Files, *The Seattle Times* Historical Archives. Alden Blethen's long-time personal secretary, Bessie Hammons, was hired in October 1897 but it is likely that she worked off the payroll prior to that. See Elizabeth Hammons Biographical File in *The Seattle Times* Historical Archives.

27. See correspondence Alden Joseph Blethen to Charles Fishback, 9 December 1896 in *The Seattle Times* Historical Archives, as well as *The Times'* stock book which details transactions among the shareholders.

28. The wrecks along highway quote is from Clarence Bagley, *History of King County*, p. 470. Quotes about Harry Chadwick's prose from "Local Boys Make Good: '30 Means Finished'" Works Progress Association (WPA) History, Washington State Historical Society. This unpublished manuscript is a fascinating history of journalism in Washington state,

written by a variety of authors who had firsthand knowledge.

29. For "Another Big Mining Deal" of Colonel Fishback, backed by "a large Syndicate," see *The Times*, 19 October 1896. This is one of many such articles promoting Fishback's activities. For Squire, see *The Argus*, 2 January 1897, and quote 9 January 1897.

30. For accusations against Alden Blethen and *The Times* concerning James J. Hill, see *The Argus*, 26 March 1898, 23 September 1899, and 17 February 1900.

31. For the Blethen/Hill friendship, see James J. Hill papers, at James Hill Library, "Railroad" Series, Hill to Blethen (Tribune Office), telegram 9 July 1887, Hill to Blethen (General Manager, Tribune, Minneapolis) letter, 15 July 1887, for instance, and into the Seattle days, James J. Hill, "Personal" Series, Hill to Blethen, letter 17 October 1901, letter 11 February 1903, and letter 25 July 1909. However, the friendship is also frankly discussed by C.B. Blethen's biography, "Alden," which described what Hill was willing to do for Blethen because of his editorial support in Minneapolis and anticipated favors in Seattle. Judge Thomas Burke was James Hill's official agent in the Northwest, and he and Hill communicated through encrypted telegrams. An example of such a coded telegram is from the James H. Hill papers, "Railroad Series," Hill's secretary to Burke, 18 August 1896, "Mr. Hill is absent and cannot conveniently be reached by wire but I know that indecent liquefy jarred unpropitious Athens viands overshoot."

32. Greatest railroad man quote from *The Times*, 9 August 1897. See *The Times*, 1 September 1896 for Blethen's delighted—and foresighted—celebration of the sailing of Hill's *Miike Maru*, the first steamer to regularly ply a route between Seattle and Japan. The good talker quote is from *The Times*, 5 October 1896, and Japanese market for grain from same article as well as from 11 January 1900. For Hill's remarks about Washington timber, see *The Times*, 15 September 1897. Blethen remained very loyal to Hill and to Hill's interests, and his good press persisted into the new century. Among dozens of articles and editorials, see *The Times'* front-page article 20 November 1901, or editorial 8 November 1903. *The Argus* referred to *The Times* as Hill's "private organ," and especially noted the newspaper's bias against the Northern Pacific. For Great Northern owning the newspaper quote, see *The Argus*, 17 February 1900. Long after Alden Blethen's financial crisis of 1896-97, James Hill trusted Blethen to look out for his interests in Seattle, writing to him, "I feel that I am entirely safe in the hands of Seattle friends who will understand the situation." James J. Hill papers, "Personal" Series, Hill to Blethen, 30 July 1909. See Upton Sinclair, *The Brass Check: A Study of American Journalism* (Pasadena, CA: self-published, 1920). See p. 125 for his general contention that newspapers represented private rather than public interests, and pp. 243-244 for brief discussion of *The Times* and *The P-I*.

33. Alden J. Blethen to Watson C. Squire, 18 October 1904, Watson C. Squire papers, Manuscripts and University Archives, University of Washington Libraries, and photocopies in *The Seattle Times* Historical Archives.

34. Blethen referred to Hill's loan in an editorial, *The Times*, 21 May 1911. See *The Seattle Times'* Stock Book, 1895-1896, in *The Seattle Times* Historical Archives. Clarance Blethen's "Alden"—as well as some friendly obituaries—tell a different story about Hill, asserting that Alden Blethen never actually borrowed any money from the railroad magnate, but that Hill simply underwrote a line of credit in Seattle for Blethen. In Coroch, "Colonel Alden J. Blethen," Blethen's daughter, Florence Blethen Duffy, maintained that her father

had a long-standing relationship with the Scandinavian-American Bank, and was able to secure financing with ease. See also correspondence, C.B. Blethen to A.F. Soelberg, 15 May 1929, Publisher's File #280, *The Seattle Times* Historical Archives, "Where you get the idea that you are in any way responsible for my Father's success in business is completely beyond my understanding. It is true that you did accommodate him as a banker, for which you and your associates were well rewarded. But it is also true that other banks would have done the same thing, and that Mr. James J. Hill stood behind Father ready to advance money to him personally should any of the Seattle bankers fail to take care of his needs." Soelberg had been an officer of the Scandinavian-American Bank.

35. For Joseph Blethen's partial ownership of the newspaper, see *The Times*, 16 January 1902, and also *The Seattle Times* Stock Book; for his literary career, see *The Times*, 29 August 1896, and numerous clippings in the Joseph Blethen Biographical File, *The Seattle Times* Historical Archives. *The Times* Historical Archives also contains a file of Joseph Blethen's short stories and some of his scripts. The engravings of Alden and Joseph Blethen appeared in *The Times*, 20 February 1897. Joe Blethen was fondly recalled as a "good fellow" in "When the Seattle Press Club Really Started," a chapter in the WPA history, Washington State Historical Society.

36. See *The Times'* editorial "Reduces Its Price," 21 April 1897 for quotes about the paper of the masses. For formation and capitalization of Times Printing Company, see *The Times*, 13 May 1897, 26 January 1898, and 9 April 1898.

37. For set up as saint quote, see *The Argus*, 9 January 1897; for promiscuous and dazzling quote, see *The Argus*, 25 September 97; for reputation quote, see *The Argus*, 2 July 1897.

38. Blethen wrote that Haskell had squandered $50,000 of his father's money and was forced into a Keeley Institute treatment program for alcoholics, and detailed Haskell's indictment for attempted blackmail by a Minneapolis grand jury. See *The Times*, 23 April 1897 or 30 September 1897. An anonymous letter (from A FRIEND) printed in *The Times*, 29 September 1897 asserted that Haskell was the landlord of a bawdy house. In *The Times*, 25 November 1899, Blethen wrote that Haskell was "DRUNK TWENTY HOURS out of every TWENTY-FOUR when connected with THE TRIBUNE." Blethen's apology to his readers ran in *The Times*, 1 October 1897. Blethen scolded Haskell until he sold *The Minneapolis Times*, an event gleefully noted in *The Times*, 17 November 1902. For contemptible whelp remarks, see *The Times*, 23 April 1897 or *The Times*, 25 November 1899. For correspondence with Albert Shaw, see telegram Edgar B. Piper, Editor, *The P-I*, to Albert Shaw, 23 November 1899, as well as an unsent letter, Albert Shaw to A.S. Capehart, 1 December 1899 which describes William Haskell's persistent inquiries, Shaw to Blethen 27 December 1899, mentioning "those matters that came within the scope of my personal knowledge" concerning the Cleveland editorial. There are also letters from Shaw to Piper, and to Haskell, during December 1899. See Albert Shaw papers, New York Public Library.

39. *The Times* made frequent comparisons between Minneapolis and Seattle during the years 1896 through 1904. In the period under discussion here, see *The Times*, for instance, 3 May 1897, 9 August 1897, 22 August 1897, or 27 August 1897. For high license as the "Minneapolis Plan," see *The Times*, 9 December 1896. For examples of provocation, see *The Argus*, 15 May 1897, 3 July 1897, and 10 July 1897. For "blackmailing sheet," see *The Times*, 17 May 1897; for filth quote, see *The Times*, 28 April 1897. See *The Times*, 8 May 1897 for "BLACKMAIL SCHEME Tried on the Editor of

The Times" or 26 June 1897 for "the whelp who demands and takes 'hush money,'" and boodler quote and Minneapolis testimonials from front page, 28 August 1897. Blethen concluded his defense with the assertion, "It [the Bank of New England] was an unfortunate business venture, but Mr. Blethen was the chief sufferer." The Bank of New England affair would continue to plague Alden Blethen, well after the turn of the century. In 1904, Minneapolis creditors revived the lawsuit against the now-prosperous Blethen, and *The P-I* publicized the case. In the context of his feud with Erastus Brainerd—that "crooked and crack-brained whelp," Blethen reviewed all the evidence yet again, in *The Times,* 22 May 1904.

40. For attacks on the Abbott Family School, see *The Argus,* 12 December 1896, 3 April 1897, 10 April 97, or 9 October 1897. For Alden Blethen and the Keeley cure, see *The Argus*, 3 July 1897 or 12 February 1898; for "tough guy," see *The Argus*, 17 July 1897; for "dissipation," see *The Argus*, 3 July 1897; for "accommodating church," see *The Argus*, 18 September 1897. The Keeley Cure was an early residential treatment program for those addicted to alcohol, opium, or other drugs. It was a franchised business, and there were Keeley homes all over the United States, including Minneapolis and Seattle. The "cure" involved daily injections of tincture of gold, and that pure metal, along with sensible diet, exercise, and a better attitude, was supposed to be efficacious. There were frequent insinuations by Blethen's enemies in Minnesota and Washington that he drank to excess, and the Keeley cure insults refer to those slurs. For *The Argus* sarcasm concerning Blethen as University of Washington regent, see 5 August 1897. Chadwick dryly informed his readers that although he could confirm Blethen's appointment to the board of regents, he was not yet aware at what prices faculty appointments would be sold.

41. For *The Times* with three mentions of Goodwin in one issue, see 5 December 1896. On 30 March 1897, *The Times* replied to Chadwick's snickering ridicule of Goodwin with a glowing *Boston Herald* review of the actor's performance, 30 March 1897. *The Times* continued to lionize Goodwin, running one of his marriages as front-page news on 22 February 1898. Blethen specifically denied Chadwick's charges that the Abbott Family School was a reformatory in *The Times* on 5 April 1897, calling Chadwick a "blackmailer and blatherskite." In 1906, after Blethen and Chadwick had buried the hatchet, *The Argus* once again told its readers about Nat Goodwin's recent visits to Alden Blethen in Seattle, and about the Abbott Family School. Goodwin early "showed a tendency for comedy work," and Blethen "sent him back to Boston but Goodwin Senior instantly bundled the boy up and fired him back to Maine" (*The Argus*, 4 July 1906). For a tantalizing description of the Abbott Family School and Alden Blethen, see Nathaniel C. Goodwin, *Nat Goodwin's Book* (Boston: R.G. Badger Company, 1914).

42. Frank A. Blethen recalled that his grandfather's cane was loaded with lead in an interview with Eldon Coroch, "Colonel Alden J. Blethen," p. 97. The story about both Chadwick and Blethen carrying revolvers and being kept separated by their friends is from the WPA history, Washington State Historical Society.

43. Animal quote, *The Argus*, 26 November 1898; block quote *The Argus*, 12 February 1898.

44. For Chadwick prose quote and Chadwick and Blethen feud story, see "Local Boys Make Good: '30 Means Finished'" WPA History, Washington State Historical Society.

45. For three spellings of "Klondike," see *The Times*, 7 July, 20 July, and 7 August 1897.

46. Excited letter home reprinted under RICHES OF

THE CLONDYKE, *Times*, 7 July 1897. This is *prior* to the arrival of the steamer *Portland*.

47. For the retrospective editorial by Alden Blethen that indicates August 1897 as the first profitable month for the newspaper, see *The Times*, 25 February 1906. It is possible that there were still some lean months to come, but the Blethen-owned *Times* turned the corner between the summer and fall of 1897. See C.B. Blethen to J. Swallwell, Chairman of Board, Dexter Horton National Bank, 21 August 1928, in *The Seattle Times* Historical Archives, which asserts that *The Times* lost a total of $60,000 between August 10, 1896 and January 1, 1898, but went "on a paying basis" in 1898, earning $13,815 in 1898, $24,477 in 1899, $38,720 in 1900, $55,432 in 1901, $71,482 in 1902, $81,405 in 1903, $93,328 in 1904, $101,320 in 1905, $182,444 in 1906, and so on through earnings of $210,024 in 1915. For population in gold rush Seattle, see Bagley, *History of King County*, pp. 441-444, and Polk's *Seattle City Directory*, for years 1897 through 1904. For 1890 to 1900 population figures, see Calvin F. Schmid, *Social Trends in Seattle* (Seattle: University of Washington Press, 1944), pp. 2-3. Joseph Blethen published "How the Trails Look Today" in *Harper's Weekly Magazine*, in 1898, under his father's name. This is probably an editing error. Both men were named Alden Joseph Blethen; briefly, the Colonel took to signing himself Alden Joseph Blethen Sr. and Joe as Alden Joseph Blethen, Jr. However, the Colonel's son began using the name Joseph Blethen in Minneapolis, probably simply to avoid confusion; it became his pen name and the name by which he is best known. Seattle Press Club and Ad Club ephemera refer to him as Joe Blethen, but other sources—for instance, the minutes of the chamber of commerce—are often confusing, using all of Joe's names, seemingly at random. For Mayor Wood's resignation to follow the gold rush to Alaska, see *The Times*, 16 August 1897.

48. For golden wave quote, see *The Times*, 23 August 1897. Such sentiments are frequent, but see 3 February 1898 for the especially clear statement, "The city's business pulse now throbs violently, with renewed prosperity, by reason of the harvest reaped by enterprising Seattle merchants. The town is overrun with strangers; the hotels are crowded; the restaurants jammed; a number of theaters are running full blast.... In the stores may be found everything needed in the gold fields, at prices which defy competition from other cities.... The coming summer will witness the greatest gold rush the world has ever seen."

49. For assignment of Costello, see *The Times*, 22 July 1897; reports quote from 23 July 1897 and fortune quote from 22 July 1897. *The Times* and *The P-I* were head to head in competing for Klondike readers, but shoulder to shoulder in boosting the city. Both worked hard to urge that a federal assay office be located in Seattle, because it would be a magnet for returning miners who had been successful. See and compare both newspapers during late July 1897.

50. See Morgan, *Skid Road*, Sale *Seattle Past to Present*, and Berner, *Boomtown*, for fine discussions of the Yukon gold rush, and its effect on the city. For Klondike industrialization of Seattle, see Bagley, *History of King County*, pp. 444, 671; Polk's *Seattle City Directory* for 1898 compared with the *Directory* for 1895. Specifically, see Berner's *Boomtown*, pp. 25-27, for discussion of Moran yards and Klondike construction. For outfitting quote, see *The Times*, 26 August 1897; for butcher quote, see *The Times*, 5 August 1897.

51. See Bagley, *History of King County*, $174 million in gold, p. 445. *The Argus* was left behind in the battle between the two major dailies over municipal leadership in Seattle, and reacted angrily to their "newspaper rivalry which borders on monomania." See *The Argus*, 1 January 1898.

52. There is no better tour of Seattle's "half-world," as *The Times'* writers awkwardly translated the notorious demimonde, than to read the microfilmed newspaper for a few months in the spring and summer of 1898. This biography cannot address the important questions of gender, race, and class raised by the reporting of those years. See *The Times*, 6 September 1897 for mention of morphine and opium; see 7 November 1897 for mention of goldseekers spending time in Tenderloin before and after their visit to the Klondike.

53. As early as August 1897, *The Times* marveled that goldseekers left more money in Seattle's Tenderloin in one night than visitors had spent during the lavish four-day Independence Day festivities, see *The Times*, 6 August 1897. For general story on Tenderloin construction projects to "handle the crowds," see *The Times*, 6 September 1897. For Considine's 1903 testimony about his earlier profits, between 1899-1901, see *The Times*, 10 February 1903. Harry Chadwick, editor of *The Argus*, was the most sincere, consistent, and articulate advocate of regulating those human vices which would never be changed, for instance, "Like other nuisances and vices that cannot be abated, the selling of liquor...should be regulated" (*The Argus*, 17 May 1902).

54. For Seattle as no longer a family town, see *The Times* throughout the municipal election campaign, and specifically 3 March 1898. For *The Times'* platform, including high license, see 10 February 1898. For "OUR WATERLOO," see *The Times*, 9 March 1898. For editorial describing the coalition that voted against *Times*-supported reform in 1900, see Blethen's editorial 1 March 1900, which reported a curious combination of the church-going moral element who reflexively voted Republican, businessmen who believed that Seattle must be "run wide open" for the sake of good business, paid voters, and every denizen of the Tenderloin. For Humes' drunken army, see *Times*, 5 March 1902.

55. Block quote from C.B. Blethen, "Alden."

56. For this story and the block quote, see Joseph Smith's reminiscence of Alden Blethen as "Story No. 1," in his series, "Statesmen I have Met, " Joseph Smith Collection, Manuscripts and University Archives, University of Washington Libraries.

57. See Percy Jefferson as told to Dorothy Daly, "I Knew the Colonel," typescript, Percy Jefferson Biographical File, *The Seattle Times* Historical Archives, for the widespread rumor that Blethen supported high license to protect his investments. For the quoted sneers of the anonymous visitor to Seattle from Minneapolis, see *The Argus*, 6 October 1900, but it is possible that he was a figment of Harry Chadwick's fertile imagination.

58. For this block quote and for a suggestive cartoon of Alden Blethen nursing a hangover on "The Morning After," see *The Argus*, 10 March 1900.

59. Edward Bemis, *Municipal Monopolies* (T.Y. Crowell, 1899), pp. 659-660.

60. This block quote is from James Wood's lengthy reminiscence of Alden Blethen, in *The Town Crier*, 17 July 1915. Wood was city editor on *The Times* for only three years, but had a longer relationship with Blethen in shared Alaska-Yukon-Pacific Exposition and chamber of commerce duties. For another reminiscence of Alden Blethen, from which smoking hot and thunder cloud quotes come, see "Local Boys Make Good," in the WPA history of journalism, Washington State Historical Society. Also, see Percy Jefferson, "I Knew the Colonel," for Blethen's unpredictable temper. *The Argus* joked that if the city council doesn't "want to all be whelps and curs six nights out of the week," they had better pave Highland Drive to please Blethen, *The Argus*, 5 January 1901. In the wake of the Cleveland editorial in Minneapolis, which was primarily considered outrageous because of its judgments about Mrs. Cleveland, Blethen was often accused by his enemies of insulting women. A good example is a run-in he had with a telephone switchboard operator, reported in *The Argus*, 10 March 1900. Chadwick's somewhat specious logic ran, "This is not the first time that Blethen has insulted women over the telephone. And if he would do that, is it not reasonable to believe that he is responsible for the insult to Mrs. Cleveland, which was published in his paper in Minneapolis?"

61. See *The Argus*, 17 December 1910, for the gibe, "There are known to be 270 active volcanoes in the world, not including Alden J. Blethen."

62. *The Argus* reported the Daniels story after Chadwick and Blethen had mended their feud, and become friends, on 16 October 1909. This headline titled an editorial that ran in *The Times*, 30 December 1896. The son of a bitch quote is from Percy Jefferson's reminiscence, "I Knew the Colonel." Jefferson also recalled that *The Times'* advertising department had no budget at this time, and that he treated a potential account to lunch at a local spot called Billy the Mug's, where a quart of beer cost a nickel, and there was a free lunch of sliced meats and cheeses, bread, pickles and hot clam nectar. See both "No Time for Ulcers" and "I Knew the Colonel," and Jefferson's oral history interview with Eldon Coroch, cited in his very useful chapter, "One Big Family," pp. 95-116, in "Colonel Alden J. Blethen."

63. See Percy Jefferson's reminiscences, and photos in *Seattle and the Orient* for the crowding, phone lines, balcony, and pot-bellied stoves of the Boston Block.

64. See Percy Jefferson's and James Wood's reminiscences, as well as M.M. Mattison's obituary, *The Times*, 13 July 1915, for the turkey marches. The schedule for Blethen's day, at least in his later years, is from *The Argus*, 17 July 1915.

65. For the Thanksgiving dinner quotes, see his obituary in *The P-I*, 13 July 1915. For an interesting article on Seattle's newsboys that predates Blethen's arrival, see *The Times*, 21 December 1895. For newsboys as street kids, see "Newsboys in Trouble," *The Times*, 1 July 1897 or 23 June 1898.

66. For the dialect humor block quote, see *The Times*, 25 July 1898. This is slightly edited for sense and style.

67. For these quotes, see Wood's reminiscence, and Percy Jefferson, "I Knew the Colonel."

68. For a description of Seattle nightspots for newsmen, see "When the Seattle Press Club Really Started," WPA journalism history, Washington State Historical Society. These informal meetings would grow into the Seattle Press Club, actually formed in 1905. *The Star* began publication in 1899; *The Seattle Times* first published a Sunday edition 9 February 1902.

69. A new Hoe triple perfecting press was added in late 1897 according to *The Times*, 9 April 1898, to meet new circulation. For common people quote, see *The Times*, 9 February 1898. For German and Norwegian columns, see, for instance, 19 February 1898. For the circulation wars, see, among many similar articles, *The Times'* editorial 1 May 1897, entitled "The P.-I. Recognizes a Great Advertising Medium," which referred to the morning newspaper's purchase of space in *The Times* to advertise its own new low subscription price. Or see *The Times*, 18 December 1897 for the monotonous to the reader quote, and for a front-page box claiming a daily average circulation 50 percent greater than any other Washington daily and a Saturday circulation of 2,500 copies more than any other paper. The Saturday edition became very much like a magazine in the first ten years of Blethen's ownership of *The Times*.

70. $1000 REWARD! block quote from *The Times*, 18 September 1897.

71. *The Times* reported on 20 September 1897 that no one had claimed the reward, and this claim was frequently repeated.

72. Battle of life block quote, *The Times*, 6 January 1898.

73. Backbone and workingmen quotes, *The Times*, 7 July 1897. Circulation of twenty-five thousand in 1901 was given in the little newspaper history printed in *The Times'* first Sunday edition on 9 February 1902. *The P-I* resisted both the new journalism and yellow journalism, even dragging its heels on purchasing a color press. But *The P-I*, after Brainerd's arrival, editorialized that "the essential characteristic of yellow journalism...[was] its reckless and impudent mendacity," which it considered *The Star* and *The Times* guilty of practicing (6 June 1904). Also see *The Argus*, 6 February 1904, for the class divisions among the three dailies, indicated by their use of "yellow journalism": "Have you read the motto for the day at the head of the editorial page of the Post-Intelligencer?...[If not], you run the risk of being classed with the middle classes who read The Times or the common herd who can afford nothing better...than the little twinkling Star." For the history of journalism and the Spanish-American War, Emery, *The Press and America*, pp. 360-375, provides a brief overview as does Frank Luther Mott, *American Journalism* (New York: Macmillan, 1941), pp. 519-545. The literature on the relationship between this war and the press is voluminous. See Charles H. Brown, *The Correspondents' War: Journalists in the Spanish-American War* (New York: Scribner's, 1967), Sidney Kobre, *The Yellow Press and Gilded Age Journalism* (Tallahassee: Florida State University Press, 1964), and Joyce Milton, *The Yellow Kids: Foreign Correspondents in the Heyday of Yellow Journalism* (New York: Harper and Row, 1989).

74. Poem reprinted in *The Times*, 6 February 1897.

75. Sinking of *Maine*, *The Times*, 17 February 1898. For two headlines that show anticipation of the news, WAR HAS ACTUALLY BEGUN!, followed four days later by WAR DECLARED!, see *The Times*, 21 April and 25 April 1898. For war bulletins in *Times* windows, see *The Times*, 4 July 1898. The war provided opportunities for brazen combinations of patriotism and merchandising. For instance, a *Times* promotion offered paper American and Cuban flags for subscribers to paste in living-room windows (*The Times*, 29 April 1898, and 9 June 1898). For scooped out of pajamas, see *The Times*, 1 June 1898. For examples of cutting-edge technology in war photography see, for instance, *The Times*, 1 July 1898.

76. For admission that *The Times* was Seattle's best evening paper, if the editorial page was removed, see *The Argus*, 7 May 1898. For Chadwick's wishful thinking that Blethen was tied to a party he detested, see *The Argus*, 26 March 1898. For Blethen as a Republican at heart, see *The Argus*, 25 August 1900 or for a similar sentiment, *The Argus*, 25 February 1899.

77. For Turner, see *The Argus*, 5 January 1898. And see *The Argus*, 26 February 1898, 16 April 1898, and 21 May 1898 for the history of Hughes' and Davies' ill-fated *Journal*. For their lawsuit against The Times Printing Company, see Alden Blethen's editorial of 26 January 1898 and the seemingly frank and detailed article of 9 April 1898. In 1895, John Collins owned *The Seattle Press-Times*, and sold it in that same year to James Woolery, taking a mortgage on the property. Hughes and Davies started a job-printing shop, and purchased 5/6 of Woolery's interest in *The Press-Times*, forsaking for a time the Associated Press franchise, and securing a United Press franchise. In March 1895, they discarded *The Press-Times* name, terminated the UP service as valueless, and

soon purchased the evening Associated Press service. The Collins mortgage, Blethen argued, could only be said to apply to property owned by *The Times* at the time the mortgage was issued, that is, prior to Collins' sale to Woolery. The Blethen family completely bought out Hughes and Davies with their contract dated 26 December 1896. In May 1897, The Times Printing Company was organized by the Blethen family, who owned *The Times* in its entirety, and had replaced all machinery, furniture, and all other items which had been covered by the mortgage. So, in April 1898, Blethen claimed that The Times Printing Company has "not one iota of anything in its possession...covered by the Collins mortgage." Davies and Hughes had interested a distant family member in investing in the purchase of the mortgage under the mistaken impression that they could make a substantial claim on the successful *Times* enterprise of 1898. "These highwaymen" were, Blethen wrote, motivated by greed and envy. This lawsuit would be appealed to the Washington State Supreme Court, and eventually decided in the Blethen family's favor. As *The Argus* later noted, "The foreclosure suit against *The Times* which has been hanging fire in the superior court for past six months, has been appealed to the supreme court.... It may not be generally known but it is nevertheless a fact, that *The Times* property was covered by a mortgage when Blethen secured control, which obligation as part of the purchase price, he assumed and agreed to pay. That the Minneapolis mountebank violated his agreement, is eloquently attested by the present action at law." *The Argus*, 23 September 1899.

78. See *The Argus*, 29 July 1899 for Blethen's visit to William Jennings Bryan and his subsequent change of heart, portrayed as remarkable for being "a flop without money and without price," generated by "a little flattery, to which he is more than usually susceptible." For maudlin and pathological quote, see Morgan, *Skid Road*, p. 180. See *The Times* throughout the presidential campaign of 1900 for Alden Blethen's support of Bryan.

79. *Seattle and the Orient*, pp. 7-11, 31-33. The book itself was described in *The Times*, 12 January 1900.

80. Quotes from *Seattle and the Orient*, p. 168, which includes a brief newspaper history.

81. For "Republican readers" buying the independent *Times*, see 23 November 1901, but this notion is frequently reiterated.

82. For Theodore Roosevelt's quote, see *The Times*, 1 November 1902. Eventually, of course, TR would bolt the Republican Party himself and run for president in 1912 as a Progressive against the Republican William Howard Taft. For C.B. Blethen running for legislature, see *The Times*, 30 October 1902; for his loss, see *The Times*, 5 November 1902. *The Argus* commented acidly on "establishing kindergartens" in the legislature for youngsters like C.B., 1 November 1902. See *The Times*, 17 May 1903 for C.B.'s position in the National Association of Democratic Clubs and his interest in founding a young men's Democratic Club in Seattle. For C.B. Blethen's bylined article supporting Hearst for president as "choice of the people," see *The Times*, 28 June 1903. For a possible alliance between William Jennings Bryan and William Randolph Hearst, see *The Times*, 15 January 1904. For *The Argus'* disappointed assertions that Blethen was, in truth, a Democrat, see 31 March 1900 or 23 April 1904. In reply to his bombast over perennial presidential hopeful William Jennings Bryan, Chadwick called Alden Blethen the "Great I Am" of the Washington State Democratic Party.

83. For prostituted his energies block quote, see *The Argus*, 10 March 1906.

84. For unanimous election of Blethen as president of

Iroquois Democratic Club, see *The Seattle Mail and Herald*, 18 January 1902.

85. For quote and Blethen's declining with thanks, see *The Times*, 23 January 1902.

86. For the new building, see *The Times*, 9 February 1902, which was the first Sunday edition and lavishly introduced readers to both its new quarters and the features they could expect each Sunday. See also *The Times* for a preview of the building, 24 January 1902. For holiday edition which featured the new *Times* Building, see *The Argus*, 21 December 1902.

87. The first Sunday edition of *The Times* really showed off what the newspaper could afford to do in illustrations, in well-known fiction, in humor, in photographs, and in every feature, from mining to the theater. For subscription figures and advertising lineage, see *The Times*, 8 October 1902. For the catchy Seven Days a Week advertising phrase, see *The Seattle Mail and Herald*, 18 January 1902.

88. For the early history of the dispute over Seattle city printing, from *The Times'* perspective, see *The Times*, 3 December 1901. For Official City Paper, see, for instance, the masthead of *The Times*, 2 January 1900. For the legal wrangling in both courts, and the outraged anger of *The Times*, see *The Times*, 14 June 1903, 29 November 1903, 8 December 1903, and 31 December 1903. For the sale of *The Bulletin* to The Times Printing Company, see 8 January 1904. For purchase of Bellingham papers, see Lottie Roeder Roth, ed., *History of Whatcom County*, Volume I (Chicago: Pioneer Historical Publishing, 1926), Chapter 29, "Whatcom County Newspapers" especially pp. 582-583, 585; also see editorial "Eight Years Ago," *The Times*, 20 October 1904. *The Morning Times'* first issue was 2 April 1907 and its last issue, 30 November 1907, according to Eldon Coroch, "Colonel Alden J. Blethen," p. 194.

89. For $1,000,000 offer, see many obituaries of Alden Blethen, including Bellingham *Reveille*, 13 July 1915; see also *The Times'* obituary, 13 July 1915, for Daniel Kelleher and the living trust. The Times Investment Company was incorporated for fifty years on 22 October 1900, to "purchase or otherwise acquire, hold, improve, lease, let, mortgage, sell, convey and otherwise dispose of" land, real property, stocks, and bonds. Of the initial $50,000 capitalization, Joe Blethen subscribed real estate and mining stocks worth $49,800, and his father and brother $100 each. All stock in this company, eventually held by Alden and Rose Ann Blethen and their four children, was entrusted to attorney Daniel Kelleher as trustee for twenty years. See "Information Regarding the Times Investment Company—Blethen Investment Company," 1921, File #471, *The Seattle Times* Historical Archives.

90. For quote describing Joseph and Clarance Blethen as live newspapermen, see *The Argus*, 14 February 1903.

91. For Joseph Blethen's career and publishing house quote, see *Seattle Mail and Herald*, 19 October 1901, in which issue he appears on the front page. For "The Alaskan," see Richard Engeman, "The Seattle Spirit Meets 'The Alaskan': A Story of Business, Boosterism, and the Arts," in *Pacific Northwest Quarterly*, Volume 81, No. 2 (April 1990), pp. 54-66. Also see *The Argus*, 24 August 1907 and 4 January 1908, as well as New York City reviews and interviews at the opening of "The Alaskan" in Joseph Blethen Biographical File, *The Seattle Times* Historical Archives. The newspaper continued to publicize Joe's stories, for instance, enthusiastically noting, 25 October 1902, the publication of "The Red Law and the White" in *Everybody's Magazine*. *The Times* reported Joe Blethen as Press Club president 5 June 1903. His tales of his European travels "Through Western Eyes" ran throughout

the spring of 1905 in *The Times*, and a typical installment is 25 June 1905. For C.B. and Joe's respective titles in early 1903, see *The Times*, 8 February 1903.

92. For a description of the T-mat award, see Christy Thomas, *Bylines and Bygones* (New York: Exposition Press, 1964), pp. 65, 77-78. Thomas was a proud recipient of this award.

93. For purchase of the four-color press—a major investment in new technology— see *The Times*, 11 June 1904. For Spanish-American War halftones, see *The Times*, July 1898; for Curtis shots of Mt. St. Helens and Mt. Hood, see *The Times*, 16 July 1898. The slogans about news and photos ran for a time at either side of *Times'* front pages, see, for instance, 25 December 1901. For a good history of *The Times'* technology, see the editorial "Eight Years Ago," 20 October 1904. For the "New Speed Record in Newspaper Pictures," see *The Times*, 2 May 1904. For the brief-lived Blethen Syndicate of Pacific Northwest news photographs, see, for instance, a front page *Times* photograph dated 11 May 1903 supplied by the service, and an advertisement in *The Times*, 15 May 1903. For the San Francisco earthquake offer, see *The Times*, 18 April 1906. For C.B.'s claim that *The Times* was first to print a photo on the day it was shot, see his obituary in *The Times* 31 October 1941.

94. The interview was provocatively entitled "Saloons Just As Numerous," and ran in *The Times*, 25 July 1902. Blethen's editorial, "A Stupid Error About High License," was published 29 July 1902.

95. For Chadwick's satire, see *The Argus*, 2 August 1902.

96. Quote from Blethen's editorial, "A Stupid Error About High License," *The Times*, 29 July 1902.

97. *The Times* toured its readers through the Queen Anne house 18 May 1901 and occasionally thereafter— it is clear that Alden Blethen was very proud of his home. For Blethen's material success, see also *The Argus*, 20 April 1901 and 25 May 1901. For the new house specifically, see *The Argus*, 21 December 1901 (photograph) and an article 15 January 1902. See also *Seattle and the Orient*, pp. 172-173. For an irreverent perspective on the Blethen mansion, see *The Tacoma Ledger* political cartoon of Theodore Roosevelt's failed attempt to visit Blethen, reprinted in *The Argus*, 6 June 1903. For Joseph Blethen's marriage to Genevieve Swadley, see *The Times*, 24 June 1899. For Masonic and club affiliations, see *The Times'* articles at Alden Blethen death, 13 July 1915 and 15 July 1915, as well as *The Minneapolis Journal*, 13 July 1915. For Blethen's increase in prosperity, see *The Argus*, 18 September 1897 and 4 January 1902, and Hanford, *Seattle and Environs*, Volume I, pp. 559-560.

98. For Blethen's assumption that he would receive patronage in a Bryan administration, see Chadwick's satirical sympathy on his not going to "Booley-booley-gaw," the week following Bryan's loss, *The Argus*, 10 November 1900. See *The Times*, May 23 and 14, 1903 for the agonized explanation of the incident. And see *The Times*, 7 June 1903, for Blethen's resentment of Tacoma editor Sam Perkins, who sat next to President Roosevelt. In this editorial, Blethen refers to John Cragwell, the African American barber whom he remembers in his final "Advice and Recommendations." Cragwell was a Republican stalwart and Blethen argued that he had more right to be seated at Roosevelt's side than Perkins.

99. For this satirical treatment of Roosevelt dropping by while Blethen was at work, see *The Argus*, 30 May 1903. *The Argus*, 6 June 1903 ran a wonderful cartoon of TR's abortive visit to Blethen's mansion.

100. The "football of fortune" remark was made by one of Chadwick's friends, see *The Argus*, 6 October 1900. For Blethenesque quote, see *The Argus*, 2 August 1902. For *The*

Times as a yellow newspaper, see *The Argus*, 9 April 1904 or 13 May 1905. As Chadwick put it 17 June 1905, "Cut out a little of the yellow, Colonel, and do not try to get that golden tint on everything that you publish, and your paper will be above criticism."

Notes for Chapter 5

1. Accounts of his daily routine, including lunch at the Butler Hotel, are in "Local Boys Make Good: '30 Means Finished,'" Works Progress Administration history, Washington State Historical Society. For a description of the Butler, see Nellie Horrocks, "Seattle Hotels and Restaurants," typescript, in Pamphlet Files, N Pam 1371, Special Collections, University of Washington Libraries. For number of employees and 1904 circulation see *The Seattle Times*, 11 August 1946.

2. *Articles of Incorporation and Minute Book*, Times Investment Company. The original minute books are held in the Thomas Balmer collection, Manuscripts and University Archives, University of Washington Libraries.

3. For early family homes see *Polk's Seattle City Directory* (Seattle: Polk City Directory Company) for the years 1897 to 1901. For extent of later land acquisitions see Times Investment Company ledger books, *The Seattle Times* Historical Archives.

4. *Articles of Incorporation and Minute Book*, Times Investment Company, especially pp. 1-31, in Thomas Balmer collection, Manuscripts and University Archives, University of Washington Libraries. The remark to the auditor is in a letter which was later uncovered by *The Seattle Post-Intelligencer*, Blethen to J.W. McComaughey, 4 February 1903, in Erastus Brainerd papers, Manuscripts and University Archives, University of Washington Libraries. An editorial cartoon making fun of Blethen's financial arrangements is found in *The Seattle Post-Intelligencer*, 16 August 1908.

5. Description of the new facility is included in various issues of *The Seattle Times* as the building approached completion. See, for example, 25 November 1901. *The Seattle Times*, 21 June 1903, discusses the purchase arrangements for the new presses. Discussion of borrowing with the Scandinavian-American Bank is in *The Seattle Times*, 6 April 1904. Blethen also recognized his long-time relationships with the bank in a *Times* anniversary speech reprinted in *The Seattle Times*, 12 August 1911.

6. The "Raise hell and sell newspapers" quote comes from a file marked "Aphorisms" kept by C.B. Blethen in the Publisher Files, part of *The Seattle Times* Historical Archives. Alden Blethen did not claim to be the originator of the phrase, but always felt it aptly expressed his philosophy.

7. Blethen as local patriot in Joseph Smith autobiography manuscript, Joseph Smith Collection, Manuscripts and University Archives, University of Washington Libraries, Box 2, folder 2-15.

8. Joseph Blethen's description of the bold type style referred to in *Reginald H. Thomson v. Alden J. Blethen et al.*, Superior Court, King County, April 1915, p. 67. See testimony given by Blethen in Olympia before a legislative committee investigating state land board chairman E.W. Ross. Blethen is questioned about the paper's investigative reporting and his own editorial practice in a meeting held 27 February 1907. Testimony was reprinted verbatim in *The Seattle Times*, 3 March 1907. Blethen stated that he read all editorial copy unless he was out of town and then C.B. would take over. The quote about his "unique personality" is from *P-I* editor Scott Bone in *The Seattle Post-Intelligencer*, 14 July 1915.

9. The number of times all four of these men are described as either hated or loved is rather remarkable. See for example

R.H. Thomson, *That Man Thomson* (Seattle: University of Washington Press, 1950), p. 1; Dale Soden, "Mark Allison Matthews: Seattle's Southern Preacher" (unpublished Ph.D. dissertation, University of Washington, 1980), pp. 361-362; Victoria Livingston, "Erastus Brainerd, The Bankruptcy of Brilliance" (unpublished master's thesis, University of Washington, 1967), pp. 126-131; and Eldon Coroch, "Colonel Alden Blethen and The Seattle Daily Times" (unpublished master's thesis, University of Washington, 1966), p. 1, for representative descriptions.

10. "School boys" quotation is from *The Argus*, 13 May 1905. *The Argus'* editor Harry Chadwick frequently commented on the feud, but claimed that the public found it foolish and boring.

11. An overall description of Brainerd's career is in Livingston, "Erastus Brainerd: The Bankruptcy of Brilliance," pp. 2-6; 21-22.

12. Blethen's assessment of the source of the feud comes from an editorial written to mark Brainerd's departure from *The Seattle Post-Intelligencer*, entitled "The Passing of Erastus Brainerd," *The Seattle Times*, 20 August 1911. Blethen makes the same claim later in a letter defending himself and circulated to members of the Commercial Club, "To Whom It May Concern," 26 November 1912, in Clarence Bagley papers, Box 8, Folder 27. For letters between the two, especially during the time of Brainerd's tenure as the secretary of the chamber of commerce's Klondike advertising committee and later bureau of information, see Brainerd Collection, Library of Congress, Mss 95-6.

13. For Wilson's career and involvement with Brainerd, see C. Brewster Coulter, "John L. Wilson, Erastus Brainerd, and the Republican Party of Washington," *Idaho Yesterdays*, vol. 4, no. 1, especially pp. 12-16. Also *The Seattle Times*, 23 May 1943; 7 March 1948; an account of Wilson's role in Republican Party politics in Washington is in Keith Murray, "Republican Party Politics in Washington During the Progressive Era" (unpublished Ph.D. dissertation, University of Washington, 1946). James A. Wood described John L. Wilson's reason for choosing Brainerd in *The Seattle Times*, 21 March 1943. The relationship of Wilson and Brainerd is discussed in Livingston, "Erastus Brainerd Bankruptcy of Brilliance," pp. 50-53.

14. See *The Times'* political reporter looking back on the state's political history in *The Seattle Times*, 14 February 1943. Description of Brainerd as a "statesman of the press" in C. Brewster Coulter, "John L. Wilson, Erastus Brainerd and the Republican Party of Washington," p. 14.

15. Quote about Brainerd's style from James A. Wood in *The Seattle Times*, 21 March 1943. See the Joseph Smith collection, Manuscripts and University Archives, University of Washington Libraries, Box 1, folder 1-20 for the "egotistic, dyspeptic" description of Brainerd.

16. See *The Seattle Post-Intelligencer*, 1 January 1904, for Brainerd's first day on the job at *The P-I*. The "vituperation" quote is from Joseph Smith papers, Box 1, folder 1-20, Manuscripts and University Archives, University of Washington Libraries.

17. Editorial comments on *The Seattle Times* as an independent, family newspaper in *The Seattle Times*, 3 March 1907.

18. See *The Seattle Post-Intelligencer*, 15 January 1904, for "katzenjammer kid" reference and 12 March 1904, for unflattering portrait of Hearst. *The Times* published the caricature-like portrait of Brainerd and its responses to *The P-I* commentary in *The Seattle Times*, 13 March 1904 and 17 April 1904.

19. The story on the neglect of the shipyard is in *The*

Seattle Times, 10 April 1904. Brainerd's use of the term knocker is in *The Seattle Post-Intelligencer*, 11 April 1904, and Blethen's editorial reply in *The Seattle Times*, 17 April 1904. Blethen continues to respond to the term knocker over the next few months. "Most offensive term" quote is in *The Seattle Times*, 8 June 1904, with more on 9 June 1904.

20. Some of the name calling can be seen in *The Seattle Times*, 21 and 24 April 1904; 8 and 9 June 1904. Chadwick's comments on the Colonel's vocabulary in *The Argus*, 4 June 1904.

21. Apologies from Blethen were in *The Seattle Times*, 8 June 1904; some of the editorials about the Wilson "organ" and its Republican bias include *The Seattle Times*, 16 and 21 October 1904. For non-partisanship see *The Seattle Times*, 20 March; 7 November 1904. For *The Seattle Post-Intelligencer* and partisanship, see *The P-I*, 2 March 1904.

22. A detailed discussion of the relationship between the Republicans and the railroad interests is in Murray, "Republican Party Politics in Washington During the Progressive Era," pp. 50-65; also Coulter, "John L. Wilson, Erastus Brainerd and the Republican Party of Washington," pp. 11-14.

23. Articles on the fraud of clerk F.F. French begin in *The Seattle Times*, 26 October 1904, and continue into early November, as do sensationalist stories of L.C. Smith's corruption. The "Desperadoes" front page announcing the libel charges is in *The Seattle Times*, 5 November 1904.

24. Editorial in *The Seattle Post-Intelligencer*, 6 November 1904. Earlier reporting on new Bank of New England lawsuit is in *The Seattle Times*, 22 May 1904. The suit was settled in Blethen's favor; see *The Seattle Times*, 20 November 1904.

25. The Chadwick comment on Brainerd's "paretic mattoid" editorial of 6 November 1904 is in *The Argus*, 12 November 1904.

26. The Blethen response to Brainerd's editorial name-calling is in *The Seattle Times*, 13 November 1904. See *The Seattle Times*, 21 November 1904, for sympathetic responses to the battle.

27. Joshua Green in a later interview made the remarks about the popularity of the rivalry. Unpublished interview of Joshua Green and Harry Broderick by Paul Andrews, no date, *The Seattle Times* Historical Archives. Chadwick's comments are in *The Argus*, 12 November 1904. Brainerd is congratulated in a letter, H.M. Lyon of *The World* to Brainerd, 30 August 1904, in Erastus Brainerd papers, Box 5, Folder 37, Manuscripts and University Archives, University of Washington Libraries. Another suspicion was that the two enjoyed their exchanges. See "Erastus Brainerd" profile by Edward H. Thomas in Works Progress Administration manuscripts, Washington State Historical Society.

28. "Hearstesque" description comes from a comment by *The Minneapolis Journal* republished in *The Seattle Times*, 18 March 1904. Chadwick often accused Blethen of yellow journalism. See, for example, *The Argus*, 17 June 1905; 21 November, 1905. Reference to color is by editorial writer Marion Baxter in *The Seattle Times*, 12 February 1905.

29. The use of color and the resistance of Wilson and Brainerd is in *The Seattle Times*, 2 May 1905; see also 21 May 1905. The "coon patch" quote is in *The Seattle Times*, 30 May 1905.

30. For *The Times'* daily and Sunday circulation in 1905, see chart in *The Seattle Times*, 11 August 1946. *The Seattle Post-Intelligencer* figure is estimated by Brainerd at 30,000 in 1907, and *The P-I* was claiming 20,000 in 1904, so the 1905 totals were no more than 25,000 and probably less. Brainerd's estimate is found in a letter of Brainerd to Melville Stone, Associated Press Manager, 24 June 1907, in Erastus Brainerd

papers, Box 5, Manuscripts Division, University of Washington. *The P-I* figure for 1904 is found in *The Seattle Times*, 9 June 1905. 318,000 column inches of advertisements ran in *The P-I* during the year as opposed to 475,000 in *The Times*. Comparative advertising lineage is in *The Seattle Times*, 7 January 1906. Offer for circulation proof is in *The Seattle Times*, 9 June 1905. The faked *Times* edition is mentioned by *The Times* in the same edition as well as 8 June 1905.

31. The winner of the "Most Beautiful Woman in Washington" contest is announced with great fanfare in *The Seattle Times*, 16 October 1904, although the series had been running for a number of months. The "Seattle Spirit" series begins in *The Seattle Times*, 25 April 1905, and the first issue of "Seattle Young Men" is 4 June 1905. Curtis photographs were frequent Sunday features. See, for example, *The Seattle Times*, 21 May 1905; 11 June 1905.

32. The new women's pages are described in *The Seattle Times*, 11 June 1904, and the debut of "Seattle Women Who Maintain Their Independence" is 7 May 1905. The "Girl in the Printing Office" ran in *The Seattle Times*, 11 June 1905. Alden Blethen quote on women, taken from *The San Francisco Examiner*, is reprinted in *The Seattle Times*, 19 March 1905.

33. Several works specifically cover the impact of progressive reform efforts in Washington state. See, for example, Murray, "Republican Party Politics During the Progressive Era"; James Donnen, "Personality and Reform in the Progressive Era: An Interpretation of Five Washington State Careers" (unpublished master's thesis, University of Washington, 1974); Mansel Blackford, "Sources of Support for Reform Candidates and Issues in Seattle Politics, 1902-1916" (unpublished master's thesis, University of Washington, 1967). For general background on historical interpretation of progressivism, see Lewis Gould, ed., *The Progressive Era* (Syracuse: Syracuse University Press, 1974).

34. Population figures for the city are available in a variety of sources. Basic figures for 1900 and 1910 in United States Bureau of the Census, *Abstract of the Census, 1910* (Washington, D.C.: Government Printing Office, 1911), p. 57. Figure for Kansas City in *World Almanac and Encyclopedia, 1913* (New York: Press Publishing Company, 1913), p. 656.

35. City poor exposé is in *The Seattle Times*, 14 May 1905. The articles on the garbage trust began in *The Seattle Times*, 13 November 1906. Crusades for Sunday saloon closings are frequent throughout the period. The sensational coverage of Ah Sou begins in *The Seattle Times*, 2 May 1905, and continues for several weeks.

36. For a major case see *R.H. Thomson v. The Seattle Daily Times et al.*, King County Superior Court, Case #91753, pp. 316-317. Copies in Washington State Archives, King County Branch. See also *Plaintiff and Defendant Indexes*, Civil Cases, King County Superior Court Records, King County Administration Building, for numerous other suits filed by Thomson against Blethen and *The Seattle Times*.

37. Biographical material in Thomson, *That Man Thomson*, p. 31. For additional press descriptions of Thomson see *The Seattle Times*, 3 November 1930; *The Seattle Post-Intelligencer*, 9 April 1976. Also, *The P-I*, 16 January 1916.

38. The "proper man" quote from *The Argus*, 4 June 1906.

39. Early debates over water issues in Seattle are discussed in Thomson, *That Man Thomson*, pp. 57-64.

40. As background for the development of the Cedar River water system see Mary McWilliams, *Seattle Water Department History, 1854-1954* (Seattle: Dogwood Press, 1955), and Myra L. Phelps, *Public Works in Seattle* (Seattle: Seattle Engi-

neering Department, 1978). Blethen's quote in *The Seattle Times*, 10 August 1901; also cited in Coroch, "Colonel Alden Blethen and The Seattle Daily Times," p. 201.

41. Coroch, "Colonel Alden Blethen and The Seattle Daily Times," p. 201, for description of lawn-watering violations; there are also repeated articles about Queen Anne street paving. See, for example, *The Seattle Times*, 28 June 1903. Comment on setting pegs wrong in H.C. Pigott to Blethen, 11 August 1911, a copy of which Pigott later forwarded to fellow newspaperman and former *Times* reporter, Joseph Smith. Pigott made the remarks in declining to attend a dinner being hosted by Blethen at the Rainier Club. In Joseph Smith collection, Manuscripts and University Archives, University of Washington Libraries.

42. A description of the 1904 city election is in Blackford, "Sources of Support for Reform Candidates and Issues in Seattle Politics, 1902-1916," pp. 27-32. For *The Times'* explanation of its pro-Moore, anti-municipal ownership stance see *The Seattle Times*, 6 March 1906.

43. For "faddists" quote see *The Seattle Times*, 7 September 1906. Brainerd's letter to John L. Wilson about Blethen and Furth is in Erastus Brainerd to John L. Wilson, no month and date, 1906, in Erastus Brainerd collection, Manuscripts and University Archives, University of Washington Libraries. There were also letters from 1901 suggesting that Blethen had asked Furth to review articles on the street railway and point out any errors. See, for example, Blethen to Jacob Furth, 29 August 1901, in Joseph Smith papers, Box 7, folder 7-4, Manuscripts and University Archives, University of Washington Libraries.

44. For pre-election attacks, see, for example, *The Seattle Times*, 2 and 7 September 1906. "The Times Wins" headlines are in *The Seattle Times*, 13 September 1906; discussion of the election results is in *The Seattle Times*, 19 September 1906.

45. Thomson description in *The Seattle Times*, 12 May 1907.

46. For cartoons, see, for example, *The Seattle Times*, 11 October 1907. Moore's mayoral support of Thomson in *The Seattle Times*, 3 October 1907. Failure in reforms is in *The Seattle Times*, 13 October 1907.

47. Thomson's private commentary is cited in Coroch, "Colonel Alden Blethen and The Seattle Daily Times," pp. 203-204; remark comes originally from Thomson to Winlock Miller, 1 December 1911, in Reginald Thomson collection, Manuscripts and University Archives, University of Washington Libraries. The Argus comment on Thomson is in *The Argus*, 5 November 1905.

48. Pigott quotation from letter, H.C. Pigott to Alden Blethen, 13 July 1911, in Joseph Smith papers, Manuscripts and University Archives, University of Washington Libraries, Box 8, folder 8-5.

49. The Chadwick quote about "interested parties" and bad advice is from *The Argus*, 16 October 1915, and cited in Coroch, "Colonel Alden Blethen and The Seattle Daily Times," p. 208.

50. Information on Seattle at the end of the Klondike era is in Janice Reiff, "Urbanization and Social Structure: Seattle, Washington, 1852-1910" (unpublished Ph.D. dissertation, University of Washington, 1981), pp. 80-81. The average amount of gold coming through the Seattle assay office from Alaska was $14 million per year; in 1908 it was $23 million. See also pp. 163-166 for new population base.

51. The effect of Matthews' height is in article on the height of prominent people in Seattle, *The Seattle Times*, 22 April 1906. For a description of Matthews' background, see Dale Soden, "Mark Allison Matthews—Seattle's Minister

Rediscovered," *Pacific Northwest Quarterly* (April 1983), especially pp. 50-52. A much more detailed version is in Soden's dissertation on Matthews, "Mark Allison Matthews: Seattle's Southern Preacher." The "smashing similes" quote is from Peter MacFarlane, "The Black-Maned Lion of Seattle," *Collier's*, vol. 50 (Dec. 1922), p. 22, and also cited in Soden, "Mark Allison Matthews—Seattle's Minister Rediscovered," p. 52.

52. *The Seattle Times*, 28 January 1902, for "storm" quote. The article by Matthews on the 1904 religious outlook is in *The Seattle Times*, 5 January 1904.

53. The "graftitis" charges were made by Matthews in January 1905, and his appearance before the council was reported in *The Seattle Times*, 31 January 1905.

54. Blethen's blast at Gill in *The Seattle Times*, 30 January 1905. Call for grand jury investigation follows in early February. Some of the cartoons of "Gill's Gang" run in *The Seattle Times*, 14, 15, and 16 March 1905.

55. Soden, "Mark Allison Matthews: Seattle's Southern Preacher," pp. 129-131.

56. *The Argus*, 26 May 1906. "Closed tight" quote is in *The Seattle Times*, 9 March 1906.

57. Background on Wappenstein's career as described by him and *The Seattle Times* is in *The Seattle Times*, 23 October 1910; see also Murray Morgan, *Skid Road* (New York: Viking Press, 1951), pp. 138; 171-172. Morgan's account of how Wappenstein obtained his position differs from other accounts. According to Morgan, Wappenstein worked as an investigator for the Great Northern and was the protégé of railroad vice-president and politico J.D. Farrell. Morgan says that Farrell asked Moore to appoint Wappenstein in return for his political support in the mayoral campaign. Wappenstein biographical description is from Dorothy Miller Kahlo, *History of the Police and Fire Departments of the City of Seattle* (Seattle: Lumbermen's Printing Company, 1907), pp. 75-76.

58. For one interpretation of the Colonel's allegiances to Wappenstein see Gordon Newell and Don Sherwood, *Totem Tales of Old Seattle* (Seattle: Superior Publishing, 1956), p. 117. The authors suggest that one of the favors performed by Wappenstein was to assign a police officer as the editor's personal bodyguard.

59. The Colonel's frequent lunches at the Italian-American Club are noted in testimony at his later trial, detailed in *The Seattle Times*, 29 November 1911.

60. Information about these Tenderloin businessmen is scattered and often difficult to find. A long article on Barberis appears in *The Times* in 1905, indicating he and Blethen were already very friendly. See *The Seattle Times*, 16 July 1905. A description of the Maison Barberis is included in a feature on Seattle's hotels and restaurants in *The Seattle Times*, 7 February 1904. Discussions of Blethen's relationship with Berryman and Dallagiovanna are contained in court documents and testimony from the later indictment and trial of Blethen for shielding vice. See *The Seattle Times*, 29 and 30 December 1911 and 1, 2, and 3 December 1911.

61. Erastus Brainerd to Rainier Club, 5 December 1908, in Erastus Brainerd collection, Manuscripts and University Archives, University of Washington Libraries, Box 6, folder 7.

62. Blethen editorial in *The Seattle Times*, 1 March 1908.

63. Alden Blethen's reversal in his support of Gill is explained in an editorial in *The Seattle Times*. For diffusion of vice problem, see, for example Coroch, "Colonel Alden Blethen and The Seattle Daily Times," pp. 219-220; Richard Berner, *Seattle 1900-1920, From Boomtown, Urban Turbulence, to Restoration* (Seattle: Charles Press, 1991), p. 114. For Gill quote see Burton J. Hendrick, "The 'Recall' in Seattle," *McClure's*, vol. 37 (October, 1911), p. 648.

64. For Gill's election victory see *The Seattle Times*, 9 March 1910. For conditions in the Tenderloin under Wappenstein, see Hendrick, "The 'Recall' in Seattle," p. 654.

65. Wilson's withdrawal from the Senate race is covered in a number of sources, including Murray, "Republican Party Politics During the Progressive Era," pp. 111-115; Livingston, "Erastus Brainerd: Bankruptcy of Brilliance," pp. 92-98. Brainerd's new policy of independence announced in *The Seattle Post-Intelligencer*, 16 September 1910. See also public response in letters sent to Brainerd, including Henry R. King to Erastus Brainerd et al., 16 September 1910; James Scott to John L. Wilson, 16 September 1910; Schuyler Duryee to Wilson, 16 September 1910. Erastus Brainerd collection, Incoming Letters, Box 6, folder 1, Manuscripts and University Archives, University of Washington Libraries.

66. Alden Blethen to Charles Wappenstein, 24 September 1910, is reprinted in *The P-I*, 24 May 1911, and appears in numerous other collections including Governor Lister papers, Washington State Archives, UW files, 1913(1).

67. For accounts of the beginning of the recall movement, see *The Seattle Times*, 8 October 1910, and after. Also, Hendrick, "The 'Recall' in Seattle," pp. 658-660. Many secondary accounts give the basic outline of the story, but some are also in error. The chronology of the recall movement is confused, for example, in Mansel G. Blackford, "Reform Politics in Seattle During the Progressive Era," *Pacific Northwest Quarterly*, vol. 59, no. 4 (October, 1968), p. 182.

68. Hendrick, "The 'Recall' in Seattle," pp. 660-663.

69. Ministerial Association participation is described in Blackford, "Reform Politics in Seattle During the Progressive Era," p. 183; see also Mark Matthews to Erastus Brainerd, 11 January 1911, in Erastus Brainerd collection, Manuscripts and University Archives, University of Washington Libraries. The most complete description of Matthews' role is in Soden, "Mark Allison Matthews: Seattle's Southern Preacher," pp. 134-140. Soden disputes earlier accounts that suggest Matthews was an avid recall promoter before the election.

70. Matthews made public his role in the Burns affair and his conversation with Gill in *The Seattle Post-Intelligencer*, 7 May 1911. McFarlane, "The Black-Maned Lion of Seattle," also quotes Matthews' offer to influence the recall. The way Matthews set up his arrangement with Burns is in Mark Matthews, "Accounting with W.J. Burns," 1 December 1910 to 1 May 1911, Mark Matthews collection, Manuscripts and University Archives, University of Washington Libraries. Quote is from William R. Hunt, *Front Page Detective: William J. Burns and the Detective Profession, 1880-1930* (Bowling Green, Ohio: Bowling Green State University Popular Press, 1990), p. 75.

71. The remarks of Burns were reported in *The Seattle Times*, 15 February 1911. A discussion of the recall Burns played in is in Hunt, *Front Page Detective*, pp. 77-78.

72. Joseph Smith to D.K. Larimer, 19 February 1911, in Joseph Smith papers, Manuscripts and University Archives, University of Washington Libraries.

73. Accusations against *The Seattle Post-Intelligencer* and *The Seattle Star* begin in *The Seattle Times*, 9 February 1911; indictments of Wappenstein are in *The Seattle Times*, 13 February 1911.

74. Blethen indictments are first covered in *The Seattle Times*, 23 May 1911, but fuller coverage is provided 24 May 1911. See also *The P-I*, 24 May 1911. Bond information in *State of Washington v. Alden Blethen, et al.*, King County Superior Court, Case #5849, 23 May 1911.

75. Blethen's first response in *The Seattle Times*, 23 May 1911; editorial in *The Seattle Times*, 24 May 1911.

76. The filing of the lawsuit against *The Seattle Post-Intelligencer* is in *The Seattle Times*, 25 May 1911. Protection of Tupper and Gideon is in Operative C reports, 5 June 1911, in Mark Matthews collection, Manuscripts and University Archives, University of Washington Libraries.

77. The courthouse sighting is in Operative C reports, 31 May 1911; Italian-American club conversation in Op C reports, 8 June 1911; quote about the fund in Op C reports, 27 July 1911, all in Mark Matthews collection, Graft Cases, Box 2, folder 2-11, Manuscripts and University Archives, University of Washington Libraries.

78. Search for public records in Op C reports, 1 August 1911; pressure on Berryman in Op C reports, 20 July 1911 both in Mark Matthews collection, Box 2, folder 2-12; 21 July 1911, Manuscripts and University Archives, University of Washington Libraries.

79. Op C report, 4 August 1911, in Mark Matthews collection, Box 2, folder 2-11, for Brainerd's help. Text of the "Nome letter," which was later used to malign Blethen's character, is in Alden Blethen to Mitchell and Steele, 1 September 1906, accompanying Blethen to "Whom It May Concern," 26 November 1912. This letter is included in Clarence Bagley collection, Box 8, folder 27, Manuscripts and University Archives, University of Washington Libraries.

80. The reports of Wappenstein's trials are covered in detail in *The Seattle Times*, May and July 1911. The story of the "Wappy Not Guilty" edition is in Op C reports, 26 July 1911, Mark Matthews collection, Manuscripts and University Archives, University of Washington Libraries.

81. Hendrick, "The 'Recall' in Seattle," pp. 655-656.

82. The lewd photographs were reported by Cotterill and also by Congressman James Bryan who read his account into the *Congressional Record* and used it in speeches against the Colonel. See, for example, *The Seattle Times*, 16 September 1913.

83. *The Argus* quote is in *The Argus*, 19 August 1911. *The Times* covered the dinner at length, reprinting all of the toasts and speeches, including Blethen's. See *The Seattle Times*, 13 August 1911.

84. The trial is covered in *The Seattle Times*, 29 and 30 November; 1, 2, and 3 December 1911.

85. Account of the resignation of Brainerd is in Livingston, "Erastus Brainerd: Bankruptcy of Brilliance," pp. 103-106. Thomson's comment about his resignation was recorded later in an interview conducted when he was 90 years old in *The Seattle Times*, 14 November 1946.

Notes for Chapter 6

1. "Educating his sons" from oral history interview with Florence Blethen Duffy, conducted by Eldon Nick Coroch, "Colonel Alden J. Blethen and The Seattle Daily Times" (University of Washington, unpublished master's thesis, 1966), cited in his Chapter V, "One Big Family." Eldon Coroch has kindly shared his notes from this and other oral history interviews, and they are held in *The Seattle Times* Historical Archives. James J. Hill to C.B. Blethen, telegram, 18 July 1915, File #45, *The Seattle Times* Historical Archives.

2. See Richard C. Berner, *Seattle, 1900-1920: From Boomtown, Urban Turbulence, to Restoration* (Seattle: Charles Press, 1991), pp. 62-63, for Seattle suburbs, and *The Seattle Times'* pro-annexation editorials, for instance, 21 June 1903, which is accompanied by an article about the positive effect annexation would have on the city. Suggestion to fill in Lake Union is from *The Argus*, 19 March 1910, to tunnel First Hill, *The Argus*, 9 April 1910, and to bridge Lake Washington, *The Argus*, 25 May 1912. For Blethen's wholehearted

support of the Lake Washington ship canal, see correspondence Alden Joseph Blethen to Miller Freeman, 17 July 1911, Freeman papers, Manuscripts and University Archives, University of Washington Libraries. See also Freeman to Blethen, 17 June 1911, commending *The Seattle Times'* editorial, "Why This Canal Fight?"

3. For "Some Things We Much Need" editorial, see *The Times*, 14 December 1901, but this laundry list of *Times* goals spans the years 1902-1915. For support for Pike Place Market, see *The Times*, 17 August 1907. For *The Times'* opposition to the Bogue plan for Seattle urban development, see recommendations, "How to Vote at Special Elections, March Fifth," *The Times*, 3 March 1912. See Minutes, Board of Trustees, Seattle Chamber of Commerce, Volume 1910-1911, 1912-1913, 1914-1915, Special Collections, Seattle Public Library. Blethen's election to the board was noted in the Minutes, 10 October 1911, and he offered his first report to the board as chair of the exploitation and publicity bureau on 14 November 1911.

4. Block quote on private and public interests from *The Times'* editorial, 14 February 1902.

5. See Coroch, "Colonel Alden J. Blethen," p. 249 for first mention of this notion of notoriety slowing growth. Mark Matthews had written an open letter, first published in *The Times*, 7 May 1911, which called Seattle a "corrupt and unholy" city. It was widely reprinted. Harry Chadwick shared Alden Blethen's worries about the effects of airing Seattle's dirty laundry too publicly, see "The Damage It Does," *The Argus*, 26 March 1910. Such concerns, however, did not restrain Blethen's own criticism during 1912 through 1914, when *The Times* portrayed Seattle as under daily siege by bomb-throwing anarchists. The infamous reputation quote is from *The Times*, 6 November 1910; the stigma quote is Blethen's from *The Times*, 9 February 1911.

6. Blethen's remark about the typographical union was quoted in *The Argus*, 9 September 1905. Chadwick wrote "h—l," but we have made this editorial change for clarity. The organized labor department was part of *The Times* throughout Alden Blethen's life, appearing in 1914 and 1915 four to six nights each week. C.D. Stratton, then editor of the labor department, did not seem to be under constraints, writing for instance a lengthy article discussing a meeting of Seattle's Central Labor Council to pay tribute "to the memory of those who have shed their life blood in the cause of industrial freedom," *The Times*, 10 February 1915. However, Stratton, like Blethen, vehemently rejected the labor militancy of the Industrial Workers of the World (IWW), or Wobblies, as criminals attempting to take advantage of legitimate labor actions.

7. Too cowardly quote from *The Times'* editorial, 12 December 1901.

8. One brick quote from *The Times*, 12 December 1901.

9. The combined birthday and Christmas party is described in *The Argus*, 3 January 1912, and the bureau of publicity event was repeated annually thereafter through 1914.

10. Blethen's Walla Walla joke from *The Argus*, 5 October 1912.

11. For the story of the hapless burglar, see *The Seattle Mail and Herald*, 23 August 1902.

12. Office coat and general reminiscence of Homer Applegate, who joined *The Times* in 1900, in the issue celebrating *The Times'* fifty year anniversary, *The Times*, 11 August 1946. Elbows out on his "old office alpaca thing" from Florence Blethen Duffy oral history interview, Coroch, "Colonel Alden J. Blethen."

13. James Wood's reminiscence of a typical Blethen tour

through the Denny Building third floor and the banter block quote is from *The Town Crier*, 18 July 1915.

14. Cheap club reference from *The Argus*, 27 May 1911; billiards at the Arctic Club from *The Argus*, 17 July 1915. According to C.B. Blethen's "Alden," a manuscript biography in *The Seattle Times* Historical Archives, his father "turned to alcohol during fits of loneliness or depression," and "frequently picked up acquaintances inferior to himself in character and position." Teacup of brandy and apple story from C.B. Blethen II, "The Moving Editor," typescript, 1970?, *The Seattle Times* Historical Archives.

15. See Col. Alden Joseph Blethen, ed., *Genealogy of the Blethen Family* (Seattle: Merchants Printing Company: 1911). This book is held by the Seattle Public Library. For C.B.'s distrust of Alden Blethen's own tales of his life, see C.B. Blethen to Marion Blethen Mesdag, 25 January 1933, File #385, *The Seattle Times* Historical Archives, "Was the real reason for his leaving there (Abbott Family School) the fact that he had determined to practice law?" For mention of Alden Blethen's membership in the New England Club and the civilizing quote, see the report of the club's resolution of sympathy to the family in *The Times*, 1 August 1915.

16. For Kent's Hill interview, grand triumphal tour, and sad story, see *The Argus*, 7 May 1911. Blethen's frequent historical editorials, both on his own general career and on the history of *The Seattle Times*, indicate his interest in shaping public perception of his past. See, among many, the historical review editorial of 21 May 1911, or the ten-year celebrations of his purchase of *The Times*, in 1906. For real candy quote, see *The Argus*, 28 September 1907. "Colonel Blethen never lived in the past. Everything was down to the minute with him," is from *The Hoquiam Washingtonian*, 13 July 1915.

17. Chadwick's quote about Blethen's public announcements of his charitable donations is from *The Argus*, 2 December 1899. However, Harry Chadwick made Alden Blethen's characteristic display a frequent target, remarking 29 November 1902, of the annual turkey purchase, "*The Seattle Times* is right. It is only just and right that the public should be let into these little matters. These heart-to-heart talks do one good.... There is a sort of feeling, however, that the Colonel's charity is not entirely disinterested.... [I]t might be mentioned that there are hundreds of papers all over the country [that do the same] but up to date *The Seattle Times* is the only one that has had the good taste to publicly call attention to the fact." Blethen was very generous to the families of those who died or were seriously injured in *The Minneapolis Tribune* fire, including the orphaned children of James Igoe, whose education he supported. For Igoe, see Joshua Green to W.K. Blethen, 10 May 1946, *The Seattle Times* Historical Archives. C.B. Blethen was clearly proud of his father's generosity when he wrote his reminiscence "Alden," in 1933, but he also remarked that his father had sometimes chosen unworthy recipients fearing that he might miss a worthy one.

18. Anecdote and quotes from the Works Progress Administration journalism history, Washington State Historical Society.

19. The phrase "worthy poor" was well-known to readers of Blethen's *Times*. See, for instance, "Coal and Wood for the Worthy Poor" signed by Blethen on front page of *The Times*, 3 January 1914. This was the fourth annual distribution of five hundred tons of coal or wood, as preferred, one ton per applicant, whose worthiness must be vouched for by a "responsible person." For Charles Alf. Williams' family, see Alden Joseph Blethen, "Advice and Recommendations," 1915, *The Seattle Times* Historical Archives.

20. Kay F. Reinartz, *Queen Anne: Community on the Hill*

(Seattle: Queen Anne Historical Society, 1993), p. 105 for Blethen's library donation.

21. For Alden Blethen on Western Advisory Board of Associated Press, see *The Times*, 12 November 1912. For AP bureau headquarters moving to Seattle, see *The Times*, 2 July 1913. For his never missing a meeting for thirty-five years, see his obituary, *The Times*, 13 July 1915.

22. For newspapermen quote, see James Wood, *The Town Crier*, 18 July 1915. Prodigal entertainer from Scott Bone's reminiscence, *The Seattle Post-Intelligencer*, 14 July 1915. This group of editors is also mentioned by Otis Moore, *The Aberdeen World*, 13 July 1915.

23. For accusations that *The Times* was a member of the Hearst chain of papers, see *The Argus*, 5 March 1904 and 12 March 1904. For comment on Blethen's denials, see *The Argus*, 16 April 1904. For personal interview with Hearst, see *The Times*, 11 July 1914, and for one of many photographs of Hearst on the paper's front page, see 12 July 1914. For Alden Blethen's Rainier Club toast to Hearst, see *The Times*, 13 July 1914. This quote is slightly edited.

24. The practical joke story about 1898 Spanish-American War news hawked as current in the 1903 *Times* is from *The Argus*, 8 August 1903.

25. See circulation chart 11 August 1946, in the Fiftieth Anniversary feature of *The Times*.

26. M.M. Mattison's reminiscence of Alden Blethen indicated that Blethen had used his influence with the chamber on Wilson's behalf, *The Times*, 13 July 1915. Eldon Coroch, "Colonel Alden J. Blethen," notes, for instance, p. 272, that *The P-I* handled Blethen's legal difficulties with delicacy and discretion. See *The Times'* editorial, 10 December 1911, for celebration of the feud's end and "discordant element" quote.

27. For account of chamber of commerce dinner, see *The Argus*, 18 November 1911. Just three months before this, Blethen had given a dinner for 250 friends and associates at the Rainier Club to celebrate fifteen years as editor of *The Times;* John L. Wilson, Erastus Brainerd, and Mark Matthews were not invited. For this dinner, see *The Argus*, 19 August 1911 and *The Times*, 12 August 1911. This occurred during the grand jury investigations, and Blethen would later write to University of Washington acting president Henry Landes that the presence of "the very cream of the membership of that club" was gratifying to him. See correspondence Alden Blethen to Henry Landes, 23 January 1914, President's papers, University of Washington, Manuscripts and University Archives. For *The Argus* front page portraits, see 3 February 1912.

28. Roger Sale, *Seattle: Past to Present* (Seattle: University of Washington Press, 1978) p. 109. For yellow quote, see *The Argus*, 22 January 1909.

29. For enviable position quote, see *The Argus*, 11 June 1910.

30. For block quote about *Times* independence, see *The Argus*, 11 September 1909.

31. For Times Square land purchase, see *The Times*, 29 March 1912.

32. For Times Square quotes, see *The Times*, 29 March 1912.

33. For general information on Alden Blethen as regent at the University of Washington, see Charles M. Gates, *The First Century at the University of Washington* (Seattle: University of Washington Press, 1961). However, the collections of the University of Washington Regents, the President, and many individual members of the faculty and the community, like Edmond Meany, Theresa McMahon, and Edwin Stevens, offer rich material, in Manuscripts and University Archives,

University of Washington Libraries. For the politicization of the board of regents between 1897 and 1902, see correspondence Blethen to John R. Rogers, 8 October 1897, Governor's papers, Washington State Archives. And see Blethen's resignation, which was not accepted, at the accession of Governor Henry McBride, 25 December 1901, cc'd to Edmond Meany, 2 December 1901, Meany papers, Manuscripts and University Archives. See Meany's letter of support for Blethen, 31 December 1901, to Governor McBride, noting that Blethen "has been one of the fairest and most non-partisan Regents that the University has ever had." For pride of my life quote, see Alden Blethen to Howard Cosgrove, 11 August 1913, Board of Regents, Manuscripts and University Archives, University of Washington Libraries.

34. Alden Blethen's speech was printed in the University of Washington *Bulletin* for 1901, quote p. 28. For description of Science Hall and cornerstone ceremony, see *The Times*, 16 October 1901.

35. For Blethen's role in UW Metropolitan Tract and the quote, see Mattison's reminiscence, *The Times*, 13 July 1915, as well as Gates, *The First Century at the University of Washington*, pp. 127-135, and Berner, *Boomtown*, pp. 82-86.

36. Quote from Alden Blethen to Thomas Kane, 15 November 1911, President's papers, University of Washington, Manuscripts and University Archives, University of Washington Libraries. This letter and others also refer to summer discussions with Rea and summer correspondence with the Meneely Company. However, it seems likely that Blethen did not personally commit to the donation until the fall, conducting these discussions and engaging in this correspondence as an agent, so to speak, of Rea's project, gathering information that might be passed to another potential donor. See Kane's reassurance in letter from Thomas Kane to Alden Blethen, 18 November 1911. In November correspondence with Kane, Blethen referred to his current court appearances, Alden Blethen to Thomas Kane, 24 November 1911, President's papers, Manuscripts and University Archives.

37. Feel them out quote from Alden Blethen to John A. Rea, 12 December 1911, cc'd to Thomas Kane, President's papers, Manuscripts and University Archives, University of Washington.

38. Supposedly C.B. Blethen tipped the Blethen hand and revealed to a journalism class his father and family's hope to soon "make an announcement that will prove our interest and warrant our permanent remembrance." See *Washington Alumnus* article in Chimes Folder, Pacific Northwest Collection, University of Washington Libraries. For announcement, see *The Times*, 24 December 1911.

39. See Meeting Minutes, 19 December 1911, Board of Regents papers, Manuscripts and University Archives, University of Washington Libraries. For Kane's gossip about Rea, see Thomas Kane to A.L. Rogers, 5 January 1912, President's papers, University of Washington, Manuscripts and University Archives. *The Argus* was quite knowledgeable about political matters, and its take on the sequence of events was "Col. Blethen refused to give the chimes, until he was assured that the entire board was favorably inclined towards receiving it. Before approaching Col. Blethen, who was unknown to him, Mr. Rea asked several men who were much more able to present it, and was turned down. Col. Blethen not only gave all that was asked, but added one bell not asked for, in order to make the chimes complete." See *The Argus*, 8 February 1913.

40. The announcement of the chimes gift and hot times quote were in *The Argus*, 30 December 1911. Quote from *The Patriarch*, 41. December 1911, clipping in Chimes File,

Pacific Northwest Collection, University of Washington Libraries. See also *The Patriarch*, 6 January 1912, for additional fulminations on "this product of plunder," the "triumph of depravity." The student who wrote this letter to *The Daily* was Glenn Hoover, and it was published 5 January 1912.

41. See an excellent survey of the Port Commission and the proposed Harbor Island development in Berner, *Boomtown*, pp. 128, 141-152. See also Padraic Burke, *A History of the Port of Seattle* (Seattle: Frayn Printing Company, 1976). For general chamber agreement on importance of waterfront development, see Minutes, 12 December 1911, Seattle Chamber of Commerce, 1910-1911. The minutes indicate agreement, specifically, between Alden Blethen and John L. Wilson on this notion. For Alden Blethen's announcement of Joe's work on the developing "deal," see Minutes, 19 December 1911. For his appointment as chairman of special committee on the Harbor Island terminal project, see Minutes, 9 January 1912.

42. For descriptions of the general plan with the Ayers investors, see Minutes, 25 January 1912 and 1 February 1912, Seattle Chamber of Commerce and *The Times*, 6 March 1912 for summary of proposal and quotes.

43. Within the chamber, there was some disagreement about whether that organization should endorse the port bonds, although they did vote to do so. See Minutes, 23 February 1912. Blethen quote about convincing voters from Minutes, 26 February 1912, Seattle Chamber of Commerce.

44. For Annual Business Edition just before port bonds vote, see *The Times*, 3 March 1912. Front-page guide to voters, see *The Times*, 4 March 1912. For Thomson, Bridges, and Chittenden as knockers, see *The Times*, 7 March 1912.

45. Headline and malcontents quote *The Times*, 6 March 1912. This is a complex story, here much condensed. The role of Scott Calhoun, attorney for the port commission, is especially interesting, as he negotiated far outside his authority and appears to have been on the Ayers' payroll while still working for the port. He soon resigned from his position with Seattle's port commission.

46. The port commission's desire to formulate its own plans is from *The Times*, 10 March 1912. The cartoon is from *The Times*, 31 March 1912. For quoted thanks, see Minutes, 7 March 1912, Seattle Chamber of Commerce, 1912-1913. Blethen was also thanked for his time and money, Minutes, 6 February 1912 and 19 March 1912. At the end of the year, the chamber's annual report noted the Harbor Island terminal effort and the passage of the bond issues as "most distinguished and enduring achievement of the year," in Minutes, 13 December 1912.

47. See Hulet Wells, "I Wanted to Work," unpublished autobiographical manuscript, quote p. 135, Wells papers, Manuscripts and University Archives, University of Washington Libraries.

48. Professor Charles McKinley, a former UW student who had been active during the chimes protest, remembered the "fan-fare about the proposal of a private outfit to lease [the Harbor Island] tract and develop a great port facility." For general account and dummy quote, see Charles McKinley to Theresa S. McMahon, 13 December 1959, McMahon papers, Manuscripts and University Archives, University of Washington Libraries. McKinley's roommate, Carl Goetz, was a summer reporter for *The P-I* and had been ordered by his editor to modify his coverage of the port hearings to make the deal look good and the port look bad. The students became convinced that John L. Wilson and Alden Blethen were cooking up a deal to make money from the waterfront development they proposed. Tam Deering, who

would lead the student protest against the Blethen Chimes, was present at the political club meeting that Blethen attended. McKinley's narrative maintained that Alden Blethen lost his temper in the meeting and "blurted out" the facts—that he and Wilson hoped for a piece of the action if the New York terminal deal succeeded. This does not seem credible.

49. For puritanical quote, see *The Argus*, 3 March 1912; for calamity quote, see *The Argus*, 3 February 1912. Also see Wells, "I Wanted to Work," pp. 9, 92, 134, 139-140.

50. For Alden Blethen in a tailspin, see Sale, *Seattle: Past and Present*, p. 109. See anti-Wobbly, anti-anarchist editorials in *The Times*, 13 and 24 April 1912. See *The Argus*, 6 April 1912, for agreement. See *The Times*, 1 May 1912 and 2 May 1912 for the May Day scuffle during the parade. Hulet Wells and others mention the suspiciously handy photographer but the photo must have run on the front page of a different edition or of an extra which has not been preserved. See Wells, "I Wanted to Work," pp. 140-141, and references throughout, for his very different memories of the parade and its aftermath.

51. For purity squad rousting the nurse, see *The Argus*, 21 September 1912. For horsewhipping quote, see *The Times'* editorial, 6 October 1912. For another purity squad error, see *The Times*, 6 October 1912. For front-page, six-frame caricature of the purity squad at this time, see *The Times*, 15 October 1912. The purity squad was Seattle's vice squad, and operated outside the strict letter of the law as the police had long done with gambling, drugs, and prostitution. As the contests for authority in the city played out, Seattle's police assigned to vice found public expectations changing radically. In November 1912, Austin Griffiths, an attorney and member of the city council, proposed an ordinance that passed unanimously making it illegal to enter any room without a search warrant—whether a hotel room on Second Avenue or a dining room on Highland Drive. See *The Times*, 14 November 1912, and Austin E. Griffiths, *Great Faith: Autobiography of An English Immigrant Boy in America, 1863-1950* (Seattle: self-published, 1958) in the University of Washington Libraries. Later, however, the purity squad was said to have been revived, for instance, *The Times*, 2 March 1914.

52. Perfect chimes quote from *The Times*, 20 October 1912. See also *The Times*, 17 October 1912. Magnificent quote from *The Times*, 27 October 1912. The chimes cost $12,000, a great deal of money in 1912. For photos of the chimes, see *The Times*, 15 October 1912 and 20 October 1912. The regents originally intended the chimes to hang in the Denny Hall cupola, but because of their size and weight, had to remodel an old campus water tower. See Minutes, 23 January 1912, Board of Regents, Manuscripts and University Archives, as well as undated typescript history, on newsprint, in the Chimes File, Pacific Northwest Collection, University of Washington Libraries. For description of reach of the chimes, see *The Times*, 21 October 1912.

53. For vast outpouring quote, see *The Times*, 22 October 1912.

54. There is a copy of the *Souvenir Program for the Installation of the Chimes* in the Chimes Folder, Pacific Northwest Collection, University of Washington Libraries.

55. Scott Bone, *The P-I*, 14 July 1915, referred to the "scant audience" and how sorry everyone felt for Alden Blethen. Public quote about wind gusts and rain, *The Times*, 23 October 1912. See Alden Blethen to Meneely and Company, the bells' foundry, cc'd to Thomas Kane, 23 October 1912, referring to the "toughest old night [that] rained cats and dogs." See Alden Blethen to Kane, 8 November 1912, President's papers, Manuscripts and University Archives.

56. Theresa McMahon's papers include much interesting

material on the 1912 chimes student protests, including the 1959 typescript reminiscence of Charles McKinley. Theresa McMahon's typescript "My Story," describes a weekly gathering of students at her home at which a chimes protest was discussed. General sense of student strategy and quotes are from that typescript, as well as from McMahon's own reminiscence. In her papers, McMahon maintained that *Pacific Northwest Quarterly* would not print in its entirety her letter protesting the July 1959 article, "The Appointment of Henry Suzzallo," by J.E. Van de Wetering which had touched incidentally—and to her mind, libelously—on President Kane's dismissal. She claimed that UW President Emeritus H. Schmitz pressured the *PNQ* editor to delete from her letter the section dealing with Kane's refusal to expel the students who protested the Blethen chimes, "purchased with tainted money."

57. The 21 October 1912 petition, signed by fifty-one students, includes the open letter, and is in the Petitions and Protests File, Board of Regents papers, Manuscripts and University Archives. See pamphlet *SUPPRESSION!* distributed on campus in lieu of *The Daily*, and containing the open letter, in Chimes File, Pacific Northwest Collection, University of Washington Libraries. See report of the Discipline Committee to the President, 8 November 1912, President's papers, Manuscripts and University Archives, for disciplinary details.

58. This poem, according to both McMahon and McKinley, was written by Raymond B. Pease, instructor in the UW Department of English. This is only one stanza of a three-stanza poem.

59. Edward Bemis, *Municipal Monopolies* (T.Y. Crowell, 1899), pp. 659-660. Brainerd quote from *The P-I*, 24 May 1911, as well as in student pamphlet. Final peal of bells quote from open letter, signed by fifty-one students.

60. Protest of Chimes Executive Committee, September 1913, Chimes File, Pacific Northwest Collection, University of Washington Libraries. Also see undated resolutions of disapproval to Washington's governor from the Young People's Society of Christian Endeavor, First Presbyterian Church, which was Rev. Mark Matthews' church, and correspondence, 28 October 1912, from Seattle Federation of Women, which endorses the students' actions, Governor M.E. Hay papers, Washington State Archives. For Commercial Club, see Alden Blethen to Whom It May Concern (at Commercial Club), cc'd to Kane, 26 November 1912, President's papers, Manuscripts and University Archives, which includes a lengthy rebuttal to charges of the circular *SUPPRESSION!.* The file Petitions and Protests, Board of Regents papers, Manuscripts and University Archives, also includes hundreds of the petitions circulated throughout the state and signed by citizens who wished to reimburse Blethen for the chimes and remove the inscription. The students and supporters held a Fumigation Day ceremony, in April 1913, to symbolically disassociate Alden Blethen from the chimes. The repayment program was revived October 1913, after the Potlatch riots, but was never completed.

61. Block quote about old hens and Commercial Club from *The Times*, 26 January 1913.

62. Retaliation and Cotterill protégés quotes from Alden Blethen to Howard Cosgrove, 11 August 1913, Board of Regents papers, Manuscripts and University Archives. Blethen's insurance communications were discussed, Minutes, Board of Regents, 26 November 1912. Alden Blethen to Howard Cosgrove, 13 August 1913, refers to torch and bomb; Secretary, Board of Regents to Alden Blethen, 14 August 1913, Board of Regents papers, accepts his offer of insurance. For renewal of insurance, see correspondence providing notification of cancellation, F.D. Hammons, Times Investment

Company to Board of Regents, University of Washington, 21 July 1916, Board of Regents papers. Percy Jefferson's "I Knew the Colonel," in *The Seattle Times* Historical Archives, claimed that the chimes tower "was set afire more than once by reformist zealots" before its final destruction in a 1949 blaze.

63. See *The Argus*, 2 November 1912. For the speckled editorial dealing with the gang of highwaymen, see *The Times*, 2 October 1912. For combine quote, *The Times*, 1 September 1912 and boycott quote, *The Times*, 9 October 1912.

64. For Blethen's "True Story of the Chime of Bells," see *The Times*, 26 January 1913.

65. Cotterill's rowdies and male fist quotes from Alden Blethen to F.A. Hazeltine, 9 June 1914, Correspondence Collected by Edwin Stevens re Thomas F. Kane, Stevens papers, Manuscripts and University Archives. For punishments given to protesting students, see report of the Discipline Committee to the President, 8 November 1912, President's papers, Manuscripts and University Archives. See also, for instance, "The Chimes Controversy," *The Washington Alumnus*, vol. 6, no. 2 (November 1912) which took an equivocal view of this major donation to the UW campus. *The Alumnus* continued to hammer away at Blethen and Kane, for instance, see "President Kane and His Critics," vol. 7, no. 1 (November 1913) or "The Inside Story of the Chimes," vol. 7, no. 2 (December 1913). The second article included an unnamed regent's protest against accepting the chimes: "Never, never, never! That obscene old rascal will never build a monument to himself on this campus while I've got a vote!" This chapter offers by no means an exhaustive treatment of the chimes controversy and its aftermath.

66. For Blethen's willingness to move the chimes to Times Square Building top, see Alden Blethen to Howard Cosgrove, 19 November 1912, Board of Regents papers, Manuscripts and University Archives. Cosgrove declined this offer, 21 November 1912, writing the Board "does not feel that any useful purpose would be served by an acceptance thereof." Correspondence, Board of Regents papers. For the cutting of Bowdoin article, see *The Daily*, 19 November 1912, Chimes File, Pacific Northwest Collection, University of Washington Libraries. For Rose Ann's protective anger, see C.B. Blethen to M. Lyle Spencer, President, University of Washington, 5 November 1931, "Mother deeply resented Father's treatment over the chimes," File #298, *The Seattle Times* Historical Archives.

67. For confidant quote, see C.B. Blethen to Edmond S. Meany, 10 June 1931, File #298, *The Seattle Times* Historical Archives. For C.B. Blethen's claim that he and his father designed the Times Square Building together, see *The Times*, 2 March 1931. See Christy Thomas, *Bylines and Bygones* (New York: Exposition Press, 1964), p. 79, for preparedness at *The Times* prior to and during World War I.

68. The Seattle Press Club's "Second WUXTRA" (Seattle, 1911?) described C.B., then managing editor, as a man who "Plays golf, toys with Winton automobiles of numerous horsepower and is the whole works in the editorial department of The Times. Mr. Blethen's favorite expression is 'All the News That's Fit to Print—And the First Pictures.' He has been around a newspaper office all his life, starting from the basement up—the mailing room." There are numerous references to C.B.'s interest in fast cars, for instance, see *The Argus*, 14 December 1912 and 7 June 1913. Edmund Burke, Seattle realtor, died in the spring of 1915 because of injuries sustained in a collision with C.B.'s Winton. For quotes, see Thomas, *Bylines and Bygones*, pp. 57-58.

69. For a daffy story about an experience of Joe Blethen's on an Ad Club excursion to Vancouver, see *The Argus*, 20

June 1914. In the wee hours of the morning, Joe and friends were playing with cars in Vancouver, and Joe leaped onto the hood of what he took to be Herbert Schoenfeld's limousine, ran across the roof and down the back, injuring his leg. For Joe Blethen's work in the chamber of commerce, see Minutes of the Board of Trustees, for instance, 18 June 1908, for his election as trustee and mention that his committee on city affairs "is one of the hardest worked committees in the Chamber." Throughout 1909, Joe Blethen seldom attended the weekly board meetings more often than once a month (17 March 1909, 3 April 1909, and 18 May 1909), and remained chairman of the committee on city affairs. He was again elected a trustee 18 June 1909, and mentioned as a trustee 9 August 1911 and 3 October 1911. The Seattle Chamber of Commerce Minutes for 16 January 1912 mention Joe Blethen as president of the Ad Club and city affairs committee chair; 28 May 1912 mention his recommendation that the chamber nominate "a tyee" for the Potlatch. See also "Second WUXTRA" (Seattle Press Club, 1911?), for a description of Joe Blethen as a "regular skyscraper full of work and enthusiasm for the club." For Joe Blethen as president of the Automobile Club and member for the previous six years, see the illustration of Joe at the wheel, *The Times*, 2 May 1915 or *The Times*, 23 May 1915.

70. For history of the Seattle Advertising Club, see Joe Blethen's "Manager's Corner," *The Times*, 11 May 1913. The first issue of the Ad Club's periodical *Organized Optimism* was mentioned in *The Times*, 7 March 1913, building toward the Potlatch. For quotes, see Joe Blethen, "The Potlatch as an Advertisement," *Bulletin*, 1912?, Department of Journalism, University of Washington. See the annual business edition, *The Times*, 3 March 1912, which was devoted to Potlatch, for village pessimist quote.

71. For all these quotes concerning 1912 Potlatch, see *The Times*, 3 March 1912.

72. *The Sun's* first issue was published 3 February 1913. See *The Argus*, 8 February 1913, "*The Seattle Sun* has commenced to shine under auspicious circumstances. Although it is only three months ago that the enterprise was first announced, *The Sun* claimed 50,000 subscribers to commence with its first number and an advertising patronage which compelled the publication of twenty-four pages.... *The Sun* has been born full grown." For Alden Blethen's quotes about *The Sun*, see Alden Blethen to Henry Landes, 23 January 1914, President's papers, Manuscripts and University Archives. C.B. Blethen's quotes about *The Sun*, from "Alden."

73. Firebrand quote from *The Times*, 23 July 1913, and Cotterill's helplessness headline, *The Times*, 21 February 1913. See *The Times*, 25 February 1913, for story about Wobblies, arrested for insulting police officers, being driven to jail in the mayor's car. For Old Soldiers, see *The Times*, 1 May 1913 and *The Times*, 22 March 1913 for "Old Glory was torn down by an alien horde." Alden Blethen's remarks about labor unions "under proper management" as distinct from those dominated by "the rabble" from 1913 interview with *The Los Angeles Times*, quoted in his obituary 13 July 1915, in *The L.A. Times*. For "good socialists," see Hulet Wells, "I Wanted To Work," for his angry memories of Socialist Judge Winsor and Blethen's respect for him, as well as many references to *The Times'* insistence that "good" regular Socialists had tried to remove the radical Wells' name from the ballot, for instance, *The Times*, 18 October 1912. For these anti-Wobbly articles and headlines four days before the fire, see 9 February 1913.

74. For general fire story, see *The Times*, 13 and 14 February 1913. Robert Herrick, assistant foreman of pressroom, remembered his experience in the fire, see *The Times*, 21 April 1940.

75. For the provocative story insinuating that the fire was incendiary, see *The Times*, 17 February 1913.

76. For posters and quotes, see *The Times*, 24 February 1913.

77. *The Argus* was in agreement with *The Times* on the issue of the Wobblies, for instance, *The Argus*, 26 December 1914, "Work is scarce. People are suffering from cold and hunger. This is not a local condition. It exists all over North America.... But there should be no place on earth for the man who will not work. He is as bad as the rat which destroys food, carries germs, and does no good to any person or anything, and which is not fit to eat, even. The world does not owe him a living. It owes him nothing. If he starves he gets just what he is entitled to.... [The] I.W.W. must move on.... They are worse than criminals. Not only parasites themselves, they are not satisfied until they have made parasites of others." *The Times* moved back into the repaired and remodeled building 30 March 1913. Industrial republic quote from "Seattle Socialist leader," quoted *The Times*, 27 July 1913, and see *The Times'* editorial, 3 October 1912.

78. For general biographical information on C.B. Blethen and his military career, see his obituaries, in *The Times* and in *The P-I*, 31 October 1941. The Clarance Brettun Blethen Biographical File in *The Seattle Times* Historical Archives includes these photocopies, as well as other materials. References to some of his semi-autobiographical fiction and non-fiction dealing with his military experiences may be found in these notes. A few pieces were published; most were not. For general military history concerning C.B. Blethen, see C. Stuart MacVeigh, "When the Bankers Marched Like Soldiers: Richard Wilson and the Businessmen's Camp," researched for inclusion in John A. Hemphill, ed., *West Pointers and Early Washington* (Seattle: West Point Society of Puget Sound, 1992). The draft chapter is in the C.B. Blethen Biographical File. C.B. Blethen spent time studying gunnery strategy and tactics at Ft. Monroe, Virginia in 1915, 1916, and 1918. In 1915, he wrote a fictionalized account of his experiences there entitled "The Officer Machine at Fort Monroe," describing Ft. Monroe's Artillery School as a machine in which "officers are the cogs and gears; officers are the raw material and they are also the finished product. It's a grinding, tearing, devouring machine that makes these fellows enormously efficient if it doesn't kill them."

79. See *The Times*, any day between 5 July 1913 and 26 July 1913, for this coverage of the Potlatch summer National Guard encampments. Although the writers do not know what D——x stands for, these photos were certainly taken by C.B. Blethen because they were found in his personal collection of hundreds of such images, annotated in his own handwriting. They are in *The Seattle Times* Historical Archives. C.B. Blethen attended the Rainier Club dinner given for the naval officers of the visiting ships in the bay, *The Times*, 16 July 1913.

80. Parade route description, *The Times*, 3 July 1913. Joe Blethen's name was mentioned nearly every other day in *The Times* in connection with Potlatch planning for the spring months of 1913. See, for instance, *The Times*, 14 July 1913, for an open house at the Savoy Hotel for booster organizations invited from other cities, like Portland, Tacoma, Yakima, Vancouver, Victoria, and Spokane. These visitors were in town during the riot.

81. For general descriptions of the 1913 Potlatch, see *The Times*, *The P-I*, and *The Sun* from July 16 through July 26, 1913. This description of *The Times'* float, and a photo, can be found 20 July 1913.

82. Blethen's editorial about Josephus Daniels and the Bremerton navy yard in *The Times*, 13 July 1913, while Daniels' quote about the fleet and the Panama Canal is 17 July 1913.

83. *The Sun*, 17 July 1913, appears to have the best and clearest description of Thursday night's events. All the newspapers printed a great many extras on Friday and Saturday, many of them with conflicting details.

84. See *The Seattle Times*—Thursday and Friday—17 and 18 July 1913, for this story. The quotes are from the front-page story in the Friday evening *Times*.

85. This soapbox speaker was a feminist, and likely a Socialist. Precisely what she said, and what was said by others in the crowd, was a matter of considerable disagreement in 1913.

86. Quotes from Friday evening *Times*, 18 July 1913.

87. For quotes and general setting, see *The Sun*, Saturday, 19 July 1913. For ads on the Red New Wagon, see Wells, "I Wanted to Work," p. 172; he discusses the riots pp. 170-174.

88. See *The Sun* for Saturday, 19 July 1913. There were at least four extras of *The Sun* on this day, as news continued to break.

89. The issue of *The Times* that Cotterill would have suppressed is 19 July 1913. For quote, see *The Sun*, 19 July 1913.

90. This description of events in Humphries' courtroom and the serving of the injunction and warrants is somewhat simplified. See *The Times*, Sunday, 20 July 1913, for mention of Joe Blethen's role in presenting the affidavit of police presence at the newspaper building.

91. Quotes from *The Times*, 19 July 1913.

92. For Daniels' denials, see *The Sun* 19 July 1913, and his autobiography, Josephus Daniels, *The Wilson Era—Years of Peace, 1910-1917* (Chapel Hill: University of North Carolina Press, 1944). For the apologies, see *The Sun*, 23 July 1913.

93. *The Times*, 20 July 1913.

94. *The Times*, 20 July 1913. George Cotterill had been born in England, and his family moved to the United States when he was a child. *The Times* would often claim that Cotterill was not an American but "a naturalized citizen" who had no real allegiance to this country.

95. See *The Sun*, 21 July 1913, for Cotterill's statement.

96. All Cotterill quotes from his public statement, reprinted in *The Sun*, 21 July 1913. Governor Lister, in an address to a municipal Democratic club, also criticized those who wrap themselves in the flag to conceal their true nature, an apparent reference to both Alden and C.B. Blethen. See Lister's remarks, first quoted in *The Sun*, 19 July 1913, and later used at the foot of the front-page *Sun* cartoon of Blethen.

97. From *The P-I*, as quoted in *The Times*, 21 July 1913.

98. See *The Times*, 21 July 1913 for the C.B. Blethen quote from Fort Worden.

99. For the total effect of these preoccupations with radical labor and militarism, see, for instance, the front page of *The Times*, 22 July 1913. See *The Sun*, 23 July 1913, for headline and editorial; see *The Times*, 23 July 1913, for casual retraction of dead soldier story.

100. For the skull and crossbones, see *The Sun*, 22 July 1913; for Blethen as an Ogre and Thing, see *The Sun*, 24 July 1913; and for front-page cartoon, see *The Sun*, 26 July 1913. See, too, *The Sun*'s summary of Seattle ministers' thinly veiled references to Alden Blethen, in *The Sun*, 28 July 1913.

101. For quote, Sale, *Seattle: Past and Present*, p. 111.

102. There are no better sources for Hulet Wells' perspective on these events than his own unpublished autobiography, "I Wanted to Work," and the play, "The Colonel and His Friends." Alden Blethen as "malevolent," from Wells, "I Wanted to Work," p. 138. For *The Times'* perspective, see, for instance, *The Times*, 18 October 1912. However, similar editorials and articles are almost constant.

103. See Wells, "I Wanted To Work," pp. 153-154, 165-167, ridicule quote p. 166. Wells wrote that the play drove Blethen to apoplexy.

104. For *The Sun*'s delighted coverage of "The Colonel and His Friends," see, for instance, 3 July 1913. For Wells' worry that Bruce Rogers, who played Blather, would be drunk at the performance, see Wells, "I Wanted to Work," p. 167. "The Colonel and His Friends" was eventually published and sold at 25 cents a copy, as "The Colonel and His Friends: A Suppressed Play," with the motto "The Issue is Not Flags But Bread" on the title page. The pamphlet is preserved in the Harry Ault papers, Manuscripts and University Archives, University of Washington Libraries.

105. For long-haired men quote, see *The Argus*, 5 August 1911. For John Cort canceling the contract at the Moore Theater, see *The Times*, 26 July 1913. For Tacoma and safety commission, see *The Times*, 28 July 1913. For Seattle Theater, University of Washington, and Everett, see *The Times*, 8 August 1913. Also see Wells, "I Wanted to Work," for his perspective on these events.

106. For Humphries' vanity, see Wells, "I Wanted to Work," pp. 158-159. For the edited testimony of the wiretapping reporter from *The Times* in Humphries' court, see *The Sun*, 15 February 1913. On receipt of a "black hand letter," Humphries handed down a blanket injunction against street speaking in the city, see *The Times*, 26 July 1913. For editing of grand jury transcript, see *The Sun*, 15, 18, and 21 July 1913. If McKinley and Theresa McMahon are correct, the easy student access to the supposedly sealed grand jury transcripts—to prepare scurrilous pamphlets during the chimes controversy—was particularly annoying to Blethen. See McKinley's typescript, and McMahon's defense of Kane, in which she wrote, "Kane was asked to appoint a faculty committee to find out where the students got the information supposedly known only to the members of the grand jury who were pledged to secrecy." McMahon papers.

107. "Citizen, Patriot, Editor" is from Alden Joseph Blethen's grave marker in Lake View Cemetery, Seattle, Washington. Harry Chadwick, in *The Argus*, remarked dozens of times on Alden Blethen's odd propensity to blurt out exactly what he would have preferred others not know. When William Jennings Bryan visited Seattle, Alden Blethen—one of his most fervent supporters—was assigned an excellent seat in one of the carriages in Bryan's entourage. But a *P-I* reporter stole Blethen's place and the publisher was forced to walk from the railroad depot to Bryan's hotel. Blethen wrote an indignant editorial in *The Times* expressing his anger and humiliation, and the *Argus* pointed out, 7 April 1900, "It might be mentioned that had Blethen not been jackass enough to himself call attention to the matter, the chances are that it would have passed unnoticed." Such incidents could be multiplied.

108. This block quote of the toast is from *The Times*, 6 July 1913.

109. This block quote of Blethen's reply is from *The Times*, 6 July 1913.

110. Bryan's recital for the *Congressional Record*, quoted by *The Sun*, 11 August 1913. See the Bryan papers, Manuscripts and University Archives, University of Washington Libraries, for clippings from various Seattle papers dealing with his conflict with Alden Blethen, as well as transcripts of three of his libel trials against Blethen in Washington's Superior Court. Unfortunately, although the photographic fake is referred to

as "the faked exhibition of degeneracy," it was not included as an exhibit.

111. See *The Times*, 20 September 1913 and 21 September 1913 for Blethen's specific remarks about Bryan. *The Argus* rallied to Blethen's support, writing 29 September 1913, that even "admitting everything which Bryan says about Blethen to be true, and adding about 60 per cent more abuse for good measure, to compare Colonel Blethen to Congressman Bryan would be like comparing a diamond to a dunghill."

112. For this second fire at the Second and Union building, see *The Times*, 6 October 1913. Also see Thomas, *Bylines and Bygones*, pp. 70-71, for description of Alden Blethen and reference to general office conviction that it was a Wobbly fire. Chadwick called for an arson investigation, see *The Argus*, 11 October 1913. In a letter to police chief Austin Griffiths in the early summer of 1914, Blethen continued to complain about "an I.W.W. or a Dynamic Socialist—I cannot tell them apart" standing on a soapbox and making a "riotous speech" right under Blethen's office window at 8:00 p.m. See Alden Blethen to Austin Griffiths, 17 June 1914, Griffiths papers, Manuscripts and University Archives.

113. See *The Times*, 31 March 1912 for land purchase and plans. Also see *The Argus*, 28 March 1914 for Blethen and shovel quote. Model office from *The Times*, 16 July 1915.

114. Scott Bone encouraged Alden Blethen to be more charitable toward the fallen foe. See *The P-I*, 20 December 1914. Assassins quote, Alden Blethen to Landes, 23 Jan 1914, President's papers, Manuscripts and University Archives.

115. See Eldon Coroch's chapter "His Troubles Are Over," in "Colonel Alden J. Blethen," for an excellent summary of Alden Blethen's final months. For the party, see *The Times*, 4 January 1915 or *The Argus*, 2 January 1915. See the year-end review, 8 December 1914, Minutes, 1914, Seattle Chamber of Commerce.

116. For Alden Blethen's request for leave of absence, see 16 February 1915, Minutes, 1915, Seattle Chamber of Commerce. See *The Town Crier*, 18 July 1915, for James Wood quote. For Blethen's dental infection, see C.B. Blethen's "Alden"; for a general infection in his lungs and liver, caused by an abscess from influenza, see Florence Blethen Duffy, oral history interview, cited Coroch, "Colonel Alden J. Blethen," p. 347.

117. See Alden Blethen's series of travel articles, *The Times*, 7 March 1915, 21 March 1915, 23 March 1915, and so forth.

118. Quote, see *The Times*, 23 March 1915.

119. Quote, see *The Times*, 28 March 1915. See *The Times*, 4 April 1915, for encounter with James Moore, an old ally and acquaintance from the Metropolitan Tract days at the University of Washington. Also see *The Times*, 18 March 1915, for mention of the William Burns libel case and Judge Ronald's warrant in that lawsuit, to be issued three days after his return to Seattle.

120. For Wood's quoted remark about Blethen's acquaintances at the AP and ANPA, see *The Town Crier*, 18 July 1915.

121. For Alden Blethen's quoted response to the Thomson verdict, see *The Times*, 2 May 1915.

122. Alden Blethen's *P-I* obituary indicated that he had returned from his trip much thinner, 13 July 1915. For doctor going to Spokane and general trip, see *The Times*, 13 July 1915. For James Wood's quoted recollection of Blethen's touring the Second and Union Building, see *The Town Crier*, 18 July 1915.

123. For this message to publicity bureau, see *The Town Crier*, 18 July 1915. For the bulletin discouraging social calls, see *The Times*, 13 June 1915.

124. The *Lusitania*'s sinking was reported in *The Times*, 7 May 1915, and a fiercely anti-German editorial was published 9 May 1915. The quoted editorial was from *The Times*, 12 May 1915.

125. See *The Times*, 13 July 1915 for the narrative of his last days and hours.

126. See *The Times*, 15 July 1915 for description of home, service, and interment.

127. See *The Times* 13, 14, and 15 July 1915 and *The P-I*, 15 July 1915.

Notes for Afterword

1. For William Henry Eustis, see Alden Blethen's obituary in *The Minneapolis Journal*, 13 July 1915.

2. The tone of Moore's signed obituary and an unsigned reminiscence in the same issue, almost certainly by him, would indicate a rift between the two men that had not been healed at Blethen's death. See *The Aberdeen World*, 13 July 1915.

3. The in harness quote from *The Hoquiam Washingtonian*, 13 July 1915, in an article written by Albert Johnson who had known Blethen in Minneapolis.

4. For *The Sun* employees' tribute, see *The Sun*, 13 July 1915. For tribute to Blethen and reminiscence of *The Minneapolis Tribune* fire, see *The Seattle Union Record*, 14 July 1915. For unkind word quote, see *The Port Orchard Independent*, 16 July 1915; for take off coat and fight quote, see *The Port Angeles Herald*, 14 July 1915.

5. See M.M. "Matt" Mattison's reminiscence, *The Seattle Times, 13* July 1915. Paul Lovering's essay is from Clarence Bagley, *History of Seattle From the Earliest Settlement to the Present Time* (Chicago: S.J. Clarke Publishing Company, 1916), p. 199. For an especially fulsome eulogy, see chamber of commerce memorial in Minutes, 27 July 1915, Seattle Chamber of Commerce, Seattle Public Library.

6. See Scott Bone's reminiscence in *The Seattle Post-Intelligencer*, 14 July 1915. Also see Chadwick's reminiscence published in *The Argus*, 17 July 1915 and James Wood, in *The Town Crier*, 17 July 1915.

7. For other uses of clichés in obituaries, see, for example, *The Othello Times*, 16 July 1915; *The Winston-Salem Sentinel*, 20 July 1915, and *Louisville Courier* 20 July 1915. These obituaries have been clipped and preserved in a scrapbook entitled "In Memoriam: Alden J. Blethen," *The Seattle Times* Historical Archives. This scrapbook includes obituaries from across the nation, including the foreign language press.

8. Picturesque character quote from Bellingham *Reveille*, 13 July 1915; throbbing West quote from *The New Orleans Statesman*, 19 July 1915. See *The Juneau Daily Empire*, 14 July 1915 for the romance of his life as a Westerner. In other commentary, his life was described as "a book of adventure" by *New York City Newspaperdom*, 29 July 1915, and he was called a "mountain man of journalism" by *The Oakland Observer*, 17 July 1915.

9. Florence Blethen Duffy remembered in an oral history interview with historian Eldon Coroch that her father considered himself a "fighting editor." See Coroch, "Colonel Alden J. Blethen and The Seattle Daily Times" (University of Washington, unpublished master's thesis, 1966), especially "One Big Family," pp. 95-113. *The Hoquiam Washingtonian*, 13 July 1915, supplied the quote about the editorial rooms versus the business office; it seems to have been written by someone who knew or worked for Blethen. *The P-I* dubbed him "a fighting editor," as did dozens of other newspapers across the nation.

10. For the Missouri Press Association, founded during Blethen's stay in Kansas City, see William H. Taft, *Missouri Newspapers* (Columbia: University of Missouri Press, 1964) and Floyd C. Shoemaker, "History of the First Fifty Years of the Missouri Press Association" unpublished manuscript at the Missouri State Historical Society, 1970. Particularly see Stephen A. Bannings, "Unearthing the Origin of Journalistic Professionalization in the Mid-Nineteenth Century" (University of Missouri at Columbia, unpublished master's thesis, 1993). This is a thoughtful reevaluation of the accepted wisdom that journalism did not develop professional standards until the Progressive Era. For the ANPA, see Edwin Emery, *History of the American Newspaper Publishers Association* (Minneapolis: University of Minnesota Press, 1950). The ANPA was founded in 1887, and much of the impetus came from the newspapers of the northern Midwest, including Chicago and Minneapolis where Alden Blethen was part owner of *The Tribune* and *The Journal* at this time.

11. Alden Blethen's "Advice and Recommendations" is held in *The Seattle Times* Historical Archives. It was dictated to longtime secretary Elizabeth Hammons on the editor's return to Seattle from his last trip to the South and East, in May and possibly into June, 1915. See editorial "Our Task and Our Pledge," *The Times*, 18 July 1915, signed by both Clarance and Joseph Blethen. They wrote that "the best of fathers" had trained them for this task, and that he had left them a great and wonderful legacy, and that they would try to live up to their heritage.

12. The difference between the brothers was noticeable even to outsiders. Enemy Hulet Wells noted, "[Alden Blethen's] place on the paper was taken by his son, Col. C.B. Blethen, who came by his title through the National Guard. This son was very much like his father, and quite different from his brother, Joseph, who had some success as a writer of magazine fiction." Wells, "I Wanted to Work," Wells papers, University of Washington Libraries, Manuscripts and University Archives, p. 178.

13. For caution on spending, see, for instance, Alden Blethen to C.B. Blethen, 3 December 1914, File #409, *The Seattle Times* Historical Archives; for soothing hurt feelings, see, for instance, Alden Blethen to Florence Blethen Duffy, 25 March 1914, *The Seattle Times* Historical Archives.

14. For "educated into the business" quote, see Florence Blethen Duffy interview with Eldon Coroch, "Colonel Alden J. Blethen," p. 2. For quotes, see editorial signed by Joseph and C.B. Blethen, "Our Task and Our Pledge," *The Times*, 18 July 1915. See C.B. Blethen to Fred Hammons, 7 April 1927, File #393, *The Seattle Times* Historical Archives - "Father's plan was for his two sons to work together dividing the business down the middle—calling one side of it 'Business' and the other side 'News and Editorial.'" See Joseph Blethen to Albert Shaw, 26 July 1915, *The Seattle Times* Historical Archives, for Joe's revealing confession to Shaw, whom he had known since he was a boy in college, "It now remains for my Brother and me to show what we are made of. The opportunity is here and we have had our training. We are not attempting to imitate my Father's methods: he was altogether too vigorous and too resourceful. But...we should be able to go ahead and make creditable records for ourselves." For masthead change after Alden Joseph Blethen's death, see *The Times*, 15 July 1915.

15. In her interview with Eldon Coroch, "Colonel Alden J. Blethen," p. 100, Florence Blethen Duffy remarked, "Father ran us all, even the boys after they were married." For Joseph Blethen's enthusiasm about his business role on the newspaper, see, for instance, Joe Blethen, "The Advertiser's Place in Journalism," *Bulletin*, 1910?, Department of Journalism, University of Washington. For Joe Blethen succeeding his fa-

ther as chair of publicity bureau, see Minutes, 29 October 1915, Chamber of Commerce, and for election to three year term as trustee, see 10 December 1915.

16. The go to it quote, encouraging Joe, is from *The Western Confectioner*, July 1915.

17. For announcement that construction would proceed apace on the Times Square Building, see *The Times*, 3 August 1915.

18. For many details and description of building, see *The Times*, 25 September 1916. For mention of models of the building floors, see *The Times*, 16 July 1915.

19. For graffiti and caricatures, see *The Times*, 25 September 1916.

20. The article about C.B. as military editor was not written by Joseph Blethen, but was accompanied by a brief statement signed by Joe, explaining the joke and how much his brother deserved this honor. This is from *The Times*, 25 September 1916, as is the "Home at Last" editorial.

21. Plaque quote from *The Times*, 25 September 1916. The birth date of 27 December 1846 is incorrect, but is repeated in many obituaries, even in *The Times* and in O.M. Moore's *Aberdeen World*. It is not uncommon for people born in November or December to shave a year off their ages, and Alden Blethen commonly did this toward the end of his life. In earlier years, he readily gave his correct birth date of 27 December 1845, but the 1846 error became very widespread as time went on. Blethen was given a "68th" birthday party in December 1914 when he was actually turning 69, and he did nothing to correct the error. The bronze plaque of commemoration in the Times Square Building, now at the Fairview and John building, is also incorrect.

22. See *The Times*, headlines of 17 September 1917, MOVING DAYS and 24 September 1916, READY TO MOVE!

23. For siren and war news, Percy O. Jefferson as told to Dorothy Daly, "No Time for Ulcers," Percy Jefferson Biographical File, *The Seattle Times* Historical Archives; for time ball, see Fiftieth Anniversary edition of *The Times*, 11 August 1946.

24. For staff shakeup, see Christy Thomas, *Bylines and Bygones* (New York: Exposition Press, 1964), p 73. For the information bureau, see *The Times*, 24 September 1916, as well as *The Times'* obituary for C.B. Blethen, 31 October 1941.

25. For an example of *The Times'* weekly National Guard feature before Alden Blethen's death, see *The Times*, 2 January 1914. For an enlistment appeal typical of hundreds, see 5 February 1915. For the Business Men's Encampment at Fort Lewis, or American Lake, see 15 or 20 August 1915, and throughout the following summer.

26. See C.B. Blethen's obituaries, *The Times* and *The P-I*, 31 October 1941. *The Times'* employees had chipped in to buy C.B. a pair of silver spurs when he went off to Washington, D.C. The clipping that mentions spurs is in C.B. Blethen biographical file, dated 9 September 1918.

27. For David Hunter's firing, see C.B. Blethen to Elmer Todd, 31 October 1932, File #292, *The Seattle Times* Historical Archives; for Hunter's inventions, see *The Times*, 25 September 1916. Bausman and Kelleher's discharge is from a memo covering the history of the association in the Daniel Kelleher Biographical File, annotated "C.B.B., President, The Times Companies, 5 March 1923." It may be that Kelleher had left the law firm prior to C.B. Blethen's discharge of Bausman and Kelleher. However, there is no mistaking C.B. Blethen's annoyance that Kelleher, when chairman of the board of Seattle National Bank in 1923, had "the habit of assuming the way and manner of one authorized to speak for

The Seattle Times." A notice, initialed CBB and dated 5 March 1923, also gives the history of the Bausman and Kelleher relationship with *The Times*, and mentions C.B.'s displeasure with Kelleher. It is in "Rules and Recommendations," a volume of briskly military directives made by C.B. Blethen to the staff at the newspaper in the late 'teens and early 'twenties, *The Seattle Times* Historical Archives.

28. For disregard for expenses, see C.B. Blethen's obituary in *The Times*. *The Argus*, before Alden Blethen's death, had wondered in print about *The Times'* advertising policies, in "The Times Should Investigate," *The Argus*, 6 February 1915. Alden Blethen's obituary in *The Grays Harbor Washingtonian*, 13 July 1915, was written by H.W. Patton who was editor of both Bellingham papers. Patton had refused to run a full-page ad at top rates for medical fakers who "claimed to be able to cure anything," and they appealed over his head to Alden Blethen who wrote to Patton "that in his opinion such advertising was legitimate." In addition to notices in "Rules and Recommendations," see "the determination to eliminate all objectionable advertising from the columns of *The Seattle Times* originated in the minds of the owners.... It is their desire to make this paper as clean and wholesome as is possible, and with that end in view they have issued orders to refuse all advertisements which concern 'female weaknesses,' 'delayed periods,' etc., etc." Business Manager, Times Printing Company, to Chichester Chemical Company, 12 June 1916, File #24, *The Seattle Times* Historical Archives. For the fraudulent and misleading quote, see F.D. Hammons to Robert F. Hanbury, 27 May 1925, File #24, and for reference to barring of psychic ads "some time ago," see "Cranage" to Fred Hammons, 19 July 1918, File #24.

29. For C.B. as publisher and editor in chief, see front page, *The Times*, 14 April 1921. For Hearst's arrival, see ENTER MR. HEARST, *The Times,* 1 May 1921. For circulation, falling dividends, and indebtedness, see loose, undated sheets, File #397 *The Seattle Times* Historical Archives, and C.B. Blethen to Fred Hammons, 7 April 1927, File #393, *The Seattle Times* Historical Archives.

30. C.B. Blethen's account of the Hearst invasion and its effect, in untitled, undated, memo to file, File #411, *The Seattle Times* Historical Archives. In 1913, *The Times'* cost of production was $924,602; in 1923, it had nearly tripled to $2,486,253.

31. For details of Joseph Blethen's gifts and sales in 1921 and 1922, see "Information Regarding the Times Investment Company—Blethen Investment Company" 1921, File #471, *The Seattle Times* Historical Archives. See also Alden Joseph Blethen, Jr. (better known as Joseph Blethen) to C.B. Blethen, 27 August 1921 File #470, written "To My Dear Brother, With Love" or to "My Dear Brother," from "Your Affectionate Brother, Joseph," and similarly affectionate correspondence from Alden Joseph Blethen, Jr. to C.B. Blethen, 5 April 1923, File #470. For Joseph Blethen joining Evans and Barnhill, see *The San Francisco Examiner*, 1 June 1923. For lovable but misled, see C.B. Blethen to S.D. Brooks, 12 October 1937, File #379. For C.B.'s insistence that Joe Blethen had never been named as a publisher of *The Times*, see C.B. Blethen to A.M. Marquis Company, 16 October 1926, File #207, concerning the Who's Who article which annoyed C.B. by making this claim for Joseph Blethen. Joseph Blethen's second wife's name was Florence Davidson Gilbert, and they married 2 March 1922 in San Francisco. They had no children. Joseph Blethen was active in San Francisco's Bohemian Club, acted as club historian, and was vice president and treasurer of Evans and Barnhill, Inc. See the Alden Joseph (Joe) Blethen Biographical File, *The Seattle Times* Historical Archives.

32. For C.B. Blethen's remembrance of his father's intent for the business, see C.B. Blethen to Fred Hammons, 7 April 1927, #393, *The Seattle Times* Historical Archives. This is a scathing letter of rebuke to Hammons, including a chart of operations for the company, at intervals between 1916 and 1927, which gave much of the history of the divided responsibilities of *The Times*, as C.B. Blethen perceived them. However, the intent of the correspondence was to inform Hammons that his work continued not to meet C.B. Blethen's expectations.

33. For C.B. Blethen's opinion of the genealogy, see C.B. Blethen to N.H. Cathcart, 9 December 1929, File #313; to Lillian M. Brown, 19 June 1929, File #107; to William F. Bliven, 28 August 1936, File #102; to Betty B. Blethen, 10 November 1931, File #381, all in *The Seattle Times* Historical Archives. Governor Roland Hartley's remark to Brigadier General Blethen is from "Local Boys Make Good: The Goose-Stepping Editor," in Works Progress Administration (WPA) History, sometimes entitled *The Press Comes West*, as Roland Hartley meets Brigadier-General Blethen. For C.B. Blethen's military career, see his obituaries in *The Times* and *The P-I*, 31 October 1941 and C.B. Blethen to W.W. Jermane, 26 August 1924, File #34, *The Seattle Times* Historical Archives.

34. For C.B.'s willingness—eventually—to confess a mistake and apologize during this early period, see "One Year Dry," a manuscript published in *Collier's* magazine, and held in typescript in *The Seattle Times* Historical Archives. For interest in radio, see handwritten note, C.B. Blethen to Hammons, attached to vendor letter, 14 October 1924, File #28, or another undated note in the same file, also C.B. Blethen to Hammons, stating "...I want an investigation made of the cost of the purchase, installation and operation of a radio station second to none in the northwest.... I think we can beat radio...without going into their own game, but if necessary, we will meet them in their own field." C.B. Blethen's first patent in color photography was issued 4 January 1921, and is entitled "The Process of Making Engravers' Plates for Reproducing Photographs in Colors in Newspapers," US Patent No. 1,364,238. His second patent issued in 1923, U.S. Patent No. 1,744,862, concerned a "Picture Printing Quality Detector Device." Copies of all known C.B. Blethen patents are held in *The Seattle Times* Historical Archives.

35. For the PLATFORM, see *The Times*, 2 June 1921.

36. For James Wood's block quote, see *The Town Crier*, 27 August 1921.

37. Telegram quoted in *The Times*, 25 September 1916.

ACKNOWLEDGMENTS

In 1950, *The Seattle Times* won its first Pulitzer Prize for national reporting. The award honored reporter Ed Guthman for his stories that finally cleared University of Washington professor Melvin Rader of allegations of Communist Party membership. Sending Guthman out to research the questionable accusations, *Times* managing editor Russell McGrath remarked, "The courts have failed to find out the truth. It's time for a newspaper to take on the job." And *Times* publisher Elmer Todd quietly observed, "This is wrong. You don't treat people like that." These are basic newspaper values: diligence, accuracy, respect, and fairness. When *The Times* has been at its best, the common sense of these simple sentiments has distinguished the newspaper as an observer, commentator, and participant in its community.

We began working with *The Times* in the spring of 1993, when the newspaper asked us to arrange their corporate archives, locate additional documentary material, and gather oral history interviews. The newspaper was planning for the centennial of Blethen family ownership in 1996, to mark the passage of one hundred years since Alden Joseph Blethen purchased his first stake in the drab little eight-page *Seattle Daily Times*.

The volume that you hold is a biography of this remarkable man, who came to Seattle late in his life and stamped *The Times* with his characteristic combination of flamboyance and combativeness gained from a lifetime of spectacular successes and failures. Indeed, Alden Blethen eagerly courted controversy. This biography frankly documents the life of a man equally notorious for his friends and his enemies, renowned for his dubious business practices and violent feuds as much as his good deeds and paternalistic care for his employees.

The Centennial Liaison Committee which supervised our work was drawn from *The Times* newsroom as well as the boardroom and, from the start, none of us was interested in a centennial publication that was overly celebratory in tone or misleading in content. All of us—family members, editors, historians—brought the same values to this book project that the daily newspaper strives to achieve: diligence, accuracy, respect, and fairness.

We all wanted to honor this newspaper's centennial with good history, as well-researched, well-written, and well-illustrated as we could manage within our deadlines, as broadly and thoughtfully interpreted as we could manage within our page limitations. Alden Blethen's life and times were complicated, rich in texture, and deserving of more attention than our time and space would allow. But we believe we have still been able to provide readers with a fair and discerning portrait of the man, neither justifying his mistakes nor exalting his successes, but recognizing his unique contributions to his community and his profession.

We did not want to mythologize a hero; happily, *The Times* agreed. Our first thanks, then, go to *The Seattle Times* Centennial Liaison Committee—Frank, Bob, and Will Blethen, Mason Sizemore, Mike Fancher, and Cyndi Nash. We could not have asked for more thoughtful, yet enthusiastic guidance.

As this biography goes to press, we are also glad to take the opportunity to thank all those who helped us to bring this research project to a conclusion. As many of you know, we could not have possibly done this without your help.

Our work began and ended in Washington state, but we were also privileged to do research in Maine, where Alden Blethen was born and spent the first thirty years of his life. We owe special thanks to Joan Roming, president of the Unity Historical Society, Bonnie Dwyer, archivist at the Kent's Hill School, and Ann Ravdin, archivist at Bowdoin College. As traveling researchers, we were grateful for the patience and hospitality of the archivists and librarians at the Maine State Archives and the Maine State Library, at the Maine Historical Society, at the Farmington Public Library—especially Jean Oplinger—and the Portland Public Library. Our appreciation also goes to Andrew Kuby of the Belfast Historical Society, Hugh Russell of the Belfast Free Library, and Farmington author Richard Mallett.

This project took us across the country, following Alden Joseph Blethen's life from threadbare obscurity to blazing notoriety. We are grateful to Dave Boutros and the staff in the Western Historical Manuscript Collection at the University of Missouri at Kansas City and the very helpful librarians at the Kansas City Public Library, as well as at the Indiana Historical Society. In Minnesota, the professional staffs at the Minneapolis Public Library, the Minnesota Historical Society, and the University of Minnesota directed us to resources we did not anticipate and helped to make our research project richer and broader.

Closer to home, we fear that we have worn out our welcome with the unfailingly helpful archivists and librarians in the University of Washington Libraries, from University Archives and Manuscripts to Special Collections to Inter-Library Borrowing. The best librarians don't just answer the questions patrons ask; they answer the questions patrons don't know they should ask. Carla Rickerson, Richard Engeman, Gary Lundell, and Karyl Winn, among so many others, have our undying gratitude, and they know how many favors we owe them.

Rick Caldwell and Carolyn Marr, at Seattle's Museum of History and Industry, helped us work in the wonderful PEMCO Webster and Stevens Collection, a treasure trove of images shot by the early staff photographers for *The Times*. The librarians at the Washington State Historical Society Archives directed us to an invaluable Works Progress Administration typescript history of journalism in Washington state and to their exhaustive index of photographs. As always, the professional staff at the Seattle branch of the National Archives and Record Service offered invaluable assistance, and we particularly want to express our appreciation to Joyce Justice for introducing us to court documents held by the Archives in the William Burns case.

We would like to thank our editor at *The Seattle Times,* Cynthia Nash, and our editor at Washington State University Press, Keith Petersen, for their encouragement, good advice, and keen eyes. Also at WSU Press we want to thank Dave Hoyt for the outstanding book and cover design, and acknowledge the efforts of Beth DeWeese, marketing and promotions coordinator. Our other colleagues at the newspaper—Gary Settle, the excellent photo editor; Lydia Chase, Sandy Freeman, Cathy Donaldson, Barbara Davis, Sue Pelton, and the entire library staff; map designers Bo Cline and Karen Kerchelich, and so many more—have each contributed their unique skills to support this project. Carolyn Dibble introduced us to *The Times* and helped us to make our way through the first months of the project; Donna Erb has cheerfully shepherded us the rest of the way, always providing us with wonderful support and valuable advice.

In addition, we both would like to offer special thanks to our students, many of whose suggestions, questions, and points of view found their way into this biography. Colleagues and friends have also made significant contributions to this book: Richard Berner, Robert Burke, Claudia Carter, Scott Cline, Eldon Coroch, John Findlay, David Freeh, Sara Ryan, and Lewis Saum, among numerous others.

Members of the Blethen family, other relatives, and associates talked with us freely, and generously allowed us to use priceless personal documents and photographs for our research. In particular, we obtained valuable family history materials and equally valuable personal reminiscences from Mr. and Mrs. Gilbert Duffy and Mr. and Mrs. Joseph Mesdag. Many thanks also to Edith Blethen Ladd and her sister in Maine and her brother Floyd Blethen in Virginia; Faith Blethen in New Jersey, and her son Randy Blethen of Clinton, Washington.

Charles H. "Dick" Todd, son of one-time *Times* publisher Elmer Todd and a former *Times* board member and corporate lawyer himself, provided us with important insights, as did his wife, Ann G. Todd. Henry MacLeod, a longtime *Times* staffer and managing editor, proved a wonderful sounding board and invaluable interpreter of the paper's "culture." Philip Wilcox, grandson of former *Seattle Post-Intelligencer* publisher Scott Bone, and William German, editor of *The San Francisco Chronicle*, both graciously helped us to search for elusive research materials. Kind assistance on a hunt to find a lost personal reminiscence by newsman William Chandler was provided by Mrs. Dean Solinsky, Jack Chandler, and Stanley Turnbull.

And we owe three more special votes of thanks.

First, we would like to thank the Seattle Public Library, not just for allowing us to research freely in their wonderful local history collection, but also for letting us shoot photographs from their bound hard copies of *The Seattle Times*. For us both, there have been no greater pleasures in this entire research project than seeing the black and white images of microfilm blaze into the gorgeous colors of the actual newspaper page itself. The Library has preserved a priceless public treasure that documents the city, county, state, and region in a way that microfilm never can.

Second, we have depended heavily throughout our project on the inter-library loan network for microfilmed newspapers and personal papers, and have never lost our delight at being able to read *The Minneapolis Tribune* at a microfilm reader-printer in Seattle. We were grateful that libraries from Maine to Colorado were willing to loan their microfilm reels to *The Seattle Times* library. Additionally, we applaud the system of trust and fair play that allows a scholar in Seattle to borrow a hundred-year-old volume of county history from Minnesota. Access to these research materials is an important but fragile intellectual privilege, and we hope that it remains available to future researchers.

And finally, we would like to thank our friends and families, whose love and patience supported us throughout this project. Above all—to Rob, Brian, and Jeff McConaghy and Will, Laine, and Luke Boswell—we owe you!

In this biography, we have tried to combine family and community history with the histories of journalism, business, and technology, and to offer a rich array of illustration. We have tried to use Alden Blethen's personal story to explore larger issues and events in American history, and to use those larger issues and events to provide a context for his personal story. We hope that readers find interest and instruction in the life of this extraordinary man.

ABOUT THE AUTHORS

Sherry Boswell and Lorraine McConaghy founded their public history firm, Partners in History, in 1987, and have specialized in historical research, writing, and education.

Sherry Boswell focuses on the history of the American West as a teacher and researcher. Two decades of living in the Pacific Northwest have also inspired a particular passion for regional history and ethnography.

Lorraine McConaghy is a historian who has long been interested in the intersection of American private lives with social history, especially in the context of twentieth century community studies. She is active in local museums and historical societies, and teaches in Seattle.

INDEX